EPHESIANS

THE NIV APPLICATION COMMENTARY

From biblical text . . . to contemporary life

KLYNE SNODGRASS

ZONDERVAN®

ZONDERVAN.com/
AUTHORTRACKER
follow your favorite authors

In appreciation to our parents

C. Sidney and Wanda V. L. Snodgrass

and

Everett Allen and Eva M. R. Parks

ZONDERVAN®

The NIV Application Commentary: Ephesians
Copyright © 1996 by Klyne Snodgrass

Requests for information should be addressed to:

Zondervan, Grand Rapids, Michigan 49530

Library of Congress Cataloging-in-Publication Data

Snodgrass, Klyne.
     Ephesians / Klyne Snodgrass.
        p.   cm.—(NIV application commentary)
     Includes bibliographical references and index.
     ISBN-10: 0-310-49340-4
     ISBN-13: 978-0-310-49340-2
     1. Bible. N.T. Ephesians—Commentaries.   I. Bible. N.T. Ephesians. English. New Inter-
national. 1996.   II. Title. III. Series.
     BS2695.3.S66   1966
     227'.507—dc20
                                                                 96–12910

This edition printed on acid-free paper.

Edited by Verlyn D. Verbrugge

Printed in the United States of America

---

10 11 12 13 14 · 21 20 19

Contents

The NIV Application Commentary Series

When complete, the NIV Application Commentary
will include the following volumes:

To see which titles are available,
visit our web site at www.zondervan.com

NIV Application Commentary
Series Introduction

THE NIV APPLICATION COMMENTARY SERIES is unique. Most commentaries help us make the journey from the twentieth century back to the first century. They enable us to cross the barriers of time, culture, language, and geography that separate us from the biblical world. Yet they only offer a one-way ticket to the past and assume that we can somehow make the return journey on our own. Once they have explained the *original meaning* of a book or passage, these commentaries give us little or no help in exploring its *contemporary significance*. The information they offer is valuable, but the job is only half done.

Recently, a few commentaries have included some contemporary application as *one* of their goals. Yet that application is often sketchy or moralistic, and some volumes sound more like printed sermons than commentaries.

The primary goal of The NIV Application Commentary Series is to help you with the difficult but vital task of bringing an ancient message into a modern context. The series not only focuses on application as a finished product but also helps you think through the *process* of moving from the original meaning of a passage to its contemporary significance. These are commentaries, not popular expositions. They are works of reference, not devotional literature.

The format of the series is designed to achieve the goals of the series. Each passage is treated in three sections: *Original Meaning, Bridging Contexts,* and *Contemporary Significance.*

THIS SECTION HELPS you understand the meaning of the biblical text in its first-century context. All of the elements of traditional exegesis—in concise form—are discussed here. These include the historical, literary, and cultural context of the passage. The authors discuss matters related to grammar and syntax, and the meaning of biblical words. They also seek to explore the main ideas of the passage and how the biblical author develops those ideas.[1]

---

1. Please note that when the authors discuss words in the original biblical languages, this series used the general rather than the scholarly method of transliteration.

After reading this section, you will understand the problems, questions, and concerns of the *original audience* and how the biblical author addressed those issues. This understanding is foundational to any legitimate application of the text today.

THIS SECTION BUILDS a bridge between the world of the Bible and the world of today, between the original context and the contemporary context, by focusing on both the timely and timeless aspects of the text.

God's Word is *timely*. The authors of Scripture spoke to specific situations, problems, and questions. Paul warned the Galatians about the consequences of circumcision and the dangers of trying to be justified by law (Gal. 5:2–5). The author of Hebrews tried to convince his readers that Christ is superior to Moses, the Aaronic priests, and the Old Testament sacrifices. John urged his readers to "test the spirits" of those who taught a form of incipient Gnosticism (1 John 4:1–6). In each of these cases, the timely nature of Scripture enables us to hear God's Word in situations that were *concrete* rather than abstract.

Yet the timely nature of Scripture also creates problems. Our situations, difficulties, and questions are not always directly related to those faced by the people in the Bible. Therefore, God's word to them does not always seem relevant to us. For example, when was the last time someone urged you to be circumcised, claiming that it was a necessary part of justification? How many people today care whether Christ is superior to the Aaronic priests? And how can a "test" designed to expose incipient Gnosticism be of any value in a modern culture?

Fortunately, Scripture is not only timely but *timeless*. Just as God spoke to the original audience, so he still speaks to us through the pages of Scripture. Because we share a common humanity with the people of the Bible, we discover a *universal dimension* in the problems they faced and the solutions God gave them. The timeless nature of Scripture enables it to speak with power in every time and in every culture.

Those who fail to recognize that Scripture is both timely and timeless run into a host of problems. For example, those who are intimidated by timely books such as Hebrews or Galatians might avoid reading them because they seem meaningless today. At the other extreme, those who are convinced of the timeless nature of Scripture, but who fail to discern its timely element, may "wax eloquent" about the Melchizedekian priesthood to a sleeping congregation.

The purpose of this section, therefore, is to help you discern what is timeless in the timely pages of the New Testament—and what is not. For example, if Paul's primary concern is not circumcision (as he tells us in Gal. 5:6), what *is* he concerned about? If discussions about the Aaronic priesthood or Melchizedek seem irrelevant today, what is of abiding value in these passages? If people try to "test the spirits" today with a test designed for a specific first-century heresy, what other biblical test might be more appropriate?

Yet this section does not merely uncover that which is timeless in a passage but also helps you to see *how* it is uncovered. The author of the commentary seeks to take what is implicit in the text and make it explicit, to take a process that normally is intuitive and explain it in a logical, orderly fashion. How do we know that circumcision is not Paul's primary concern? What clues in the text or its context help us realize that Paul's real concern is at a deeper level?

Of course, those passages in which the historical distance between us and the original readers is greatest require a longer treatment. Conversely, those passages in which the historical distance is smaller or seemingly nonexistent require less attention.

One final clarification. Because this section prepares the way for discussing the contemporary significance of the passage, there is not always a sharp distinction or a clear break between this section and the one that follows. Yet when both sections are read together, you should have a strong sense of moving from the world of the Bible to the world of today.

 THIS SECTION ALLOWS the biblical message to speak with as much power today as it did when it was first written. How can you apply what you learned about Jerusalem, Ephesus, or Corinth to our present-day needs in Chicago, Los Angeles, or London? How can you take a message originally spoken in Greek and Aramaic and communicate it clearly in our own language? How can you take the eternal truths originally spoken in a different time and culture and apply them to the similar-yet-different needs of our culture?

In order to achieve these goals, this section gives you help in several key areas.

First, it helps you identify contemporary situations, problems, or questions that are truly comparable to those faced by the original audience. Because contemporary situations are seldom identical to those faced in the first century, you must seek situations that are analogous if your applications are to be relevant.

Second, this section explores a variety of contexts in which the passage might be applied today. You will look at personal applications, but you will also be encouraged to think beyond private concerns to the society and culture at large.

Third, this section will alert you to any problems or difficulties you might encounter in seeking to apply the passage. And if there are several legitimate ways to apply a passage (areas in which Christians disagree), the author will bring these to your attention and help you think through the issues involved.

In seeking to achieve these goals, the contributors to this series attempt to avoid two extremes. They avoid making such specific applications that the commentary might quickly become dated. They also avoid discussing the significance of the passage in such a general way that it fails to engage contemporary life and culture.

Above all, contributors to this series have made a diligent effort not to sound moralistic or preachy. The NIV Application Commentary Series does not seek to provide ready-made sermon materials but rather tools, ideas, and insights that will help you communicate God's Word with power. If we help you to achieve that goal, then we have fulfilled the purpose for this series.

—The Editors

General Editor's Preface

THE GOSPEL HAS ALWAYS BEEN about change and choice. *Change* from an old way of life without Jesus Christ to a new way of life with Jesus Christ is a staple of God's message to us in Scripture. *Choice*, however, regarding what we do with our new status in Jesus Christ has been an equally important part of the message. Does it really make a difference, this new status, in the way we live? Do choices really reflect the change adequately? Change and choice might be called the twin pillars of the Good News.

Ephesians is one New Testament book that emphasizes these twin pillars. Although Klyne Snodgrass, the author of this excellent commentary, warns about a too easy dichotomy between the first three chapters that describe the change from life in the darkness to life in the light and the second three chapters that talk about hard choices that this new order demands, the subject matter does lend itself to recognizing at least an emphasis on change in the first half and choice in the second half. Salvation, conversion, or change, Paul tells us, is a gift of God: Formerly you were of the "uncircumcised," now you are of the "circumcised." You used to be "foreigners and aliens," now you are "fellow citizens." This change in status demands choices—choices between disunity and unity, good and bad family life, good and bad social structures.

This talk about changes and choices does indeed make Ephesians read like a contemporary letter. Almost everything in it rings a bell for anyone concerned about modern culture. The words themselves—change and choice— are buzz words in contemporary self-help psychology, education, and vocational guidance. Application in such a climate seems like a no-brainer— except for one consideration. Is it possible that the relative emphasis between change and choice is different for twenty-first century readers and first-century readers? Both are interested in change and choice, of course. But would a first-century reader look at the relationship between change and choice a bit differently?

It is possible that for a first-century reader, the miracle of change, of salvation given freely as a gift from an omnipotent God, was the focal point of this kind of discussion. That God (or the gods) existed would have been assumed as a matter of fact. That these gods controlled both the exceptional and the everyday—weather, crops, war—was likewise beyond question. But would such a God take the time to bring about change in me, an individual sinner? Most first-century gods were shorthand for Fate, an inevitable, unchangeable destiny to which I was born and, if I was smart, resigned. That God would actually put in place a mechanism to provide lasting change in my life—this was the unthinkable. The choices of life follow hard on the "change" of conversion; a God that can work such a change is fully capable of giving us an inspired guidebook, a Bible, to outline the choices we must now make.

For moderns, change is not all that unthinkable. Go into your local bookstore and go to the self-help psychology section. The rows and rows of books you find there are all about change: Change your body shape in thirty days; change from a business failure to a business success by following these seven key principles. No, change (even if it is human-initiated change) is pretty much assumed by modern individuals. The focal point for moderns is choice. Because we have relocated the capacity for change from an all-powerful God to human reason, the choices of "how we should then live" are as varied as the number of human beings who propose them. If God does not change, then choices become central. And moderns are besieged, literally overwhelmed, with the variety of choices we face in everything—from how to raise our children, to how we should love our neighbors, to what we should eat, to whom to vote for in political elections.

The great wisdom in Ephesians, as Professor Snodgrass so ably shows us, is its emphasis on both change and choice as the twin pillars. One cannot exist without the other. And the place that change and choice ever and again come together is in our liturgy and worship. Ephesians is filled with prayer and praise for our great and sovereign Lord, who shows us, as we worship him, that one cannot become a new creature without acting like one, and that knowing how to act can only come if one recognizes the great change brought about in the new life in Jesus Christ.

—Terry C. Muck

Author's Preface

THE LETTER WE KNOW AS EPHESIANS has always been a magnet for me. Its description of life with and in Christ has intrigued and challenged me. Part of the challenge was to understand; part was to obey. Ephesians has also provided a sense of peace and hope, surely one of the reasons the apostle Paul wrote the letter. Upon invitation to write for the NIV Application Commentary Series, I did not have to wonder which New Testament book to select. I chose Ephesians, or rather Ephesians had chosen me years earlier. Even the mission statement of the school where I teach, North Park Theological Seminary, focuses on Ephesians 1:10: "to bring all things in heaven and on earth together under one head, even Christ."

My first serious work on Ephesians started in seminary, and for almost thirty years since this letter has been a topic of interest. I have taught it often in seminary and in churches, and it has been the focus of my preaching more than any other New Testament book. Yet I have no illusion that I have grasped all the letter has to offer. Many other questions could have been treated. The issues I did treat are ones I felt most important for pastors and church leaders. Discussion of more technical items can be found in the major critical commentaries.

My explanation of the NIV translation is based on the Greek text; in fact, during the course of the study I became even more convinced of the value and importance of working with the original languages when studying Scripture. In their effort to help, all translations mislead. I have tried to be as explicit as possible to help readers of the NIV know how the Greek text functions and where questions need to be addressed.

I am fully aware how much about Ephesians I have learned from others, both from teachers and especially from commentaries and monographs. I make no claim to originality. Even where my sources are not specifically cited, they have contributed to my thinking.

I must express gratitude to several people. My work has been supported by both the administration and the faculty of North Park Theological Seminary. This community and the biblical faculty of the college provide a collegial context for my work. My colleague in theology, John Weborg, has been a particularly helpful dialogue partner. Sonia Bodi and Ann Briody, North Park librarians, went well beyond the call of duty in helping to locate resources. Nathan Pawl, my teaching assistant and friend, saved me an enormous amount of time and helped make the work enjoyable. In addition to expected responsibilities, he read and commented on the entire manuscript and prepared the indices. John Painter of LaTrobe Universitiy in Australia read an early version of the treatment of chapter one and made several helpful suggestions. Carey Newman of Southern Baptist Theological Seminary, who has done his own extensive study of Ephesians, also graciously read almost the entire manuscript and made copious notations. Such investment from colleagues is of enormous benefit. I have also profited from my discussions with students at North Park as we have worked on Ephesians together. The editors on this project—Terry Muck, Marianne Meye Thompson, and Scot McKnight—and the people from Zondervan—Jack Kuhatschek and Stan Gundry—all helped in clarifying my thinking. Particular thanks go to Marianne for reading several early sections and pushing me not to be so abstract. Appreciation goes as well to Verlyn Verbrugge, who helped make the commentary more readable. To all these people I express my thanks.

Most of all I thank my wife, Phyllis, for supporting me for many years now. She has done way more than anyone could ask and has made the journey fun along the way.

Klyne Snodgrass
Paul W. Brandel Professor of New Testament Studies
North Park Theological Seminary
Chicago, Illinois

Abbreviations

BJRL	Bulletin of the John Rylands University Library
CBQ	Catholic Biblical Quarterly
ExpTim	Expository Times
GTJ	Grace Theological Journal
JBL	Journal of Biblical Literature
JSNT	Journal for the Study of the New Testament
JTS	Journal of Theological Studies
KJV	King James Version
LXX	Septuagint
NASB	New American Standard Bible
NCB	New Century Bible
NEB	New English Bible
NIV	New International Version
NRSV	New Revised Standard Version
NTS	New Testament Studies
RevEx	Review and Expositor
RSV	Revised Standard Version
SJT	Scottish Journal of Theology
TDNT	Theological Dictionary of the New Testament
TrinJ	Trinity Journal
WTJ	Westminster Theological Journal

Introduction

"POUND FOR POUND" Ephesians may well be the most influential document ever written. Within the history of Christianity, only the Psalms, the Gospel of John, and Romans have been so instrumental in shaping the life and thought of Christians, but all three of these works are much longer than the few pages of this letter. Ephesians has justly been described as "the Switzerland of the New Testament," "the crown and climax of Pauline theology," and "one of the divinest compositions of man." The explanation of the gospel and of life with Christ provided here is powerful and direct. If read receptively, it is a bombshell.

This letter is the most contemporary book in the Bible.[1] Apart from a few terms and the treatment of slavery, Ephesians could have been written to a modern church. It is about *us*. It describes human beings, their predicament, sin, and delusion, but much more it describes God's reaching out to people to recreate and transform them into a new society.[2] Most of the letter is about two subjects: *power* and *identity*. It describes the power God's Spirit gives for living. It shows who we really are without Christ and who we become both individually and corporately with Christ. It is about how we understand ourselves and how we can get along with each other and God. The focus on God's new society also makes Ephesians one of the most important works for understanding the church.

Modern society is in a mess. For all the good things we enjoy, we seem to have lost all sense of definition and direction. Who are we really, and what holds us together? We all have a need to belong, but to what? Is there anything that merits our commitment? This life is hard. Where will we find the resources to make it? Our society's moral guidelines have been erased. Are there boundaries and values that function as legitimate guides? What is a human life for anyway?

The church is supposed to have answers to such questions, but in our day it has lost both its direction and its voice. The lives of Christians are too often no different from the lives of non-Christians. The gospel has been

---

1. John Mackay, *God's Order: The Ephesian Letter and this Present Time* (New York: Macmillan, 1953), 19.

2. *God's New Society* is the title of John R. W. Stott's commentary on Ephesians (Downer's Grove, Ill.: InterVarsity, 1979), now published under the title *The Message of Ephesians: God's New Society*. Note the similarity to John Mackay's *God's Order*.

diluted to ineffectual pabulum and so garbled by cultural trappings that it bears little resemblance to the pages of the New Testament. The Western church, including the American church, is not the—or even *a*—New Testament church.

We need nothing less than a new reformation, and Ephesians is the document to bring it about. This short little letter is a surprisingly comprehensive statement about God and his work, about Christ and the gospel, about life with God's Spirit, and about the right way to live.

The Message of Ephesians

THE LETTER IS consistently theocentric and Trinitarian. Its message about God's grace and love is encouraging and rewarding. God is not some remote being; he is the prime actor throughout the letter. From the beginning the letter shows we were always meant to belong to God and that God has been and is at work to make the reality of our relationship with him happen. In Christ and by the Spirit God brings us to himself and gives us what we need for life.

All the privileges of life are found in *union with Christ* and conveyed by the Spirit. Ephesians presents a gospel of union with Christ more powerfully than any other New Testament letter. Nothing short of attachment to him will rescue us from the human plight, and nothing can define us as human beings more than attachment to him. From living with him we learn how to live for him.

The understanding of the gospel in Ephesians challenges and redefines the superficial understanding of the gospel prevalent in our day. This gospel requires people to act; this faith works. Believers have a responsibility to make choices and to change the pattern of their lives. An easy believism or passive faith cannot survive under the penetrating message of this letter.

Repeatedly Ephesians distinguishes one's former way of life with life in Christ. These *formerly-now* contrasts offer a painful but realistic assessment of life without God, and they also give engaging descriptions of conversion and its effects. Nowhere else in the Bible is conversion so clearly described as here. In fact, the contrast in 5:8 functions as a summary of much of the letter: "For once you were darkness, but now you are light in the Lord. Live as children of light." Such portrayals of life before and with Christ are designed to keep people from living like everyone around them and to call them to mirror their relation with Christ in their daily lives.

Consequently, Ephesians provides some of the most direct and practical guidelines for living found in Scripture. Not every subject is covered by any means, but the foundation and guidelines are so clear that application to other issues follows directly. Be warned, however: Ephesians does not give a list of rules to follow, nor can response be superficial or easy. This letter requires us to change our inner being and character in a radical way. Life can no longer merely happen, for all our activity must now take place in, to, and for the Lord. Truth and love as defined by Christ become the twin forces guiding all else. In fact, Ephesians has more focus on truth and love than nearly all other New Testament documents.[3]

The concern for truth and love undergirds an emphasis on relationships, both between God and human beings and among people. Ephesians is relentlessly relational. All relations in this letter are viewed—not individualistically—but from the perspective of union with Christ. From life with Christ we relate to God and to others. We are part of Christ and part of each other (cf. 4:25; 5:30), a statement that also functions as a fitting summary of what it means to be a Christian. Not surprisingly, then, the themes of unity, peace, and the body of Christ have a dominant role in the letter. We come to God bound to Christ and to the other believers in him. God is honored in the company of people bound together in Christ.

In explaining what this group is and how it functions, Ephesians provides some of the most insightful theological thinking on the church in the New Testament. Various images—body, building, family, and marriage—combine to stress interrelatedness, belonging, connection, and mutuality. Our world is fractured by racism, individualism, and classism, and all of us know the pain and the enormity of these problems. Ephesians holds up another model, one that destroys racism and divisions, for it tells of God's providing a wholeness that binds us together. Our churches need to recover their identity as corporate representations of people being joined together in Christ. Ephesians tells us how to be the church.

One of the largest failures of the church is in worship and prayer. Ephesians does not discuss these subjects; rather, a good deal of Ephesians *is* worship and prayer. The first chapter is entirely praise and prayer, a primer on worship that demonstrates how to worship and engages us in worship. Possibly the first three chapters are prayer. Also, Ephesians throughout incorporates worship language from the early church, so much so that large chunks of the letter have been identified by scholars as tradition or hymns that Paul borrowed from earlier sources. Not all such identifications are convincing, but Ephesians is prime material for learning how to worship and pray.

Furthermore, Ephesians focuses on evangelism, though the focus is much different than the halting attempts of the modern church. The theology of

---

3. Among the letters, only 1 John has more focus on both, and only 1 Corinthians has more focus on love.

the gospel and the understanding of the church presented in Ephesians require us to rethink how evangelism is done. This letter has the potential to revitalize how we do evangelism.

With all the concern about Christian identity, Ephesians also has a pervasive emphasis on the mind. The revelation that comes in the gospel changes our thinking process. Conversion is a renewal of the mind, a transition from a darkened stupor to alert and enlightened wisdom. Too often Christians neglect the treasure of their own minds, and our churches and our society show it. Life's problems are large, and threats to life and right living are real, but Ephesians will not allow us to fear or retreat. Rather, it calls us to think, to learn, to become wise, and to act. If you are not willing to work mentally, Ephesians asserts that Christianity is not the religion for you.

Ephesians truly is the letter for today.[4] This is the message we need, for it tells us who we are, who God is, and what we are to do. It tells us that for Christians the origin and recipient of every act is Jesus Christ (see esp. 6:5-9). This letter, almost two thousand years old, comes as the word of God, seeking entrance with us and response from us. It offers both direction and confidence for living. We and our churches need to make this letter part of our very being.

What Is This Letter?

DESPITE THE GRANDEUR of the letter and the breadth of its influence, Ephesians is something of an enigma. We do not know to whom the letter was sent, from where it was sent, or why it was sent. (Those who do not accept Paul's authorship would add *by whom it was sent*.) All of Paul's letters include a co-author like Timothy or Silas except Romans and Ephesians, the two most influential Christian letters. It is startling that precisely for these two New Testament letters their purpose continues to be a matter of serious debate.

More detailed treatment of introductory issues may be found in the standard New Testament introductions and technical commentaries. In this commentary a summary of the most important issues is provided, as well as an assessment of the options and an indication of how decisions affect the application of the letter. The most important subjects requiring analysis are the letter's destination, purpose, and authorship, which are to some degree intertwined.

---

4. See the treatment by Neil Alexander, "The Epistle for Today," *Biblical Studies: Essays in Honour of William Barclay*, eds. Johnston R. McKay and James F. Miller (London: Collins, 1976), 99–118.

Destination

TWO FACTORS MAKE Ephesus unlikely as the destination of the letter. (1) The words "in Ephesus" are omitted in several early witnesses, including p46, which dates to the beginning of the third century and is the earliest manuscript we have of this letter. A few scholars argue that Ephesus was the original destination and that the city's name has been removed to make the letter acceptable to a broader audience. Most scholars, however, recognize that "in Ephesus" has been added later to the text. The problem is that without the "address," verse 1 does not make much sense.[5] Several emendations have been proposed, but although interesting, none is convincing.[6] The suggestion that the letter is a circular letter to be read in more than one place is probably correct, but the hypothesis that the original letter left a blank to be filled in by Tychicus, the letter carrier (cf. 6:21–22), is without foundation.

(2) Most likely the author did not know the readers personally. The statements in 1:15; 3:2–4; and 6:23–24 do not sound like comments of someone with firsthand knowledge of his readers. According to Acts, Paul spent better than two years in Ephesus and was emotionally attached to the believers there.[7] If this letter were to Ephesus, one would expect it to have more of the warmth evidenced in Philippians instead of the general tone it has.

Obviously then, specific knowledge of Ephesus—as amazing as this ancient city was—does not help us much in interpreting the letter. We may safely assume that the letter was a general letter to Gentile believers in southwestern Asia Minor and that it became identified with Ephesus as the most important city between Rome and Antioch.[8]

The Purpose of the Letter

THE PURPOSE OF the letter is directly tied to the question of authorship. Over a century ago Adolf Jülicher felt constrained to accept Pauline authorship because no convincing hypothesis could explain why a Pauline disciple would compose such a letter.[9] This is still the case, and the strained explanations of

---

5. Especially the Greek text, which translated literally reads: "Paul, an apostle of Christ Jesus through the will of God, to the holy ones who are and faithful in Christ Jesus."

6. The most attractive of these emendations are: (a) "Asia"; (b) "Hierapolis and Laodicea"; (c) "the holy and faithful who are in Christ Jesus." Hierapolis and Laodicea were two cities near Colosse, forming a "tri-city" complex. Marcion labeled Ephesians as the letter to the Laodiceans (cf. Col. 4:16).

7. See Acts 18:19–21; 19:1–41; 20:17–38.

8. It is also possible that Ephesus was one of several cities to which the letter went.

9. Adolf Jülicher, *An Introduction to the New Testament*, trans. Janet Penrose Ward (London: Smith, Elder, 1904), 146–47.

purpose by those advocating authorship by a Pauline disciple show how embarrassing the problem is. The suggestion of E. J. Goodspeed, for example, that Ephesians was intended to introduce a collection of Paul's letters, is rarely accepted.[10] What would motivate a pseudonymous author to write just this general material for an unspecified audience?

The difficulty is obvious in the discussion of A. Lincoln, who believes the letter was written by someone other than Paul. After summarizing the letter, he admits this "summary may appear not to amount to very much, hardly to have been worth the effort. . . . "[11] He suggests its original readers needed to be reminded of the debt they owed to Paul, but why was that important twenty or more years after his death, and is this letter the way to achieve the goal? Lincoln further suggests that the local concerns that prompted Colossians were still around and needed addressing,[12] but the more Ephesians is brought into the context of the situation in Colossians, the more likely it was written by Paul at about the same time.

R. Schnackenburg's solutions are no more helpful. In his view the author addresses pastoral concerns of his time, which are not easy to determine. He suggests a *crisis* of leadership that the author of Ephesians noted in a *nonspecific* manner because of diverse local conditions, but which he nevertheless considered *ominous*. Schnackenburg concludes that "we are justified in talking of a 'spiritual crisis' which is mirrored in the muted admonition of Eph."[13] The juxtaposition of "muted" and "crisis" shows the improbability of the hypothesis.

No crisis appears to be addressed in Ephesians, and no specific opponents are attacked. Why would a pseudonymous author write a general letter with no particular purpose? Until a convincing explanation surfaces as to why someone would compose a letter like Ephesians and what that person was trying to accomplish by sending it out as a letter of Paul, the explanation of non-Pauline authorship cannot be judged as attractive or compelling.

On the other hand, if the letter is from Paul, its purpose is still difficult to detect. It is so general that it almost appears to be a sermon or tract dressed up as a letter. In fact, some have suggested Ephesians is a baptismal homily or a sermon for renewing baptismal vows. This is unlikely, although 4:22–24 is probably a baptismal confession. Even though the subject matter in this document is general, this is a genuine letter and its form should not be slighted.

---

10. Edgar J. Goodspeed, *The Key to Ephesians* (Chicago: Univ. of Chicago Press, 1956).

11. Lincoln, *Ephesians*, lxxix.

12. Ibid., lxxxii.

13. R. Schnackenburg, *Ephesians: A Commentary*, 23, 34–35 (italics mine). See also Werner Georg Kümmel, *Introduction to the New Testament*, trans. Howard Clark Kee (Nashville: Abingdon, 1975), 364, who suggests Ephesians was addressed to a "general spiritual crisis." But can a crisis be general?

The key to understanding the purpose of Ephesians lies in Colossians. There Paul did address a problem, one in which Christians were being belittled and disqualified and were in danger of being led astray by other religious teachings (Col. 2:4–23). The problem was exacerbated by the embarrassment of Paul's imprisonment. The Colossians also were Christians Paul had not met, but notice the depth of feeling expressed for these Gentile believers in 2:1–5. Even though he did not know them, they belonged to his ministry. His desire for them was that they would be *encouraged and united in love and would understand* fully the mystery of God in Christ. That is precisely the purpose of Ephesians.[14] After addressing the specific problem in Colosse, and with the same depth of feeling for Gentile Christians, Paul wrote a more general letter to encourage, unite, and inform all the believers in that area.

Ephesians, then, has as its main purpose *identity formation*.[15] It seeks to shape believers by reminding them how wonderful God's work in Christ is, how significant their unity with Christ is, and what living for Christ looks like. It is a letter of definition and encouragement.[16] Paul sought to ground, shape, and challenge his readers so that they might live their faith.

Authorship

THE WITNESS OF the early church for the influence of Ephesians as a letter from Paul is extensive. It was referred to early and often, from Clement of Rome (A.D. 95) on. It is quoted by Ignatius and Polycarp and included both in Marcion's canon of Paul's letters (about 140) and in the Muratorian Fragment (usually dated about 180).

Moreover, Ephesians claims to be by Paul and has Pauline language and theology. Not until the nineteenth century was its authenticity as a Pauline letter questioned.

Yet in our day, the authorship of the letter is heavily debated, and in academic circles it is increasingly not respectable to argue for Pauline authorship.[17] However, despite the frequency with which Pauline authorship is denied, the case against Ephesians is *not* obvious. The situation is not like

---

14. Cf. Colossians 2:2 and Ephesians 6:22.

15. J. Paul Sampley, "Ephesians," *The Deutero-Pauline Letters* (Minneapolis: Fortress, 1993), 23.

16. Nils A. Dahl similarly suggests that Ephesians is a letter of reminder and congratulations; see his "Interpreting Ephesians: Then and Now," *Currents in Theology and Mission*, 5 (1978): 133–43.

17. Two massive studies of authorship should be consulted: C. Leslie Mitton, *The Epistle to the Ephesians*, presents the case against Pauline authorship, while A. Van Roon, *The Authenticity of Ephesians*, argues for it.

---

the Pastoral Letters, where major differences in language exist. The language and thought of Ephesians are still very much Paul's own. Even those who reject Paul's authorship speak of the writer as pondering Paul's letters (especially Colossians) so intimately that they became part of the equipment of his mind.[18] But if Ephesians is so Pauline, why was the authorship ever questioned?

Usually obstacles to Paul's authorship are divided into several categories:

(1) *Linguistic and stylistic arguments.* For example, Ephesians uses "in the heavenly realms" (which Paul's other letters only use as an adjective) and "the devil" instead of "Satan" (as in his undisputed letters). Ephesians is much more liturgical and expansive, having long sentences and numerous prepositional phrases and genitive ("of") constructions.

(2) *Historical arguments.* The Jew-Gentile controversy is settled, and "the barrier" broken down in 2:14 is easier to understand after the destruction of the temple in A.D. 70.

(3) *Literary considerations.* The relation of Ephesians to Colossians and other New Testament letters suggests dependence of the author on these other writings. Furthermore, the comments in 2:20 and 3:1–13 suggest too lofty a view of the apostles and of Paul to be understood as coming from Paul. Would Paul have spoken of the "*holy* apostles" (3:5)?

(4) *Theological differences with the authentic letters.* The word *church* in Ephesians refers to the universal church, whereas in Paul's other letters it usually refers to a local church. The death of Christ is supposedly diminished. The terms *body* and *mystery* are supposedly used in slightly different ways from other Pauline letters.

Such issues are not irrelevant, but they are not difficult to treat. The linguistic and stylistic variations are not out of bounds, particularly given the subject matter and the fact that much of Ephesians is doxology and prayer. If the letter was written around A.D. 60, the problem of the Judaizers would not be at the fore. In fact, the tone of Romans is already different from Galatians, and the concern for the unity of Gentiles and Jews in Ephesians is similar to Paul's concern in Romans. The other theological differences can be accounted for if the letter was intended as a circular letter and if a primary concern was unity. The death of Christ is still very much a theme of Ephesians, despite assertions to the contrary (see 1:7; 2:13–16; 5:2).

---

18. Mitton, *The Epistle to the Ephesians*, 261. See Ernst Käsemann, "Ephesians and Acts," *Studies in Luke-Acts*, eds. L. E. Keck and J. L. Martyn (London: SPCK, 1968), 288, who says that the craftsmanship of the author leads us very close to Paul!

True, Ephesians *is* different in some respects, but most of the objections raised are a smokescreen. At bottom, the rejection of Pauline authorship is based on two items: its relationship with Colossians and the description of Paul and the apostles and prophets in 2:20 and 3:1–13 (especially 3:4–5), which seems to exalt Paul's own role and that of the apostles excessively. Decisions on these items usually determine conclusions about authorship.

The relation to Colossians. Colossians should be read repeatedly when interpreting Ephesians, for the two are intimately related, somewhat like the relation of Romans and Galatians, (though the parallels there are not as extensive). Approximately 34 percent of Colossians is paralleled by about 25 percent of Ephesians. The parallels are not exact and rarely exceed five words in succession.[19] The one exception to this is—of all places—the instructions to Tychicus, for which the two letters have thirty-two words in common and are almost in verbatim agreement.[20]

These are the facts; all else is theory. Are the parallels evidence of one mind (Paul's) writing two letters in the same time frame—one addressed to a specific church with a specific problem and the other more general and addressed to a broader area? Or are the parallels evidence of a Pauline disciple who is responsible for one or both letters?[21]

The description of Paul and the apostles (2:20 and 3:1–13). The description of the apostles and prophets as part of the foundation of the church (2:20) is understandable, at least as long as metaphors are not viewed inflexibly. The apostles and prophets do have a founding role, as evidenced also in Revelation 21:14, where the wall of the heavenly city is said to have twelve foundations, on which are the names of the twelve apostles. The focus of Ephesians 2:20 is not on the apostles and prophets personally, but on their contribution as teachers who established the faith. The intent with this verse is no different from Colossians 2:7 ("rooted and built up in him,

---

19. Compare Eph. 1:1–2 and Col. 1:1–2, which is not too important; Eph. 1:7 and Col. 1:14; Eph. 2:5 and Col. 2:13; Eph. 3:2 and Col. 1:25; Eph. 3:9 and Col. 1:26; Eph. 4:16 and Col. 2:19; Eph. 4:32 and Col. 3:13; Eph. 5:5–6 and Col. 3:5–6; Eph. 5:19–20 and Col. 3:16–17; Eph. 6:1–4 and Col. 3:20–21; Eph. 6:5–9 and Col. 3:22–4:1. More detailed comparisons can be found in the *Zondervan NIV Bible Commentary* (Grand Rapids: Zondervan, 1994), 2:758-759, and in Abbott, *A Critical and Exegetical Commentary on Ephesians and Colossians*, xxiii.

20. See Eph. 6:21–22 and Col. 4:7–8.

21. Most scholars assume that Colossians was written first and served as a model for Ephesians. Those arguing Ephesians was not written by Paul would not argue the author copied from Colossians; they would say the writer was so enamored with Colossians that its wording became his wording. Other scholars challenge this reconstruction by arguing Ephesians was first and served as the model for Colossians, while some even question any literary relation at all.

strengthened in the faith as you were taught"), even though Colossians makes no reference to the people doing the teaching.[22]

The material in 3:1–13 presents at the same time the strongest argument against Pauline authorship (3:5) and some of the strongest arguments for Pauline authorship. The seemingly self-centered statements about Paul's own apostolic role, for example, have led those who reject Pauline authorship to conclude these verses are the attempt by a pseudonymous writer to claim Paul's authority and theology for himself. At the same time, they see the self-identification in 3:8 ("less than the least of all God's people") as "theatrical ... artificial exaggeration ... forced and unnatural."[23] On the other hand, those who accept Paul's authorship reject such judgments, see the description in 3:8 as the "very hallmark of apostolic authenticity," and argue no disciple of Paul would dream of giving him so low a place.[24] At least we must recognize that the tone and attitude of verse 8 is close to the words in 1 Corinthians 15:8–10 and 2 Corinthians 10–12.

Tension clearly exists between Paul's exaltation of his apostolic office (3:3–7) and his humility (3:8), but this phenomenon is common in his unquestioned letters. Paul had a high view of his apostolic office, insisted on the legitimacy of that office, and would take a backseat to no one. In 2 Corinthians 3:1–4:6 he even saw the revelation in his gospel as superior to the revelation to Moses and comparable to the creation of light![25] His rank as an apostle depended on the revelation of the risen Lord to him, and both the book of Acts and his letters insist that the revelation to him included a call to take the gospel to the Gentiles (see Acts 9:15; 22:21; 26:17; Rom. 1:1–5; Gal. 1:15–17). At the same time he knew he was unworthy of this ministry, for he had persecuted the church (1 Cor. 15:8–10).

The most troublesome language is the expression "*holy* apostles and prophets" (3:5), for which no parallel exists in Paul's letters. Is this indication of a later age venerating people like Paul? At first glance this seems convincing and would explain 2:20 as well, but a closer look diminishes the force of this argument. The worrisome word is *holy,* but that is because we read into that word an aura that suggests exaltation, reverence, and veneration. Remember that Paul's most common way to refer to Christians is *the holy ones* (NIV *saints*). The word means nothing more than "those whom God has set apart."[26] If that is the connotation in 3:5, then no veneration by a past age

22. For further discussion of 2:20, see pp. 136–37.

23. Mitton, *The Epistle to the Ephesians,* 15, 136, 152.

24. Bruce, *The Epistle to the Ephesians,* 63.

25. See also Romans 1:1–17; 10:5–8; 15:15–21; 1 Corinthians 3:10–11; 9:1–27; 15:1–11; 2 Corinthians 10–13; Galatians 1:15–24.

26. Paul does speak of the Holy Scriptures (Rom. 1:2) and of the law as holy (7:12), but

is present. The word *holy*, in other words, is not a sufficient basis to reject Pauline authorship.[27] I would suggest that nothing more is intended by 3:5 than one finds in Romans 1:1–5, where Paul describes himself as "called to be an *apostle* and *set apart* for the gospel of God" and as one who has received "grace and apostleship" to bring about the obedience of faith among the Gentiles. This description of the apostles and prophets in Ephesians 3 fits with the purpose of encouraging the readers and should be compared to Paul's self-description as an ambassador of Christ in 6:20.

Moreover, what would a pseudonymous writer have gained by using such language (including 3:1–13)? Why would he refer to Paul as a prisoner and make nothing of his imprisonment? We can understand Paul's feeling deeply about his Gentile mission and trying to emphasize it, but why would a pseudonymous author do that? Nor may we argue that pseudonymity is a mere innocent literary device with no intent to deceive, and yet say that statements such as those in 3:1, 13 and 6:19–20 are "attempts at verisimilitude."[28]

In fact 3:13 and 6:19–20 may be keys in this discussion. If they are from Paul, these verses show the same concern he has in Philippians that Christians not be depressed because he is in prison. If written by a pseudonymous author, these verses accomplish little. Why warn people not to be discouraged over a man who has long been dead or ask people to pray for him?

In the end a decision about authorship will be made on some understanding of why 3:1–13 is included. In my opinion these verses express ideas passionately held by Paul and are paralleled in his unquestioned letters. Why they would be included by a later pseudonymous writer is unclear.[29] I have a hard time imagining such an author investing so much and making so little of what he wants his readers to do with the material.

Other factors. Three additional factors deserve consideration. (1) Although pseudepigraphy is a proven literary device in the ancient world, too little attention has been given to the subject of pseudepigraphal letters.

---

he also refers to a holy kiss (16:16, et al.) and in many manuscripts of 1 Thessalonians 5:27 to the holy brothers. If this latter were the correct reading, it would be a telling argument.

27. See Barth, *Ephesians*, 1:335.

28. Similar to 3:1, Paul refers to himself by name within the body of other letters (see 2 Cor. 10:1; Gal. 5:2; 1 Thess. 2:18). Note Lincoln, *Ephesians*, 455, on 6:19-20, who claims that Paul's request for prayer, although he is deceased, is supposed to be both a literary device and a request by the real author for prayer for his own proclamation of the gospel. Lewis R. Donelson, *Pseudepigraphy and Ethical Argument in the Pastoral Epistles* (Tübingen: J. C. B. Mohr, 1986), 10–11, questions the frequent claim that pseudonymity was an innocent literary device with no intent to deceive.

29. Note how Schnackenburg, *Ephesians: A Commentary*, 135–36, struggles to answer this question, but not too convincingly. The same can be said for Lincoln, *Ephesians*, 171–72, 193–95.

Paul warns about the possibility in 2 Thessalonians 2:2 in such a way that it is clear he does not condone the practice.[30] Also, from all the evidence we have, the early church rejected known pseudepigraphal writings.[31] Until we do a better job explaining both the specific motivations of a pseudepigraph, who the real readers are, and how the letter addresses them, any theory of pseudonymity must be viewed as inadequately based.[32]

(2) The hypothesis of an imitator of Paul creates problems. The author would be a person who had read Paul's letters, especially Colossians, so much that he (or she) became a *mirror* of Paul, not just someone who sounds a bit like Paul. Does the human mind even operate this way, particularly on the basis of a letter as short as Colossians? Would a first-century imitator even attempt to adhere to the style of his source? No evidence exists that this happened.[33] Who is this marvelous mystery theologian who mirrors and even exceeds Paul, but has left no other known trace? Why would this person copy verbatim the instructions to Tychicus, the least important part of the letter? As G. B. Caird indicated, there are difficulties in attributing Ephesians to Paul, but these are insignificant in comparison with the difficulties of attributing it to an imitator.[34]

(3) Most important, Ephesians has extensive parallels in language and style with the Qumran scrolls. Despite the fact that these extensive parallels were detailed over thirty-five years ago,[35] few people have done justice to their implications. No other document in the New Testament is as close to the Qumran material as Ephesians, especially in the liturgical sections. These parallels not only show the writer was Jewish, they virtually require an early

---

30. Many, of course, deny the authenticity of 2 Thessalonians as well.

31. See Donelson, *Pseudepigraphy*, 11, who assumed several New Testament letters are pseudonymous, but was unable to find a single example of someone accepting a document known to be a forgery. For a survey of recent discussion of pseudepigraphy, see Thomas D. Lea, "Pseudonymity and the New Testament," *New Testament Criticism and Interpretation*, eds. David Alan Black and David S. Dockery (Grand Rapids: Zondervan, 1991), 535–59.

32. This is especially true for a letter that emphasizes truth as much as Ephesians does. See also Richard Bauckham, "Pseudo-Apostolic Letters," *JBL* 107 (1988): 469–94, who points out that addressees of pseudepigraphs cannot be the real readers; they must be later people in an analogous situation. A pseudepigraph cannot perform the same function as a real letter (p. 475). He also points out how rare apocryphal apostolic letters were.

33. See the comments of H. J. Cadbury, "The Dilemma of Ephesians," *NTS* 5 (1958–1959): 95–96.

34. Caird, *Paul's Letters From Prison*, 29.

35. See Karl Georg Kuhn, "The Epistle to the Ephesians in the Light of the Qumran Texts," *Paul and Qumran: Studies in New Testament Exegesis*, ed. Jerome Murphy-O'Connor (Chicago: Priory Press, 1968),115–31 (originally published in *NTS*, 7 [1960–61]: 334–46), and Franz Mussner, "Contributions Made by Qumran to the Understanding of the Epistle to the Ephesians," in the same volume, 159–78.

date for the letter.[36] The later the date of Ephesians is set and the more the letter is removed from a Jewish context, the more difficult it is to account for the parallels.[37] The Qumran community was destroyed in A.D. 66, and Judaism changed significantly after A.D. 70. If the letter is dated between A.D. 80 and 95, what made a Jew in Asia Minor sound so much like the Judaism of Qumran?

Options concerning authorship. Various possibilities exist for resolving the authorship question. Alternatives include the following:

(1) The letter was written by Paul. Whether an amanuensis was used is of little relevance. The date of the composition depends on which of Paul's imprisonments are alluded to:
(a) if Ephesus, the letter would date about A.D. 55;
(b) if Caesarea, about A.D. 58;
(c) if Rome, about A.D. 60.
While a case can be made for any of these imprisonments, the Roman imprisonment is most likely.
(2) The letter was written by Paul, but has additions added by another hand. This is unlikely, but evaluation of such hypotheses depends on the specific form the suggestion takes. On this approach, the main part of the letter would stem from one of the dates above.
(3) The letter was written by a close disciple of Paul under his direction and/or following his intent, either while Paul was still in prison or closely after his death.[38] The date again would be between A.D. 60 to 64 or in some variations as late as the early 70s.
(4) The letter was written by a disciple and imitator of Paul some distance removed from his death. Often this person is left anonymous, but others suggest this disciple was Onesimus or Tychicus. On this approach the date of composition is assigned as early as A.D. 80 and as late as 95.

Almost forty years ago H. J. Cadbury asked cogently, "Which is more likely—that an imitator of Paul in the first century composed a writing ninety or ninety-five percent in accordance with Paul's style or that Paul himself wrote a letter diverging five or ten percent from his usual style?"[39] For me, the answer is obviously the latter.

---

36. See Barth, *Ephesians*, 1:21.

37. This also negates earlier attempts to find Gnostic influence behind Ephesians.

38. See Ralph P. Martin, "Ephesians," *The Broadman Bible Commentary* (Nashville: Broadman, 1971), 11:129, who thinks Luke is that disciple. Luke Timothy Johnson, *The Writings of the New Testament: An Interpretation* (Philadelphia: Fortress, 1986), 369–372, suggests a Pauline school active with Paul during his ministry.

39. Cadbury, "The Dilemma of Ephesians," 101.

What Difference Does it Make?

WHETHER EPHESIANS IS from Paul or a disciple of his is of major importance for two reasons. (1) If it is not by Paul, it cannot be used to reconstruct Paul's thought and that of the earliest church. Even if only subconsciously, all readers of the Bible carry in their heads a framework by which Scripture is understood. Assumptions about the occasion and time in which a document was written determine how it is understood. We do not read 1 Thessalonians the same way we read Philippians because of differing ideas about Paul the missionary in A.D. 50 and Paul the prisoner in A.D. 60. Do we include Ephesians in the attempt to understand Paul? Numerous books written on Paul's theology disregard Ephesians completely. If Ephesians is by Paul, the picture these works present is skewed.

(2) If Ephesians is not by Paul, it will likely be considered less important than Paul's other letters and will be used with less confidence. Those who date Ephesians to the latter part of the first century often see Ephesians as a movement toward "early catholicism" (usually a negative connotation). On this approach Ephesians is less focused on the Spirit, has less concern for the Parousia, salvation by faith, and Christology, and has more concern with ecclesiology and order. True, Ephesians does show development, but it is not early catholicism.

Those who reject Pauline authorship often argue that no devaluing of Ephesians should result. In reality, however, most of these scholars do consider it less authoritative. So while decisions about authorship and purpose do not necessarily make Ephesians less authoritative, in practice Ephesians is given less attention and less voice. But Ephesians is "the real thing," and it deserves maximum attention and application.

Outline

WHILE EPHESIANS IS easily divided into large sections, disagreement exists over how the first three chapters should be outlined. Paul's doxology and prayer could extend from 1:3 to 1:23, to 2:10, to 2:22, or all the way to 3:21. Although the second half of the letter focuses on ethics, Ephesians should not be halved into theological and ethical parts. The second half is also theological and the first half is also ethical.

    I. Salutation: Identification of Author, Recipients, and a Greeting (1:1–2)
   II. The Body of the Letter (1:3–6:20)
      A. A Meditation on God's Gift of Salvation (1:3–3:21)
         1. Doxology (1:3–14)

Annotated Bibliography

Commentaries on Ephesians

THIS LIST OF works on Ephesians is by no means exhaustive. Only those works most likely to be helpful for those working in the church are included.

Modern Comprehensive Commentaries

THREE COMMENTARIES STAND as the primary explanations of the letter. A fourth is expected to join this group when Ernest Best's forthcoming commentary in the New International Critical Commentary series appears.

Barth, Markus. *Ephesians*. Volumes 34 and 34A of The Anchor Bible. Garden City, N.Y.: Doubleday, 1974 (labeled vol. 1 and 2 in the footnotes). Barth's commentary is without equal. Over 800 pages are devoted to explanatory notes, extensive theological comments, and bibliographies. Greek words are transliterated and translated. Even when choices taken are not convincing, the information provided is a rich resource for reflection. Barth accepts Pauline authorship.

Lincoln, Andrew T. *Ephesians*. Vol. 42 of Word Biblical Commentary. Dallas: Word, 1990. Lincoln's commentary is comprehensive (468 pages), summarizes the issues well, and provides good bibliographical material for further work. The commentary is based on the Greek text, but translations are provided. Lincoln rejects Pauline authorship.

Schnackenburg, Rudolf. *Ephesians: A Commentary*. Trans. Helen Heron. Edinburgh: T. & T. Clark, 1991. Although somewhat briefer (345 pages), this major technical commentary, originally published in German, is from a Catholic scholar. Some decisions may be questionable, but they always merit consideration. If Greek is used, it is translated. Schnackenburg rejects Pauline authorship.

Older Comprehensive Commentaries

Abbott, Thomas K. *A Critical and Exegetical Commentary on the Epistle to the Ephesians and to the Colossians*. International Critical Commentary. New York: Scribner's, 1902. This work is not as comprehensive as the three listed above, but is still helpful. It is based on the Greek text, but does not translate Greek or foreign language quotations.

Eadie, J. *A Commentary on the Greek Text of the Epistle of Paul to the Ephesians*. 2d ed. New York: Carter, 1861. This lengthy commentary (485 pages), although dated and sometimes taking unusual turns, is still insightful and worth reading. Foreign languages are usually translated.

Hodge, Charles. *A Commentary on the Epistle to the Ephesians*. New York: Robert Carter and Brothers, 1864. Often reprinted, this commentary provides 389 pages of exegetical and theological analysis. Greek is usually translated.

Robinson, J. Armitage. *St. Paul's Epistle to the Ephesians*. London: Macmillan, 1903. Of the older commentaries, this one is probably the most significant. Actually it is two commentaries in one, for the author goes through the text of Ephesians twice: once to provide an English exposition and a second time to provide a technical commentary on the Greek text. Foreign language material in the second section is not translated.

Westcott, Brooke Foss. *Saint Paul's Epistle to the Ephesians*. London: Macmillan, 1906. A lot of information is packed into this commentary on the Greek text. Although cryptic because of its brevity, it deserves attention. Information on the theology of the letter and on a sizable number of specific phrases make up the last 75 pages of the commentary.

Shorter but Helpful Commentaries

Bruce, F. F. *The Epistle to the Ephesians*. New York: Revell, 1961. This is the shorter of Bruce's two commentaries (136 pages) and is based on the English text. Like all of Bruce's works, it is straightforward and provides good information.

_____. *The Epistles to the Colossians, to Philemon, and to the Ephesians*. The New International Commentary on the New Testament. Grand Rapids: Eerdmans, 1984. As is to be expected, there is some overlap with the shorter commentary. This one is almost 200 pages in length and has much more involvement with secondary sources. Greek is usually confined to the footnotes.

Caird, G. B. *Paul's Letters from Prison*. Oxford: Oxford Univ. Press, 1976. This short commentary has 94 pages of small print devoted to the English text of Ephesians. Although brief, Caird is often extremely insightful. This commentary merits use.

Foulkes, Francis. *The Letter of Paul to the Ephesians*. The Tyndale New Testament Commentaries. 2d ed. Grand Rapids: Eerdmans, 1989. The discussion is based on the English text. Occasional comments of real insight make this commentary worth reading.

Hendriksen, William. *Exposition of Ephesians*. Grand Rapids: Baker, 1967. This commentary is longer than most in this category (286 pages). Capable exegetical work stands behind the theological and expositional discussion of the text. Greek words appear occasionally, but are confined to the footnotes.

Mitton, C. Leslie. *Ephesians*. New Century Bible. London: Oliphants, 1976. A practical treatment of the English text of Ephesians by a scholar who has worked extensively on the authorship question. See below.

Stott, John R. W. *God's New Society*. Downers Grove, Ill.: InterVarsity, 1979. Also published as *The Message of Ephesians*. This is probably the most helpful of all the nontechnical commentaries on Ephesians. Stott is a master preacher, but he is also a careful scholar. In this commentary he provides almost 300 pages of valuable discussion of the English text. If Greek is brought in, it is translated.

Zerwick, Max. *The Epistle to the Ephesians*. Trans. Kevin Smyth. New York: Crossroad, 1981. Zerwick is best know for his work on Greek grammar, but this commentary is nontechnical. It was originally published in German. Frequently Zerwick offers insights that others miss.

Expositions and Sermons

Calvin, John. *Sermons on the Epistle to the Ephesians*. London: The Banner of Truth Trust, 1973 (reprint of 1577). Calvin, of course, also has a commentary on Ephesians that merits attention, but this is a collection of 48 sermons on Ephesians that cover over 700 pages! The sermons are discursive, but it is interesting to watch the Reformer in Geneva give major witness to the importance of Ephesians.

Chrysostom, John. *Homilies on Ephesians*. *Nicene and Post-Nicene Fathers of the Christian Church*. Edited by Philip Schaff. Grand Rapids: Eerdmans, 1988. Chrysostom has 24 homilies on Ephesians. They are similar to those of Calvin, but usually Chrysostom stays closer to the biblical text.

Mackay, John A. *God's Order: The Ephesian Letter and This Present Time*. New York: Macmillan, 1953. This book contains the text of lectures on Ephesians originally given at the University of Edinburgh. The material here is insightful theologically and is presented in compelling fashion. This book deserves to be read.

Moody, Dale. *Christ and the Church: An Exposition of Ephesians*. Grand Rapids: Eerdmans, 1963. Like Mackay, Moody was a theologian. His preaching on Ephesians provided the substance for this exposition. He communicates well the intent and value of Ephesians.

Morris, Leon. *Expository Reflections on the Letter to the Ephesians*. Grand Rapids: Baker, 1994. This book reads like a Bible study being led by a scholar— which is exactly what it is. It is nontechnical, but well-informed and a practical, sane exposition of the text.

Helpful Monographs

Arnold, Clinton E. *Ephesians: Power and Magic: The Concept of Power in Ephesians in Light of Historical Setting*. New York: Cambridge Univ. Press, 1989. This is an important book on an important topic. Ephesians emphasizes power and spiritual forces, and Arnold helps the reader understand the significance of this topic in the first-century church. Exegetical attention is given to all pertinent texts in Ephesians.

Caragounis, Chrys C. *The Ephesian Mysterion: Meaning and Content*. Lund: C. W. K. Gleerup, 1977. This monograph is more than an investigation of the term *mystery*, for the author analyzes several major sections and subjects of Ephesians.

Hanson, Stig. *The Unity of the Church in the New Testament: Colossians and Ephesians*. Uppsala: Almquist, 1946. Although the subtitle suggests the focus is on Colossians and Ephesians, this book provides a technical discussion of unity in the New Testament, with about forty pages being devoted to Ephesians. Despite, or possibly because of, the broader focus, this book makes a helpful contribution to understanding the theme of unity in Ephesians.

Lincoln, Andrew T. *Paradise Now and Not Yet*. Cambridge: Cambridge Univ. Press, 1981. This is a general study of Paul's thought about heaven and his eschatology. Only about 35 pages focus explicitly on Ephesians, but the importance of "the heavenly realms" in Ephesians makes this book worth mentioning.

Lincoln, Andrew T. *The Theology of the Later Pauline Letters*. Cambridge: Cambridge Univ. Press, 1993. About 90 pages are given to an explanation of the theology of Ephesians, how it (understood as a pseudonymous writing) relates to Paul's theology, and how it may be appropriated in the modern period.

Rader, William. *The Church and Racial Hostility: A History of Interpretation of Ephesians 2:11–22*. Tübingen: J. C. B. Mohr (Paul Siebeck), 1978. This book provides a chronicle of the interpretation of 2:11–22 from the Apostolic Fathers right up to the modern period and brings this history into the modern discussion about race relations.

Major Treatments of Authorship

Mitton, C. Leslie. *The Epistle to the Ephesians*. Oxford: Clarendon, 1951. Mitton's study is the classic treatment of the argument from one who rejects Pauline authorship. He makes too much of the parallels between Ephesians and other New Testament letters (excluding Colossians) and does not do justice to early Christian tradition behind all the writings.

Annotated Bibliography

Van Roon, A. *The Authenticity of Ephesians*. Leiden: E. J. Brill, 1974. This massive study is of benefit not only for its argument in favor of Pauline authorship, but also because about 150 pages are devoted to investigation of cosmic and anthropological expressions in Ephesians (e.g., "heavenlies," "powers," "fullness," "body," and "head").

Ephesians 1:1-2

P AUL, AN APOSTLE of Christ Jesus by the will of God, to the saints in Ephesus, the faithful in Christ Jesus: ²Grace and peace to you from God our Father and the Lord Jesus Christ.

LETTERS IN THE ancient world followed a set form. They began by identifying the writer and the readers or addressees. This was usually followed by a greeting and a prayer or wish for health (even in secular letters), then the body of the letter, and finally the closing, which contained any details about the sending of the letter and another greeting. An example of this form appears in Acts 15:23–29 (without the prayer).

Christian writers adapted this set form to their purposes, "christianizing" it by changing or expanding the traditional elements. The author and recipients are not merely identified; they are also described by their relation to Christ. The greeting was also made specifically Christian. Instead of merely "Paul to the Ephesians, greetings," Paul described himself as "an apostle of Christ Jesus by the will of God" and his readers as holy (NIV, "saints") and "faithful in Christ Jesus." And instead of using the standard word "greeting" [*chairein*], through a play on words Paul changed his greeting to read "grace [*charis*] and peace to you from God our Father and the Lord Jesus Christ."

An apostle of Christ. Paul's identification of himself as an apostle appointed by God is his customary way of beginning his letters. (Cf. the exact parallels in 2 Cor. 1:1; Col. 1:1; 2 Tim. 1:1.) Often Paul had to defend his legitimacy as an apostle, but here the tone is merely descriptive. The term *apostle* carried several connotations in the early church, all of which were true of Paul. It referred to someone who had seen the risen Christ (1 Cor. 9:1), to those sent out by the church with a missionary task, or more broadly to anyone who functioned as an agent or representative. This self-description emphasizes the authority with which Paul wrote. If he was an apostle because of the will of God, what he wrote must be seen as communication from God.

The will of God is an important theme in Ephesians, appearing more frequently here than in any other letter. The concern is not about Christians finding the will of God; rather, the emphasis is on God's *purpose* with his actions for humanity. The point here is that Paul was an apostle because God wanted him to be.

In Paul's letters, "Christ" (meaning "the Anointed One") is often no longer a title as it was in a Jewish context. Particularly among Gentile Christians it became a name, linked with the name "Jesus." But of the forty-six occurrences of the word "Christ" in Ephesians, twenty-three have the article in Greek, some of which may still point to the role of the Jewish Messiah in the salvation of the Gentiles (see 1:10; 2:13; 4:20).

The holy ones. The identification of the recipients as "saints" (lit., "the holy ones") is Paul's usual description of Christians. "Saints" is not a helpful translation, for this English word usually refers to extraordinarily pious people. Paul's first intent was not that these people lived especially holy lives—he described the Corinthian Christians the same way (1 Cor. 1:2), and yet he had no illusions about the sanctity of their lives. Rather, his primary concern was to emphasize that just as he had been appointed by God to be an apostle, they too had been separated to God (separation is the key idea in the word "holy"). Paul's addressees were holy because God had set them apart to be his people. The focus is entirely on God's action and the reference is to God's saving work.[1]

The recipients[2] of this letter are also described as "faithful in Christ Jesus" (cf. Col. 1:2). "Faithful" can refer either to someone who has proven *to be faithful* or to someone who is a believer, someone who *has faith*. The latter seems the better choice here (cf. John 20:27; Acts 10:45; 16:1, 15; 2 Cor. 6:15).

With the expression "in Christ Jesus" we encounter one of the most significant and difficult points in Paul's writings. Paul is not merely saying these people believed in Christ; rather, they were *in* Christ *positionally*. This concept of being in Christ is one of—if not *the*—most important parts of Paul's theology, for this is the center from which he understood and explained salvation. The thirteen Pauline letters use "in Christ," "in the Lord," "in him," or some similar expression 164 times to express a variety of ideas. "Christ" is usually used in contexts talking about salvation and its benefits, whereas "Lord" is usually used to talk about Christian behavior and life. Sometimes these terms are used to convey what believers obtain in Christ (as 1:7: "in him we have redemption"), at other times "in Christ" describes what a person does (4:17: "So I tell you this, and insist on it in the Lord"), and at still other times the focus is directly on the fact that a Christian is a person who is *in* Christ. This language expresses the oneness and the identity that a believer shares with Christ. Paul's gospel is a gospel about union with Christ, and this is the

---

1. See 1 Corinthians 6:11, where "sanctified" is the verb form of the word "holy." In the Old Testament both Israelites and angels were sometimes called "holy ones." Such language was adapted to describe God's people in the New Testament.

2. On the textual question of whether "in Ephesus" belongs to the original text and the question of the destination of the letter, see p. 21 in the introduction.

meaning in 1:1. Ephesians focuses more on union with Christ and on being *in Christ* than any other letter (36 times).[3]

The greeting. The wording in this verse is paralleled exactly in seven other Pauline letters. "Grace and peace" are important themes throughout Ephesians: Both are key words that describe God's initial salvation, and both describe God's continuing work among his people. As we will see in 1:3–14, "grace" is one of the most important words in Paul's theology. Even though other writers use this greeting (1 Peter 1:2; 2 Peter 1:2; Rev. 1:4), no other writer comes close to placing as much emphasis on grace as Paul. Not by accident, he begins and ends every letter with "grace," as if to emphasize that all of life is lived in the parameters of grace. Though not used as frequently, "peace" too has a foundational role in Paul's theology. God alone is the one who conveys grace and peace, and Paul wants his readers to experience this.

"God our Father and the Lord Jesus Christ" are together the source of grace and peace. Right from the beginning Paul's thought is theocentric, focusing on God's activity in Jesus Christ. The apostle had no hesitation in linking Jesus Christ with God, but he also maintains a healthy demarcation between them. Usually he used the terms *God the Father* when speaking of God and *Lord* or *Christ* when referring to Jesus. "Lord" was used in the Old Testament in reference to the God of Israel, and the appropriation of this title for Jesus is striking.

Bridging Contexts

THE FOREIGNNESS OF Paul's thought to our culture is apparent. Already in this section we face vocabulary, a christianized letter form, and theological assumptions that require bridging.

Vocabulary. Expressions such as "apostle," "saints," "in Christ," and "grace" are not common language, and the realities to which they point will occupy us through much of this commentary. While we struggle to grasp Paul's intent, for him they were the breath of his life, and he was confident that his readers understood them well. But most churchgoers today would have a difficult time explaining such concepts with any depth. Bridging has to convey the theology of these words, a task that will begin when we treat 1:3–14.

Letter form. The way Paul adapted the form of letters in his culture to make them specifically Christian is impressive, but it also creates a problem for us. When modern believers attempt to christianize letters or other aspects of our culture, the result is often archaic and artificial. We may copy Paul's theological language without grasping its depth or finding adequate words

---

3. See especially comments on 1:3–14; 2:5–7, 11–22.

to convey it. The difference may be that we are imitating something we have not experienced. Paul is not merely using nice theological words, but expressing his encounter with, and his life with, the God that confronted him on the Damascus road.

If we are to bridge the years and cultural differences in biblical texts, we must do more than merely copy theological words. We must experience the reality to which the words point and find contemporary ways to describe it. We must not only ask what the text *teaches* about God, humanity, life with God, and other subjects; we must *own* what it teaches and create language to give the reality a home in our own souls.

Theological assumptions. Especially in a short section like this, texts often assume more than they express. If we can see the assumptions by which Paul lived and thought, we have important material for reflecting on our own life with God. Two assumptions dominate this introduction: the activity of God and Paul's sense of "geography."

(1) As will be shown in detail in 1:3–14, Paul viewed God as intentional, purposeful, and working at great lengths to bring humanity to himself and to equip people for life. Paul saw his own life as part of God's plan of salvation. His ministry was not merely a job or a choice he made, but part of God's work to bring salvation to humanity. The rest of the letter will detail this activity and how people should respond.

(2) To speak of Paul's sense of "geography" is an attempt to describe the "place" where he thought Christians live. In Paul's mind, just as these Christians live literally in the region near Ephesus, they also live in Christ. The terrain, climate, values, and history in which people grow up and live helps to define who they are. As really as this region near Ephesus defines who they are, Christ defines who believers really are. He is the "sphere of influence" or "power field" in which they live and from which they benefit and are transformed. That is, his Spirit, values, character, history, and purposes shape their lives. People can live in other spheres (cf. 2:1–3), but Christians live in Christ. Jesus Christ must never be depersonalized by such language, but we will not understand Paul unless we learn to think of life as lived *in* Christ. As the 1:3–14 will show, the implications of this are enormous.

PAUL'S RELATION TO Christ changed even the form of his letters. How can we show the reality of Christ in our lives? We must do this not merely by using external language, so that we appear pious, but by actual transformation resulting from our relationship with Christ.

Gospel and culture. Paul used his culture's letter form to write specifically Christian letters, but his method raises a crucial question: How do culture and gospel relate? The gospel defines life for Christians, but that life is always lived out in a culture, a culture that also seeks to define us. Christians must therefore understand the culture they live in and must decide what in culture may be legitimately adapted and enjoyed and what must be rejected.

All too often we confuse our cultural expression of Christianity with the gospel itself. The early Church faced this problem in Acts 6 over the distribution of food and in Acts 15 with the "Jerusalem Council" over the necessity of observing Jewish legal practices. In a similar manner, we must separate the heart of the gospel from our cultural expression of the gospel. Christianity in African tribal communities, for example, does not need to look like Western Christianity.

We must also determine how to relate to our culture. Will the use of religious language help or hinder a conversation? Given the religious fanaticism and the division between the "religious right" and other groups in the United States, for instance, religious language often *hinders* communication about Christianity. Acts 17 and 22–26 present a much different tone from Paul in addressing non-Christian audiences from what appears in his letters to Christians. Sensitivity to the reception of the message determines the selection of the words.

The primary ingredient for Christians in relating to culture surely is authenticity. We should not try to communicate Paul's experience of Christ; we must communicate our own. We learn from Paul, but our own experience of the gospel must be lived out authentically before God and people. This is not to elevate experience over Scripture, but we cannot live out a theology that we do not know firsthand. Anything less is a sham and will not convince. Our expression of the gospel in our culture must be a natural flow of the depth of our relation with Christ, not the borrowing of mere words that we have labeled religious.

If God is active, what are we doing? Every writing necessarily assumes numerous ideas or facts as obvious. Otherwise each writing would be intolerably long. Therefore, reflection on assumptions in a text is an important part of application. Of course, the assumptions need to be justified, preferably drawn from other parts of the same letter. The present text assumes that God is actively setting a people apart for himself. In other words, grace, salvation, human responsibility, and ethics are already in view even before we begin reading this letter.

Too often people relegate any sense of God's activity or planning to the distant past, as if he worked in the first century but not now. Yet God still sets people apart for salvation and still calls some to be his special agents. Whether we assume God is active or passive determines our own expectation and readiness to respond. *By believing God is active, we precondition ourselves for healthy response to God.*

Caution is in order, however, for any idea may be taken to an extreme. Unfortunately, some people conclude that since God set them apart, they are superior to others. Some conclude that since God is active, solutions to life are simple, or that every act is the result of God's action. But the Bible is not so simplistic, and application of the biblical text should never be merely application of individual texts. Texts should be applied within the frame of the entire Scriptures. Other texts prevent the abuse of individual passages. As 1 Corinthians 1–4 points out, for example, the message of the cross does not allow feelings of superiority. Or as Job, Habakkuk, and the psalmists lament, God often appears inactive, and life has no easy solutions. Only against such a backdrop can we apply a specific text.[4]

Paul's sense of geography—in Christ and in the world. Paul's assumption about "geography"—about living both in a specific place and in Christ—is a profound insight into life with God. The Christian faith is not an attractive set of ideas or a nice avenue to follow. Rather, it is so deep an engagement with Christ, so deep a union with our Lord, that Paul can only describe it as living *in Christ*. To live in Christ is to be determined by him. He shapes who we are. A person cannot be conscious of being enveloped by Christ and behave in ways totally out of keeping with his character. Later we will see that this theology is the basis of Paul's understanding of salvation, but clearly it drives his ethics and is his most appropriate description of Christians.

This sense of "geography" is important. What is the significance of the fact that Christians live in two places at the same time? Paul's readers lived both in the region of Ephesus and in Christ. What was the significance for this locale that they were in Christ and what was the significance for Christ that they were in this locale? Each Christian must personalize that question in deciding how to live. We can neither avoid the place where we live nor betray the Christ in whom we live. The rest of Ephesians does not focus on the responsibility of the readers to their locale except in the most general way. Most of the attention will be on the significance of being in Christ for salvation and for life in the Christian community. Both are important, but in applying the text we need to extend the theology. We must also put into practice the significance of being in Christ for relations outside the Christian community.

---

4. On the subject of such tensions in the biblical material, see my *Between Two Truths* (Grand Rapids: Zondervan, 1990).

Ephesians 1:3-14

PRAISE BE TO the God and Father of our Lord Jesus Christ, who has blessed us in the heavenly realms with every spiritual blessing in Christ. ⁴For he chose us in him before the creation of the world to be holy and blameless in his sight. In love ⁵he predestined us to be adopted as his sons through Jesus Christ, in accordance with his pleasure and will—⁶to the praise of his glorious grace, which he has freely given us in the One he loves. ⁷In him we have redemption through his blood, the forgiveness of sins, in accordance with the riches of God's grace ⁸that he lavished on us with all wisdom and understanding. ⁹And he made known to us the mystery of his will according to his good pleasure, which he purposed in Christ, ¹⁰to be put into effect when the times will have reached their fulfillment—to bring all things in heaven and on earth together under one head, even Christ.

¹¹In him we were also chosen, having been predestined according to the plan of him who works out everything in conformity with the purpose of his will, ¹²in order that we, who were the first to hope in Christ, might be for the praise of his glory. ¹³And you also were included in Christ when you heard the word of truth, the gospel of your salvation. Having believed, you were marked in him with a seal, the promised Holy Spirit, ¹⁴who is a deposit guaranteeing our inheritance until the redemption of those who are God's possession—to the praise of his glory.

Original Meaning

AS INDICATED IN the discussion of 1:1–2, ancient letters followed a stereotyped form, just as our letters do today. After the initial identification of the author and recipients and the greeting, letters usually contained a prayer. This prayer was most often a health wish. All Paul's letters except Galatians contain a prayer. His prayers are not wishes for good health, however, but expressions of praise for God's work in Christ (doxologies) or thanksgiving for his readers and prayers of intercession for their lives as Christians. These opening prayers form an important part of each letter for several reasons. (1) They provide information about the concerns of the letter, functioning almost as an introduction to the topics to be treated. (2) With them Paul expressed his love and concern for his Christian friends. (3) Paul also entered into the worship experience of his readers as they gathered for worship, at which time his letter would be read. In effect he led them in worship by modeling worship for them.

The prayer in Ephesians is unusual, for it contains a long doxology (actually a blessing, 1:3—14), a thanksgiving (1:15—16), and an intercessory prayer (1:17—20). No other New Testament letter has *both* a doxology *and* a thanksgiving-intercession. A problem exists in knowing where the prayer ends. The whole of the first three chapters of Ephesians is filled with worship and liturgical expressions, using language familiar to the church. It is virtually doctrine set to music.[1] But does Paul's prayer end at 1:23 or does it extend all the way through 3:21? Note that 3:14—21 is clearly a prayer and that the themes of the intercession in 1:15—23 are present in 3:14—21 (wealth of God's glory, Spirit, power, faith, knowing what one possesses in Christ, filling and fullness, and the church). Are the first three chapters an expression of prayer and praise?[2] At the very least we must say that in Ephesians 1—3 the line distinguishing theology and prayer is very thin. In praying we convey our understanding of God back to God.

In this introductory prayer, we do gain insight into Paul's concerns in writing Ephesians. He does not address a specific theological or ecclesiastical problem. Rather, this is a general letter that explains the wonders of salvation in Christ and helps people know the significance of the gift of life with Christ. In focusing on these issues, the doxology in 1:3—14 presents a theologically *loaded* and structurally *complex* summary of God's work in Christ.

Themes and Structure. Several key ideas give this section its power. Most important is the expression "in Christ," which, along with expressions like "in him" or "in whom," appears eleven times in the Greek text (nine times in the NIV). As we have already seen in connection with 1:1,[3] the idea of being "in Christ" is one of the most important components in Paul's theology. Paul also emphasizes here the praise of God's glory (vv. 6, 12, 14), God's pleasure (vv. 5, 9), salvation, the plan of God (election), and revelation of the divine mystery.

This section has a Trinitarian focus, with verses 3—12 concentrating on the Father and Christ and verses 3 and 13—14 on the Spirit. Three perspec-

---

1. See Mackay, p. 17, who uses this phrase as a description of the whole letter.
2. A similar situation exists in 1 Thessalonians 1—3, where it is also difficult to know where Paul's prayer stops.
3. See pp. 38—40, 42.

tives on time also appear: God's activity in eternity (vv. 3–5, 9, 11), God's activity in human history in Christ and in those who believe (vv. 6–8, 11–14), and the end of history, when all is summed up in Christ (v. 10).

While most English translations do not show it, the Greek text of 1:3–14 is *one* unusually long sentence, presenting one cascading description of God's work in Christ after another. Every new element provides a further explanation about what God has done. Paul felt the richness of God's grace, and the exuberance of his language shows it. The rhythm, recurring phrases, and exalted theology make this doxology one of the most impressive expressions of praise ever written. Its purpose is praise to God for binding us to himself by the grace he has shown in Christ.[4]

It is best to structure this section according to the three Greek participles by which the text unfolds: "blessed us" in 1:3, "predestined us" in 1:5, and "made known to us" in 1:9. These participles emphasize one major point: the goodness of God revealed in his desire to choose a people for himself. Verses 3–4, in which the first participle occurs, *function as the thesis of the whole letter;* the rest is commentary. That is, this letter is about God's blessing us in Christ and choosing us so that we might live holy and blameless lives before God. The remaining chapters unfold this twofold emphasis on God's saving us and the change in conduct it produces. In the immediate context (1:5–14) the second and third participles explain God's salvation. Attention does not turn to holy living before God until chapters 4–6.

This initial section may be thus outlined as follows:

A. Blessed and chosen by God to live blamelessly before him (*thesis*) (1:3–4)
B. Chosen by God for adoption and forgiven through grace (*explanation*) (1:5–8a)
C. God's plan for eternity revealed and his Spirit given as a guarantee (*explanation*) (1:8b–14)

God's election is the central idea (vv. 4–5, 9–12), and the grace experienced in Christ (vv. 6–8) and the gift of the Spirit (vv. 13–14) flow directly from his choice and purpose. Note how Paul's worship—like his greeting in 1:2—is *theocentric*. The three main participles all describe God's actions. He has exalted Christ and made him Lord, but God is still the primary actor. God is not a distant being who waits to see what humans will do. God is the beginning, the one who works through Christ and the Spirit for humans and with humans, and the goal.

---

4. The doxologies in 2 Corinthians 1:3–7 and 1 Peter 1:3–9 begin the same way: "Praise be to [Blessed is] the God and Father of our Lord Jesus Christ."

God Blessed Us in Christ to Be Holy (1:3–4)

THE GOD WHO acted in Christ and chose Christians to live before him deserves praise. The words translated "Praise be to God" are actually, "Blessed is the God." By using the word "praise" the NIV loses the play on three occurrences of the root "bless": *"Blessed* is the God who *blessed* us with every spiritual *blessing."* To use the same word both for our worship of God and of God's showering us with spiritual gifts is foreign to us, but this double meaning of the word *bless* is common in both the Old and New Testament. For example, note "The LORD bless you" in Numbers 6:24 and "Bless the LORD" in Psalm 103:1.[5] The worship of Zechariah in Luke 1:68–75 is similar to Ephesians 1:3–14, in that it begins with "Blessed is the Lord God of Israel"[6] and goes on to explain all God has done to save his people. Such a blessing concludes each of the five books of the Psalms.

"Every spiritual blessing" has been granted to us in Christ (see 2 Peter 1:3). "Spiritual" does not mean these gifts are "otherworldly," nor does it suggest the spiritual gifts listed in 1 Corinthians 12:3–11, 28. Rather, the expression refers to all that God's Spirit brings to enable life.[7] The letter will unfold all these blessings, but the immediate context mentions election, adoption, grace, forgiveness, revelation, the gospel, and the Holy Spirit. As verses 13–14 show, the Spirit is the primary gift and the source of all the others.

The expression "in the heavenly realms" is difficult. Paul does not mean that spiritual blessings are to be enjoyed later in heaven, for the focus of this text is on the *present* enjoyment of God's gifts. In fact, focus on "getting into heaven" in the future is not the primary concern of the New Testament. The concern is much more for the present life with God and in Christ. While *the coming age* is important in Ephesians, only 5:5 and 6:8 give any focus to gaining future salvation, and both of these verses mention the future only as a prod for present living. Literally, the text reads only "in the heavenlies"; and although this word occurs elsewhere as the adjective "heavenly," it has the sense of "the heavenly realms" only in Ephesians. The term is not, however, merely a synonym for "heaven," as an examination of the four other occurrences in Ephesians shows. This phrase can refer to:

(1) the place of exaltation for Christ (1:20) and believers (2:6)
(2) the place for revelation of God's wisdom to the rulers and authorities (3:10)

---

5. NIV: "Praise the LORD."

6. NIV: "Praise be to the Lord." See also Romans 1:25 and 9:5.

7. See Gordon D. Fee, *God's Empowering Presence: The Holy Spirit in the Letters of Paul* (Peabody, Mass.: Hendrickson, 1994), 666–67.

---

(3) more negatively, the place of battle between believers and evil spiritual forces (6:12).

In other words, "heavenly realms" does not refer to a physical location but to a spiritual reality—God's world, in which believers have a share and which evil forces still seek to attack. It includes all of the believer's relation to God and the church's experience.[8] It is a way of saying that this world is not the only reality. A larger reality exists where Christ is already exalted as Lord, where believers participate in his victory, and where spiritual forces are opposed. Though believers live physically on this earth, they receive spiritual resources and their identity from a higher plane. The spiritual blessings given to Christians are enjoyed in the present life, for they derive from what God has done in Christ *in the heavenlies*.

"In Christ" and related expressions, as already noted in our comments on 1:1, are among the most important components of Paul's theology, especially in Ephesians.[9] Every element in Paul's teachings flows from his understanding about our union with Christ. Note how these expressions dominate this section. God's purpose and election take place in Christ (1:4, 9, 11). God's grace and redemption are found in Christ (1:6–7). All things in heaven and on earth are summed up in Christ (1:10). People hope in Christ, hear the word in Christ, and by faith are sealed in Christ (1:12–13). Remember that this whole section is worship: God is being praised, and the focus of that praise is what God has done in Christ and what is available in Christ.

No simple definition of "in Christ" will do, and each occurrence must be analyzed individually and in context. At times, "in Christ" functions instrumentally to convey that something happens *by* Christ or *through* his work, such as "through Christ Jesus the law of the Spirit of life set me free ..." (Rom. 8:2).[10] At other times the expression is used adjectivally in the sense of "Christian" (see 2 Cor. 12:2). In other places it qualifies an action, such as in Ephesians 6:1: "Children, obey your parents *in the Lord*."

But the most important use of "in Christ" has a "local" sense and points to incorporation into Christ. That is, Christ is the "place" where believers reside, the source in which they find God's salvation and blessings, and the frame-

---

8. See Stott, *God's New Society*, 35, who suggests "the unseen world of spiritual reality," and Schnackenburg, *Ephesians: A Commentary*, 51, who offers "the area and effectiveness of God's activity or of that of the ungodly 'powers.'"

9. In addition to the 164 times that "in Christ" occurs in Paul's letters, the Greek equivalent for "in the Spirit" occurs 22 times (5 in Ephesians) and "in God" occurs 3 times (none in Ephesians). Note that 23 of the 36 occurrences in Ephesians are in the first two chapters. Ephesians is above all else *the* letter explaining union with Christ.

10. The text rendered more literally is: "For the law of the Spirit of life in Christ Jesus freed me. ..."

work in which they live and work. It is as if Christ were a vast repository holding the gifts of God, but, of course, without losing any sense of Christ as person. Christ is the source of all spiritual blessings, and because believers reside in him they can enjoy those blessings. Just as Christ's personhood is not lost, neither is the believer's individuality lost. This is not some eastern religious thought of absorption into the deity. Rather, Christ and the believer are bound into a unity in which Christ sets the parameters for life and makes available God's provisions for life. The logical conclusion of this thinking is Paul's use of the *body* imagery, which is of major importance in Ephesians.

The origin of Paul's *in Christ* thinking is uncertain. The only other New Testament documents with anything similar are the Johannine writings, with their focus on the reciprocal idea of believers remaining in Christ and his remaining in them. This suggests the roots of this thinking may stem from Jesus, though Paul's usage cannot be traced to explicit words of Jesus. Some scholars suggest the origin is in Old Testament texts that speak of Abraham as the one *in whom* all nations are blessed.[11] Christ, the one who has taken on the task of Israel, has become the new representative head in whom all will be blessed. This may be a factor, but Paul's theology of baptism as dying and rising with Christ is also probably behind the idea of being in Christ (see Rom. 6:3–8).

We should note that in 1:4,[12] Paul's concern from the first is ethical transformation, although he does not explore that issue until chapters 4–6. Paul sought to encourage believers by telling them of the grandeur of salvation, but he also wanted to challenge them to live in keeping with God's grace. Life from God results in transformed life with God. This expectation of "holy and blameless" living flows from God's choosing people and separating them to himself. This thought is commentary on the title "saints" or "holy ones" in 1:1 and is paralleled by the expectation in 5:27 that the church be holy and blameless.

Election (1:4–6)

JUST AS 1:1 emphasized God's activity in making Paul an apostle, so this section emphasizes God's activity in planning and choosing people in Christ. Election means that God chooses people, and this teaching cannot be turned around to the thought that people choose God. Election means that the existence of the people of God can be explained only on the basis of God's character, plan, and action, not on some quality in the people who are cho-

---

11. See Galatians 3:8 in the context of Genesis 12:3; 18:18. Cf. also the contrast between being "in Adam" and being "in Christ" in 1 Corinthians 15:22.

12. The teaching on election in 1:4 will be treated with 1:5–6, even though it belongs with 1:3 as part of the main statement of the letter.

sen. The initiative is always God's based on his "grace" (vv. 6–7; "grace" is not a change of subjects but a continuation of the same theme, using different words). Salvation is not some accident or afterthought on the part of God. His purpose *always* was to draw humanity to himself. "Before the foundation of the world" does not mean "just prior to creation"; rather it expresses that God's purposes are rooted in the depths of his nature. God is the kind of God who loves and seeks a people (cf. Deut. 7:7–9). The accent falls also on God's eternal plan, a theme that reappears in verses 9–11.

This is one of the most important texts on election in the Bible. Election is not some strange, unnecessary doctrine, but merely another way of speaking of God's grace and salvation. Words like "chose" and "predestined" underscore God's activity in setting apart a people for himself. Election results in "saints" (1:1; i.e., "the holy ones," "the set-apart ones").

The emphasis on adoption in 1:5 shows that the purpose of election is relational. God, for no other reason than that he is a loving God, chose to adopt people *into his family* through Jesus Christ. *Adoption* is family imagery used to explain the salvation experience, both present (cf. also Rom. 8:15; Gal. 4:5) and future (Rom. 8:23).[13]

Usually when people speak of divine election, they think of the election of individuals and the benefit to them. But biblical texts have a different emphasis, for election is primarily a corporate term. Nothing in Ephesians 1 focuses on individuals; rather, the text focuses collectively on those who are in Christ. This changes the theology. People become elect only in the Elect One—Christ. Whereas Israel was chosen to convey the blessings of God to the world, now Christ has taken on that task. He is the "seed of Abraham" par excellence, who fulfills Israel's election (cf. Gal. 3:7–29). Election takes place *in him* (Eph. 1:4) and *through him* (1:5). Individuals are not elected and then put in Christ. They are in Christ and therefore elect.[14]

Election does indeed bring privilege, but not so that people can bask in privilege or disdain others. Election always brings responsibility; God has chosen us to do something—namely, to live holy and blameless lives before him (1:4;

---

13. The focus on "inheritance" and "God's possession" in 1:14 continues this thought (cf. Rom. 8:14–15, 28–30).

14. T. F. Torrance ("Universalism or Election," *SJT* 2 [1949]: 315) defined election as "the love of God enacted and inserted into history in the life, death and resurrection of Jesus Christ so that in the strictest sense Jesus Christ is the election of God." Note the similar ideas in 1 Peter 2:4–8 and the use of "the chosen" to describe Jesus in Luke 9:35, a term borrowed from Isaiah 42:1. On the subject of election, see A. A. Solomon, "The New Testament Doctrine of Election," *SJT* 11 (1958): 406–22; H. H. Rowley, *The Biblical Doctrine of Election* (London: Lutterworth, 1953); William W. Klein, *The New Chosen People: A Corporate View of Election* (Grand Rapids: Zondervan, 1990).

cf. 5:27). Other biblical texts on election have the same understanding, whether they refer to Israel, the remnant, or an individual like Paul or Jeremiah. God's choosing enlists people in his work and gives them responsibility.

A punctuation problem exists at the end of verse 4: Does "in love" go with verse 4 (so that Christians are "holy and blameless before God in love") or with verse 5 (as the NIV, "in love God predestined us")?[15] Scholars are divided on this issue. Either rendering of 1:4–5 is true, but since the focus here is on God's activity, the NIV choice is preferable.

The ultimate aim of election is the glory of God, as the recurring phrase "to the praise of his glory" shows (1:6, 12, 14). Exact parallels to this phrase do not appear in the New Testament or the LXX. The idea is not that God wants to praise himself. Rather, the purpose of God's electing activity is to reveal his own character as a loving, saving God. When God is revealed—and "glory" is primarily a word about revelation—praise is the inevitable result.

Inundated with Grace (1:6b–8a)

THE NEW TESTAMENT meaning of the word *grace* (*charis*) combines elements from two Old Testament words: *hen*, which focuses on the mercy of a superior to an inferior, and *hesed*, which stresses covenant faithfulness. The basic connotation of the Greek word is whatever causes delight and rejoicing: beauty, kindness, charm, favor. *Grace*, then, refers to God's unbelievable acceptance of us. It is not something God gives us; rather, it is *God's giving us himself*.[16] It is his coming alongside us to embrace us and work for our benefit. Grace is the Judge of the universe asking criminals to sit down to a meal in his home. The initiative always belongs to God, who grants people the gift of eternal life in Christ.

Grace is the power that works salvation (2:5–8) and is a summary word for the gospel (2 Cor. 6:1). Elsewhere in Paul's letters, grace conveys a broad range of ideas. Grace does not refer just to the entrance to the Christian life; it covers the whole of life (Rom. 5:2; 6:14). We are not only saved by grace, we live by grace. The word is also used for God's giving a ministry to Paul (Eph. 3:7–8) and to Christians (4:7), as well as for the *benefit* that Christians give each other with edifying speech (4:29). It is even used for the collection of money for the poor (2 Cor. 8:1–19) and as an expression of thanks (2 Cor. 8:16).

Of the twelve times "grace" occurs in Ephesians, only 4:29 refers to grace from humans; the other eleven occurrences focus on grace that saves or

---

15. The same problem recurs in 3:17 with "in love" and in 1:8 with "in all wisdom and understanding." In 4:2 and 16 "in love" comes at the end of the phrase or clause.

16. See Harold H. Ditmanson, *Grace in Experience and Theology* (Minneapolis: Augsburg, 1977), 57–59.

involves us in ministry. In 1:6–8 emphasis is placed on God's saving grace with four statements:

(1) God's choosing people leads to the praise of his grace.
(2) God's grace "graced" us in the One he loves. (The NIV's "freely given us" is actually the verb form of the word "grace"; a literal translation would be "the grace with which he graced us in the Beloved.")
(3) Salvation derives from the wealth of his grace (cf. 2:7—"riches" also appears at 1:18; 3:8, 16).
(4) Grace was lavished on us.

With this exuberant language Paul enables his readers to feel deeply the value and importance God has placed on them.

"The One he loves" refers to Christ. In the Synoptics this expression (lit., "the Beloved") is—or at least approaches—a messianic title (cf. Matt. 3:17; 12:18). The use here is similar. The same word is used of Christians (Rom. 1:7) and of Jews (11:28). It is virtually a synonym for "the elect." Election cannot be separated from Christ or from God's love.

As election takes place in Christ, so is "redemption" found in Christ. The term *redemption* has its roots in the Old Testament idea of the covenant and in the language of the ancient marketplace; in both instances it involved the idea of purchasing or buying back some item or person that would otherwise be lost, taken prisoner, or destroyed. Boaz, for example, redeemed the land belonging to Naomi's husband and with it the right to marry Ruth (Ruth 4:1–12), and people sold into slavery because of poverty could be redeemed (bought back) by a relative. This language was adapted to explain God's redeeming Israel from the Egyptians (2 Sam. 7:23) or for saving people from distress (Ps. 72:14; Jer. 15:21). In the first-century Hellenistic world "redemption" was used relatively rarely, but it was used in connection with the purchase of a slave's freedom.

Of the ten times "redemption" occurs in the New Testament, seven are in Paul's letters, three of these in Ephesians. Paul's readers understood the word to signify release from bondage through the payment of a price. The price paid is clearly the "blood" of Christ, which is merely a shorthand way of pointing to his sacrificial death and the new covenant it established with God. Redemption is seen here as a present possession, although the emphasis elsewhere is future (e.g., 1:14; 4:30). This tension between the present and the future is one of the most consistent parts of Christian thinking. All of the Christian faith is a blend of *the now* and *the not yet*, of what we already possess in Christ and what we still await.[17]

---

17. Note the recent book by C. Marvin Pate, *The End of the Age Has Come: The Theology of Paul* (Grand Rapids: Zondervan, 1995).

"Forgiveness of sins" is added as further explanation of redemption. The word used for "sins" is more literally "transgression" (*paraptoma*), but no distinction seems intended from the more frequent word for sin, *hamartia*. Paul uses the Greek word *aphesis* for forgiveness only here and in the parallel passage in Colossians 1:14. The corresponding verb occurs in Romans 4:7 as part of an Old Testament quotation. The apostle does use a different word for forgiveness in a few other passages (e. g. Eph. 4:32), but his thinking about salvation did not usually focus on forgiveness. Paul was more concerned with sin as a power or a tyrant than with specific erroneous acts, even though the latter are important. In other words, the apostle thought of salvation primarily in terms of release. *Aphesis* often carries the connotation of release,[18] and the connection to "redemption" shows that is the nuance here.[19] Paul's thought is about *release* from sins and the indictment they bring. Because of grace Christians no longer live in sins or under their indictment. Instead they live in Christ.

The Revelation of God's Will (1:8b–1:12)

WHEREAS THE FOCUS in 1:4–6a was on God's choice of people in Christ, Paul now shifts to the revelation of God's plan and how that plan centered on Christ. Words for God's will, purpose, and desire dominate verses 9 and 11. Paul emphasizes that God's work in Christ was not an afterthought or an incidental event in the universe. Rather, it is what God intended all along.

Two problems surface with the phrase "in all wisdom and understanding" (v. 8b). (1) Does it belong to verse 8b or verse 9a? Does Paul mean that God's grace was lavished on us in all wisdom and understanding, or that with all wisdom and understanding God made known to us the mystery of his will? Either is possible, but the latter seems more fitting (cf. a similar theme in 1:17; 3:10–11). (2) Does Paul mean that God exercises *his own* wisdom and understanding when he makes known his will, or does he refer to the wisdom and understanding *given to human beings* when he makes his will known? Ephesians 3:10–11 would suggest the former; 1:17 the latter. "Wisdom" often refers to wise living by humans, but it is also used of God's wisdom, especially in passages that speak of his saving plan.[20] A decision between the two options is difficult, and perhaps both ideas should be included. Each option implies the other, though the focus here seems to be on the display of God's own wisdom and understanding. No distinction is intended between the terms "wisdom" and "understanding." The two words form a *hendiadys*—one idea conveyed through two words.

---

18. See, for example, its use in Luke 4:18.
19. The same connection exists in Colossians 1:14.
20. See also 1 Corinthians 1:21–30; 2:7.

The gospel is first of all a revelation about God's purpose and work, and here his revealing activity is a cause for praise. Paul's own ministry is evidence of God's revelation, both in his calling and in his responsibility. The term *mystery* emphasizes the revelation theme further. Whereas in modern usage *mystery* refers to what is unknown, in Jewish and early Christian literature this word refers to the hidden divine plan now revealed by God (cf. 3:3–9; 6:19).[21]

In this passage all the attention is on God's completing his plan of salvation at the end of time. Some scholars see 1:10 as the key to the whole letter, but as important as it is, this verse is difficult to understand because of two words. (1) *Oikonomia* is rendered in the NIV as "to be put into effect," but this translation suggests that Paul's focus is only on the end time, which is debatable. More commonly this word means "management" or "steward-ship."[22] Some translations use "administration" or even "plan," but the latter is not well attested in the New Testament period. Paul uses the term in 3:2 of his own work and in 3:9 of his responsibility for the revelation of God's hidden mystery. The point in 1:10 is that God desired Christ to administer or rule "the fullness of the times" (lit.).[23] This text is about the eternal Lordship of Christ.[24] (2) *Anakephalaioo* has been translated in the NIV as "bring together under one head," but whether the word involves any connotation of "head" or "headship" is doubtful. The word means "sum up" or "recapitu-late."[25] The whole universe is to be brought together in Christ. He is the focal point that gives all creation coherence. One day every knee will bow (Phil. 2:10) and God's creation will be unified around Christ. Both troublesome words, then, focus on Christ as Lord of all.[26]

The NIV understands verse 10 to refer to the end of time. Literally the text reads "the fullness of the times." Does this point to the end of time or does it include the entire period since Christ's coming (see Mark 1:15; Gal. 4:4)? Any period of time can be said to be fulfilled.[27] Apocalyptic writers spoke of periods of time set by God, and clearly "the fullness of the times" points to the climax of God's working. Even in Ephesians, although Christ is Lord, all things in heaven and earth are not yet summed up in Christ (1:20–21; 5:16; 6:10–12). While the primary intent in this text does concern the ultimate

---

21. See Raymond E. Brown, *The Semitic Background of the Term "Mystery" in the New Testament* (Philadelphia: Fortress, 1968); Chrys C. Caragounis, *The Ephesian Mysterion.*

22. Several nuances are possible: the act of managing, the responsibility of managing, or the office responsible for managing (see Luke 16:2; 1 Cor. 9:17).

23. Probably Christ, rather than God, is viewed as the one who administers.

24. Cf. Colossians 1:25–26.

25. See Romans 13:9, the only other New Testament occurrence of the word.

26. Cf. Colossians 1:20.

27. See Acts 7:23 or 9:23, both of which have the Greek word for "fulfill."

fulfillment of God's purpose at the end of time, Paul viewed that fulfillment as already having begun in Christ's life, death, and resurrection. He is already Lord of all times. Just as redemption is both present and future, the revelation of God's will points both to the present and the future.

One of the difficulties in understanding Ephesians is the way the author changes from "we" and "our" to "you" and "your." The first such difficulty occurs in 1:11—14. "We" in 1:11 and "our" in 1:14 clearly refer to all Christians, and "you" in 1:13 describes the Gentile recipients of the letter. The difficulty comes in 1:12, with the words "we who were the first to hope in Christ." Some scholars argue the word translated "first to hope" has no temporal focus and see 1:12 as referring to all Christians. As the NIV stands, the reference is to Jewish Christians. Since Ephesians is concerned about the relation of Jewish Christians and Gentiles, this inference is probably correct.

The Spirit: The Benefit for Christians (1:13—14)

THE DOXOLOGY TURNS from focusing on God's plan to the reception of the gospel, "the word of truth."[28] The gospel is about truth from God that gives life. Truth is one of the foundational ideas in this letter and in Paul's theology.

Paul's persistent emphasis in 1:3—14 on being "in Christ" receives further explanation here. As a result of faith, people in Christ are sealed with the Holy Spirit. This statement describes conversion, not baptism or a second experience after conversion. At conversion, all believers receive the Spirit as both a "seal" and a "deposit" guaranteeing future life with God.

Seals were used in the ancient world in ways similar to today. Cargo was sealed before shipping or letters were sealed to guarantee the validity of the contents. A seal conveyed authenticity and ownership. In this case, the Spirit is the seal given to believers to verify that they belong to God.[29] The Spirit is called "the promised" Holy Spirit because of texts like Ezekiel 36:26—27 and Joel 2:28, which speak of an end-time outpouring of God's Spirit. The coming of the Spirit, along with Jesus' resurrection, convinced the early church that the end times had begun.

The Spirit is also a "deposit." The Greek word used here (*arrabon*) indicates a down payment that guaranteed complete payment (see also 2 Cor. 1:22; 5:5; cf. Rom. 8:23).[30] The Spirit, in other words, is God's first installment on

---

28. Whenever "of" constructions occur in Greek, a decision must be made about the nuance intended. While "the true word" is a possible translation, more likely the intent here is "the word about the truth."

29. See 4:30; 2 Corinthians 1:22.

30. On the Spirit in Paul, see Gordon Fee, *God's Empowering Presence.* A textual question exists in 1:14 about the gender of the Greek pronoun referring to the Spirit. This should

our salvation and the guarantee that the full future inheritance will be delivered. The NIV correctly translates 1:14 so that the possession is seen as God's possession of his people, not their possession of salvation. Otherwise the use of redemption language does not make sense. The language of God's possessing a people is paralleled in Malachi 3:17. As this whole context shows and as 1:19 will verify, Paul thought it of great significance that God had acquired a people, especially a people that included Gentiles.

To EXPLAIN PAUL'S thought for today we must explain unfamiliar or archaic ideas. Even more important, however, is the process of *theologizing*, whereby we understand the theology at work in a text, whether implicit or explicit. The theology of a text is what we really apply. If we grasp what a text teaches about God, Christ, salvation, or other subjects, we can apply that understanding to life.

Building blocks. Especially in a passage as theologically loaded as 1:3—14, we must not only deal with particular topics like in Christ and grace, but we must also stand back and view the text as a whole. By looking at the "building blocks" of the text, a larger theological perspective comes in view. At least three building blocks should be noticed: the focus on all three persons of the Trinity, the threefold perspective on time, and the theology of worship.

(1) Much of this section contains unfamiliar thought. We are not accustomed to focusing on God and his plan. Ideas such as election are foreign to us and require "translation," while other ideas require the rearranging of our whole worldview. In our contemporary perspective, we as human beings are the primary actors on the stage of history, but Paul's doxology asserts that God is the primary actor. No bridge exists from his worship to our worldview. A change of perspective is required before we can begin to apply the text. We need Paul's sense of God at work for us in Christ and through the Spirit.

(2) God's character is best described as a "God for us" (cf. Rom. 8:31), the one who has chosen us. God has always been and always will be this kind of God. God is the God of past, present, and future, and in all three he is at work for us. Our security rests on what he did before the foundation of the world, on what he did and continues to do in Christ and in the Spirit, and on what he has promised for the future. God has intentionally chosen and planned to go to great lengths to achieve salvation for people. This is not an afterthought on his part, but the very essence of who he is. God is a gregarious God, who

---

not be seen as a question of the personhood of the Spirit, but a question about which noun is the antecedent of the pronoun.

created people for relation with him. The outcome of creation is not in doubt, for God has been at work from the beginning and has already set Christ as the one who will accomplish his purposes. God will have a people for himself. When that happens, people will see how loving and relational he is. The language of Ephesians 1:9-14 looks forward to that day.

(3) Since this text is a doxology, obviously its first importance is what it teaches about worship and about the God who is worshiped. As in the Psalms, Paul's praise is *descriptive* of God and his actions. Worship always has this "narrative" quality, recounting the actions of God. For Christians, while they do not ignore other actions of God, the center is always on God's work *in Christ,* as the doxology shows. Though we do not know precisely where Paul's prayer stops, it is clear that his prayer includes a recounting of God's actions and that it is theological by its very nature. Doxology is theology and vice versa. This is obviously no cold recounting, however, for the reality of God's work for us creates deep emotion that energizes us.

In Christ. The New Testament writers groped for words to explain the reality they found as believers in Jesus as the Messiah and Lord. No single explanation or image was adequate, and consequently they used a variety of figures and sometimes even created new expressions. "In Christ" is just such a creation.

We assume that reality is the physical world around us, which we see and experience. The doxology—as all the Bible—asserts that reality is much larger, that it also includes God and his actions and what takes place "in Christ" and "in the heavenly realms." In bridging contexts we must expand our thinking to do justice to this "larger reality." Christians live in two realities at the same time: their physical world and in the heavenlies in Christ. We live in the reality of God's work in Christ and the gift of his Spirit. What we need for life is found in Christ, or, as Colossians especially emphasizes, Christ is all and all you need.

The idea of being "in Christ" presents one of the most difficult bridging tasks in Ephesians. How could early Christians think they were "in" a person who had been alive with them only a few years earlier and whose brothers they knew? They did not speak of being in James, nor do we speak of being in John Wesley or Martin Luther. The difficulty in our comprehending the idea of being in Christ is compounded by typical evangelical language about conversion. Christians today usually speak of inviting Christ into their hearts in order to be able to go to heaven, but language about "Christ being in us" and a concern over our going to heaven are relatively rare in the Bible, especially in Paul.[31]

---

31. Only *five* texts in Paul's letters refer to Christ in us: Romans 8:10; 2 Corinthians 13:5; Galatians 2:20; 4:19; Ephesians 3:17. Colossians 1:27 should be understood as "Christ among you, the hope of glory," i.e., Christ among the Gentiles.

Scholars often debate which theological idea is central in Paul's thought. Some choose justification by faith, but the verb *justify* only occurs four times outside Romans and Galatians and not at all in Ephesians. "In Christ" with its 164 occurrences, 36 of which are in Ephesians, is much more likely the central motif, or at least *a* central motif. Just as redemption is "in Christ" (1:7), so justification and every other act of God take place in Christ.[32] In fact, the only way that the atonement makes sense, the only way that Christ's death is effective for us, is if the union between Christ and believers is so strong that in some way his death is our death and his life is our life. This solidarity is achieved by a double identification via the Incarnation and faith. In the Incarnation Christ identifies with us and by faith we identify with him.

Closely related to the idea of being "in Christ" is the language of doing something "with Christ" or of "dying and rising with Christ."[33] The result is that believers are so closely connected to Christ that the "body" image is one of the most expressive pictures of the relation. *Christians are part of Christ (5:30) and part of each other (4:25).* Much of Ephesians is summarized with these two statements.

The statement that Christians are part of Christ has enormous implications for how we understand salvation and Christology. (1) With regard to salvation, Paul teaches that we are embodied in Christ and share his death and resurrection. Evangelicals usually focus on Christ's substitution for us as the key idea in salvation. As important as substitution is (see 5:2), it is only *one* aspect of the explanation, not the whole teaching. In fact, the way people understand substitution often militates against Paul's emphasis on being in Christ, for substitution suggests that Christ takes our place and we are removed from the picture, whereas in Paul's view we are caught up into Christ and made one with him. (2) With regard to Christology, Paul's Christ is no longer viewed merely as a human being. He is the cosmic Christ, the focus of God's activity from eternity (1:4), the one who embodies and represents all humanity (1:6–7), the one in whom all God's good gifts are available (1:3), and the one in whom all creation can be summed up (1:10). Without using Christological titles, Paul's in Christ thinking expresses a full Christology.[34]

Election. If "in Christ" is difficult to explain to a modern culture, surely election is as well. At first glance election seems to be an archaic idea, confined

---

32. See Galatians 2:17 for justification taking place "in Christ."

33. See e. g., Romans 8:1–4; 2 Corinthians 5:14–21; Galatians 2:19b–20; Philippians 3:8–10; Ephesians 2:4–10.

34. See James S. Stewart, *A Man in Christ* (London: Hodder and Stoughton, 1936), 154: "When we speak of being 'in Christ' we are consciously or unconsciously making a confession of faith; we are framing a Christology."

to the biblical mindset and more troublesome than helpful for modern audiences. We have difficulty thinking that God chooses some and ignores the rest. How can God be a God of love and do this? But such conclusions run far beyond the text of Ephesians.

At the same time, perhaps election is not as foreign as first thought. Being selected for a team or an organization, being admitted to a school, or being chosen by someone of the opposite sex are all affirmations of value. In recent times black Muslim extremists have argued that the Jews are not God's chosen people, but that blacks are. Similarly, white supremacists have argued that not Jews but whites are God's chosen race. Both groups are seeking to coopt language for valuing themselves. Election, *as it relates to humans*, expresses two ideas: the value given to human beings by God and responsibility they owe to God. Both are still important.

The election language in Ephesians 1 *is primarily about God* and shows why God should be praised. Any conclusions drawn must derive from the fact that this is a doxology, not a systematic theology. This is not to ignore the theological significance of doxologies, but to stay within Paul's intention with his worship. His purpose is to focus on God at work, planning and drawing people to himself through Christ. If the focus is corporate rather than individual and if people are elect only in the Elect One, Christ, then this text has nothing to do with our fear that God chooses some and ignores others. That is a nonbiblical conclusion about the *result* of election and the question who is elect. The focus of the biblical text is on the *cause* of election—God—and its *purpose*—that Christians live holy and blameless before God. God values human beings and draws them—both Jews and Gentiles—to himself in Christ. The focus is God's grace, and this text will not support any discussions about arbitrary decisions from God.

Numerous questions remain about election, and Christians will no doubt disagree on the answers. Can election be lost? Is it possible to have once been in Christ and then be out of him? But this text (and most others) do not treat our questions and suggest they may be misguided. Paul was more interested in praising God for his grace. While granting an element of mystery in the subject of election, certain points must be emphasized:

(1) Election is God's grace in action.
(2) God chose Abraham and then Israel for a task—to bless all the nations of the earth (Gen. 12:3).
(3) Jesus took on the task of Israel as God's Elect One.
(4) People are elect in Christ for relation to God.
(5) While God chooses, people still have choice and are responsible for their decisions.

(6) Election does demonstrate God's favor, which can be a strong support in a time of difficulty, but it is never to be treated as a sign of superiority.

(7) More important, *election always implies responsibility.* People are chosen to do something.

(8) The ultimate goal of election is the revelation of God's own character, which Ephesians expresses as *the praise of his glory.*

Consequently, most of the debates about election should be politely set aside. If we focus on praising God for valuing us and if we realize the responsibility that his valuing brings, we have understood Paul, and the other questions on election recede in importance. No one should worry whether he or she is elect. The main question is: "Are you in Christ and one with him?"

The responsibility election brings in this text is ethical: We are to live holy and blameless lives before God. Some will blanche at the call to be holy and blameless. While Paul rejected his so-called blameless experience as a Jew, he still called on Christians to live blamelessly (cf. Phil. 2:15 with 3:6). This text does not promote perfectionism, but it does call for Christians to live lives of service to God.

Salvation language. Paul described his message as "the gospel of salvation" (1:13), but many in our culture have no sense of danger or do not feel any need for salvation. Specific words for salvation may complicate our attempt to understand. Words like "grace," for example, communicate hardly any content today, and even familiar words such as "adopted" and "inheritance" seem strange in discussions about God. Bridging contexts requires patient effort to unpack the words and to discuss both the human plight and God's work to deal with the problem. In the end, all salvation language seeks to describe God's dealings with human sin and alienation from him in order to restore people to himself.

In describing this saving work, the doxology presents a constellation of the main ideas in Paul's theology. Of course, not everything is included, but Paul uses five key words to describe Christianity—grace, truth, faith, love, and hope. All five appear in 1:3—14[35] and in key passages throughout the letter. There is a logical order to the five. Grace always comes first; that is why it receives so much attention at the beginning of this letter. It describes God's action and is foundational for understanding the other terms.

But grace is a difficult word.[36] People know it is important, but too often it carries little meaning (in spite of the popularity of the song "Amazing Grace") and has only a "liturgical" function. Grace is the reality we need for

---

35. Faith is the noun form of the word "believed" in 1:13.
36. See pp. 50–51.

life. It emphasizes that God values us and seeks us despite our failure and sin. It underscores that God is the one who always takes the initiative and who empowers us. Even when human beings ignore him, God still seeks people and draws them to himself. "Grace" is too important theologically to drop, but it is so hard to grasp that it may have to be modeled before it can be understood.

Another word of salvation that requires bridging is *redemption* (cf. 1:7). The word has little current use, and its theological content is not easily recognized. What people need to know is that they belong to God and always have. Further, God has gone to great lengths—he has paid a price—to identify with humanity through the life, death, and resurrection of his Son and to bring people back to himself. Redemption means that God is at work getting people back to himself. We should not speculate to whom the price is paid. This is a figure of speech, and Scripture never discusses the idea of a literal payment.

A sense of time. Hearing this passage also requires us to reflect on time. We tend to think only about the present, but any sane life must focus on past, present, and future. People need to know their roots and ultimate destination as well as their present. For Christians all this is heightened. We need a deep sense of God's whole story: his activity in Israel, especially his foundational work in Christ, and his comforting promise for the future. But we may not abdicate the present for either the past or the future. Christians are people who live in the present, founded on the past, and pulled by the future. Moreover, the future is not merely "out there"; it is already experienced. The ultimate promises of God are already being enjoyed in the present, even though their completion is still to come. This "already-not yet" understanding of time must dominate Christian living.

The most important aspect of this "already-not yet" thinking has to do with the Holy Spirit. In addition to the activity of God the Father and the Christological implications of this text, both 1:3 and 1:13–14 reveal important information about the Spirit. Though promised at the end of the age, the Spirit has already been given to us by the resurrected Christ. He both conveys God's present blessing to us (v. 3) and is proof that we belong to him (v. 13). Through the Spirit, Christians already now enjoy the privileges of life with God. And the Spirit also guarantees what is still future, when life with God is brought to fulfillment in future salvation.

APPLICATION OF A doxology cannot be done in a direct way. This passage asks nothing explicitly of the readers, but the implicit message suggests application on two levels. At one level the application is imitation. The readers should do just what Paul did—worship and praise God. Any attempt to analyze and explain this passage falls far short of the exuberance of Paul's praise. But at the second level the implications of the theology of this passage for Christian living are enormous. We will reflect on some of them here; others will be explained by the rest of the letter.

Reality and worship. Why do people fail to live in relation to God and to serve him? Is it not because most of the time we view God as a remote being, cut off from us and not involved with us—a being whose expectations are not important, at least not in the reality we know? Ephesians more than any other book seeks to show that God is not remote, that he has been and is active for us, and that he will affect both individuals and the church by what he does.

The gospel is an expression of reality, actually an assault on the reality we know. Reality is not just this world, but includes God's purpose in this world and the next. As Walter Wink reminds us, "To worship is to remember Who owns the house."[37] If we have some perspective that the "real reality" in which we live has to do with a God who values us and has been active for us, our lives by necessity change. Suddenly, what God expects becomes important.

This is the reason why worship and praise are so crucial. They give opportunity for us to tell the truth about ourselves and God. In worship a community recreates its own soul;[38] it reestablishes who it really is. In worship we reject what is pseudo-real and inadequate to define us, and we affirm the "real reality" of God, his salvation, and human responsibility.

Any persecuted group knows this, but perhaps no church group knows this better than the black church. Black Christians for generations have maintained that the defining reality in the world they experience is a pseudo-reality, seeing that blacks too are God's privileged children and that God will one day see to it that justice will prevail. Worship is the place where the dream has been kept alive. Unfortunately, churches now—both black and white—too often buy into the pseudo-reality of this world to such an extent that God's intent is blurry at best. Many have accepted the view that sin will win. True, worship is always cultural in that it uses culture for expression, but worship is also always countercultural, for it refuses to accept the pseudo-reality of its time. We need to keep the dream alive of God's "real reality," and therefore we need to worship with the focus and intensity that Paul does in his doxology. God will win, not sin. In worship we acknowledge God because he has acknowledged us (cf. Rom. 1:21, 28).

---

37. Walter Wink, *Engaging the Powers: Discerning and Resistance in a World of Domination* (Minneapolis: Fortress, 1992), 160.

38. This description comes from Émile Durkheim, *The Elementary Forms of the Religious Life*, trans. Joseph Ward Swain (Glencoe, Ill.: The Free Press, 1947). Unfortunately, in actuality too many communities only mirror themselves in worship and do not encounter God.

Prayer and praise are the activities that hold the "real reality" before us. As Karl Barth put it, "To clasp the hands in prayer is the beginning of an uprising against the disorder of the world."[39] Consequently, our prayer and worship must always have a *theological* character, reminding us who God is. Rather than prayer being our list of needs for this pseudo-reality, it must describe God and his reality and thereby draw us closer to God.

This God we worship is not a remote God. He is a Father to us (1:3), and we are his children (1:5). Life is lived *before* him (1:4), and his Spirit has been given to us (1:13–14). *Life is relational*, both in relation to God and in relation to other people. This text focuses on life as relation with God. People often fear they will miss something in life if they live in relation to God. What they will miss is the distortion and perversion of life without God and the heartbreak that results. Life with God is not some minimalist approach to life; rather, God's Spirit has brought every privilege.

I have a sense that the church of our time has forgotten how to worship. The old forms of worship do not fit, and the new forms do not convince. How will we recover the depth and spontaneity of Paul's doxology? I offer no fix-it plan for worship, but I am convinced that the key to worship is not in procedures, but in experiencing God; not in a plan for worship, but in time for worship and eyes sensitive enough to discern God and his work. Knowledge of God leads to wonder and worship. There is no way to learn to worship apart from doing it. Abraham Heschel understood well the character of worship:

> Prayer is *our* humble *answer* to the inconceivable surprise of living. . . . Only one response can maintain us: gratefulness for witnessing the wonder, for the gift of our unearned right to serve, to adore, and to fulfill. It is gratefulness which makes the soul great.[40]

Furthermore, you must worship something, and you will by giving yourself to it. But nothing or no one else besides God merits such a level of attention. Nothing else offers so much in return; in fact idols usually require costly sacrifices—your dignity, your freedom, your integrity, and healthy relations for a start. Further, as Tom Wright points out, "You become like what you worship."[41] Devotion shapes us, but since we were created in the image of God,

---

39. Quoted without reference in Richard Foster, *Prayer: Finding the Heart's True Home* (San Francisco: Harper, 1992), 243.

40. Abraham Joshua Heschel, *Quest for God: Studies in Prayer and Symbolism* (New York: Crossroad, 1990), 5 (italics his).

41. Thomas Wright, *Bringing the Church to the World* (Minneapolis: Bethany, 1992), 51. Wright also discusses the high cost of idolatry.

only God has the right to shape us. All else is distortion and sin. Worship is our breath, our hold on life. Learn to worship.

The reality of being in Christ. Most important, we live *in Christ*.[42] Awareness of the presence of God and of living in Christ are the keys to all of life. People sin because they forget God. How strange that we forget the "place" we live. If we know we live before God and in Christ, we know we live in a defining presence. Our lives become determined by the character of Christ and God. It becomes increasingly difficult to say, "I know I live in Christ, but I am going to do the opposite of what Christ expects." Christian ethics are grounded in our being in Christ. The alternative, rule-keeping, is always an inadequate foundation for Christian ethics, because it asks the individual to conform to an external norm. If one lives in Christ, however, Christ is that person's environment. Christians must live out of their environment, out of an inner definition that comes from being in Christ and empowered by his Spirit. The expectation in 1:4b that people live holy and blameless before God flows from this understanding.

Without ignoring the importance of Christ's being in us, the neglected idea of our being in Christ is much more significant. If we emphasize only that Christ is in us, we define reality, and Christ is about one inch tall. If we realize we are in Christ, he determines reality and encompasses all we are.

For Paul faith is incorporation into Christ, a fellowship with him that determines life. The Christian religion is far more than merely believing certain facts, as a recent news magazine claimed. Fellowship with Christ cannot be reduced to belief in certain doctrines about Christ. We cannot appropriate Christ's death for us personally apart from our being in Christ. Participation in Christ is destructive of wrong allegiances, tyrannies, and misdirection, and it is dynamic and creative so that one becomes a "Christ-bearer." Being in Christ is another way to talk about the fact that Jesus is Lord. He determines our being.

Christians must live like people who know their "geography," who know they live in Christ and consequently are part of him. As a result, Christians should never view themselves merely as individuals. Yes, they are still individual persons, but not *merely* individuals. They are part of Christ, and as will be developed in the letter, also part of other people in Christ. As such, they should always act in accord with who he is. Everything they do—whether good or bad—involves Christ. Knowing that we are part of Christ brings ethical transformation.[43]

---

42. Compare Acts 17:28, which says that in God we live and move and have our being.

43. See Paul's treatment of these ideas in reference to sexual conduct in 1 Corinthians 6:15–20.

Paul's "in Christ" theology will inevitably change the way we do evange-lism. The standard line of "asking Jesus into your heart so you can go to heaven" is weak in comparison to what Paul describes, and there is little evidence this was his procedure. Clearly Paul asked for faith in Jesus, but what did this mean? Other passages in Ephesians will help us answer this question (see on 2:8), but what is clear already is that for Paul, faith brought about a unity with Christ.

What language shall we use to invite people into Christ? Possibly the discipleship imagery of following Jesus or attaching oneself to him is a good place to begin. Paul's language of dying and rising with Christ may prove effective. Whatever language is used, people need to be encouraged to know that faith is relational and means that they merge their lives into Christ's and become part of his body. Attaining salvation, in other words, does not result from believing enough facts, but from being joined to Christ. The emphasis on going to heaven needs to be placed in perspective so that present life with Christ and life in the Spirit receive proper attention. Such evangelism may require more thought, but it almost certainly will have more effect in changing lives.

The reality of being blessed and valued. The emphasis in 1:3 on God's blessing us with every spiritual blessing can easily lead to misunderstanding. We think of blessing primarily in terms of health and material things, but this is *not* a health and wealth theology. Also, sometimes when we read a text like this, we are tempted to say, "But I don't feel blessed." Remember that this text was written to a general audience about whom Paul may have known little or nothing. He is not describing how well off they were from this world's perspective or how happy they felt. As already mentioned, the physical world is not the limit of his reality. His statement of being blessed in Christ is just as true even if his addressees were enduring persecution. It is as true of Christians being tormented in a war-torn African nation as it is of overly indulgent American Christians. Paul's focus is on what God has provided with his Spirit and in Christ. The text is not "otherworldly" in contrast to this world, but it does focus on "the other reality" *and its impact in this life.* The blessings are the values and salvation described in the rest of the passage.

Election. Election may seem to have little contemporary significance, and nothing is gained by trying to force this language on people. In fact, election language may mislead, for it suggests voting on the basis of value, merit, recognition, and accomplishment—none of which pertain to God's election. On the other hand, the language may be too valuable to give up, for the doctrine of election removes the idea that we are in control. We must never think we do all the choosing and assume God is waiting like some wallflower to be chosen. We want to be in control; election says otherwise.

Regardless of what words we use, the *function* of the election language is important. It both rooted the Christian movement squarely in God's dealings with Israel—which should never be minimized—and emphasized the activity and valuing God does in drawing people to himself. The moment people take seriously the fact that God values them, their whole outlook on life changes. If God gives himself to us, always giving us freedom to choose and act independently, but always wooing us and accepting us, then a dignity and value is placed in us that nothing else can achieve. Such valuing motivates all of life.

All the focus on God's choosing and acting should not be taken to an extreme. As one theologian put it, "With theology you always have to pay."[44] He meant that if we pay too much on one theological idea, we do not have enough left for other necessary truths. People often pay so much for ideas like election that they have nothing left to pay for other necessities like human freedom and responsibility. Biblical ideas must always be held in tension with other biblical ideas. Paul's discussion of God's choosing has nothing to do with fatalism or a determinism that diminishes human action and responsibility. The tendency to ask how much of salvation is God's part and how much is the human part is misguided. It assumes that human beings and God stand in isolation. The truth is that salvation is entirely a work of God in which humans are totally involved. If God is the one in whom we live and move and have our being (Acts 17:28), we do not stand isolated from him in making a decision for him. God is the one who works in and through us even as we choose him.

Wendell Berry grasped this intertwining of God's life and ours:

> The problem, of course, is that we are *not* the authors of ourselves. Each of us has had many authors. … We could say that the human race is a great coauthorship in which we are collaborating with God and nature in the making of ourselves and one another. From this there is no escape.[45]

We collaborate with God to make ourselves and one another. This is Paul's argument in Ephesians. But Paul makes a prior point: God acted first. He created us, he gave us all we need in Christ, and he housed his Spirit in us so that we can collaborate with him to live holy lives. Christianity is a marvelously freeing and creating faith.

Blessed to be holy. Sometimes Christians debate whether the church is a company of freed believers or a hospital for sick souls. This is not an either-

---

44. The comment is from conversation with a Swedish theologian, Runar Eldebo.

45. Wendell Berry, "Men and Women in Search of Common Ground," *Home Economics* (San Francisco: North Point Press, 1987), 115 (italics his).

or choice, for surely the church is made up of believers who have been given freedom in Christ in order to be a community of healing for the broken. Our text, however, forces us to rethink the character of the church, one of the central themes of the letter. Christians are to live in a holy and blameless manner before God (1:4). This is not an oppressive weight, but as much privilege as it is responsibility. We are called to live in keeping with God's intent for us.

Whatever else the church is, it must be a community of *changed* people, a community focused on ethical living before God. The concern is not "do-goodism" or keeping rules, but being people who live out their relation to God. People both in and outside the church have the right to expect changed behavior from Christians. Purity—or right living—is not an option.

Nowhere is proper conduct more needed than in the lives of church leaders and pastors. We live in a time when virtually all respect for pastors and church leaders has been lost, for too many of these people have abused their positions for selfish reasons or have shown that their relation with God made no difference. Ethical living that flows from life with God is the responsibility of all Christians, and leaders must demonstrate that or resign. To be blessed and valued by God demands life in keeping with God.

Grace. This text is one of the most expressive texts on *grace* in the New Testament. The wealth of God's grace is lavished on us (1:6–8) and is a main reason for praise to God. Paul's theology of grace will be expanded in 2:4–10; 3:7–10; 4:7–10, 29–32, but already here the implications are clear. The primary application has to do with how we view ourselves and our own egos. A sense of being inundated with God's grace rules out any negative self-perceptions or devaluing and any sense of the meaninglessness of life. How can we call meaningless what God has valued so greatly? How can we count worthless what God has chosen and invested in? At the same time there can be no arrogance or overestimation of self because all the value comes from God. Grace eliminates both egotism and self-deprecation.

Paul does not spell out here the responsibility that comes with grace, but clearly "cheap grace" is not a viable option. If God has lavished so much value on us, we cannot devalue his efforts by ignoring him or the implications for life. Grace must lead to the very place it does in this text—to gratitude, a gratitude that is both spoken and lived. For Christianity, *religion is grace and ethics is gratitude.*[46] The first response to God's valuing us must be thanks and praise to God. All the rest of Christian living flows from this.

As the language of grace and election shows, most of this doxology is really about God's valuing of us. God blessed us, chose us from eternity,

---

46. Karl Barth, *Ethics*, ed. Dietrich Braun, trans. Geoffrey W. Bromiley (New York: Seabury, 1981), 499.

graced us, planned for us, sent Christ for us, revealed to us, will sum up all things in Christ in whom we have a part, gave us the Spirit as a guarantee, and will redeem us as his own people. The threefold repetition *to the praise of his glory* (1:6, 12, 14) shows the only possible response—worship and thanks to the God who values us and acts for us. The text is both a call to worship and a classic example of what worship should be.

People who know the value God has for them find both worship and obedience natural—not necessarily easy, but natural. The problem is that so many of us have difficulty believing that God really does value us personally and individually. Mere words about God's valuing will not change the perception of those who already have negative self-images or who have been beaten down by life. The church has a responsibility in valuing people. With their worship Christians attest to the "real reality" where God values and seeks each human, and with their own actions Christians convey value to others by the way they live.

As indicated above with election, *any* theological point can be taken to an extreme. When too much or the wrong kind of emphasis is placed on value from God, the danger is arrogance and pharisaism. Focus on the privilege of revelation and election led Jews in the ancient world to develop disdain for non-Jews. Christians have been guilty of the same sin. Value from God can get translated as inherent superiority to other people. Such an attitude cannot legitimately exist with a proper understanding of grace.

The reality of God at work. Clearly this text emphasizes the activity of God with regard to the past, present, and future. All too easily people assume God is not active because they do not see obvious actions from him. But God is rarely "public" in his actions. In fact, Isaiah 45:15 says that God is a hidden God, or as one scholar put it, "an elusive presence." God does not force himself on us, but this hidden God does reveal himself and is active in making his grace and his purposes in Christ known. We almost need a sign that reads "Slow down—God at work." Confidence that God is at work fulfilling his purposes preconditions us to anticipate his work and be receptive to it. Correct theology about an active God leads to godly living.

Care must be exercised, however, in language about God's actions. Convinced that God does work, people assume that all that happens is his action, which is not true. We live in a contingent world, where good and bad things happen to both good and bad people. God does not *cause* everything that happens. Such an idea overemphasizes the sovereignty of God. God may allow events to occur, but he does not manipulate them like some puppeteer. The problem why God allows horrible acts to happen to human beings will remain with us. Ephesians 2:1–3 refers to a "ruler of the kingdom of the air" who is also at work among the disobedient, and 5:3–16 points to human evil. Sickness and the violence of nature only compound the problem.

Most important, we as believers may be confident that no matter what does happen, it does not happen merely to us. We are not alone. In everything that happens we have to deal with God, especially when we live in Christ. We came from God, all of us. Whatever we do, even if it is sin, we are dealing with God. We are never alone and out of his sight or concern. And we are going to God; his plan is for a future with him. This is precisely the implication of the doxology with its focus on God's planning in eternity to have a people for himself, on his work in Christ and in the Spirit, and on God's future redemption and summing up all things in Christ.

This text is concerned about God's future triumph, not about our getting into heaven. We should remember that this victory has already been demonstrated by his work in Christ. Ephesians 1:18–23 and 2:4–10 will develop this thought, but already in the doxology the future is not merely an event in some later time. This future has moved into the present and changes how Christians live. We both have and await redemption (1:7, 14). That means that Christians belong to God now and that his ownership will be finalized when Christ sums up all things. Christians must live as people who belong to God—people who know what is already theirs because they belong to God and what is still to come.

Nowhere is the future triumph of God conveyed so clearly as with the gift of the Holy Spirit. Ephesians will later develop several aspects of a theology of the Spirit, but 1:13–14 focuses on the Spirit as the verification that we belong to God and that God will complete his promise to us. Texts like this show that the gift of the Spirit is not some second blessing or higher stage of the Christian faith and life—something for the spiritually elite. Rather, the Spirit is the possession—the necessary possession—of all Christians. He is God's gift to us showing that we are his, and he bestows on us a sense of God's presence and involvement in our lives.[47] The obvious benefit of having the Spirit is a sense of peace and security that comes with belonging to God. How does a person know he or she has the Spirit? Primarily in the change that is brought into life, especially love. Change is both the work of the Spirit and the evidence of the Spirit.

The reality of belonging to God is the reality in which we must live. God is at work, planning, blessing, valuing, and loving people, and his work in Christ and in the Spirit are both the means and the proof of his work. With this description of reality the doxology has already set the direction for the Christian life described in the rest of the letter. This is the reality from which

---

47. Cf. Romans 8:9-15; 1 John 4:13.

Christians must understand themselves and from which they must live. We close with a doxological paraphrase of Ephesians 1:3–14.

How marvelous God is! His Spirit has provided everything needed for life. Every good thing has been made available in Christ. We praise such a God.

Right from the first God has been busy devising a way to draw us home to himself so that we may live with him and for him. Through Jesus Christ he has made us family. As a result we owe God praise for the way he freely gave himself to us in Christ. In Christ's death God's abundant care for us is known; God gave himself for us to bring us back and make us his people. What lavish love he has for us! We honor you, God.

In his unfathomable wisdom God has made known his plan and desire to bring all things together in Christ. This includes everything in our world and everything in God's world. Amazingly God's plan includes us and gives us a share in what he is doing. For this we owe God praise for the hope that is ours in Christ. When we heard about the truth from God and believed the good news about his plan, God marked us as his own by giving us his Spirit. The Spirit's dwelling in us is a pledge from God that he will complete his plan and that one day we will truly live with God. For this we owe God praise. Our God, we do worship you.

Ephesians 1:15–23

FOR THIS REASON, ever since I heard about your faith in the Lord Jesus and your love for all the saints, [16]I have not stopped giving thanks for you, remembering you in my prayers. [17]I keep asking that the God of our Lord Jesus Christ, the glorious Father, may give you the Spirit of wisdom and revelation, so that you may know him better. [18]I pray also that the eyes of your heart may be enlightened in order that you may know the hope to which he has called you, the riches of his glorious inheritance in the saints, [19]and his incomparably great power for us who believe. That power is like the working of his mighty strength, [20]which he exerted in Christ when he raised him from the dead and seated him at his right hand in the heavenly realms, [21]far above all rule and authority, power and dominion, and every title that can be given, not only in the present age but also in the one to come. [22]And God placed all things under his feet and appointed him to be head over everything for the church, [23]which is his body, the fullness of him who fills everything in every way.

THIS IS THE only Pauline letter to combine both a doxology and a thanksgiving-intercession. Paul's petition for the continuing work of God in his readers grows out of his thanks for what God has already accomplished in them. Since the themes of the intercessory prayer of 1:15–23 are present in 3:14–21, the two passages should be compared.[1] Note too the extensive parallels between this passage and Colossians 1:4–12, 15–19.

Structure. Similar to the previous passage, the Greek text of 1:15–23 is one long sentence. The process of thought is clear:

A. The report Paul has of their faith and love (1:15)
B. Affirmation that he gives thanks and prays for them (1:16)

---

1. Note "wealth of his glory," "Spirit," "power," "belief," knowing what one possesses in Christ, "fill," "fullness," and "church."

C. Intercession for the gift of revelation (1:17–23)
  1. The primary request is that God will give his revealing Spirit (1:17)
  2. The goal of the prayer is that the revelation will bring a three-part knowledge of God (1:18–19)
    a. To know the hope of his calling(1:18a)
    b. To know the riches of *his* glorious inheritance in the saints (1:18b)
    c. To know his incomparably great power (1:19)
  3. Description of the working of God's power in Christ (1:20–23)
    a. Resurrection from the dead (1:20a)
    b. Exaltation to God's right hand and above every ruler or force (1:20b–21)
    c. Scripture proof of the submission of all things to Christ (1:22a)
    d. Christ as head of all things for the church, his body (1:22b–23a)
    e. The fullness filling all things (1:23b)

A reminder is in order that chapter and verse divisions were late additions to the biblical text (thirteenth and sixteenth centuries respectively). Although a shift occurs at 2:1, a chapter division at this point is unfortunate, for the next section (2:1–10) is a continuation of this text. The description of the ruler of the air in 2:2 develops the thought of "all rule and authority" in 1:21, and 2:5–6 extends to believers what is affirmed of Christ in 1:20.

Introduction to the Prayer (1:15–16)

"FOR THIS REASON" points back to the doxology, which affirms the foundational character of that passage. The theology of the doxology motivates everything else in the letter and should be reread in connection with each new section. The way God has worked to accomplish salvation motivates both Paul's praise and his intercession. The intent of this prayer is that people will know in their own lives the benefits mentioned in the doxology.

"Faith in the Lord Jesus" is not Paul's usual way of talking about Jesus as the object of faith, though other passages in the Pauline letters do occasionally speak of Jesus in this manner (1:13; Col. 1:4 [cf. Philem. 5]; likely Rom. 3:25; Gal. 3:26; 1 Tim. 3:13; 2 Tim. 3:15). The designation "the Lord Jesus" appears in Ephesians only here, but it does occur in Paul's other letters, especially the Thessalonian correspondence. At times the name "Jesus" may carry an emphasis on the historical character of the person, but no such nuance seems intended here. Variations in the names for Jesus and their order occur with no distinction intended.

Faith in Christ leads unavoidably to "love" for others whom God has set apart for himself in Christ. Note the trilogy of faith, love, and hope that appears here and in at least nine other New Testament passages.[2] Whereas in this text Paul has heard of his addressees' faith and love and prays they may know hope, in Colossians hope seems to be the basis of faith and love. A variety of nuances exists in the ways the trilogy is used. That these three occur together so frequently in early church writings is no accident. They are foundational terms for Christianity, and along with grace and truth, summarize the gospel and its consequences.[3]

Verses 15–16 suggest Paul may not have even known the recipients, but he has heard of their faith and life. On that basis he has a rapport with them and intercedes for them. That Paul does not stop praying for them is a figurative way of saying that he prays for them regularly. Similar ideas are expressed in many of the opening prayers of his letters (see esp. Rom. 1:9–10).

Paul's Intercession (1:17–19a)

"THE GLORIOUS FATHER" (NIV) is literally "the Father of glory." Though this is a legitimate way of translating a Greek "of" expression (a genitive case), "glorious Father" is probably too weak. "Glory" often refers to that which makes God visible or to his activity of making himself visible. Note, for example, the classic description of the revelation of God in Exodus 33:17–34:7, in which Moses asks to see God's glory.[4] Given the context in Ephesians, the nuance seems to be "the Father who shows his glory," that is, the Father who reveals himself.[5] As in the doxology, God is viewed as a giver, who by giving makes himself, along with his *character* and plan, known.

The intent of Paul's prayer is clear: that people will receive revelation to know what they have in Christ. Questions arise, however, over the intent of specific words. How, for example, should "Spirit of wisdom and revelation" be understood? Does it refer to the Holy Spirit (so NIV) who brings wisdom and revelation or to the human spirit enabled by God to see the wisdom and revelation he gives?[6] Some commentators say both ideas are present,

---

2. Romans 5:1–5; 1 Corinthians 13:13; Galatians 5:5–6; Ephesians 4:2–5; Colossians 1:4–5; 1 Thessalonians 1:3; 5:8; Hebrews 6:10–12; (cf. 10:23–24); 1 Peter 1:21–22. The textual question as to whether "the love" belongs in Ephesians 1:15 should be answered in the affirmative.

3. See p. 59. As in the doxology, all five terms appear in Galatians 5:4–7; Ephesians 4:2–15; Colossians 1:4–6.

4. See also Romans 6:4; 8:18; 2 Corinthians 3:18.

5. Technically, this may be a Hebraic genitive: "the Father characterized by glory."

6. The Greek word *pneuma* ("spirit") occurs fourteen times in Ephesians, twelve of which refer to the Holy Spirit (1:13, 17; 2:18, 22; 3:5, 16; 4:3, 4, 30; 5:18; 6:17, 18). This word is used of the ruler of this world in 2:2 and of the human spirit in 4:23. In Ephesians the Holy

---

but this is probably not Paul's intent here. The themes of wisdom and revelation were emphasized already in 1:8–9. Paul focuses here on what is accomplished for humans, but as 3:16 shows, he is thinking of the Holy Spirit as the one who performs this task (see also 1 Cor. 2:10–12).[7]

Ephesians 3:5 speaks of revelation given by the Spirit to the apostles and prophets, but here revelation is open to and needed by all. Just as 5:18 encourages believers to be filled with the Spirit (who is already theirs as a guarantee, 1:13)), so here Paul prays that the Spirit will continually reveal to them knowledge about God (the "him" in 1:17 refers to God, not Christ). As in the doxology, this text is *theocentric* and *Trinitarian*. Some sections of Ephesians (e.g., 2:11–22) are primarily Christocentric, but most of Ephesians, especially 1:3– 2:10, is theocentric.

The connection of 1:18 to 1:17 is problematic. Whereas the NIV has "I pray also that the eyes of your heart may be enlightened," literally the text reads, "having the eyes of the heart enlightened." Also, this participial phrase is in the accusative case with no obvious grammatical connection to the rest of the text. The NIV suggests Paul prayed for two gifts to be given: (1) the Spirit of wisdom and revelation, and (2) enlightenment of the heart. This is possible, but one would have expected such an idea to be expressed differently. Alternatively, but no easier grammatically, this phrase parenthetically provides an explanation of "Spirit of wisdom and revelation."

Despite the grammatical difficulties, Paul's intent is clear—that God's Spirit, already given to his readers, will continually give wisdom and revelation for life and understanding. The result is that the "inner eyes," the instruments of sight and understanding for the inner being, will receive light by which to see. In other words, the apostle prays the lights will go on inside people so that they know God and understand the benefit of the gospel.

As to the content of Paul's intercession, he wants his readers to know three realities about God: the hope of his calling, the riches of his inheritance in the saints, and the incomparable greatness of his power for us. The relation of these three to each other is unclear. Are these three different items? or one with two explanations? or one from three vantage points? Since the second item deals with the wealth of God's inheritance and the other two with benefits for believers, it is best to see the focus on three different items. This is not to suggest that other items are unimportant, but only that these three are the focus here.

Spirit is the guarantee of salvation (1:14; 4:30), a revealer (1:17; 3:5), the basis of unity (2:18; 4:3–4), the builder of the church (2:22), a present power (3:16), the source of life (5:18), and the means of ministry (6:17–18).

7. See the discussion in Gordon Fee, *God's Empowering Presence: The Holy Spirit in the Letters of Paul* (Peabody, Mass.: Hendrickson, 1994), 674–76.

(1) That Christians should know "the hope to which [God] has called" them means that they should know the significance that God's call has for their future. In effect Paul prays they will know the significance of God's choosing them—one of the themes of the doxology. The focus here is not on the fact of God's choosing, but on the outcome, the consummation of God's plan in eternity. Paul wants believers to know that God's call makes a radical—and *positive*—change in what the future holds for them. Correspondingly, their understanding of that hope will change the way they live. In 4:1, 4 Paul will expand this focus on the ethical implications of God's call for their daily life and for unity.

Hope is an important theme in this letter, despite the fact that the word occurs only here and at 2:12 and 4:4.[8] The content of hope is already implied in the word "faith." In fact, C. F. D. Moule rightly defined "hope" as "faith standing on tiptoe."[9] In Romans 8:24 Paul even wrote that we are saved by hope. An essential characteristic of Christianity is its *tilt* toward the future, and Paul desires his readers to have a sense of what God's present call means for their future.

(2) The way the NIV translates the second reality is questionable. "The riches of his glorious inheritance in the saints" (1:18b) is literally, "the wealth of the glory of his inheritance in the holy ones." These kinds of liturgical combinations create difficulty for translators (see 2 Cor. 4:4, 6), but even if "of the glory" is to be taken as the adjective "glorious," it should modify "riches" rather than "inheritance." However, "the wealth of the glory" is more than either of these ideas. Paul points to the tremendous glory that is present when God inherits the people he has set apart for himself. It is the *Father's* inheritance that Paul refers to, *not* that of believers (cf. 1:14). "In the saints" means that the inheritance is found in, or consists of, these people. The revelation of who God really is and enjoyment of him will take place when God inherits his own people. His glory will then be made manifest.

(3) The third reality believers should know is God's "incomparably great power" for people with faith. With the mention of *power* Paul makes explicit a subject that has been implicit from the first and is central to the letter. In fact, statistically Ephesians focuses on words for power more than any other New Testament letter. In verse 19 alone four different words for power occur, emphasizing God's activity in people's lives. Here the apostle emphasizes what God's power has accomplished in the resurrection of Christ and in his

---

8. Several other passages also focus on the future (see 1:10, 12, 14; 2:7; 3:11; 4:13, 30; 5:5; 6:8–9).

9. C. F. D. Moule, *The Meaning of Hope* (Philadelphia: Fortress, 1963), 11, quoting M. Warren.

exaltation to God's right hand. Paul desires that believers will know this great power is available *for them*.

Significantly, the focus on God's power here is not on God's inherent power or on some cosmic display of force. Rather, it is on God's life-giving power as it is specifically available for believers. In this way the prayer looks back to the emphasis in the doxology on God's activity of planning and working for us and our salvation.[10]

The Exaltation of Christ (1:19b–23)

IN VERSE 20 the NIV, as most translations, reads "raised him from the dead." The Greek text actually uses the plural, "from the dead ones" (as do most passages in the New Testament referring to Christ's resurrection). The point is not that Christ was raised from a state of death, but that he was raised *out from* the dead ones. This is an important difference, for it suggests that his resurrection was not viewed as an isolated event, but as the first stage in the future resurrection.[11] His resurrection is an inauguration of the final resurrection.

Christ has been raised and is now exalted "in the heavenly realms." The words express the dignity and honor that God's power has given Christ (Phil. 2:9–11). As indicated above,[12] "in the heavenly realms" does not point to heaven or to a literal location; its use in connection with the rulers and powers (3:10) and spiritual warfare (6:12) precludes this. "In the heavenly realms" here points to Christ's presence with God and to the larger reality of life with God. That Christ is exalted to the highest position possible shows the importance of his life, death, and resurrection. Further, his exaltation shows that a shift has taken place. Life's center of gravity is not earthly life; it is in the heavenly realm with Christ and God. As the Exalted One, Christ is Lord, and his exaltation is determinative for life and for the church. The implications of this exaltation will be unfolded throughout the letter (esp. in 2:5–6; 4:7–16).

Paul's language here was used frequently by the early church to refer to Christ's resurrection and exaltation, so much so that some scholars make the unlikely suggestion that an early Christian hymn lies behind this text. The imagery in 1:20 of Christ seated at the right hand of God and exalted over the powers is drawn from Psalm 110:1.[13] Paul goes on in 1:22a to connect the

---

10. See pp. 45–54.

11. Cf. Acts 4:2; 1 Corinthians 15:20–24.

12. See pp. 46–47.

13. The New Testament refers more frequently to Psalm 110:1 than to any other Old Testament text; see Matthew 22:44/Mark 12:36/Luke 20:42–43; Matthew 26:64/Mark 14:62/Luke 22:69; [Mark 16:19]; Acts 2:34–35; Romans 8:34; Colossians 3:1; Hebrews 1:3, 13; 8:1; 10:12–13; 12:2; 1 Peter 3:22.

subjection of the powers with Psalm 8:6b. These two Old Testament texts were also used to describe Christ's resurrection and exaltation in 1 Corinthians 15:25–28 and Hebrews 1:13–2:9.

Obviously this Old Testament verification of Christ's resurrection and exaltation was important for the early church in order to show that Christ was alive and that he is the Lord, the One who is able to save and from whom no one can separate. In Psalm 8 all things are subjected already; in Psalm 110 they are in the process of being subjected. Similarly some New Testament texts see the subjugation of powers as not yet complete (cf. 1 Cor. 15:25–28; Heb. 2:5–9); others assume the subjugation of all things is already complete (cf. Eph. 1:20–22; 1 Peter 3:22). This again illustrates the tension between the already and the not yet: Christ's resurrection and exaltation as Lord have already given him all power and authority, but all things have not yet been summed up in him (Eph. 1:10). As 2:1–3 shows, other forces are still at work.

A concern for spiritual power is evident throughout the letter, climaxing in a discussion of spiritual warfare in 6:10–20. A recent study of Ephesians argues that the letter was written to address attitudes and beliefs about spiritual powers in first-century Asia Minor and that Ephesians was the result of a pastoral concern to instruct readers about the relation of Christ and believers to spiritual powers.[14] The emphasis on magic and spiritual powers in and around Ephesus gives some plausibility to this view (cf. Acts 19:11–41, with its focus on miracles, exorcism, the burning of magical books, and the riot over offense to Artemis, the primary deity in Ephesus, with whom astrological beliefs were associated). On the other hand, this letter cannot be subsumed entirely under this one theme.

The powers (1:21–22a). The five categories of powers mentioned in 1:21—"rule," "authority," "power," "dominion," and "title"—are a stacking of terms to emphasize that Christ's victory over them is total. No certain conclusions can be drawn about distinctions between these terms, and no hierarchy of the powers is in mind.[15] In fact, precise definition of the five terms is difficult for three reasons: (1) New Testament discussions of the powers is brief and general, (2) most of the terms are used of both humans *and* spiritual beings, and (3) prior use of some of the terms provides little insight. For example, "rulers and authorities" is used of humans in Luke 12:11 and 20:20. "Authority" (*exousia*) is not used of angelic or demonic powers prior to the New Testament, and "dominion" (lit., "lordship") does not occur prior to its Christian usage. The meaning of "ruler" (*arche* or *archon*) is debated. Does

---

14. Clinton E. Arnold, *Ephesians, Power, and Magic: The Concept of Power in Ephesians in Light of its Historical Setting* (Grand Rapids: Baker, 1992), who suggests that the goal of Paul's prayer here is the appropriation of the unsurpassed power available to Christians.

15. See the discussion of 6:10–20, pp. 334–46.

1 Corinthians 2:8 refer to humans or spiritual powers who crucified the Lord of glory? Similarly, does "authorities" in Romans 13:1 refer to human political leaders or, as O. Cullmann argued, to human authorities *and* the spiritual beings that stand behind the humans?[16]

Without doubt, the five terms in 1:21 refer to spiritual beings, as the further development of the idea in 2:1–3 shows. But do they include human rulers as well? M. Barth affirms that these terms refer to spiritual beings, but he also writes, "Paul had in mind at the same time both visible, specific governors *and* the invisible authority exerted by them; concrete conditions and manifestations of life *and* the invisible mystery of the psyche." By this he means the very structures of life, whether they be political, financial, biological, or historical.[17] Walter Wink in his three volumes on the powers takes a similar approach, arguing that "principalities and powers" refers to the inner and outer aspects of any manifestation of power.[18]

But it is not so clear that Paul also has human authorities in mind. His emphasis seems to be on spiritual beings. In any case, even though we cannot define precisely the five categories, the intent of the passage is clear. Whatever powers exist—real or imaginary, human or nonhuman—they are *all* subject to Christ. In fact, the New Testament shows little interest in the powers other than to say they have been defeated, as a variety of texts affirms.[19] In Colossians 2:15 the defeat of the powers occurs at the cross; in the other texts, including those in Ephesians, the defeat occurs in the resurrection. The stress in Colossians 1:16 (where three of the five terms of Eph. 1:21 occur) is on the inferiority of the powers in that, like all other things, they were created by and for Christ and therefore subject to his control (cf. also 6:10–18). The powers are not in control. He is. The powers are not equal combatants on the stage of life. They are subject, and the only one in control is Jesus Christ.

"Every title that can be given" is literally "every name being named." With this phrase Paul was trying to be inclusive, as if to say, "If there is anything else there, it too is subjected to Christ." In addition, calling on names was important in exorcisms and magical practices in the ancient world and especially in and around Ephesus.[20]

---

16. Oscar Cullmann, *The State in the New Testament* (New York: Charles Scribner's Sons, 1956), 95–114.

17. Barth, *Ephesians*, 1:154, 174–75 (italics his).

18. Walter Wink, *Naming the Powers*, vol. 1, *The Powers* (Philadelphia: Fortress, 1984), 5.

19. See especially Romans 8:34–39; 1 Corinthians 15:20–28; Philippians 2:9–11; Ephesians 3:10; 4:8; 6:10–20; Colossians 2:10, 15; 1 Peter 3:22.

20. Clinton E. Arnold, *Ephesians*, 54–56. Knowledge of the Ephesian "letters" was believed to give one magical powers. Note also Acts 19:13.

The expression "the present age ... the one to come" occurs in some apocalyptic writings and in rabbinic literature, but it does not occur prior to the teaching of Jesus. G. E. Ladd suggests that Jesus was the first to use the expression.[21] These phrases show a belief in the demarcation of time between this age and God's future. Some scholars have argued that Ephesians focuses only on the present and champions a realized eschatology in which all is already fulfilled. Texts like this one, however, demonstrate that Ephesians has both a realized and a future eschatology. We have seen this already in comparing 1:13 and 4:30, but the focus on God's future occurs throughout Ephesians.[22]

Christ, church, body (1:22b–23). The statement that "God placed all things under [Christ's] feet" (1:22) leads naturally to the thought of Christ as "head" and to the image of the body. The second half of 1:22 emphasizes that Christ is "head over everything for the church." While the idea could be "head over all things in relation to the church," the NIV translation is surely correct. The point is that Christ is head of all things *for the benefit of the church.* The church is in a position of privilege because Jesus Christ is Lord (cf. also Col. 1:15–20).

With this first occurrence in Ephesians of the word "church" (*ekklesia*), a subject is introduced that becomes one of the main emphases of the letter. No other letter is so specifically focused on the theology of the church as Ephesians, and no other letter expresses such a high regard for the church (see esp. 5:23–33). Whereas Paul's other letters normally use "church" to refer to an individual congregation, all occurrences in Ephesians are universal in scope.

The word "head" has been the subject of heated debate in recent decades, particularly because of the description of the husband as head of the wife (see comments at 5:22). The debate is whether the word "head" means "source" or "authority." Here, however, no doubt exists. Paul intends to assert the idea of authority, that Christ is *Lord over all things.*

In 1:23 the concept of *the body* is introduced for the first time. This concept is one of the foundational features of Paul's thinking and will be important in the remaining chapters (except chap. 6). Elsewhere in Paul, the body image also plays a significant, but sometimes different role.[23] Paul uses the body image to express a variety of theological points. His focus here is nei-

---

21. George E. Ladd, *The Presence of the Future* (Grand Rapids: Eerdmans, 1974), 90, 115. Note Matthew 12:32 and the similar phrases in Mark 10:30 and 1 Timothy 4:8.

22. Note the expectation that all will be summed up in Christ (1:10), the concern for the coming ages (2:7), the reference to eternity throughout all generations (3:21), final unity (4:13), the kingdom (5:5), and judgment (6:8).

23. See Romans 12:3–8; 1 Corinthians 6:16; 10:14–17; 11:23–34; 12:4–31; Colossians 1:18–24; 2:6–19; 3:15.

ther on the church nor on the body, but on Christ, who is Lord of all things. Both the authority of Christ and his close relationship to the body are stressed.

While the transition from feet and head to body is natural, Paul's use of the head and body images in Ephesians and Colossians is different from his other letters and reflects a later development of his thought. In the discussion of the body in 1 Corinthians 12:21, for example, the head of the body was not Christ but another human member in the body. Paul had already referred to Christ as head in 11:3, but apparently the two images had not yet been brought into relation.

When Paul uses "head" in Ephesians and Colossians, "body" always occurs in the same context (though "body" is used at times without mention of head). This has led to debate as to whether there are two different meanings of "body" and how "head" and "body" are related. But to ask whether Christ as head is part of the body may well be an overreading of the metaphors. The main point is that Jesus' position as "head" stresses that he is Lord; the image of the "body" stresses his unity with believers and their unity with each other.

The origin of Paul's use of the body image is uncertain.[24] More important is the question of intent. The body image is a development of Paul's "in Christ" thinking. It expresses what we have already seen—that Christians live in Christ and take their identity from him. They are part of him (see 5:30; cf. also Gal. 3:26–28, which speaks of being baptized into Christ, of putting on Christ, and of being one with those in him).

The most difficult part of this passage (indeed, of the entire letter) is 1:23. Four issues must be settled: (1) the meaning of "fullness"; (2) The referent of "fullness"—does it describe Christ or the church? (3) the proper understanding of "fills," which can be understood as a Greek middle voice ("fills") or a passive ("is being filled"); (4) whether "everything" should be understood as referring to "all things" or adverbially as "in every respect."[25]

Among other possibilities, decisions on these issues yield the following options:

(1) the church is the fullness of God, who *fills all things*
(2) the church is the fullness of Christ, who *is being filled in every respect by God*
(3) Christ is the fullness of God, who *fills all things*.

---

24. Suggestions have been made that it derived from Gnosticism, Stoicism, Semitic ideas of corporate solidarity, the Eucharist, or physiological insights from ancient medical thinking. While Gnosticism is discounted today as a source of Paul's thinking, any or all of the other possibilities could be instrumental in Paul's thinking.

25. The difference between "all things" and "in every respect" is minimal, but is tied to the decision whether "fills" is middle or passive. If "fills" is passive, the adverbial "in every respect" must be chosen as well.

Fullness (pleroma) can express a variety of nuances, but the primary idea seems to be "completeness." The word can mean "totality" or "full number" (Rom. 11:25), "that which fills" (e.g., 13:10: "Love is the fulfillment [lit., fullness] of the law"), or "that which is filled" (rare or nonexistent in the New Testament). This term occurs only seventeen times in the New Testament, and no other New Testament writing makes as much theological use of the word as Ephesians. Of the three other occurrences in Ephesians, 1:10 speaks of the fullness of times and does not offer much help for interpreting this text. Ephesians 3:19, however, is close in theme to this one and emphasizes the importance of knowing Christ's love so that "you may be filled to the measure of all the fullness of God" (lit.: "that you may be filled into all the fullness of God"). Ephesians 4:13 speaks of the maturity of attaining "to the whole measure of the fullness of Christ." In understanding *pleroma*, the parallel in Colossians 2:9–10 is helpful: "For in Christ all the fullness of the Deity lives in bodily form, and you have been given fullness in Christ."[26] In these texts "fullness" is used of both God and Christ. Christians are filled by living in relation to Christ; they draw from his fullness (cf. John 1:16).

The Old Testament provides the proper background for understanding "fullness." God's presence, his glory later referred to as his Shekinah, filled the tabernacle and temple, and the Spirit of God and the wisdom of God filled individuals.[27] "Fullness," in other words, refers to God's making his presence and power felt. Whereas in the Old Testament he filled the temple, now he fills Christ, and Christ in turn fills his own so that the church partakes of the divine fullness. The focus is on the gift of God's own being in revelation and salvation.

Given this Old Testament background and the other uses of "fullness" in Ephesians and Colossians, it seems unlikely that "fullness" refers to the church (options 1 and 2). Understanding the term in that way would give the church an elevated status that it has in no other letter (even though Ephesians does have an exalted view of the church; cf. 3:21). "Fullness" instead refers to Christ (option 3), and as C. F. D. Moule suggested,[28] the phrase "which is his body" in 1:23a is merely understood as a parenthetical comment about the church. In 1:19–23 God is the prime actor. He raised and exalted Christ,

---

26. The Greek text does not use *pleroma* for the second occurrence of "fullness" in the NIV, but a participle, "You have been made full in him."

27. See Barth, *Ephesians*, 1:203–5. The attempt to find a background in Gnosticism is misguided. Only the second-century Valentinians used *pleroma* in a technical sense; see the arguments of P. D. Overfield, "Pleroma: A Study in Content and Context," *NTS* 25 (1979): 384–96.

28. C. F. D. Moule, *The Epistles to the Colossians and Philemon* (Cambridge: Cambridge Univ. Press, 1962), 168.

subjected all things to him, and gave him as head to the church. Accordingly, 1:23b is further description of Christ and his relation to God. He is the fullness of God, who fills all things. Christ is the place where God's presence, power, and salvation are known, and the church draws from this fullness (see also 4:15–16).

BRINGING THIS PASSAGE into our modern world involves analysis of both the biblical culture *and* our own. In bridging by necessity we look at ourselves. Sometimes the ancient culture is not distant, and the process seems more like looking in a mirror. That will partly be the case in this passage.

Paul's prayer in 1:15–20 is directly relevant and easily appropriated—as relevant for us now as it was when it was first written. It reveals both a conviction about the importance of prayer and a commitment to other believers. The emotional tone of 1:15–16 shows how encouraging the news was that Paul had received about his readers' faith and love. It also shows the depth of relation he felt with people he probably had never met. They were important to him and his faith, and they were an occasion of thanksgiving that bound him closer to God. Paul's example encouraged his readers to pray continually for all of God's people (cf. 6:18, where this becomes an exhortation).

Paul speaks of the love his readers have "for all the saints" (1:15). Did they *limit* their love to the saints? Some critics complain that the New Testament authors were too internally directed. But letters like Ephesians are not full explanations of the church's thinking. Especially in writings directed to believers, we should expect to hear of love for believers, and surely it is appropriate for them to take the approach reflected in Galatians 6:10 ("Let us do good to all people, especially to those who belong to the family of believers"). People concerned to share the message cannot remain focused on their own little group (see 3:8–9; 6:18–20). But we cannot know and care for everyone at the same level. Knowledge about people and respect for them leads to commitment to them and concern for them. That is what is reflected in this prayer.

Like the doxology in 1:3–14, Paul's prayer is theocentric and Trinitarian. His understanding of God and of God's actions is the basis of his prayer and shows through in his prayer. True prayer is always this way; it expresses a theology and therefore requires careful reflection and meditation on the kind of God to whom we are praying. We must examine the theological assumptions on which the prayer rests.

The Spirit and insight. Paul's request that God give a Spirit of wisdom and revelation is not a prayer for a second work of the Spirit or for something special for a few Christians. Rather, he wants *all* his readers to know the continual revealing work of God's Spirit and by that *know God*. One of the main tasks of the Spirit is to help Christians know what God has given them (1 Cor. 2:12). Philip Melanchthon said, "To know Christ is to know his benefits."[29] Paul's prayer in effect says, "By knowing God's benefits, you will know God." As in the doxology, God is viewed as a giver, who by giving makes himself known. Knowing God happens neither accidentally nor by magic. The Spirit makes possible knowledge of both God and his benefits.

The Spirit has both been given to us as the seal and guarantee of salvation (1:13–14) and is being given to us as the one who helps us understand God. Christian living requires a continual openness to the Spirit and his communication to us, not about strange mysteries, but about what Christians have in the gospel and about its significance for life. The gospel tells us what God has revealed about his character and his intent for humans.

Christians continually need insight into the faith, for they have a darkness that needs enlightening (1:17–18). This darkness is the result of sin as well as a human inability to grasp the magnificence of God and the enormity of his work in Christ. Despite our twentieth-century advance of knowledge, this is as true now as it was in the first century. God addresses our limitation and darkness and through his Spirit helps us to overcome this deficiency and to keep us ever learning about God and Christ.

Hope. Our culture offers no basis for hope. Meaninglessness we know; hope we do not. Death haunts all of us. For all its advantages, our society is frayed and has problems so enormous we have given up on solving them. Crime, poverty, human stupidity, racism, terrorism, and various other "isms" threaten to undo us. The elderly read the obituaries first. The young have lost a sense of hope of making a difference or of being "successful," and their music shows it. Middle-aged people are bored. In other countries the addition of war and famine to the list make the situation absolutely stifling. We have a sense that we cannot solve our problems—either individually or socially. This loss of hope for the present is based on a loss of hope for the future. It is as if society has AIDS and seeks only to drain out of the present all it can. Is hope possible?

Hope was as rare a commodity in the first-century world Paul addressed as it is today. Fate, determinism, and despair dominated the ancient world. People had little hope of being able to better their situation. A common epi-

---

29. See *The Loci Communes of Philipp Melanchthon*, trans. Charles L. Hill (Boston: Meador, 1944), 68.

taph read, "I was not, I was, I am not, I don't care." Life—for all its joy—has always been difficult and oppressive. People felt manipulated by unseen forces, and religion was a only way to find protection from bad luck, sickness, and evil powers.

Religion has always been and still is the means by which people attempt to deal with meaninglessness and evil, and rightly so. Karl Marx is noted for saying, "Religion is the sigh of the oppressed creature, the heart of a heartless world and the soul of soulless conditions. It is the opium of the people."[30] The truth is that all humans live as oppressed creatures, oppressed by meaninglessness and evil—both our own and that of other people. In our society we attempt to insulate ourselves from despair with movies, television, and other forms of entertainment. We are taught from an early age that "they all lived happily ever after," and we pursue this illusion. While life and God's creation are good and are to be enjoyed, we must always remember the truth that *there are no happy endings*—at least in this life. We must all deal with meaninglessness, evil, sickness, and death.

God's work in Christ addresses our meaninglessness, the problem of evil, and death. Christianity is a great religion for people who know they are desperate, and the truth is that all humans feel desperate—even when they try to deny it. Even Martin Luther's last words on his deathbed were, "We are all beggars."

But death is not the end. We can look forward to a happy ending of life with God. Hope is therefore a positive force. God has built a bridge from no hope to hope in his creation of life in the midst of death. Hope is a life-changing experience. Paul does not present an other-worldly, pie-in-the-sky theology, but he does view God's work in the resurrection as a cosmic event that has changed the course of history. He therefore prayed that people might know what God's call meant for their future and, therefore, for their present. In our society, people—including Christians—care primarily only for the present. But if God has called us to be among his future people, hope changes everything and becomes the basis from which we live in the present.

Paul's prayer points to God's power to bring life from death—a power available both now so that we can deal with the death in which we live and for the future when the dead are raised. In 1:21 Paul points to the present age and the one to come. The early church believed that the new age had already begun because of two events—the resurrection of Jesus and the pouring out of the Holy Spirit (see 1:13–14, 20–21; cf. Acts 2:17–36; 1 Cor. 15:20–28). The hope was grounded in Christ's resurrection and in Pentecost. Because of

---

30. See his *A Critique of Hegel's Philosophy of Right*, ed. Joseph O'Malley (Cambridge: Cambridge Univ. Press, 1970), 131

their hope Christians live "between the times"—residents of both this age and of the coming age. The next chapter (2:6) will assert that Christians too have already been raised and exalted with Christ. The future has already been set in motion by God's resurrection of Christ, and *Christians live from their future*, the future God has established for them. This requires a change in our worldview—a change from meaninglessness to an awareness that God's new age has begun and hope is given to us.

Power and the powers (1:19–21). Perhaps the greatest difficulties in hearing this text come at two points: belief in the power of God, and the question of the relevance of the rulers and powers. (1) Belief in God's power may be easy in the abstract, but can people today really believe in the resurrection or in the availability of God's power for living? Christianity is a religion about power,[31] for it focuses on the resurrection and exaltation of Christ. Modern Christianity sometimes makes the mistake of focusing on the death of Jesus or on various ethical ideas, treating the resurrection as almost an afterthought. Instead, the focus must be on the "twin event"[32] of the death and resurrection, with the understanding that a third event, the pouring out of the Spirit, flows directly from the resurrection. All else derives from these three events.

The ancient world was no more eager to believe in the resurrection than we are, for it did not fit their worldview. But we must not judge this teaching from our old worldview. The death and resurrection of Christ assault our worldview and value system and replace them with a worldview and values that do justice to the God who gives life in the midst of death. Faith affirms the life-giving power of God, available both for living and dying, and looks beyond death to resurrection and future life. This conviction rests on the witness of the early church, the Scriptures, and the present work of God, though it awaits verification at the end of time.

(2) The text does not give a full explanation of power and its effect in the lives of believers. Rather, the focus is on freedom from spiritual powers. In the ancient world people had an extraordinary fear of hostile spiritual powers. Health, love, and success were all at the mercy of spiritual influences. This is the reason that magic, amulets, charms, astrological beliefs, and certain religious practices were so important, especially in Ephesus. "Less advanced" cultures today may still have similar attitudes, but much of the modern Western world has nothing matching this inordinate fear.

At the same time, surprisingly, our culture is schizophrenic in its attitude toward spiritual powers. On the one hand, our "scientific" worldview rejects

---

31. See Hans-Reudi Weber, *Power: Focus for a Biblical Theology* (Geneva: WCC Publications, 1989).

32. See Paul S. Minear, *To Die and To Live* (New York: Seabury, 1977), 49.

any belief in spiritual beings, demons, angels, and the like. On the other hand, much of our society still is superstitious, accepts astrology, and is fascinated with thought about spiritual beings. The "psychic network" is a multimillion dollar industry. The recent influence of the new age movement has made language about "spirit guides" and angels common. Right in the middle of our "scientific" culture, major news magazines and television series focus on angels. In most cases, however, despite movies about demon possession, our culture focuses only on positive spiritual powers. Our society does not fear spiritual forces or blame them for things that go wrong; rather, it looks to them for assistance and good luck.

On the other hand, some Christians in recent years, unlike the surrounding culture, have focused more on the negative role of spiritual forces. Instead of helpers, Christians view these forces as oppressive and threatening beings, and they become concerned with "binding Satan," identifying "territorial spirits," and wrestling with evil. This current focus does not derive from the Bible, or it is at least unbalanced. Far more attention is being given to demons than the New Testament evidence warrants.

How should we deal with the New Testament evidence of spiritual powers? Is our atmosphere filled with good and evil forces that impact our lives? Or should we "demythologize" principalities and powers and understand that we are not dealing with spiritual beings, but with structures and systems in society and in life—governments, political structures, the character of companies or industries, historical constraints, racism, and the like?

As might be expected, these subjects are receiving increased scholarly attention. The largest recent study is the three-volume work by Walter Wink.[33] He has tried to deal with principalities and powers without demythologizing them, but in the end he does. He brackets the "ontological" question of whether such spiritual beings exist so that he can deal with the *fact* of evil and spiritual realities. One can appreciate his attempt. All of us—regardless of our beliefs—have to deal with the fact of evil. But, we cannot investigate spiritual powers by any empirical method, and therefore we can never prove or disprove their existence. No appropriate lab exists in which to do the research. However, we cannot bracket the ontological question, for if we do so, we can as easily bracket the ontological question with regard to the existence of God.

The problem is that we think we must explain all things. We cannot. Being human means being incomplete and not knowing all the answers. This

---

33. In addition to his *Naming the Powers* (n. 18 above), see Wink's *Unmasking the Powers*, vol. 2: *The Powers* (Philadelphia: Fortress, 1986) and *Engaging the Powers*, vol. 3: *The Powers* (Minneapolis: Fortress, 1992).

is one area where answers are difficult to find, and the danger is always of saying more than we are entitled to say. Especially with this subject, we should "not go beyond what is written" (1 Cor. 4:6), for when we do, we are almost certainly wrong. Frank Peretti's novels focusing on demons and angels are a violation of Christian thinking, for they engage in speculation that does not do justice to the balance and reserve of the Bible.[34] Christian thinking must always ask, "Where is it written?"

The problems increase when our experience of evil goes beyond what the text treats. Not everything is in the Bible, but we must be careful of canonizing experiences we may have interpreted through distorted lenses and under the influence of ideas derived from other people, be they Dante or Peretti. Anchoring our thinking to the biblical concerns will not be as much fun, but it will give us what we need for life.

We will be facing principalities and powers elsewhere in this letter, but here the issue is clear. Without doubt, Paul thought about spiritual beings, but their existence is of little consequence for him. He *hardly cared* about the principalities and powers in and of themselves. His main goal was to show their subjection and defeat, as if to say, "Whatever is there has been defeated by and is under Christ's control." We need to put the emphasis precisely where he did.

Christ and his church (1:22–23). These two verses may seem largely irrelevant, especially with the difficulty in knowing how to take verse 23. That Christ is called the head over all things is a metaphorical way of emphasizing one of the most important confessions of the early church—"Jesus is Lord." If our interpretation of verse 23b is correct, Christ is the one who conveys God to us. This is a crucial theological conviction, for if Jesus is Lord and embodies the fullness of God, then he defines reality with clarity so that people know what life is really about.

Furthermore, these verses emphasize that Jesus is Lord over all things *for the benefit of the church*. The church is so intimately bound to Christ that it is his body and participates in his life and reign. The intimacy of this relationship goes well beyond what most Christians think they are doing when they "make a decision" to believe in Christ. If this theology is taken seriously, the church—and its individual members—occupies a place of privilege and benefit that is astounding. We are intimately involved with the One who embodies and communicates the very fullness of God.

Summary. In sum, Paul's prayer for understanding in 1:15–23 expresses a theology that embodies the following:

---

34. Frank E. Peretti, *This Present Darkness* (Westchester, Ill.: Crossway, 1986), and *Prophet* (Westchester, Ill.: Crossway, 1992).

An ecclesiology of interrelatedness, shown both at the beginning with the focus on love and prayer and at the end with the mention of the body drawing from the fullness that is in Christ

A theology of the Spirit as the revealer, continually at work in the lives of believers to help them understand what they have from God and thereby to know God

A theology of God, who wants his people and works to bring them to himself

A Christology of exaltation, emphasizing the resurrection and the exaltation of Christ to the highest honor with God; he is Lord, and all that exists is made subservient to him.

THIS TEXT DOES not give specific directions for life, but it mirrors life and lays a foundation for life. The focus on the cosmic nature of God's work in Christ will not allow an individualistic appropriation of the text. The text implies the kind of *community* the church should be.

(1) **The church is a worldwide caring community**. Markus Barth is correct in saying that we cannot love everybody.[35] Our minds are too small to have a frame of reference so inclusive. But our love cannot be confined to the limits of our own specific community. We need a sense of a larger and broader movement of God and of our own involvement with other Christians. Note how Paul cared for and invested in Christians he did not even know. He was not just attempting to build an empire for himself, but he took seriously his belief in the body of Christ. Those other people were intimately involved with him because of their mutual faith. Such involvement with other Christians keeps us from being myopic and parochial, and it keeps both churches and pastors from being "lone rangers." Loneliness, a sense of being too small for the task, and pride all have a difficult time surviving when a person has a sense of being involved with other Christians in the body of Christ.

Paul felt a deep attachment to Christians everywhere, and so should we. Although we should be involved with non-Christians, the focus in this text is on the depth of sharing with other believers that comes from belonging to Christ. Being part of Christ means being part of the others in Christ and working with them in behalf of God's kingdom.

(2) Because Christians care for other people, **the church is a praying community**. To pray is to remember "who owns the house."[36] This is God's

---

35. Barth, *Ephesians*, 1:147.
36. Wink, *Engaging the Powers*, 160.

world and the people in it are his. The church is not an independent, self-determining group; it is a community that acknowledges it is owned and therefore under direction. Our regular practice should include praying for other Christians—even ones we do not know. Through such prayers we acknowledge we all belong to the same God and that we participate together in a common God-given mission. Knowledge of the faith and love of others should lead to thanksgiving, for we benefit when they succeed. We are one with those in Christ and share life in Christ with them.

(3) **The church is a thinking community.** The focus on the enlightenment of the mind in verse 18 introduces an important, but too frequently ignored, part of Paul's thinking. Too many Christians are passive in their thinking and learning or have an anti-intellectual bias. Part of this is understandable, for "intellectualism" has often been destructive and arrogant, but Christians have recoiled with an anti-intellectualism that leads to ignorance. We do not ward off intellectual attack by being less thoughtful!

Christians are not the only ones guilty of anti-intellectualism. We live in a society that has largely stopped thinking. The complexity of life and the overload of information available today has driven us to trite television shows and spectator sports as our main areas of mental stimulation. This text does not suggest we should all be academics or that the solutions to life are all academic. But Christians must always grow in wisdom and in their understanding of life, God, and the relevance of their faith. Wisdom is practical knowledge for right living. *The church should first of all be a community of thinkers—* not thinking in distinction from action, but thinking as the basis for action. Ignorance is an *ethical* issue.

Historically, Christianity has led the way in promoting education and in starting colleges and universities. Now most of those previously Christian institutions have lost their attachment to the faith and are little different from secular schools.[37] Pastors used to be respected as the intellectual and moral leaders in society. Now the intellectually gifted tend to go into business or science, and pastors are less and less competent leaders in any area. In the past, when the church has made significant progress—for example, at the Reformation or the great revivals—the best thinkers of the day provided the direction and force for the movement. People like Martin Luther, John Wesley, or Dietrich Bonhoeffer were *thinking* pioneers who would not accept the status quo, but applied their minds to understanding the implications of

---

37. See George M. Marsden, *The Soul of the American University: From Protestant Establishment to Established Nonbelief* (New York: Oxford Univ. Press, 1994). See also the lament over the church's failure with regard to the mind in Mark A. Noll's *The Scandal of the Evangelical Mind* (Grand Rapids: Eerdmans, 1994).

the gospel. This kind of inquiring, analytical devotion to the gospel and life still is needed from *all* of us.

Unfortunately, much of modern Christianity is guilty of a drippy sentimentality, or worse, of sensationalism. With the latter, preachers sound more like religious professional wrestlers hyping an audience. We seem more interested in trying to create emotional feeling than in providing an understanding of God and wisdom for living. As a result, many of the world say to Christians, "Your thinking is too superficial for the complexity of the world in which we live." Christians have reacted against the extremes of this world without thinking through the implications of their choices. This needs to change. A church should be a place for analysis, reflection, and reasoned discussion about the significance of the gospel. Christians should have a reputation as people who think.

This text focuses on the gift of insight that the Spirit brings to enlighten our hearts, but he does not usually just zap people with understanding. Openness to the work of the Spirit is surely required, but so is investment in thinking and learning. Nowhere is the adage "garbage in, garbage out" more true than when dealing with our own minds. If we invest our minds in pornography, sitcoms, and movies, we will not end up with knowledge of God. This is not to suggest a narrow focus on certain "spiritual" ideas. Rather, we should focus on the broadest and most complex subjects known—God, human life, and what God has done for humanity in Christ. From that foundation every other subject needs investigation, and Christians should be at the forefront of an analysis of every subject important for human life—medical ethics and medical research, theology and business, enjoyment and suffering, to name a few. We need to have the "eyes of [our] heart" enlightened to drive out the darkness and to energize us for the task.

We must remember two important facts here. The thinking called for is based on *revelation* and leads to *knowledge of God*. The goal of reflection on Scripture is not theological academics—knowing about God—but knowing God, being in relation to him, and understanding his purposes and desire for his people. From that all other knowledge derives. While no human can know God fully, we can know God really—we can relate to God and experience his presence and work in our lives.

(4) **The church is a community that understands time**. Like the doxology (1:3–14), this passage focuses on understanding the past, the present, and the future. This letter will frequently contrast the hopeless past of the recipients with their present and future privilege in Christ. Here it looks to the specific past event of God's work in Christ—his life, death, and especially resurrection as events that have changed the course of history and determine the future.

In a world that knows no time except the present, Christians must remind people about the future—something we have failed to do. We too have been caught up by the present, emphasizing only the here and now in our preaching and teaching. But if there is no future, there is no gospel. The brevity, injustice, suffering, and dying in this life cry out for the ultimate victory of God, for God to do something. Christians are eschatologically oriented because they know that God has done something marvelous and is not finished. The new age has come in the midst of the old, and one day the new age will be all that is left.

Christians must know both what they already have in Christ and what still awaits them. We too groan with creation, awaiting God's final redemption (Rom. 8:19–24). It is part of understanding time. We live between the times of the beginning of the resurrection and its end. Christians—even in their frustration—know the patience that comes from faith. As Tertullian put it, "Faith is patience with the lamp lit."[38]

Too often, however, we are comfortable enough with the present that we do not care about the future. For those attempting to focus only on pleasure in this life, Christianity has the responsibility of removing society's insulation from the truth of the hardship of life and of death. Without being morbid and without neglecting the legitimacy of pleasure and life, we must face and embrace both suffering and death. The gospel allows us to do just that.[39]

For those who know this life is temporary and feel its meaninglessness, we convey the hope of God's future, when he has a people for himself. Even those looking into death's face can have hope. Without diminishing the awful pain of diseases like AIDS and cancer, people can know God is bigger than disease, that he does not leave them, and that he holds out his future to them. That does not change the reality of death, but it does reduce it from being ultimate and final to an enemy God has defeated in the resurrection. Dying may be horrendous, but it cannot separate us from God's love and it is not the last word. Even in death, God stays with us and gives us hope.

(5) **The church is a confident community**. Surely the reason why Paul prays that his readers will know hope, God's inheritance, and power is so they may live confidently. If the Christ to whom they are connected has been exalted over every other power, we as Christians do not need to worry about the powers. Nothing can separate us from Christ, disqualify us, or condemn us (Rom. 8:31–39). If Christ is the one who conveys the fullness of God, we do not need to worry about having missed something. We know of our own

---

38. Tertullian in response to his own question "What is faith?" Quoted without reference in James S. Stewart, *The Wind of the Spirit* (Nashville: Abingdon, 1968), 53

39. Compare 1 Corinthians 3:21–23 and 2 Corinthians 4:7–15.

value and place in God's purposes. We are the beneficiaries of his lordship and we live under his lordship.

The church's confidence ought not, however, be misunderstood as triumphalism—the sin of overemphasizing "victory" so that sin, difficulty, and pain are not acknowledged and dealt with. Triumphalism in its arrogance forgets the cross and God's identification with the pain of the world. It also forgets what is still awaited—the complete victory of God in the future. The Corinthian community was guilty of the sin of triumphalism, but Paul reminded them of the cross and of the fact that God's power is made complete in weakness, a weakness that identifies with the self-giving love of the cross (esp. 2 Cor. 12:9; 13:4). Such confidence does not gloss over life's problems, but it is defined by the resurrection and lordship of Jesus Christ.

(6) **The church is a community of power.** The power Christians have is not intrinsic power, something they have in themselves, but a power that comes from God, defined by the resurrection of Jesus and his exaltation as Lord over every other power, both now and in the future. Because no other power can rival him, and because in him the fullness of God lives, Christians do not have to look elsewhere to find what they need for life. What they need is in Christ. This power, however, is not power in the abstract; it is *relational power*—power that is known because of being bound to the one in whom power resides.

But looking elsewhere is precisely what many people do. A strange temptation prevails to mix faith in Christ with some other ingredient—such as works, a second blessing, power over the demonic, or astrology—to mention only a few options in the syncretistic brew. But Christ is sufficient and nothing else is needed. *To attempt to add to Christ is to take away from him.*

We must remember this when we seek to apply the language about spiritual powers in 1:21. The purpose of this verse is not to provide information about spiritual beings so that Christians can worry about them or seek to name them and bind them. Its purpose is that people may focus on Christ, rejoice, and live confidently. To focus on the demonic is to lose focus on Christ—precisely what happens in Frank Peretti's novels. Such a focus is out of bounds, as are Walter Wink's suggestions of talking to the demonic.[40] Evil is real, and as far as we can tell, so are spiritual beings, but they are not mentioned in this passage because they are a threat or should be a cause of concern. Instead, they are defeated and we need not worry.

The real issue here and throughout Scripture is the question, "What determines who we are? Where do we get our identity?" Christians are defined and

---

40. See n. 18 and Wink, *Unmasking the Powers*, 57, 77. Wink even discusses approvingly people who talk to the "angels of the plants" (156).

shaped by Jesus Christ and his life, death, and resurrection; demons and spiritual forces are not determining or shaping factors. They have an extremely limited role. This is not to be cavalier with the reality of evil, for evil is very real (as the rest of Ephesians will show), but the application of *this* text gives no license for focusing on spiritual beings.

Two additional points need to be addressed. (a) A focus on power does not suggest a focus on "power religion"—the contemporary movement focusing on miracles, predictive prophecy, and exorcism.[41] Ephesians will provide little support for such a movement. On the other hand, neither should we accept the view that miracles were confined to the first century, for the same God who intervened in Scripture can intervene today.[42]

(b) If the power Christians have does not focus on miracles and the like, what good is it? If power is available, why do we not see it more? Of course, we live between the times, and Paul acknowledges in this letter that evil is still with us. The new age has come in the midst of the old (2:1–3; 4:17–19; 5:3–17; 6:10–20), but his point is *not* that God's power is limited by present evil. Rather, Ephesians underscores that God's power has invaded this present evil age in the resurrection *for us* (1:19–21). The theology here is precisely that announced in Romans 8:31–39: God's power does not remove us from persecution, danger, difficulty, and death, but makes us more than conquerors in all such things. This is not a power to work magic and escape difficulty, but *a power to live in an evil world*. This power is for godly living. Much of the letter will address these issues and the change that God produces in his people. This is where application of the discussion of power must focus.

A glaring question still remains: If God's power is directed at change in his people, why do we not see that change more frequently in people's lives—including our own? The question is painful and cannot be set aside, but it is also—at least implicitly—the problem that Ephesians addresses. Ephesians holds up what God intends. May it also be the instrument through which God's intention is made reality.

---

41. See the critique of this movement in Michael Scott Horton, ed., *Power Religion: The Selling Out of the Evangelical Church?* (Chicago: Moody, 1992), and a defense in Gary S. Greig and Kevin N. Springer, eds., *The Kingdom and the Power* (Ventura, Calif.: Regal Books, 1993).

42. While most of this subject is outside the concerns of Ephesians, we will deal with this issue again in chapter 6.

Ephesians 2:1–10

A
S FOR YOU, you were dead in your transgressions and sins, ²in which you used to live when you followed the ways of this world and of the ruler of the kingdom of the air, the spirit who is now at work in those who are disobedient. ³All of us also lived among them at one time, gratifying the cravings of our sinful nature and following its desires and thoughts. Like the rest, we were by nature objects of wrath. ⁴But because of his great love for us, God, who is rich in mercy, ⁵made us alive with Christ even when we were dead in transgressions—it is by grace you have been saved. ⁶And God raised us up with Christ and seated us with him in the heavenly realms in Christ Jesus, ⁷in order that in the coming ages he might show the incomparable riches of his grace, expressed in his kindness to us in Christ Jesus. ⁸For it is by grace you have been saved, through faith—and this not from yourselves, it is the gift of God—⁹not by works, so that no one can boast. ¹⁰For we are God's workmanship, created in Christ Jesus to do good works, which God prepared in advance for us to do.

THIS PASSAGE IS one of the clearest, most expressive, and most loved descriptions of salvation in the New Testament. It contains the first of five explicit "formerly-now" contrasts, which distinguish a life of sin and alienation before Christ from a life of faith in Christ. These contrasts constitute one of the main subjects in Ephesians.[1]

The number of oppositions in this passage is striking: living in transgressions and sins versus living in good works prepared by God; this world versus the heavenly realms; death versus life; sinful nature (lit., "flesh") versus union with Christ; wrath versus mercy and salvation; under the "ruler" versus seated with Christ; by nature versus by grace; not from works versus through faith.

Most of the major themes of Paul's salvation theology are present in 2:1–10. In fact, 2:8–9 (or better, 2:8–10) has often been singled out as

---

1. See 2:11–13, 19–22; 4:17–24; 5:8; also expressing the same idea are 3:5 and 4:28. Cf. also Romans 8:9-15.

"the most effective summary we have of the Pauline doctrine of salvation by grace through faith."[2] Whether a continuation of the prayer in chapter 1 or the beginning of a new section describing Christians, this section provides foundational theological ideas on which the rest of the letter will build. The past, present, and future of God's salvation in Christ are all in view here.

We make several observations at the outset. Although the NIV introduces 2:1 with "As for you," the Greek text has only "and," which binds this section closely to 1:15–23.[3] Significant parallels exist between 1:18–21 and 2:1–7: "raised," "seated in the heavenly realms," "riches," "ruler," "this age and the coming age(s)," and the idea of God's having a people. What was said about Jesus in 1:19–21 is now being applied to Christians: God raised and exalted Christ and he has raised and exalted Christians with him (cf. also Col. 2:12–13; 3:1–4).

Structure. The Greek text of 2:1–7 is one long sentence. Paul began writing about being dead in transgressions and sins in 2:1, was diverted to write more about life in sins and the merciful love of God in 2:2–4, and then started over with his thought of being dead in transgressions in 2:5.[4] Clearly Paul's intent in 2:1–10 is to say: "*And you too* were involved in God's act. When Jesus was raised from the dead, you also were raised from death to life." This section is made up of three movements:

A. The former way of life in sins (2:1–3)
B. God's merciful salvation in Christ and its purpose (2:4–7)
C. Further explanation of salvation by grace (2:8–10)

Repetition of key ideas underscores items the author gives prominence: "dead in transgressions" (vv. 1, 5); "formerly" (vv. 2, 3; NIV: "used to" and "at one time"); "lived" (vv. 2, 10; NIV: "live" and "do"[5]); "age" (vv. 2, 7; NIV: "ways" and "ages"); "with Christ" (vv. 5–6); "it is by grace you have been saved" (vv. 5, 8); and "in Christ Jesus" (vv. 6, 7, 10).

---

2. C. L. Mitton, *Ephesians*, 155. See the discussion by Andrew T. Lincoln, "Ephesians 2:8–10: A Summary of Paul's Gospel," *CBQ* 45 (1983): 617–30. Neither author accepts Pauline authorship of Ephesians, however, and Lincoln attempts to identify shifts from Paul's style as proofs that someone else wrote the letter.

3. Some have even suggested 1:23 should end with a comma instead of a period, but this is unwarranted.

4. In fact, the RSV borrows the words "he made alive" from 2:5 and duplicates them in 2:1 to try to smooth out Paul's thought.

5. Literally "walked" in verses 2 and 10. This word will dominate the ethical discussions in chapters 4 and 5 (see 4:1, 17; 5:2, 8, 15).

The Former Way of Life in Sins (2:1–3)

NOTE THE VARIATIONS in the pronouns in this passage, a feature that occurs regularly in Paul's letters and throughout Ephesians.[6] Sometimes the change indicates that two different groups are being referred to; at other times no reason for the shift is discernible. Especially because of the focus on Gentiles and Jews in 2:11–22, some scholars view "you" and "your" in 2:1–3 as referring to Gentiles and "us," "our," and "we" as referring to Jewish Christians.[7] But a closer reading of the text argues against this approach. Similar changes appear in 2:5–10 for no discernible reason. If any explanation can be made for the changes of pronouns in this passage, probably Paul uses the second-person pronouns where he is attempting to emphasize the relevance of his statements for his readers.

Dead in transgressions and sins (2:1). Looking back from the perspective of life in Christ, Paul viewed the former life as death, that is, spiritual death,[8] life without God, or a meaningless life hardly worth living.[9] For those who think life comes from God and is experienced in relation to God, separation from God is equivalent to death (cf. 4:18).

Elsewhere Paul views death as a tyrant that dominates unredeemed humanity, both in their present living and in their destiny in the grave.[10] Ernest Best describes the view in 2:1 as "a realized eschatological conception of death."[11] In other words, the end result has invaded and permeated the present. Death controls life. It is nonrelational, powerless, and corrupting. As a consequence of sin, people have no relation to God and distorted relations with each other. They are powerless to change and are being pulled down to destruction.

As in Romans 5:12–21, death is a result of sin. The expression "dead in your transgressions and sins" suggests that sins both cause death and are evidence of death. No attempt should be made to distinguish between

---

6. E.g., Romans 7:4–5; 8:12–16; Galatians 3:29; 4:6. In Ephesians see 2:11–22; 4:1–16; 5:1–2; 6:11–12.

7. See Barth, *Ephesians*, 1:212, 216.

8. Both *nekros* and *thanatos* are used in the New Testament to express this metaphorical death.

9. This language was fairly common in both Old and New Testaments and in other Jewish sources (see Ps. 88:3–6; 143:3; Ezek. 37:11–14; Matt. 8:22; 23:27; Luke 15:24; Rom. 5:12–21; Eph. 5:14; esp. 1 Tim. 5:6 [referring to the pleasure-seeking widow who is dead while living] and Rev. 3:1 [referring to the church at Sardis, which had a reputation for being alive, but was dead]).

10. See especially Romans 5:12–21; 6:15–23; 7:5, 24; 8:6–13.

11. Ernest Best, "Dead in Trespasses and Sins," *JSNT* 13 (1981): 16.

"transgressions" and "sins;" for both words are used to express one idea concerning the variety and dominance of sins.[12]

Living in sins (2:2–3). The word translated "live" is actually "walk," a word used frequently in New Testament texts to describe a way of life. The instructions in chapters 4 and 5 are framed around this word. While more frequent in Ephesians than other Pauline letters, this word is at the center of Paul's ethical thinking.[13] The metaphor has its origin in the Old Testament idea of walking in the way of the Lord (e. g., Deut. 5:33; Ps. 1:1; Isa. 30:21.)

Particularly with this letter's focus on being in Christ, the description of the former life as *in* transgressions and sins is significant. These words describe the path in which people walk and the boundaries that shape their lives. As we have seen, Paul has a "spheres of influence" theology.[14] People live in one of two spheres or environments, either in Christ or in sin(s). Transgressions and sins determine the environment in the former way of life (cf. 1 Cor. 15:17).

Two other descriptions of this former life are given in 2:2: following "the ways of this world and of the ruler of the kingdom of the air." "The ways" of this world is an appropriate translation, but a nuance is lost from the more literal *"age* of this world"—the same word used in 1:21 of the present and the coming age, and in 2:7 of the coming ages throughout which God's grace will be demonstrated. The former way of life of these believers involved conformity with the present worldly age.[15] "World" has a broad semantic range in the New Testament, covering creation, people, and a world system that either leaves God out of the picture or is openly hostile to him. Clearly Paul's intent here is to focus on this world system, a way of life shaped by a system that does not consider God (similar to the expression "living according to the flesh").[16]

---

12. The two words are used interchangeably both in the singular and in the plural (e.g., Rom. 5:20; Col. 1:14; 2:13. Regarding the word "sin" (*hamartia*), 48 of the 64 Pauline occurrences of this word are in Romans, of which only three are plural. In Romans Paul views sin not so much as individual misdeeds as the tyrant that dominates human life. Of the 16 occurrences outside Romans, 9 are in the plural.

13. See Romans 6:4; 8:4; 1 Corinthians 3:3; 7:17; 2 Corinthians 4:2; Galatians 5:16. This use of "walk" also occurs in the Johannine literature and elsewhere in the New Testament (e. g., John 8:12; 11:9–10; 1 John 1:6–7; Acts 21:21).

14. See pp. 40, 42, 47–48, 56–57, 63–64.

15. The attempt by Schnackenburg, *Ephesians: A Commentary*, 91 and 96, to see "age" in 2:2 as pointing to a personified being does not do justice to the temporal meanings of the word in 1:21 and 2:7.

16. Compare Galatians 1:4, which speaks of Christians being rescued from the present evil age, and Romans 12:2, which cautions Christians not to be conformed to the present age (NIV, "the pattern of this world").

Living in sins is also living in conformity with "the ruler of the kingdom of the air." Christ is exalted over all the powers and fills all things (1:21–23), but another power is also at work. Although Paul does not name this ruler, he is clearly talking about a life that follows the evil one (6:16) or the devil (4:27; 6:11).[17]

Exactly what is intended with "the ruler of the kingdom of the air" and how it relates to the words that follow are unclear. The word translated as "kingdom" is actually the word usually translated by "authority."[18] Colossians 1:13 has a similar theology; Christians are delivered from the realm or dominion of darkness. According to 3:10 and 6:12 the domain of the rulers and powers is in the heavenly realms. The ancient world apparently viewed the air between heaven and earth as the domain of spirits.[19] From a biblical perspective, this may have been enhanced by Job 1–2, which speaks of Satan appearing before the throne of God, though that is uncertain. The ruler has control of this godless domain, the atmosphere, and instead of living in accord with God's domain, people choose a tyrant instead of the God who created them.[20]

"The spirit who is now at work in those who are disobedient" can be taken in various ways.[21] The "spirit" likely refers either to the "ruler" or the "kingdom." If the former, the ruler is the spirit now at work. If the latter, "spirit" describes that over which he rules, and his realm is at work. The difference is significant, for in the first case, the ruler is personal, referring to the devil at work in disobedient people, while in the second it is impersonal, meaning the world order at work (note similar ideas and questions in 1 Cor. 2:6–8, 12). The NIV has interpreted "spirit" as describing the ruler himself. This is supported by the fact that it is easier to see a ruler at work than a kingdom. But even if reference is to the world order at work, the evil one is still ruler over that world order.

---

17. Compare "the prince of this world" in John 12:31; 14:30; 16:11, and "the prince of the demons" in Matthew 9:34; 12:24, in which the word "prince" (*archon*) translates the same word rendered "ruler" here. References to "rule" or "rulers" in Ephesians 1:21, ; 3:10; 6:12 use a related word *arche*.

18. *Exousia*; the NEB translates this singular word as a collective noun, "spiritual powers," but that is without warrant.

19. See Clinton E. Arnold, *Ephesians, Power, and Magic*, 60–61; Everett Ferguson, *Demonology of the Early Christian World* (Lewiston, N.Y.: Edwin Mellen, 1984). 45–47, 75–86

20. Walter Wink, *Naming the Powers*, Vol. 1: *The Powers* (Philadelphia: Fortress, 1984), 83. It is possible that *exousia* ("authority," the word translated "kingdom") is a genitive of apposition. If so, we should translate, "the ruler, the authority of the air."

21. Such a negative use of the word "spirit" is rare in Paul's writings (seen only in 1 Cor. 2:12; 2 Cor. 11:4; 2 Thess. 2:2 [NIV, prophecy]; 1 Tim. 4:1).

Disobedience and unbelief are often equated in the New Testament,[22] enough so that translations sometimes use "unbelievers" when the Greek actually has "disobedient" (cf. NIV at Rom. 15:31). Disobedience and life in sins are contrasted with living in good works prepared by God in Ephesians 2:10.

Sinful nature and wrath (2:3). As if to avoid the suggestion that the readers were a uniquely evil group, Paul switches to the first person plural and affirms that all of us at one time lived among the disobedient. His concern is not that Christians merely lived *among* the disobedient, but that they also lived *like* them, determined by the old order. The blame is *not* placed on the ruler of the old realm, even though he is at work. Rather, it is placed on the "sinful nature" (*sarx*; lit., "flesh"). The translation of *sarx* as "sinful nature" avoids misleading ideas that suggest humanity or the material is negative, but it creates confusion with the second occurrence of the English word "nature," which renders a different Greek word.

Paul uses *sarx* in various ways in his letters, usually with negative ethical connotations as here. It usually refers to that which leaves God out of the picture, that which is *merely human* and left to its own devices. Implicit is the thought that without God, desires are the lord in control. They must be gratified and followed. In the former life we lived *by* our sinful desires, doing whatever they told us. "Cravings" and "desires" refer to legitimate human needs that are distorted, subverted, and heightened to produce an irrational self-centeredness (see comments on 4:17–19, 28–29). Once again Paul focuses on the mind. The former life is marked by a misaligned reasoning process that causes people to do what the sinful nature says. Sin causes a distortion in the mind (see esp. Rom. 1:21-22, 28).

The result is that all people are "by nature objects of wrath." That is, all people are headed for an encounter with God's wrath. "Objects of wrath" is literally "children of wrath." "Children of" (or "son of") is a Semitic way of saying "characterized by" or "described by."[23] These people are under God's wrath, both his present wrath (cf. John 3:26; Rom. 1:18)[24] and his future wrath (cf. Rom. 5:9; Eph. 5:4). Both are implied here. Paul is not thinking of uncontrolled outbursts of angry passion on God's part nor of some impersonal wrath; rather, wrath points to God's constant displeasure and reaction against sin.

"Nature" (*physis*) has a variety of meanings: for example, the order of nature (Rom. 1:26; Rom. 11:21; 1 Cor. 11:14[25]), every *kind* of animal (James

---

22. See John 3:36; Romans 2:8; 10:16, 21; 15:31; Hebrews 3:12, 18–19; 4:2, 6, 11.

23. Compare Deuteronomy 25:2, where "deserves to be beaten" is literally "a son of stripes," and 1 Samuel 26:16, where "deserve to die" is literally "sons of death."

24. The contrast with the mercy of God in verse 4 seems to require that the wrath in verse 3 is also present.

25. The meaning here is virtually "custom" and is the loosest use of this term.

3:7), and what one is by constitution rather than from experience or circumstance (e.g., Rom. 2:27; Gal. 2;15; 4:8; 2 Peter 1:4). The use in Ephesians 2:3 falls into this third category. By their very nature human beings in this fallen world are sinful and therefore under God's wrath, even though the text does not explain how this came about.

This text speaks of the universality of sin, but it *does not reject the value of humanity*. It points to *pervasive depravity*, a depravity that extends to all human thought and action, but it does not suggest *total depravity* in the sense of absolute worthlessness. All humans—whether believers or not—are created in the image of God and have enormous value and capability. Despite depravity, God finds something worth loving.[26]

The picture the text paints is bleak. Because of sins, humans are the living dead. They live in keeping with a world order that ignores God and in keeping with a tyrant who works to cause disobedience. In their enslavement they follow desires and distorted reasonings that leave God out of the picture and, therefore, they are under God's wrath. But, the main point of Ephesians—and especially of 2:1–10—is that *God will not stay out of the picture.*

God's Merciful Salvation in Christ and Its Purpose (2:4–7)

MANY SUGGEST AN early Christian hymn or creed stands behind 2:4–10, possibly an initiation hymn used in connection with baptism. Ephesians clearly uses earlier liturgical traditions, most obviously in 4:22-24 and 5:14. Dependence on a hymn or creed is difficult to prove, for Paul was certainly capable of both the theology and the style of this passage. A similar theology is present in Romans 7:4-6 and Titus 3:3-7. Although dependence on a baptismal hymn is unproven, baptismal *ideas* are clearly behind this text (cf. the parallel passage in Col. 2:12–13). Romans 6:2–11 also makes explicit reference to baptism in connection with dying and rising with Christ (see also Gal. 3:27).

The mercy and love of God. While the NIV does not show it, 2:4 begins with an emphasis on God. The picture was bleak, *but God* acted because of his love and mercy. That salvation is a gift and does not come as a result of anything in the receiver is made explicit in 2:8–9, but it is already implicit

---

26. Whether "by nature objects of wrath" was intended to teach a doctrine of original sin is debated. The Semitism "children of wrath," which stands behind this expression, does not refer to babies. Paul is describing adults, not children, so this part of the statement is not about original sin. The key word is the word "nature." It is probably better to say this text assumes a doctrine of original sin than teaches it. How sin gains entrance or is transmitted is not discussed here or elsewhere; that sin has infected the human race is presupposed. This text is similar to Paul's discussion in Romans 5:12–14. The strongest recent argument for the relevance of Ephesians 2:3 to the doctrine of original sin is that by David L. Turner, "Ephesians 2:3c and *Pecattum Originale, GTJ* 1 (1980): 195–219.

in 2:4. Mercy and love are revelations of God's being, not a response to something that merits love in the individual. God acts in mercy because he is that kind of God.

The word "mercy" (*eleos*) does not often occur in Paul's letters. The importance of this theme for Paul, however, is evident in its use in Romans (9:16–18, 23; 11:30–32; 15:9) and in descriptions of his own conversion (1 Tim. 1:13–16). Numerous other Scriptures focus on the mercy of God, such as Exodus 34:6; Deuteronomy 4:31; 7:7–9; Psalm 78:38; Isaiah 55:7; Jeremiah 31:20; Micah 7:18 in the Old Testament, and Matthew 5:7; 9:13; 23:23; 1 Peter 1:3 in the New Testament. Apart from God's mercy, no hope exists for humanity.

The "love" of God is a major theme in Paul's understanding of salvation.[27] Once again, the theocentric focus of Ephesians is emphasized. God is not an onlooker in the salvation process or in an "angry huff" waiting to be appeased. Rather, he is the primary actor, the one who by his love deals with his own wrath and shows mercy to his people.

"Mercy," "love," "grace," "kindness," and "gift" in 2:4–10 are obviously closely related and show that Paul is stacking words in an attempt to describe adequately the reality of the gospel. While each of these words carries a nuance different from the others, their meanings shade into each other. They come as a cascade of expansive language attempting to describe the grandeur of God's care for and commitment to human beings expressed in his action in Jesus.

The expansive language is also evident in the words "rich" (2:4) and "riches" (2:7), used to describe the incomprehensible and inexhaustible supply of some trait or gift of God (see Rom. 2:4; 11:33). Ephesians uses this language more than any other letter and emphasizes the riches of God's grace (1:7; 2:7), his mercy (2:4), his glory (1:18; 3:16), and the riches of Christ (3:8). God's "wealth" is his resources for caring for his people and for revealing his nature.

Raised with Christ from death to life. Almost as if he cannot believe the depth of God's love, in 2:5 Paul repeats the statement from 2:1: "even when we were dead in transgressions." The two verbs in 2:6 ("raised us up with Christ and seated us with him") provide a commentary on "made us alive with Christ" in 2:5. These expressions do not refer to future resurrection, but to our being raised with Christ in the past, to being "co-resurrected" with Christ. Paul's theology asserts that Christians were included in the redemptive events of Christ's death and resurrection. The threefold repetition of

---

27. The love of God appears in 1:4, 6 and 5:1; the love of Christ appears in 3:18–19; 5:2, 25. See also Romans 5:5, 8; 8:35, 39; 15:30; 2 Corinthians 13:11, 13; Colossians 3:12; 1 Thessalonians 1:4; 2 Thessalonians 2:13, 16.

"with" is significant and underscores the Pauline emphasis on participation with Christ. To enjoy salvation requires being joined to the Savior (cf. Rom. 7:4.) The gift cannot be separated from the Giver.[28]

The language here is reminiscent of Romans 5:6–10, which speaks of God demonstrating his love even while we were weak, sinners, and his enemies. Salvation exists because God created life in the midst of death. Without the resurrection there would be no salvation. Romans 5:6–10—like other texts—emphasizes the death of Christ as the means of salvation, and the resurrection is implicit. Here in Ephesians 2 Paul does not mention the death of Christ, focusing instead on his resurrection (cf. 1 Peter 1:3).

How we are "raised up" is not explained. Physical resurrection is not meant, but this co-resurrection is real nonetheless. If humanity's plight is a living spiritual death (2:2–3), the solution is a spiritual resurrection. Life must be infused. Several facts suggest that the Holy Spirit is the one who makes the dead live. The seal of the Spirit in 1:13 apparently refers to the same event as 2:5, and 2 Corinthians 3:6 speaks of the Spirit making us alive (see also John 6:63).[29]

Some have charged that Ephesians has lost the focus on the cross, but such a complaint reveals a failure to understand the movement of Ephesians and ignores texts that do focus on the death of Jesus.[30] Ephesians 2:5–6 merely extends to believers God's act of resurrection and exaltation mentioned in 1:19–20. Paul does not focus on dying with Christ here because he uses the imagery of our being dead already in transgressions. The next section (2:13–16) will suggest that by his death Christ both deals with our "living death" and puts to death all enmity (both that between humans and God and that among humans). The point here is that when God raised Christ from the dead and exalted him, he raised and exalted Christians with him.

Neither here nor elsewhere does Paul view Christ's death and resurrection apart from each other.[31] Salvation depends on both, for when we believe, we participate in the twin event of the death and resurrection of Jesus. Parallels to participation in or identification with these two events of Jesus

---

28. Ernst Käsemann made this expression popular. See his "The Righteousness of God" in Paul," *New Testament Questions of Today* (London: SCM, 1969), 174–76. Barth's attempt (*Ephesians*, 1: 220) to suggest that "made alive together with" has a double meaning referring to resurrection with Christ and to the joining of Jews and Gentiles is unconvincing.

29. Other texts emphasize the role of the Spirit in salvation too (e.g., Rom. 5:5; 8:9–17 [note the death-life contrast in 8:10]; 1 Cor. 6:11; 12:3, 13; Gal. 3:2–6; Eph. 2:18).

30. See 1:7; 2:13, 15–16; 5:2.

31. See p. 84 for the importance of referring to the "twin event" of the death and resurrection of Christ.

appear frequently.[32] While this theology is implicit throughout the New Testament (e.g., Matt. 16:24–25), outside the Pauline letters it is explicit only in 1 Peter 2:4–5, 24.

Not only have Christians been raised with Christ, they have also been seated with him in the heavenly realms. What is true of him (1:20) is true of us. If he is exalted to God's right hand, so are we. We are joined to him so that we are where he is. Several other texts speak of being exalted with Christ (see Rom. 8:37; 1 Cor. 15:48; 2 Cor. 2:14; Gal. 4:26; Phil. 3:20; Col. 3:1–4), but no text states this idea as forcefully as Ephesians 2:5-6. The intent here is to underscore the life believers now have with Christ, and with that life come privilege, honor, security, and responsibility.

This is *not*, however, the same as saying we are actually seated in heaven. As we saw in connection with 1:3,[33] "in the heavenly realms" is not merely a synonym for "heaven." The use of the term in 3:10 for the place of revelation to the powers and in 6:12 for the place of battle with evil forces prohibits this. The phrase points to the heavenly—i. e., the spiritual—reality of God and his work in Christ. Leon Morris suggests "the realm of spiritual realities."[34] The "heavenly realms" are not separated from this world; on the contrary they are determinative for this world.

Being raised with Christ and being seated with him are conditioned on being "in Christ Jesus." The threefold repetition of this phrase underscores once again the centrality "in Christ" has for Paul's theology.[35] "Being in Christ is not only the fundamental fact of the individual Christian's existence, it is the whole reality."[36] In Paul's mind, Christ's death and resurrection are not merely events that produce benefit for believers, they are events in which believers are included.[37] According to Paul's "spheres of influence" theology, people either live in sin and under its influence or in Christ and under his influence. It is a question of serving the tyrant sin or the Lord Christ. Conversion is a transfer from one sphere to the other, a change of lordships, and being raised with Christ is the language Paul uses to describe this transfer from the realm of death to the realm of life.[38] Anything short of such a theology fails to understand Paul.

---

32. See Romans 6:1–14; 7:4; 8:11–13; 1 Corinthians 10:16; 2 Corinthians 4:10–12; Galatians 2:19–20; 6:14; Philippians 3:9–10; Colossians 2:12–13; 3:1–4; 2 Timothy 2:11–13.

33. See pp. 46–47.

34. Morris, *Expository Reflections on Ephesians*, 50–51.

35. See pp. 38–40, 42, 47–48, 56–57, 63–64.

36. Lewis B. Smedes, *Union with Christ: A Biblical View of New Life in Jesus Christ* (Grand Rapids: Eerdmans, 1983), 59.

37. See Robert C. Tannehill, *Dying and Rising with Christ* (Berlin: Verlag Alfred Töpelmann, 1967), 1.

38. See Käsemann, "The Righteousness of God' in Paul," 170–76; E. P. Sanders, *Paul and*

Saved by grace. As the NIV indicates, the words "by grace you have been saved" interrupt the flow of thought and show the astonishment Paul has that God should save people out of their living death. The language of having been saved and the use of the perfect tense do not follow Paul's normal pattern. Outside this passage Paul does not use the perfect tense for the word "save" (*sozo*).[39] This tense points to a past event and its continuing results. Salvation is viewed here as something that has occurred and is currently experienced by those who are in Christ.[40] Salvation language points primarily to the idea of rescue from danger, but this is, of course, only one of several ways Paul speaks of God's redeeming activity. No single image—justification, salvation, redemption, reconciliation, freedom, or any other—is adequate by itself to explain the reality God has worked for us.

Surely the most significant word in Paul's discussion of salvation is "grace" (cf. 1:6–8). We have already pointed out that five key words (grace, truth, faith, love, and hope) encapsulate the Christian gospel.[41] Grace is the key ingredient and by necessity comes first; everything else flows from and builds on a theology of grace. Grace means the completely undeserved, loving commitment of God to us. For some reason unknown to us, but which is rooted in his nature, God gives himself to us, attaches himself to us, and acts to rescue us. Though wrath should have come, saving grace comes instead. This action is rooted in God's very nature.[42] The initiative always lies only and completely with him. No human action could remove us from the plight in which we are found. If grace is God's giving himself to us, this text underscores that grace *connects* us to Christ.

Palestinian Judaism (Philadelphia: Fortress, 1977), 463–72, 506–8; *Paul, the Law, and the Jewish People* (Philadelphia: Fortress, 1983), 4–10. Morna Hooker has several articles promoting "interchange" as a helpful explanation of salvation. "Interchange" is best summarized by the statement, "He became what we are in order that we might become what he is" (from Irenaeus, *Against Heresies*, Preface). See her "Interchange in Christ," *JTS* 22 (1971): 349–61; "Interchange and Atonement," *BJRL* 60 (1978): 462–81; "Interchange and Suffering," in *Suffering and Martyrdom in the New Testament*, ed. William Horbury and Brian McNeill (Cambridge: Cambridge Univ. Press, 1981), 70–83; and "Interchange in Christ and Ethics," *JSNT* 25 (1985): 3–17. Cf. John 5:24; 1 John 3:14.

39. The Pauline letters use the verb "save" (*sozo*) 29 times and the noun "salvation" (*soteria*) 19 times. Usually Paul has in mind our future salvation (Rom. 5:9–10), but he also uses it to refer to an event of the past (Rom. 8:24) or something being experienced in the present (1 Cor. 1:18; 2 Cor. 6:2).

40. The future component, the "not yet" part of Christianity is not mentioned here but is present elsewhere in Ephesians (1:10, 14; 4:30; 5:5).

41. See p. 59.

42. These statements do not deny the importance of humans being created in the image of God or their potential value. Instead, they proceed from a sense of the seriousness of the human plight.

Demonstration for the coming ages (2:7). The purpose of God's action in saving us is to demonstrate in the coming ages how rich his grace is; in intervening for us, God shows his own character (cf. Rom. 3:25–26). By its very nature the gospel is a revelation.[43] The revelation of God's character will continue throughout eternity, and the primary evidence of his grace and kindness are the people who have received life in Christ Jesus. We should also remember the expression "to the praise of his glory" in 1:6, 12, and 14. God's saving work shows who he really is and results in worship, both now and throughout eternity.

Further Explanation of Salvation by Grace (2:8–10)

THIS SECTION PROVIDES commentary on the insertion in 2:5 ("it is by grace you have been saved"), repeated in 2:8 but with "through faith" added to show how this salvation is appropriated. This further explanation also shows the relevance salvation has for the readers; note the change to "you." Two other subjects are introduced in verses 9–10, which will be expanded in later passages—new creation and the ethical impact of God's work. The combination of ideas makes 2:8–10 one of the most effective summaries of Paul's gospel of salvation by grace through faith.[44]

Faith. Romans 1:17 and Galatians 3:11 both show the importance of Habakkuk 2:4 for the origin of Paul's understanding of "faith," and an allusion to that Old Testament text is possible here. Up to this point in the letter "faith" and its cognates have served only to identify the readers as believers (1:1, 15, 19) and to indicate their reception of the gospel (1:13). Verse 8 is similar to 1:13, describing the *means* by which salvation is appropriated. Language is especially important here. Christians are saved by God's grace, not by their faith. Faith is the only *means* by which this grace is received. The rest of the letter underscores the importance of faith and its cognates for salvation and life (3:12, 17; 4:5, 13; 6:16, 21, 23).

Faith (*pistis*) cannot be limited to mental assent or to believing certain ideas. The Greek noun can mean "faith," "faithfulness," "reliability," "promise," "pledge," "proof," "trust," and "confidence." In addition, it can be used of the act of believing, the content of what is believed, or as a word that encapsulates all the gospel stands for—in essence, "the faith religion" (cf. Gal. 3:23; Eph. 4:5). The verb *pisteuo* can mean "trust," "give credence to," "be convinced that," "entrust," and "have confidence." Primarily, this word group treats *that*

---

43. See my discussion of this issue in "The Gospel in Romans: A Theology of Revelation," *Gospel in Paul: Studies on Corinthians, Galatians and Romans for Richard Longenecker*, eds. L. Ann Jervis and Peter Richardson (Sheffield: Sheffield Academic Press, 1994), 288–314.

44. See n. 2.

on which one may rely or *the act of relying on something believed reliable.* Both sides of the coin are present—relying on something or someone believed reliable. As always, context—not a catalogue of possibilities—determines meaning.

Paul assumes this two-sided nature of faith in his discussions of salvation. *Faith is relational,* describing reliance on a reliable God. Faith is a *covenant* word, expressing the commitment and trust that bind two parties together. Throughout Scripture, God by his grace makes promises and commits himself to his people. They in turn are to trust those promises and live in light of them. God shows himself faithful and people are to respond in faithfulness. To say "I have faith" does not so much say anything about oneself; rather it says, "God is a trustworthy God."[45]

People who believe do not merely assent to certain ideas; they are bound to God and live in response to him. Paul's frequent use of phrases such as "with Christ" and "in Christ" show his conviction that faith joins them to Jesus Christ so strongly that they are in him and that what is true of him is true of them. Christ's past is their past, and he determines their present and future. Faith has an *adhesive* quality to it;[46] it binds the believer to the one who is believed. Salvation does not come from believing ideas or an emotional decision, but from being bound to Christ.

A problem emerges in the middle of verse 8: What is the antecedent of "this" in the statement, "and this not from yourselves." Though other texts may refer to faith itself as a gift of God (see Acts 3:16; 14:27; 18:27),[47] that is not Paul's point here. The word "this" is neuter, whereas "faith" is a feminine noun. Since there is no neuter noun is in the previous clause as the obvious antecedent of "this," the word most likely refers to the *whole process* of God's saving people by grace. (Note the parallel between "not from yourselves" and "not from works.") Paul's point is that salvation is a gift from the trustworthy God, whom we believe.

Works and boasting (2:9). Paul is no longer dealing with the problem of the imposition of the Jewish law on his converts as he was in Romans, Galatians, and—to some degree—in Philippians. In these letters Paul resisted forcefully any grounding of salvation in "works of law." No doubt behind "not by works" (2:9) stands this longer expression "works of law" from those

---

45. See D. H. van Daalen, "'Faith' According to Paul," *ExpTim* 87 (1975–76): 83–85.

46. See William Sanday and Arthur C. Headlam, *The Epistle to the Romans* (Edinburgh: T. & T. Clark, 1896), who define faith as "the lively act or impulse of adhesion to Christ" (11) and the "*enthusiastic* adhesion, personal adhesion; the highest and most effective motive-power of which human character is capable" (34, italics theirs).

47. Possibly Acts 15:11 can be read to suggest grace enables belief. Obviously theological systems that emphasize "irresistible grace" are attracted to the idea that faith itself is God's gift.

earlier debates, though its meaning is not limited to the specific "boundary markers" that distinguished Jews from Gentiles (e.g., circumcision, Sabbath keeping, and food laws).[48] "Works" refers to any human condition or accomplishment by which one thinks to gain status or privilege before God. In reality, however, nothing we do grants standing before God. Humans in and of themselves have no claim on God.

Boasting is actually a determinative part of Paul's theology. Much of his concern is to make sure that praise goes only to God. He seeks to destroy any conceivable ground for human beings boasting in themselves. Humanity is left with every mouth silenced and no claim or defense before God.[49] The only legitimate boasting is in what God has done (1 Cor. 1:31), a theology Paul adopted from Jeremiah 9:24. This Old Testament text provided a foundation for Paul's worship, ministry, and self-understanding.[50] "Works righteousness" is not a problem the letter addresses, but Paul cannot speak of salvation without excluding the possibility of personal boasting. Such rejection, however, does not entail a rejection of human competence. Rather, it is an insistence that all we are and do comes as a gift of God.

God's new creation (2:10). Note the switch back to "we." One obvious reason why no room exists for human boasting is that Paul views salvation as God's new creation. People do not contribute to their rebirth any more than they did to their natural birth. The emphasis on the activity of God, which began in 1:1, comes to a crescendo here. "We are God's workmanship" can well be translated, "We are the result of his activity." Salvation and new life are God's work, and human beings are recipients, not causative agents. That creation language is used should not be taken lightly (see also 2:15; 4:24). The New Testament assumes that God's act in Christ is parallel to creation itself.[51] This new creation—like everything else in Ephesians—

---

48. As James D. G. Dunn argued. See his "Works of the Law and the Curse of the Law (Galatians 3.10–14)," *NTS* 31 (1985): 523–42; "Yet Once More—The Works of the Law': A Response," *JSNT* 46 (1992): 99–117. But Romans 4:2–4 refers to Abraham's works before any thought of "boundary markers." Romans 9:32 also seems to contrast works in a general sense with faith. See Douglas J. Moo, "'Law.' 'Works of the Law,' and Legalism in Paul," *WTJ*, 45 (1983): 73–100; C. E. B. Cranfield, "'The Works of the Law' in the Epistle to the Romans," *JSNT*, 43 (1991): 89–101.

49. See especially Romans 3:19, 27; 4:2; 1 Corinthians 1:18–29; 3:21; 4:7; Galatians 6:14.

50. This theology of boasting (both negatively and positively understood) is a recurrent theme throughout the Corinthian letters. The positive sense of boasting is often lost in translations by the substitution of *rejoice* for boasting (cf. NIV in Rom. 5:2, 3, 11).

51. See 1 Corinthians 15:20–24, 45–49, where the resurrection is viewed as the inauguration of a new order and Christ is a "new Adam" (cf. Rom. 5:12–21). In 2 Corinthians 4:6 the coming of the gospel is equivalent to the creation of light, and in 5:17 those in Christ are a new creation. Colossians 1:15–20 emphasizes the relation of creation and redemp-

takes place "in Christ Jesus." The new creation is based in Christ's resurrection, the creation of life in the midst of death.

Good works prepared beforehand. The purpose of God's creative activity is not merely to have a people, as if he were constructing a work of art. Rather, this new creation is to be active and productive like the Creator. Christians are "to do good works, which God prepared in advance for us to do" (contrast to 2:2).[52] Salvation is not from works, but it surely is *for* works, that is, living obediently and productively. In keeping with 1:3–14 on God's planning, choosing, and acting, this verse shows God planned and acted not only to save, but also to mark out the way we should live. John Stott's words are not too strong: "Good works are indispensable to salvation—not as its ground or means . . . but as its consequence and evidence."[53]

Paul does not normally speak of "good works." "Works" has such a negative connotation for him from his debates about works of the law that he rarely uses the plural of this word in a positive sense (elsewhere only in Rom. 2:6, an Old Testament quotation, and in the Pastorals[54]). When he does use "works" positively, he adds the adjective "good" to prevent misunderstanding.[55] No focus on self for reasons of pride is permitted; attention to self to ensure ethical responsibility is required.

AT TIMES BRIDGING contexts is required because of the foreignness of beliefs and practices in an ancient culture, because of the newness of the worldview Christianity brings, or because of the distortion of the beliefs and practices of modern culture, including the modern church culture. Sometimes the bridge has been broken from our side. All three of these gulfs exist in understanding this text.

The main problem in appropriating this passage is for us to take it seriously. For the most part, we do not believe the picture of ourselves is as bad as Paul says. Are the lives we so carefully groom meaningless—a living

---

tion (see also Rom. 8:18–23; Eph. 3:9; 4:24; Col. 3:10). Each of the Gospels—especially John—draws parallels between its account and Genesis. See Paul S. Minear, *Christians and the New Creation: Genesis Motifs in the New Testament* (Louisville: Westminster/John Knox, 1994).

52. This statement has already been anticipated in 1:4: "he chose us in him [Christ] before the creation of the world to be holy and blameless in his sight."

53. Stott, *God's New Society*, 84–85.

54. See 1 Timothy 2:10; 5:10, 25; 6:18 (NIV has "good deeds"); Titus 2:7, 14; 3:8, 14 (NIV has "doing what is good"). Note the similarity of 2 Timothy 2:21 to Ephesians 2:10.

55. Conversely, the singular "work" in Paul's letters is always positive except for two texts: 1 Corinthians 5:2 (NIV, "this") and 2 Timothy 4:18 (NIV, "attack"), both of which are clearly negative—the one defined by context and the other by the addition of the word "evil."

death—without God in the picture? On the other hand, we find it hard to believe that the facts are as good as Paul says. Does God really love us so deeply and are we actually exalted with Christ in the heavenly realms? The passage is about value and hope: Without God humanity has little of either; with God humanity is given immense hope and lasting value.

Two wrong turns (2:1–3). The process of application must always follow the intent and function of the passage. In doing so, we must avoid wrong turns. (1) The first wrong turn is *overreading* the text. These verses must be taken for what they are—a dramatic description of the former life, not a full theology of humanity. (2) The second wrong turn is *overreacting* to the text. The description of the world and of humanity is bleak; consequently, it would be easy to reject the world and all association with unbelievers. But a healthy theology of creation does not allow rejection of humanity or the material world and enjoyment of it. God announced his creation good (Gen. 1), and this assumption is fundamental to Paul's theology (see 1 Cor. 10:26; 1 Tim. 4:4). "Separation from the world" is not to be taken lightly, but that teaching does not mean disrespect for or distancing ourselves from unbelievers (1 Cor. 5:9–10). The attitude that God's people take toward unbelievers must mirror the love described in Ephesians 2:4–10.

Can it be this bad? (2:1–3). At first glance Paul's description of life without Christ appears too harsh. Is everyone as degraded as he suggests? Does not life also have joy and happiness in it? Are there not many good, ethical people for whom this description does not fit? Is everyone destined for God's wrath? Paul is not denying the value of creation or of humanity created in the image of God. He is not saying all human beings are worthless, nor is his primary concern what will happen on Judgment Day. His concern is to contrast the plight of humanity without God with the privilege of humanity with God and in Christ.

Unfortunately, Paul's estimate of humanity without God is not unduly harsh. People in both the ancient and modern worlds—even apart from religious conviction—have come to the same conclusion. Some ancient Greeks knew living death so well they coined the proverb *Soma sema*—"The body is a tomb."[56] Old Testament passages like Psalm 90, Ecclesiastes, or Isaiah 40:6–8 reveal the same awareness of the brevity and meaninglessness of life apart from God. Religions like Hinduism seek nirvana through escape from this life and its cycle of reincarnation.

If all this sounds too morbid for modern Western culture, we need only to reflect on the evil in our own society, our suicide rate, the enormous prob-

---

56. Cf. our earlier description of the prevalence of meaninglessness in the ancient world as witnessed by the common epitaph "I was not, I was, I am not, I don't care" (see pp. 82–83).

lems caused by escapism through alcohol and drugs, and the meaningless-ness that challenges all of us as we face injustice, disease, and our own death.[57] Death haunts us and is our destiny. If we also remember that fully one bil-lion people live in dire poverty and that war and terrorism afflict the planet, "living death" may be too soft a description.

Ephesians 2:1–3, however, does not merely address the human plight in general terms; it speaks specifically of being dead *in trespasses and sins*. Sin is the act of choosing our own way and leaving God out of the picture. That is why Paul can say that "everything that does not come from faith is sin" (Rom. 14:23). If God is the giver of life, every act that ignores God is sin. We have tried to find life in ourselves and our own desires, and in the process have cut ourselves off from the Giver of life and have crippled our relations with other people. Death—non-relational by definition—is the result.

But note that this text does not merely address evil sinners—the other people. It addresses all of us. Religious people too can be dead in sins. Remem-ber Jesus' complaint that the Pharisees were like whitewashed tombs full of dead bones (Matt. 23:27–28). All of us are guilty of living without God. Yes, there is decency and goodness in many people. That too is temporary and meaningless without God and does not alter the fact of universal sinfulness.

A kind of blindness makes appropriation of this text difficult. It says that we live in keeping with the world and its "ruler," but we are deluded into believing we determine ourselves. We tell ourselves we are not susceptible to peer pressure, that we do what we want, without ever asking what or who determines our wants. All of us are children of our time, and the truth is that our time is geared away from God and towards sin and meaninglessness. Evil is a force that determines us—whether it be the evil in our own self-seeking souls, the evil that grips our self-seeking society, or the evil that the "ruler" seeks to accomplish.

The ruler. Paul's statement that the "ruler" is at work—apparently to cause disobedience—is not open to empirical investigation. Balance is crucial in this discussion, and care should be taken not to read into the Bible the mythol-ogy that has grown up around the devil. The Bible says much less about the devil than some Christians do. Without doubt, Paul believed in a being that fostered evil. Can modern people really believe in such a being? Or can the ancient idea of the devil be reduced to the *force* of evil in the world?

Walter Wink thinks so. He brackets the ontological question, "Does Satan exist?" in order to deal with the *fact and experience* of evil.[58] He is correct at one

---

57. Courses on death and dying are the most popular electives on several college cam-puses (see Nathaniel Sheppard, Jr., "Popular College Courses Reflect Students' Changing Vaules," *Chicago Tribune*, May 7, 1995, sec 1, 13).

58. See the discussion of this in the previous section, pp. 85–86.

level, for all of us must face the reality of evil in the world and in ourselves. His descriptions of Satan are thought-provoking: "the archetypal representation of the collective weight of human fallenness, the symbol of the spirit of an entire society alienated from God"; "the real interiority of a society that idolatrously pursues its own enhancement as the highest good"; and "often experienced as an actual force of evil craving annihilation."[59] On the other hand, the ontological question about the existence of the devil may not be shelved any more than the question of the existence of God. Why is it relatively easy for us to believe in a beneficent being but difficult to believe in a malevolent one?

Questions about the existence of God and the devil are really variations on the questions "Are we alone?" and "Could we get in this human plight by ourselves?" As this relates to God, the issues have to do with creation, its purpose, and the resulting life with God. As it relates to the devil, the issues have to do with human sin and depravity. The Bible points to the tempter (i.e., the devil) for the entrance of sin. By far, however, it stresses human sin—not the devil—as the cause of the difficulty and evil in the world. The devil is only mentioned three times in the Old Testament,[60] and while New Testament references are more frequent, the devil's standing is limited.[61] He is not the "marquee player"; most of us do evil well enough by ourselves.

In other words, any overemphasis on the role of the devil is wrong. This passage intends to remind its readers of their former plight, not to magnify the illegitimate ruler. We must recognize a tension in relation to belief in the devil. The more we emphasize the devil, the less we emphasize human depravity. An overemphasis on the devil is a way of overvaluing ourselves so that we escape the blame. In the New Testament the devil is not presented as the problem for which we need a solution. Our own sin and this evil age are. Moreover, to overemphasize the devil is to underemphasize Christ. In effect, this would-be ruler does not deserve our attention—a threat yes, but a minor player.

Many modern Christians give far too much attention and power to the devil, almost as if he were omnipresent. The Bible does not present a cos-

---

59. Walter Wink, *Unmasking the Powers*, vol. 2: *The Powers* (Philadelphia: Fortress, 1986), 10–11, 24–26. On p. 30 he asks, "When we tear the mask away from Satan, do we find ourselves?" In *Engaging the Powers*, vol. 3: *The Powers* (Minneapolis: Fortress, 1992), 8, Wink suggests it is merely a habit of thought that makes people think of powers as personal beings and states his preference of considering them as impersonal entities.

60. 1 Chronicles 21:1; Job 1–2; Zechariah 3:1–2 (cf. also the account of temptation in Gen. 3). Isaiah 14 and Ezekiel 28 refer to the kings of Babylon and Tyre respectively, not to the fall of Satan. Evil spirits and demons are also rarely mentioned in the Old Testament (Deut. 32:17; 1 Sam. 16:14–23; 19:9; Isa. 65:11).

61. The Pauline letters refer to Satan only ten times and to the devil eight.

mological dualism, as if God and the devil were virtual equals wrestling for humanity. Only one supreme being exists—God. The force of this whole passage is to underscore God's triumph in Christ (1:18–23). Ephesians does recognize another power at work, but not as a threat to God's purposes or, at least as far as 2:1–3 is concerned, even to Christians (cf. also 4:27; 6:10–20). Fear or anxiety about the devil and his forces does not derive from Scripture, nor does fascination or preoccupation. Obviously balance is required. Paul does see a threat here, but he is more concerned that people have aligned with the ruler of this world than that they will be overpowered by him.

In the end, the blame is not placed on the ruler, but on us. We have chosen to follow our own desires, and our society has reinforced the choice. But rather than bringing satisfaction, it has made us subject to the wrath of God.

Does God get angry? (2:3). The idea of God's wrath causes problems for us in the twentieth century. It seems theologically unsophisticated and offensive. How can a loving God get angry? Yet in some ways the Bible—from Genesis 3 to the end of Revelation—is the story of the wrath of God, of God's reaction to disobedience and sin. Is God a doting parent who ignores wrongdoing? In reality, the wrath of God is an essential doctrine. Wrath and judgment are the presupposition of salvation. If God does not have wrath, salvation is not needed.

Careless language about God's wrath leaves the impression that God is angry at humans, but Christ loves them and gains God's favor for them by dying on the cross. But the cross does not gain back God's favor. Rather, God's favor was the *basis* of Jesus' death. Romans 5:8 reminds us that *God demonstrated his love in sending Christ, while we were still sinners.* No division exists in the Godhead between the Father and the Son or between the wrath of God and the love of God. Love is not the opposite of wrath. As difficult as it may be to conceive, the wrath of God is an expression of his love and deep attachment to his people. Already in the third century, the theologian Lactantius wrote that "he who does not get angry does not care."[62] If God can look at the sin and injustice in this world and not get angry, he is not much of a God! The God of the Bible is not some unmovable, unfeeling force, but a God who cares.

The story of the Bible is the story of God himself taking action to keep his anger from destroying humanity. After the Fall, in the wilderness, with the sacrificial system, with the prophets, in the Exile and Return, and most of all on the cross, God was at work dealing with his own anger and showing

---

62. See his *A Treatise On the Anger of God,* secs. 5–6, 16–17.

mercy.[63] Yes, God gets angry. He cares deeply, and his anger is both an expression of his love and the context in which his love is demonstrated.

Can it be this good? (2:4–7). Application of these verses is difficult because they sound too good to be true. Two questions present themselves: (1) Can we seriously believe God loves *us*? 2) Were we really involved in events that happened to Christ? In both cases appropriation of the message depends on hearing the Word (Rom. 10:17) and on the work of the Holy Spirit.

(1) That God loves and shows mercy is a truism. The problem is that we either take God's love for granted with no impact on our lives or we reject that God could love someone as sinful and/or insignificant as we are. The good news is that God knows how bad things are, but changes them. Where wrath should have come, mercy comes instead. Awareness of the enormity of the plight helps prevent taking God's love for granted, but the love of God must be appropriated individually. This is why Paul emphasized the *wealth* of God's mercy and love. His resources for loving are not limited, and his love extends even to the least deserving. The Holy Spirit is the one who conveys the love of God to us as we open ourselves to the gospel message (Rom. 5:5).

(2) Possibly the most difficult task of bringing Ephesians into our lives is in understanding how we are involved in events that happened to Christ. How can it possibly be true that what happened to Christ happened (past tense) to us at the same time? We were not even born then, and we are now separated from him by two thousand years, culture, geography, race, and every conceivable reality. Both Jesus and we are individuals. Does that not preclude our being involved in actions specific to him?

Help for understanding these ideas is already in the Old Testament and in Greek thought. The reality we need to grasp in order to feel the force of Paul's statements is that of living in God. This notion is not entirely new. A psalmist prayed: "Lord, you have been our dwelling place throughout all generations" (Ps. 90:1), and a Greek poet is quoted approvingly by Paul for his statement: "For in him we live and move and have our being" (Acts 17:28).

The "corporate solidarity" of the Old Testament and Semitic culture provides further background.[64] Focus was placed on the oscillation between the individual and community so that what the individual did impacted the community and vice versa. Titles like "son of man," "servant," and "son of God" were all corporate terms used of Israel or the remnant as well as of individ-

---

63. Passages like Psalm 78, Hosea, Romans 1–3 (especially 3:21–26), and our text present in moving fashion God's dealing with his anger and showing mercy.

64. Formerly called "corporate personality." See Russell Philip Shedd, *Man in Community: A Study of St. Paul's Application of Old Testament and Early Jewish Conceptions of Human Solidarity* (Grand Rapids: Eerdmans, 1964; H. Wheeler Robinson, *Corporate Personality in Ancient Israel* (Philadelphia: Fortress, 1964).

uals. These titles were taken over by Jesus because of his identification with Israel's task in God's purposes. In effect, he became Israel, the Elect One of God (Luke 9:35).

When the early Christians tried to describe Jesus and his work, they did not merely describe him as an individual to whom certain things happened. They saw him as the beginning of a new order, as a new Adam heading up a new race. Consequently, they no longer saw themselves merely as individuals, but as individuals taken up in and involved with Jesus.

Moreover, though the cross and resurrection are historical events, they are not merely historical events. They are also eschatological and inclusive events—the death of death and the firstfruits of the end-time resurrection.[65] As R. Tannehill says, "Christ's death and resurrection are not merely events which produce benefits for the believer but are events in which the believer himself [or herself] participates."[66]

Similarly, though Jesus is a historical person, he is not merely a historical person. Rather, he is the one in whom humanity is represented and included. Since this whole new order is embodied in Christ, time is both transcended and maintained. Jesus identified with the plight of humanity and the task of Israel for humanity. He became one with humanity and took on the penalty of sin. In conversion and baptism we identify with Christ's death and resurrection, and we live out the pattern of death and resurrection in our lives. Christianity is not primarily a religion of ideas, but a religion of participation, of involvement, and of fellowship with God in Christ. Christians are called into fellowship with God's Son, have been crucified with Christ, have been baptized into his death, have put off the old being and have put on Christ himself, and will be united with him in resurrection (Rom. 6:2–11; 13:14; 1 Cor. 1:9; Gal. 2:19–20; 3:26–27).

But how is this participation to be understood? It cannot be literal, for we were *not* there when Jesus was crucified. On the other hand, to say it is metaphorical seems to rob it of its force. This language of participation with Christ points to the solidarity we experience with Christ by the grace of God and through faith.[67] We are attached to him by faith and partake of

---

65. See 1 Corinthians 15:20–23; 2 Timothy 1:10; Hebrews 2:14–15; see Tannehill, *Dying and Rising with Christ*, 123.

66. Ibid., 1. See also Ben Witherington, III, *Paul's Narrative Thought World* (Louisville: Westminster/John Knox, 1994), who suggests conversion is being put into the story of Christ.

67. Note John Calvin's comment: "... as long as Christ remains outside of us, and we are separated from him, all that he has suffered and done for the salvation of the human race remains useless and of no value for us" (*Institutes*, 3.1.1). For discussion of union with Christ and participationist categories, in addition to the works by Smedes, Tannehill, Sanders, and

him. The Spirit is the one who causes that union with Christ (see 1:13; Rom. 8:1–17; 1 Cor. 12:13).

Our exaltation with Christ in the heavenly realms is merely an extension of this solidarity. This too is a reality, although not literal. It is Paul's way of saying Jesus is victorious and that his victory—not the human plight—determines who we really are. This is a direct implication of the early Christian confession, "Jesus is Lord." The emphasis on realized eschatology is strong.

Yes, the gospel is as good as 2:4–7 says. Anything less than the affirmations in 2:4–7 is not the gospel and does not do justice to the God who binds himself to us in Jesus Christ.

The church's failure with faith (2:8–10). A colossal problem exists in moving from faith as used in this text to faith as understood in the modern world. What pernicious and devious force has so subverted the meaning of the word "faith?" As pointed out above, Paul's understanding of "faith" includes attachment, union, and solidarity with Christ, whereas in much of the church—including the evangelical church—"faith" means assent, decision, or the teachings one affirms. Whereas in Paul's thought "faith" is life-changing and productive of good deeds, for much of the church change is desirable with faith, but not necessary, and "not by works" means one does not have to do anything. A decision, the right prayer prayed, is enough to go to heaven. How did faith in Christ get perverted into thought about Christ? How did all the focus get placed on getting into heaven? How did anyone read the New Testament and conclude we do not have to do anything?

Many Christians have reacted against the idea that salvation is some transaction with God to ensure going to heaven.[68] Martin Luther and the Reformers, of course, reacted against the excesses of indulgences and the thought that people could gain their access to God by what they did. Much of Paul's thought, including this passage, is designed to prevent any such idea. But we distort the very idea of faith when we fail to see that it joins us to Christ and affects the whole reality of our lives. The faith that many people profess is nothing more than a false and *groundless* hope of escaping judgment. We do nothing to gain our salvation and life with God, *but such a joining to God does everything to us.* To build a bridge from the text to our situation we must recover and proclaim a biblical faith, one that involves us

---

Shedd, see James S. Stewart, *A Man in Christ* (London: Hodder and Stoughton, 1936); Michel Bouttier, *Christianity According to Paul*, trans. Franke Clarke (Napierville: Allenson, 1966); Albert Schweitzer, *The Mysticism of Paul the Apostle*, trans. William Montgomery (London: A. & C. Black, 1931).

68. Notably, P. P. Waldenstrom; see Axel Andersson, *The Christian Doctrine of the Atonement According to P. P. Waldenstrom*, trans. G. F. Hedstrand (Chicago: Covenant, 1937). Waldenstrom's recoil from such ideas led to several wrong emphases in his own explanation.

with Christ, effects a new creation in us, and propels us into doing the good things God expects. Faithfulness in Christian living is not an optional part of the faith.

THIS PASSAGE DOES not instruct the readers to *do* anything; it only states what God has done in Christ. The implications, however, are enormous for what Christians should do and think. Surely proper application of this text starts with *speechlessness*, then moves to wonder and worship, and finally to obedience and service. The astonishment reflected in the repetition "dead in transgressions" (vv. 1 and 5) and the expansive language describing God's grace should be confessed. The contrast between the plight of humanity without God and the privilege of humanity with God is remarkable. The salvation and grace described here are the reasons why the letter started in 1:3 with the doxology. Worship—a worship that embraces all of life—is the proper response.

This passage contrasts two ways of living, the former life in sins and the present life in Christ. By implication the text asks, "Where will you live?" What are the defining markers of the path along which we walk and who laid out the path?[69] This passage provides a description of reality, as if to say, "This is what life in the world is really like and this is what life with God is really like." The focus of the text is identity. Who are we and who is God? From knowing who we are, we know how to live. This passage thus reveals the identity of people without God, the identity of people in Christ, and the identity of God.

Geography determines identity: The former life (2:1–3). Who are we? We are all people with a past, a past marked by disobedience and failure, which demonstrates something is very wrong at the core of our being. This is true of all people. None of us can escape the indictment; we are geared to self-seeking and the satisfaction of self-centered cravings, whether we make this obvious or covert in our lives.

We spoke earlier of Paul's "sense of geography," referring to his "spheres of influence" theology, which views life as lived either in sin or in Christ.[70] That theology is expressed in this text. If one lives in sin, one's identity is determined by sin, the old world order, and the "ruler of the kingdom of the air." Such a person is controlled by sinful desires and reasonings and, consequently, lives under the wrath of God.

---

69. Remember that the verb for "live" (v. 2) and "do" (v. 10) is actually "walk."
70. See pp. 38–40, 42 and 63–64.

As a result, this text requires us to take sin more seriously than we usually do. As to the plight of humanity, sins cannot be thought of merely in terms of the individual and choices that one makes. Rather, we must think first of a world order and a power of evil dominating our perspectives and actions. The world in which we live seeks to stamp us with its assumptions and character. Clearly Paul believed people need deliverance from an evil realm or age (cf. Gal. 1:4).

How, for example, did Germany become so pervasively distorted to follow Nazism? Not because German people are more sinful than other people, but because a whole self-seeking order grew up in the chaos after the Depression and deceived millions, including many in the church. Germans were seeking what all of us seek—security, respect, and economic prosperity.

How did the United States become so distorted with racism and the Vietnam war? Why does materialism have such a deep grip on modern society? How do needs become cravings? How does sexual practice become so distorted as to be idolatrous? The good is distorted by a world system that leaves God out of the picture, which is what sin always does. Isaiah's confession is descriptive of us all: "I am ruined! For I am a man of unclean lips, and I live among a people of unclean lips" (Isa. 6:5). Sin is personal, individual, and corporate, and a consent to a manipulative age without God.

The problem for Christians is that two overlapping realms or ages exist (compare 1:21 and 2:2). Though a new age exists in Christ, the old age is still with us and at work. Which realm will define us? This text attempts to describe what was formerly true (2:2–3), but for many Christians that is still their reality. A break with the past has not really occurred. They are attracted to the glitz and glitter of the world. One can understand that people who do not know God are stranded in a living death, but how can one comprehend Christians who have found life still turning back to death? Christians need to be much more aware that the old order still wants to define who we are. If the desires of Christians are the same as those of non-Christians and if the desires are fulfilled the same way, the gospel is useless.

To live out the implications of this text requires self-analysis and defiance. Christians must always distinguish between life with and without God. Again the focus is on our minds. What belongs to life as God created it and gave for our enjoyment? What belongs to the world as an attempt to find life in one's self and without God? On first glance the two may look the same—all humans have the same needs and drives—but the two approaches are miles apart. We must distinguish the world that God created from the world that human beings subvert to their own purposes. The former leads to worship of God; the latter leads to the wrath of God. Once we have distinguished God's order from the old order, we are obligated to defiance, a defiance rooted in the confession "Jesus is Lord." If Jesus is Lord, sin and the old world order cannot be our geography, and Christians must say a constant "No" to their attempts to define us.

Geography determines identity: Life in and with Christ (2:4–10). A Christian's self-understanding is found outside the Christian,[71] and conversion is a transition to a new identity.[72] Our true identity is not determined by personal characteristics, experiences, and abilities, even though those items are important. It is determined by life in and with Jesus Christ. He is the environment that shapes us. Paul felt this so forcefully that he said: "I have been crucified with Christ and I no longer live, but Christ lives in me" (Gal. 2:20). Specifically, Christ's death and resurrection are events reproduced in our lives. We die to the old world and its tyrannies of sin and self and rise to life in the Spirit (6:14–15). As important as imitation of Jesus is, identification with Christ is much more important. Our culture will always shape us, but Jesus Christ must be our primary culture.[73] That is the force of the "co-resurrection" language.

To be *in* and *with* Christ means that ours is no longer an individual identity. We are in solidarity with Christ, or as 5:31 puts it, "we are members of his body." Life is relational, and our primary relation is with Jesus Christ. So what is this new identity? Because of our attachment to Christ, believers are people about whom it must be said:

(1) They have experienced resurrection. Their living death has been turned into true life.[74] They experience salvation as a present reality.
(2) Their new lives are the very creation of God.
(3) Exalted with Christ their Lord, they enjoy unparalleled privilege, honor, and security. They are not held back by fear or vulnerability; rather, they have what they need for life with God.
(4) They experience God's abundant kindness throughout eternity.

In essence this passage screams out "Get a life!" Too often we have become spectators of life and spend enormous amounts of time on trivialities. Is not the fascination with the lives of the "rich and famous" due to our triviality? Why does our society spend so much time watching talk shows that discuss the banal and bizarre? We need to live out the transition from death to life (2:1–10) by turning from banality to life with Christ.

---

71. Smedes, *Union with Christ*, 109.

72. See the discussion in Beverly Roberts Gaventa, *From Darkness to Light: Aspects of Conversion in the New Testament* (Philadelphia: Fortress, 1986), 9.

73. See the discussion of separation and culture in 5:6–14.

74. Romans 6:13 describes Christians as those who have just emerged from the grave and are looking for something to do.

So why is the identity question so important? An understanding of identity is not some philosophical or theological question for idle musing. It is an understanding of who we are—whether consciously or unconsciously known—and it determines how we live.

Three more wrong turns. Knowledge of our new identity can lead to pride, escapism, and perfectionism. Each of these is a wrong turn in our walk with God. Each is also a variation on the Christian sin of triumphalism. We as Christians must learn to distinguish our legitimate triumph (e.g., Rom. 8:37; 2 Cor. 2:14–3:6) from the arrogant sin of triumphalism.

(1) The privileges we have from God by virtue of our salvation can easily be turned into pharisaic *pride* and an accompanying disdain for other people who do not know these facts. If we do that, we forget that all our privileges are due to association with Christ, not to ourselves. Pride is as wrong after conversion as before. Worship and obedience are the only proper responses to God's call.

(2) The ideas of privilege and exaltation with Christ can lead to spiritual *escapism*, as if to say that because we are exalted with Christ, we need have nothing to do with this world. Nothing could be further from Paul's mind, as the paraenetic sections show. Paul does not support mystic narcissism or ethical passivity; rather, he promotes new creation and identity with Christ as the shaping factor in our lives. Being in Christ affirms that he gives us our identity and determines who we are. As James Stewart points out, union with Christ is the foundation of Paul's ethics.[75]

(3) Texts like this have led some to the delusion of *perfectionism*. If we are exalted with Christ, should we not be free from all sin? If we are in Christ and he is in us, then should not sin be impossible for us? Again, balance is required. Most of us assume that sin is just a necessary part of life. Our expectations are low in our fight against sin. But Paul's expectations were high. He was optimistic and fully confident believers would live godly lives. But he did not believe in or hint at perfectionism (see 1 Cor. 13:8–13; Phil. 3:12–16).[76] To believe in perfectionism is to forget the now and not yet character of biblical Christianity. We do live in two ages, and the reality of the old age and its impact on us cannot be ignored. Worse, to believe in perfectionism is to be blinded by one's own spiritual arrogance.

In addition to the wrong turns a *caution* is in order. This passage presents a picture of radical change in moving from death to life. While this picture is true in reality, not all people experience such a dramatic conversion, nor

---

75. Stewart, *A Man in Christ*, 194.
76. Elsewhere in the New Testament, see especially 1 John 1:8–10.

should they be expected to.[77] People who grow up in godly families may not even be able to identify the time of conversion. Some conversions, like Paul's (Acts 9), are dramatic, other, like Timothy's (2 Tim. 1:5), are gradual; some are revolutionary, some evolutionary—though in both cases the movement is from death to life, dealing with the same theology of sin.

Eternal security? The theological question concerning eternal security is prompted by the triumphal tone of the text and the emphasis of Ephesians on being "in Christ." If one is in Christ, can one move out of Christ? If one is seated with Christ in the heavenlies, can that position be lost? It is tempting to assume that the logic behind this text presupposes eternal security. If we have been saved, does that not presuppose eternal security?

Such a conclusion is unfair. In the New Testament salvation is past, present, and future.[78] Salvation certainly is enjoyed in the present, and Paul was confident—but not presumptuous—about future judgment. But he is not dealing here with the possibility of apostasy, which the New Testament views as a real threat. Rather, he is describing the privilege of being joined with Christ. Whether that union can be broken has to be addressed from other texts.[79]

We should ask, however, if the anxiety over eternal security does not emerge from an inadequate view of the gospel, one that fails to do justice to Paul's theology of union with Christ. A weak view of faith is propped up with overemphasis on "once saved, always saved." Such preaching has too often resulted in people "making a decision" and not taking faith seriously ever again. Nothing could be further from Paul's understanding of faith, and no one should proclaim such a gospel.

The identity of God: The persistent, loving God. A modern singer has commented: "I feel that the greatest gift you can give another person or an audience is a revelation of what's in your heart and soul."[80] God gave just such a gift of self-revelation. In giving his gift of salvation, God revealed a heart

---

77. See the discussion in Gaventa, *From Darkness to Light*, 10–14.

78. C. F. D. Moule, *The Meaning of Hope* (Philadelphia: Fortress, 1963), 5, tells an (apocryphal) story about B. F. Westcott, a famous nineteenth century New Testament scholar, being asked by a Salvation Army lass if he was saved. He replied, "My dear, do you mean *sotheis, sesosmenos,* or *sozomenos?* Is it the aorist participle of the Greek verb that you mean, or the perfect, or the present?" All three are true—the past act, the past act and its present effect, and the present reality. Conversion is a process still taking place and moving toward completion.

79. See the discussions in I. Howard Marshall, *Kept By the Power of God* (Minneapolis: Bethany, 1969); Judith M. Gundry Volf, *Paul and Perseverance: Staying In and Falling Away* (Louisville: Westminster/John Knox, 1990); Gerald L. Borchert, *Assurance and Warning* (Nashville: Broadman, 1987).

80. Larry Katz, "Between the Lines," *Chicago Tribune*, May 7, 1995, sec. 13, p. 21, quoting Carly Simon.

---

and soul full of mercy, love, grace, and kindness. If God has done all this to change our death to life, what a wonderful and loving God he shows himself to be! This section provides a great summary of Paul's gospel, because it expresses poignantly that *God is for us*. We can almost hear Romans 8:31–32: "If God is for us, who can be against us? He who did not spare his own Son ... how will he not also, along with him, graciously give us all things?" To apply this passage is not merely to think about the past or about God in the abstract, but to know the identity of God as *God for us*. As one person stated, "God takes no action that does not have man as its object."[81] God is the persistent, loving God, rich in mercy and grace.

Over and over in Ephesians Paul reveals God as showering people with grace. He is not the Deist God who sits afar off and waits. He is the active God, who will not stay out of the picture; he is *Immanuel—God with us*. Such a God brings joy and rejoicing to our lives.

Two more wrong turns. It is easy to presume on the mercy of God and forget God's judgment and our responsibility. (1) The person who says, "I like committing crimes. God likes forgiving them. Really the world is admirably arranged,"[82] is reckless and in danger. (2) At the same time, texts like this one emphasizing the love and activity of God can also easily be twisted into a "health and wealth" theology, as we have already seen. The love of God does not work like magic to remove the problems from the world and put all Christians on easy street. The love of God is present in the midst of problems and difficulty (see Rom. 8:35–39).

Salvation without works. If salvation is a gift of grace, then human beings can do nothing to achieve it. It is God's work, a gift extended to everyone. Its cause is purely in God's character, not in the character or conduct of any person. No act or virtue can be presented to God to gain acceptance. But for many grace is so hard to believe or accept. Virtually all our experience tells us that we have to earn acceptance, love, and respect. We spend our lives seeking self-actualization, some act or fact that will give us significance and standing. If we have self-confidence, we see no need to be stripped of all our hard-earned value. Other people are worse than we are, so why shouldn't God accept us? If we lack self-confidence, we find it hard to think God will accept us under any circumstance. Either way, grace is so hard to take.

But remember that grace is God's giving us himself. He accepts us without precondition or complaint. We are given significance and standing by our relation to God. We are valued by grace, but the attention is not placed on

---

81. Jack Miles, *God: A Biography* (Knopf, 1995), quoted in a review by Ross Miller, *Chicago Tribune*, May 7, 1995, sec. 14, p. 4.

82. The words are from Herod in W. H. Auden's "For the Time Being." See his *Collected Longer Poems* (New York: Random House, 1965), 189.

us, but on the God who loves so deeply. Grace moves us to worship and true humility. If all the initiative comes from God and all the praise belongs to him, no room is left for either pride or self-depreciation.[83] But if grace is taken seriously, the focus is moved off ourselves, and pride does not have a leg to stand on. Dealing with grace and pride is, of course, a daily task and part of our ongoing identification with the death of Christ.

Unfortunately, Christians have as hard a time with pride as anyone. We tend to think that grace is only for salvation, and then we have to work to prove ourselves, or that by working we prove ourselves better than others, especially non-Christians. Accomplishment is important, but not to make us more acceptable to God. Furthermore, our good deeds never make us more important than other people. Grace is not just the beginning of Christian life, but the whole. We live in grace (Rom. 5:2) and we are to mirror grace to others. The dynamic that produces salvation is the dynamic by which we live (Gal. 3:3).

A terrible wrong turn. Does not all this lead to "cheap grace" and a do-nothing religion for many people? Unfortunately it has, but this practice distorts the gospel. To think that Paul's words about grace and faith apart from works could lead to a religion in which people do nothing shows ignorance about the meaning of all three words. For Paul grace is a power that put him to work (1 Cor. 15:10). When he wrote against "works," he was combating the idea that certain practices—especially Jewish ones—were necessary for people in order to be acceptable to God. Ephesians 2:10 shows salvation is not from works, but it is *for* good works. God saves people so that they might live productive lives in keeping with what God intended for humanity. With "good works" Paul was not thinking about "do-goodism," but about a life reflective of God's love (see chaps. 4–6).

A recovery of the New Testament faith described here will reconfigure the church. Imagine a church in which people knew they were bound to Jesus Christ, lived in union with him, reflected his death and resurrection, and, conscious of their new creation by God, lived productive lives. That is what Paul was describing, and that is what we are called to be.

A faith worth having—and sharing. In these pages I have reacted against a superficial understanding of faith because much of what passes for faith in modern churches is not worth having. It evokes no deep commitment, no deep thought, and no significant change. The faith discussed in 2:4–10 is a faith worth having, for it is relational. The gift it brings ties us to the Giver so that grace becomes a power within us. The gift takes possession of us[84] and brings change.

---

83. Note 1 Corinthians 15:10, where Paul wrote, "But by the grace of God I am what I am."
84. Käsemann, "The Righteousness of God' in Paul," 173.

Surely if Ephesians 2:4–10 is the best summary of the gospel, this passage is of primary importance for evangelism. People in the former way cannot be left there missing out on God's mercy. To know the Giver giving himself creates a contagious joy. The power that creates life from death cannot be hidden. The transformation from 2:1–3 to 2:4–10—if experienced—must be revealed in both word and life.

Often Christians are sure neither how they should do evangelism nor that they want to. Opportunities for evangelism are more likely to cause embarrassment, uncertainty, and guilt than spontaneity, confidence, and love. The reasons for our failure at evangelism are many, including revulsion at the tactics some people use and the illusion that we need to produce decisions from people as quickly as possible. Surely, however, success in evangelism depends on a right understanding of God and his gospel—the focus of 2:1–10. What if people experienced Christians as those joined to the loving Giver? What if they saw grace extended from people who had experienced grace? What if they saw evidence of the movement from disobedience to obedience and from death to life? What if they saw a faith worth having? Evangelism needs to be a conscious activity, but it does not need to be forced. Evangelism should be the natural expression of a life joined to a loving God, the sharing of a faith worth having.

Ephesians 2:11–22

THEREFORE, REMEMBER THAT formerly you who are Gentiles by birth and called "uncircumcised" by those who call themselves "the circumcision" (that done in the body by the hands of men)—¹²remember that at that time you were separate from Christ, excluded from citizenship in Israel and foreigners to the covenants of the promise, without hope and without God in the world. ¹³But now in Christ Jesus you who once were far away have been brought near through the blood of Christ.

¹⁴For he himself is our peace, who has made the two one and has destroyed the barrier, the dividing wall of hostility, ¹⁵by abolishing in his flesh the law with its commandments and regulations. His purpose was to create in himself one new man out of the two, thus making peace, ¹⁶and in this one body to reconcile both of them to God through the cross, by which he put to death their hostility. ¹⁷He came and preached peace to you who were far away and peace to those who were near. ¹⁸For through him we both have access to the Father by one Spirit.

¹⁹Consequently, you are no longer foreigners and aliens, but fellow citizens with God's people and members of God's household, ²⁰built on the foundation of the apostles and prophets, with Christ Jesus himself as the chief cornerstone. ²¹In him the whole building is joined together and rises to become a holy temple in the Lord. ²²And in him you too are being built together to become a dwelling in which God lives by his Spirit.

Original Meaning

MARKUS BARTH CALLS this section "the key and high point of the whole epistle,"[1] and justly so. In fact, it is perhaps the most significant ecclesiological text in the New Testament. Although it deals with the division between Jews and Gentiles, no specific problem is being addressed. Rather, the description of blessings in Christ, which began

---

1. Barth, *Ephesians*, 1:275.

in 1:3, continues here. Salvation and Christology are also important, but the nature of the church is the key theme. Ephesians gives more attention to and makes loftier statements about the church than any other letter, despite the fact that the word *ekklesia* occurs only three times outside the husband-wife analogy in chapter 5.[2] This section sketches out the theology on which the other passages build.

This is the second of the explicit "formerly-now" contrasts that form the backbone of the letter.[3] Whereas the first such contrast (2:1–3) focused on sins, evil, and the "ruler of the kingdom of the air," this one focuses on division, alienation, and deprivation of privileges. Evil is present by implication, but the ruler is left out of the picture.

Items given prominence provide a pathway to the author's intent. One of these is lost in the NIV. The phrase *en sarki* (lit., "in the flesh") appears three times in the Greek text (twice in v. 11—NIV, "by birth" and "in the body"— and once in v. 15). The third occurrence is set over against the first two to show that the source of the problem (Gentiles and Jews being both "in the flesh") is also the source of the solution: Jesus, by his death *in the flesh*, destroys the barrier that divides. Other words given prominence are "foreigners," "far," "near," "peace," "both," "Spirit," and as one can expect, "in Christ." The NIV has seven such expressions (e.g., "in Christ," "in him," or "in one body"), though the Greek text actually has eleven such phrases. Once again Paul is emphasizing that everything of consequence for belief takes place "in Christ."[4]

Isaiah 52:7 and 57:19 were important in the composition of this text; 2:13–18 is to some degree an interpretation of these two Old Testament passages,[5] both of which were important in Judaism and in the early church's understanding of the gospel and its proclamation.[6] Dependence on Isaiah 9:6; Micah 5:5; and Zechariah 9:9–10 are not so commonly mentioned, but the complex of ideas associated with these texts has probably helped in shaping Paul's thought. Note also that while most of the text centers on what Christ has accomplished in the past and on the privilege that results in the present,

---

2. 1:22; 3:10, 21; in chapter 5 the word occurs six times: 5:23, 24, 25, 27, 29, 32.

3. See p. 93.

4. Remember that 23 of the 36 occurrences of "in Christ" and related phrases take place in the first two chapters; Paul demonstrates the solidarity Christians have with Christ and the privileges that come with that union.

5. Lincoln's view (*Ephesians*, 138) that Isaiah 57:19 is not already in mind in 2:13 is unlikely. See Peter Stuhlmacher, "'He is Our Peace' (Eph. 2:14): On the Exegesis and Significance of Ephesians 2:14–18," *Reconciliation, Law, and Righteousness: Essays in Biblical Theology* (Philadelphia: Fortress, 1986), 182–200, who argues Ephesians 2:14–18 is a Christological exegesis of Isaiah 9:5–6; 52:7; 57:19.

6. See Acts 2:39; 10:36; Romans 10:15; and especially Ephesians 6:15.

the future is still in view. The temple is in the process of being built, but its completion is still future.

The variation in the pronouns "you" and "we/us" continues in this text and has encouraged some to suggest a hymn stands behind this passage. Elaborate theories have been developed, suggesting a possible Gnostic hymn about a cosmic reconciliation of two spheres. Evidence for such hypotheses is slim, and these theories are not convincing.[7]

Structure. This passage falls easily into three sections:

A. Distance from God and his purposes, privileges, and people until made near in Christ (2:11–13)
B. Peace with God and his people because Christ has brought peace (2:14–18)
C. The people of God as the dwelling of God (2:19–22)

Verses 14–18 provide commentary on verse 13, with "he himself is our peace" being the primary statement in this section. The rest is an explanation of Christ's work of peace or its consequence. The structure of verses 14–16 is fairly elaborate in that "he is our peace" is followed by three participles ("made," "destroyed," and "abolishing") and two purpose clauses ("to create" and "to reconcile"), each ending with a participle ("making" and "put to death"). This yields the following pattern:

He himself is our peace
who *made* both one
... *destroyed* the barrier, the dividing wall of hostility
and *abolished* the law
to create one new being
making peace
to reconcile both to God
having put to death the hostility

Verses 19–22 provide the summary conclusion of the whole passage and show how the plight of alienation is overcome by the privilege of life with God.[8]

---

7. For a summary of this debate, see William Rader, *The Church and Racial Hostility*, 177–201. Lincoln, *Ephesians*, 127–34, rejects a background in Gnosticism, but views 2:14–16 as hymnic and as reflecting Hellenistic Jewish cosmological speculation. Stuhlmacher, "'He is Our Peace,'" 182–200, rightly rejects speculations about both Gnosticism and hymnic reconstructions.

8. This passage is largely chiastic, a form of inverted parallelism in which the first line mirrors the last, the second the next to last, and so on (note how v. 12 is mirrored in v. 19, v. 13 in v. 17 and v. 14 in v. 16). However, elaborate explanations of a chiastic structure

Distance From God Until Made Near in Christ (2:11–13)

THE REAL REASON for the "formerly-now" contrasts in Ephesians is made clear. Paul wants his readers to remember the change effected by Christ. The command "remember" in 2:11 is the only imperative in chapters 1–3. This remembering covers all the material in verses 11–13, not merely the former life. Continual awareness[9] of what they were and what they have now become will enrich both their thanks to God and their obedience.

The former plight (2:11–12). Verses 11–12 focus on the deprivation and distance of the former life. As indicated above, "by birth" and "in the body" in the NIV translate *en sarki* ("in the flesh"). Exactly what nuance to put on this phrase is debated. The difficulty comes because of the remarkably complex ways in which Paul uses the Greek word *sarx* ("flesh"). "Sinful nature" (a common meaning for *sarx* in Paul) is not the intended meaning in 2:11 for either Gentiles or Jews. On the other hand, more is implied than mere physical origin and physical circumcision. When Paul uses *sarx*, he often points to the frailty of humanity apart from God. Here, therefore, the word refers to the merely human realm in which people live in contrast to life in the Spirit or in Christ, so that the connotation is more pejorative than the NIV suggests. Paul wants his readers to remember that they were Gentiles, confined to that which is weak and merely human, being bad-mouthed by Jews, who labeled them "the uncircumcision" and themselves "the circumcision." But, as we will see, the Jews were no better off; they too needed the gospel.

The labels "the uncircumcision" and "the circumcision" were common *Jewish* ways of referring to Gentiles and Jews respectively.[10] The former expressed disdain for the nonelect and disobedient, while the latter was a title of honor and privilege for those belonging to God's covenant. In Philippians 3:2–3 Paul even co-opts "the circumcision" as a title of honor for his *Gentile Christian* friends, and via a wordplay,[11] refers to the Jews as "the mutilation." The disdain of Jews for Gentiles and the corresponding disdain of Gentiles for Jews is well attested in the ancient world.[12]

---

involving each line of the passage are forced. See, e. g., J. C. Kirby, *Ephesians, Baptism, and Pentecost* (London: SPCK, 1968), 156–57.

9. This is the force of the present tense in the imperative.

10. E. g., Acts 10:45; Romans 2:26–27; 3:30; Galatians 2:7–9, 12; Colossians 4:11; Titus 1:10. Circumcision was the mark of belonging to the covenant and the primary symbol of obedience to God's law.

11. *Katatome* ("mutilation") and *peritome* ("circumcision"). This co-opting of the term "circumcision" seems to be based on the thinking of Colossians 2:11, which speaks of the spiritual circumcision Christ works on Gentiles.

12. Barth, *Ephesians*, 1:254–55. See also the balanced discussions in Scot McKnight, *A Light Among the Gentiles* (Minneapolis: Fortress, 1991), 11–29; John G. Gager, "Judaism as

Although the Jews were bad-mouthing the Gentiles as "the uncircumcision," in Paul's mind Jews were no better off, for the circumcision in which they boasted was a mere human circumcision. They too were "in the flesh." They lived in the same realm as the Gentiles, even with their circumcision. "By the hands of men" stresses the human origin of their circumcision; God was not involved.[13]

Verse 12 describes five elements in which the Gentiles were deprived, disconnected, and distant:[14]

(1) They had no relation to Christ; this contrasts with their present position in Christ.[15]

(2) They were "excluded from citizenship in Israel." Does "Israel" refer to historic Israel, spiritual Israel, or Jewish Christians? Probably Paul thought generally of exclusion from God's people; that is, the Gentiles had no part in God's purposes with Israel.

(3) They were "foreigners to the covenants of the promise." This phrase emphasizes the same distance and disconnection as "excluded." Precisely which covenants Paul has in mind is not clear. Surely the covenants with Abraham and David are included, and likely also the promise of the new covenant in Jeremiah 31:31–34. No doubt for Paul the "covenants *of promise*" focused primarily on the Messiah and the Holy Spirit, the means by which the covenants with Abraham, David, and Jeremiah were fulfilled (see 2 Cor. 3:3–18; Gal. 3:14).

(4) They were "without hope." They had no hope of escaping the human plight and could not anticipate any relief (cf. 1 Thess. 4:13).

(5) They were "without God." This does not mean they were atheists (although the word can be used this way), nor that they did not have

---

Seen by Outsiders," *Early Judaism and its Modern Interpreters*, eds. Robert A. Kraft and George W. E. Nickelsburg (Philadelphia: Fortress, 1986), 99–116. Not all relations between Jews and Gentiles were marked by hostility, but one has only to read *The Letter of Aristeas*, 134–39, which views the law as preventing mingling with other nations, and Tacitus, *Histories*, 5.5, which harshly describes Jews as hating non-Jews, to see Ephesians 2:11 mirrored. Frequent conflicts between Jews and the Roman authorities in Palestine and several expulsions of Jews from Rome (cf. Acts 18:2) only heightened the tensions. Note too the patience of the Jews listening to Paul's defense until he mentions his mission to the Gentiles (Acts 22:21–23).

13. The opposite, "not by the hands of men," is used to describe what God does, such as a temple God will build (Mark 14:58), our eternal dwelling in heaven (2 Cor. 5:1), or the spiritual circumcision Christ effects at conversion (Col. 2:11, which should be compared to Eph. 2:11).

14. These elements assume the privileges Jews enjoyed (cf. Rom. 3:1–2; 9:1–5).

15. The word "excluded" is the same word translated "separated" in 4:18 and "alienated" in Colossians 1:21, the only other times the word occurs in the New Testament.

gods (ancient Gentiles had plenty of gods). Rather, they did not have *God* (cf. Acts 17:23). In addition to being in the flesh, these Gentiles were "in the world" (a pejorative term that picks up the meaning of "world" in 2:2). The sphere in which they lived was isolated from God and what he was doing.

God's solution to the human plight (2:13). If the plight was estrangement and distance, the solution is nearness and belonging. In 2:4–10 God's grace is described as overcoming our plight of sin and establishing us in the heavenly realms with Christ. In this text the blood of Christ brings people in Christ near to God. Since Paul's "spheres of influence" theology dominates the first two chapters of Ephesians, it is not surprising to see the solution presented in such terms. The formerly distant Gentiles have been brought near to God in Christ. Who was the agent in the process? Either Christ himself (see 2:14–18) or possibly God (if the passive verb "have been brought near" is a "divine" passive, describing actions that God has performed).

It is no afterthought that Gentiles are now included in God's purposes. This theme may be secondary in the Old Testament, but it is there. God's covenant with Abraham had in view the blessing of the Gentiles (Gen. 12:2–3), the prophets anticipate the day when Gentiles will stream to worship God in Jerusalem (esp. Isa. 2:2–4; 56:6–7; Jer. 3:17), and the Psalms assume all the nations should worship God (Pss. 22:27; 86:9; 117:1; 148:11). In Paul's understanding of the gospel, what had been secondary— the inclusion of the Gentiles—has *now* become primary. Frequently Paul uses "now" to mark off the newness of what God has done in Christ and the present conditions that result. In doing so he points to the eschatological character of God's work and to the breaking in of the new age in the midst of the old.[16]

The language of "far" and "near" is derived from Isaiah 57:19 (quoted in Eph. 2:17). "You who once were far away" refers to Gentiles who have been brought near in Christ. The terms *far* and *near* in Isaiah 57:19 both refer to Jews during the Exile, but later Jewish interpreters sometimes understood this text of proselytes.[17] If this interpretation was prevalent in the first century, the step from understanding the text of proselytes to Gentiles would have been easy.[18]

---

16. Not all occurrences of "now" (*nun* and *nuni*) have this meaning, but many do (see Rom. 3:21; 5:9–11; 7:6; 8:1; 16:26; 1 Cor. 15:20; 2 Cor. 5:16; 6:2; Eph. 3:5; Col. 1:22, 26; 2 Tim. 1:10).

17. See Lincoln, *Ephesians*, 146–47. Note also Psalm 148:14; Acts 2:39; 22:21; 26:23.

18. See Romans 9:24–26; 11:30–32; 1 Peter 2:10.

Sacrificial ideas are present in the thought that "the blood of Christ" brings people near. This phrase focuses on life violently taken.[19] Sacrifice is not the only conceptual mode by which salvation is understood, but no one can deny that sacrifice is a necessary and important part of New Testament thinking on salvation (see 5:2). The implication of the sacrificial language is that Christ has died *for us*, which means both he died in our place and for our benefit.[20]

In sum, the human plight is caused by separation from God. Life comes from him and is to be enjoyed in his presence. The only solution to the plight, then, is proximity to God, and Christ is the one who takes us there.

Peace with God and His People Through Christ (2:14–18)

THIS SECTION EXPANDS on the brief statement in 2:13. Note the change to the first person in verse 14, to the second person in verse 17, and back to the first person in verse 18. The occurrences of the first person are required because Paul is emphasizing the union of Jews and Gentiles. As before, the second person emphasizes the relevance of the comments for the readers.

Christ our peace (2:14a, 17). "He himself" attempts to do justice to the emphasis on the pronoun in the Greek text. "*He* is our peace" serves as a heading for 2:14–18. As Barth points out, "To say Christ—that is to speak of peace. To speak of peace—that is to speak of Christ!"[21]

The impact of Isaiah 52:7 and 57:19 is clear in 2:13 and 17, but a much larger theology of peace associated with the Messiah stands behind this section. Judaism had linked Isaiah 9:6 with 52:7,[22] but also texts like Micah 5:5a and Zechariah 9:9–10 focused on the Messiah as the bringer of peace. Micah 5:5a, portraying a messianic shepherd ruler, is virtually identical to Ephesians 2:14a and seems to be the origin of Paul's wording.

Peace dominates this section both explicitly (vv. 14, 15, 17 [twice]) and implicitly (unity, destruction of division and hostility, access, and reconciliation). Christ is our peace, makes peace, and proclaims peace. Paul seeks to connect Christ and peace as comprehensively as possible. He is the one who

---

19. Note the parallel between "blood" and "death" in Romans 5:9–10 (cf. also 1 Cor. 11:25–26; Col. 1:20). See the discussion in Leon Morris, *The Apostolic Preaching of the Cross* (Grand Rapids: Eerdmans, 1965), 112–28. Is there an allusion to the blood of the new covenant?

20. See Ernst Käsemann, "The Saving Significance of the Death of Jesus in Paul," *Perspectives on Paul* (London: SCM, 1969), 39.

21. Barth, *Ephesians*, 1:295.

22. See 2 Baruch 29 and 73; Testament of Levi 18.4. Note also the use of Isaiah 52:7 in 11Q Melchizedek. See Stuhlmacher, "'He is Our Peace,'" 188.

makes peace possible, who announces its availability, and in whom peace is enjoyed. This theology of peace is both a Christological and a soteriological statement.

The word for peace (*eirene*) occurs forty-three times in Paul's letters, eight of which are in Ephesians (1:2; 2:14–17; 4:3; 6:15, 23). Peace is a central and fundamental component of Paul's theology. Virtually every topic of doctrinal significance is brought into relation to peace. In addition to occurrences in greetings and blessings, note the following:

> God is a God of peace (Rom. 15:33; 16:20; 1 Cor. 14:33; 2 Cor. 13:11; 1 Thess. 5:23).
> Christ is the Lord of peace who gives peace (2 Thess. 3:16).
> The gospel is a gospel of peace (Eph. 6:15).
> The mindset of the Spirit is life and peace (Rom. 8:6),
> Peace is an eschatological reward (Rom. 2:10),
> Peace is equivalent to salvation and describes relation to God (Rom. 5:1),
> The kingdom is righteousness, peace, and joy in the Holy Spirit (Rom. 14:17),
> Peace is the goal for human relations (Rom. 14:19; Eph. 4:3; 2 Tim. 2:22).
> Peace is the foundation for problem solving (1 Cor. 7:15; 14:33).
> The fruit of the Spirit is peace (Gal. 5:17).
> Peace guards our hearts (Phil. 4:7) and rules in them (Col. 3:15).

With such varied use it is not surprising that Paul summarizes the gospel by saying, "*He* [Christ] is our peace." Peace is not merely the cessation of hostility; it is a comprehensive term for salvation and life with God. The background to this use is the Old Testament concept of *shalom*, which covers wholeness, physical well-being, prosperity, security, good relations, and integrity.[23] David even asks about the *shalom* of his war (2 Sam. 11:7; NIV, "how the war was going")! *Shalom* is much more positive than merely the absence of conflict. It refers to the way life should be and is a gift of God that is received only in his presence. In various texts *shalom* is equated with righteousness, justice, salvation, and the reign of God.[24] Yahweh *is* peace (Judg. 6:24), makes a covenant of peace with his people, and promises one who will

---

23. As examples, see Genesis 37:14 (NIV, "well"); Psalm 38:3 (NIV, "health"); 73:3 (NIV, "prosperity"); Leviticus 26:6; Judges 4:17 (NIV, "friendly relations"); Zechariah 8:16 (NIV, "sound" judgment). For good discussions of peace see Ulrich Mauser, *The Gospel of Peace* (Louisville: Westminster/John Knox, 1992); Perry B. Yoder, *Shalom: The Bible's Word for Salvation, Justice, and Peace* (Newton, Kans.: Faith and Life, 1987).

24. See Leviticus 26:3–23; Psalm 34:14; 37:37–40; 85:10; 119:165; Isaiah 32:16–17; 52:7 (to which allusion is made in Eph. 2:17).

bring peace.[25] Peace is what God wills for his people, as can be seen in the great prophecies about the future.[26]

In 2:14–18 peace is unexpectedly both a destructive and a constructive act. Division and hostility had to be destroyed, and unity and peace established. Peace and reconciliation (v. 16) take place on both horizontal and vertical levels. Most of the focus initially is placed on the horizontal peace established between Jews and Gentiles. "The two" (v. 14) refers to the two parties mentioned in verses 11–12, the Jews and the Gentiles,[27] and the mention of the law (v. 15) and of Gentiles being included with God's people (v. 19) is further confirmation. In Christ, Jews and Gentiles are made into one new being.

At the same time, "he himself is our peace" describes the vertical dimension. We have peace with God (Rom. 5:1). Hostility between humanity and God is at least implied here and may be explicit in 2:16 with the words "put to death their hostility"[28] (if this does not refer again to the hostility between Jews and Gentiles; see Rom. 5:8–10). Christ not only joins Jews and Gentiles into a new being, but he ushers both of them in one body into God's presence.

Christ's preaching of "peace to you who were far away and peace to those who were near" (v. 17) refers to the preaching done by the apostles and missionaries to Gentiles and Jews respectively, not literal preaching by Jesus. But this phrase does show how much Paul viewed himself and other proclaimers as representatives of Christ. "Preached peace" is adopted from Isaiah 52:7 (cf. also Zech. 9:10).[29]

The destruction of the barrier that divides (2:14b–15). The identification of the "barrier, the dividing wall of hostility" and how it relates to the "law with its commandments and regulations" is difficult. The problem is

---

25. See Numbers 6:26; 25:12; Isaiah 54:10; Ezekiel 34:25; 37:26; Malachi 2:5; for the promise of one who will bring peace, see Isaiah 9:1–7; 11:1–9; Micah 5:2–5; Zechariah 9:9–10.

26. Such as Isaiah 2:2–4; 11:1–9; Jeremiah 29:11 (NIV, "prosper"). The theological significance of peace in the New Testament is no less important. Not surprisingly, the first word of the risen Christ to his disciples in the Gospel of John is "peace."

27. That the neuter is used for "the two" (rather than the masculine as in 2:16 and 18) is no proof that reference was originally to two parts of the cosmos (contra Lincoln, *Ephesians*, 128–29). The neuter and the mixing of genders often occur in reference to people (note, e.g., John 1:11; 6:39–40; 1 Cor. 1:27–28).

28. Literally, "having killed the hostility in himself." The phrase means that the killing takes place in his own being, not that the hostility is his.

29. Koshi Usami, *Somatic Comprehension of Unity: The Church in Ephesus* (Rome: Biblical Institute Press, 1983), 53–55, suggests that Paul intentionally avoided the pronoun "we" in verse 17, in order not to express an attitude of superiority.

compounded by uncertainty over whether "hostility" should be taken with the dividing wall (NIV) or with the law (NASB), and whether "in his flesh" should be taken with "destroyed" in verse 14 (NEB) or with "abolished" in verse 15 (NIV).[30] How does "abolishing ... the law" (v. 15) relate to "destroyed the barrier" (v. 14)? Is "the barrier" only a way of referring to "the law," or is something different intended?

To some degree the answer to these questions depends on the identification of the "barrier, the dividing wall." Five options are usually suggested:

the flesh
the cosmic barrier between heaven and earth referred to in Gnostic texts
the law
the curtain separating the Holy Place and the Most Holy Place in the temple
the barrier in the temple between the Court of the Gentiles and the Court of the Israelites

The first two have little to commend them.[31] The other three options all focus on the law in some way. The law was referred to as an "iron wall" surrounding Israel and a "fence" separating them from people of other nations.[32] The idea of access to God in 2:18 could allude to the temple curtain, torn at Jesus' death, though this is unlikely, since "the dividing wall" is a strange way to refer to the curtain of the temple.[33] Most older commentators accepted that Paul had in mind the fifth option, the barrier in the temple. Both Josephus and Philo describe a barrier separating the Court of the Gentiles from the Court of the Israelites; signs were posted in Latin and Greek, warning Gentiles not to go farther into the temple precincts under penalty of death. Archaeological and literary evidence confirms the existence of these signs.[34] It is worth remembering that Paul was arrested in Jerusalem on the specific charge that he had taken an Ephesian named Trophimus into the restricted temple area (see Acts 21:28–29). If Paul is not referring to this literal barrier in the temple, it is at least a striking example of the division caused by the law. On the other hand, if "the dividing wall" does refer to the

---

30. The NRSV moves "in his flesh" forward so that it relates to both the action of making one and the action of destruction.

31. See Barth, *Ephesians*, 1:285–87; Schnackenburg, *Ephesians, A Commentary*, 111–16.

32. *The Letter of Aristeas*, 139, 142.

33. Note the use of "curtain" (*katapetasma*), not "barrier" (*mesotoichon*) or "dividing wall" (*phragmos*), in Matthew 27:51; Mark 15:38; Luke 23:45; Hebrews 6:19; 9:3; 10:20.

34. See Josephus, *The Jewish War*, 5.193–94.; 6.124–26; *Antiquities of the Jews*, 15.417; Philo, *Embassy to Gaius*, 212. See the discussion in Robinson, *St. Paul's Epistle to the Ephesians*, 59–60.

temple barrier, it is in essence a symbol of the law itself as a tool of division (cf. Eph. 2:15).[35]

In other words, if Paul is referring to the temple barrier, the words "has destroyed the barrier" (2:14) have a narrower, specific focus while "abolishing in his flesh the law" is broader and more general. If "barrier" refers to the law generally, then the two phrases are parallel. In either case the law itself is viewed as an instrument of division, which it surely and intentionally was. Israel saw its election and its laws as separating her from the surrounding nations, especially after the Exile. Circumcision, Sabbath keeping, and food laws were all primary indications of the distinctions between Jews and other people, leading to arrogance and name-calling.

"Abolished the law" is strong language and can easily mislead. But note the qualifiers to this text: "the law with its commandments and regulations." Paul does *not* abolish the law as the Word of God or as a moral guide (cf. his quoting one of the ten commandments in 6:2). What is abolished is the law as *a set of regulations that excludes Gentiles*.[36] The moral instruction of the law continues, but Paul will tolerate no practice of the law that excludes Gentiles or forces them to become Jews. One of the main messages of Ephesians is that Gentiles are accepted by God in Christ on an equal footing with Jews.

The destruction of the barrier takes place "in his [Christ's] flesh." As we have already pointed out, the source of the problem is "in the flesh" for both Jews and Gentiles (v. 11), and now God's solution is also "in the flesh," which refers to the Incarnation and specifically to the death of Jesus on the cross (see vv. 15–16).[37] Jesus took the hostility of both Jews and Gentiles into himself, and when he died it died. As Paul wrote in Galatians 3:13: "Christ redeemed us from the curse of the law by becoming a curse for us."[38] With good reason M. Barth points to the priestly overtones of this section

---

35. Schnackenburg, *Ephesians, A Commentary*, 113–14, assumes the temple is in ruins at the time of writing and thus rejects the temple barrier option. Stott, *God's New Society*, 91–92, 98–99, following Robinson, accepts the temple barrier interpretation and assumes the temple is still standing. For Christians the temple was no longer an obstacle preventing access to God after the crucifixion. But nothing can be determined from this verse about whether the temple was still standing.

36. The Greek word for "abolish" (*katargeo*) appears in Romans 3:31, where Paul states he does *not* abolish (active voice, NIV: nullify) the law. In Romans 7:6 he uses the passive voice of the same word to say "we have been *released* from the law." Paul both had to affirm the law and to prevent it from being a source of division or a means by which people presented themselves to God.

37. This view of flesh as both the source of the problem for humans and the solution in the Incarnation and death of Jesus is paralleled in Romans 8:3 (see also 7:4).

38. See the discussion of solidarity with Christ, pp. 112–14 .

and the resulting conclusion that Christ is presented both as priest and as sacrifice.[39]

The unity of the new being. Reconciliation is both a destructive and a constructive act, and verses 14–16 use four expressions to state that both take place in Christ: "in his flesh;" "in himself;" "in one body;" "by which" (lit., "in him"). Not only does Christ take the hostility *into himself* and destroy it, but also *in himself* he creates a new being. Implicit in this language is a theology of the resurrection, for that is the source of the new creation.

Notice that the new being (NIV, "one new man") is a *corporate* idea.[40] Jesus Christ in his death and resurrection identified with and represented humanity. People are incorporated into him, and when he is raised to new life, a new being comes into existence, one in which people are one with Christ and one with each other in him. Grace not only connects us to God and Christ, it connects us to each other.

This assumption is the basis of Paul's use of the "body" (v. 16). Does "body" refer to Christ's body on the cross or to the church as his body? Usually "body" in Ephesians refers to the church,[41] but would these two uses have been kept separate? As Schnackenburg argues, "The Church is thereby pulled into the vicinity of the Cross, exists in fact in the Crucifixion-event. . . . So close is the connection of the Church to Christ that she already appears in the Cross as a New Creation, the one redeemed humanity."[42] The new being[43] is Christ himself, into which people are incorporated as his body.

The purpose of the new being is the creation of peace and unity between Jews and Gentiles. Unity is a major theme of this letter.[44] Four affirmations of unity exist in 2:14–18:

"made the two one" (2:14)
"to create in himself one new man out of the two" (2:15)
"in this one body to reconcile both of them" (2:16)
"we both have access to the Father by [in] one Spirit" (2:18)

The two groups of people are made one. God's purpose for the unity of all things, introduced at 1:10, treated briefly in 1:22–23, is now expanded.

---

39. Barth, *Ephesians*, 1:267, 300.

40. Cf. 4:13, where the "not yet" character of this reality is expressed.

41. 1:23; 4:4, 12, 16 (twice); 5:23, 30. The word also occurs in 2:16 and 5:28, the latter referring to physical bodies.

42. Schnackenburg, *Ephesians: A Commentary*, 117.

43. The only other texts that mention the new being (man, self) explicitly are 4:24 and Col. 3:10.

44. The theology of Galatians 3:28 flows through this text: "There is neither Jew nor Greek, slave nor free, male nor female, for you are all one in Christ Jesus." Note that "one" (*heis*) in this verse is masculine—one person—not neuter.

Divided humanity is reconciled in Christ and joined into a unified, worshiping community. In effect, Paul suggests that Christians are a "third race" beside Jews and Gentiles;[45] the two are one in Jesus Christ. The name-calling of 2:11 is over.

Reconciliation. This passage is one of the few that discuss the doctrine of reconciliation, which focuses on the restoration of broken relations. In the New Testament this language appears only in Paul's letters, and then only infrequently.[46] The verb to "reconcile" (*apokatallasso*) does not occur prior to Paul's use, and in the New Testament appears elsewhere only in Colossians 1:20 and 22.[47] In each reconciliation passage the focus is different. Romans 5:10–11 focuses on reconciliation between God and sinners who are enemies. In 2 Corinthians 5:18–21 God reconciles us/the world to himself and gives us the ministry of reconciliation. In Colossians 1:20–21 God reconciles to himself all things on earth and in heaven. In Ephesians 2:16 a *double reconciliation* occurs— that between God and humanity and that between Jews and Gentiles.

In New Testament texts, God is always the one who does the reconciling. Human beings are reconciled; God (or Christ) reconciles. The initiative always lies with God. The cross is God's act to reconcile people to himself, not an act by which he is reconciled. Even when people are hostile to God and God is angry, he loves and works to restore relations.

The result of reconciliation is "access" (2:18), the privilege of entering into God's presence.[48] The term was used of an audience with a king, but the more likely nuance derives from temple ideas of access to God (see Heb. 6:18–20; 10:19–22). The temple language is obvious in this text, especially in 2:19–22 (cf. also Isa. 56:6–8). The Spirit is brought into the picture as the means of access to the Father.[49] The Spirit is the agent of incorporation

---

45. See the discussion in Rader, *The Church and Racial Hostility*, 228–32; Lincoln, *Ephesians*, 134, 144.

46. See Romans 5:10–11; 11:15; 2 Corinthians 5:18–21; Ephesians 2:16; Colossians 1:20–22. Still, Ralph Martin considers it the center of Paul's theology. See "Center of Paul's Theology," *Dictionary of Paul and his Letters*, eds. Gerald F. Hawthorne and Ralph P. Martin (Downers Grove, Ill.: InterVarsity, 1993), 92–95; see also his *Reconciliation: A Study of Paul's Theology* (Atlanta: John Knox, 1981); Peter Stuhlmacher, "Jesus as Reconciler, Reflections on the Problem of Portraying Jesus Within the Framework of a Biblical Theology of the New Testament," *Reconciliation, Law, and Righteousness*, 1–15.

47. Paul may have coined the word; other Pauline texts use the verb *katallasso* and the noun *katallage*

48. The word "access" (*prosagoge*) occurs elsewhere in the New Testament only at 3:12 and Romans 5:2. The verb form is used in a similar way in 1 Peter 3:18.

49. It is not impossible that the Greek for "by one Spirit" should be understood as it is in Philippians 1:27 of the unity of humans, but this is not likely, given the focus on the Holy Spirit in 2:22.

and union and the one who mediates the presence of God to us (see also 1 Cor. 12:13).

The People of God as the Dwelling of God (2:19–22)

THIS SECTION PROVIDES a summary conclusion to the preceding material, but also extends the ideas by developing the building and temple imagery. The alienation and separation of Gentiles described in 2:12 are reversed in 2:19. (Note the switch back to "you.") Gentiles are "no longer foreigners and aliens,"[50] outsiders cut off from God's purposes; rather, they are citizens along with God's people and are part of God's household—in effect, family members.[51]

The language in 2:20–22 shifts without warning from speaking of a family to describing a building, which is then defined more narrowly as a temple. This shift is facilitated in the Greek by a multiple wordplay on the *oikos* ("house") word group. Gentile Christians are no longer "aliens" (*paroikoi*); they are "members of God's household" (*oikeioi*), "built on" (*epoikodomethentes*) a sure foundation, and the "building" (*oikodome*) . . . is "built together" (*synoikodomeisthe*).[52]

In 2:5–6 we noted three "with" (*syn*) words associating Christ and believers. Here in 2:19–22 three more "with" words appear: "fellow citizens" (**sympolitai**), "joined together" (**synarmologeo**), and "built together" (**synoikodomeo**). The focus is not on being joined to Christ, however, but on being joined to God's people.[53]

The expression "God's people" (2:19) is literally "the holy ones." Is Paul referring to spiritual Israel, to Jews, to Jewish Christians, to all believers, or even to angels? The NIV's "God's people" is appropriate. Paul's intent is merely that those excluded are now included in the privileges Israel has enjoyed. In this text he is not discussing the implications of Israel's failure to believe. It is fair to say the Gentiles do not become Israel; they share with Israel.

The new temple (2:20–22). Jewish and early Christian tradition viewed the people of God as a spiritual temple, focusing on several Old Testament quotations about stones—texts understood as referring to the end time and the Messiah.[54] The building is "built on the foundation of the apostles and

---

50. This expression is a hendiadys—two terms to express one idea. "Aliens" is a negative word here, but note it is used positively of Christians in 1 Peter 2:11 to stress that Christians do not belong to this world.

51. The description of the church in family terms reappears in 3:14–15; 5:1.

52. Note the similarity of language and mixing of metaphors in 4:16.

53. "With" compounds are used fourteen times in the letter to underscore unity with Christ and unity in Christ. The uses in 5:7 and 10 are to prevent union with unbelievers.

54. Note the similarity between 2:19 and 1 Peter 2:4–6, both alluding to Isaiah 28:16. The Dead Sea Scrolls likewise interpreted this verse in Isaiah as referring to a spiritual tem-

prophets" (2:20). "Prophets" almost certainly refers not to Old Testament but to New Testament prophets. This is demonstrated both by the order ("apostles and prophets") and by the reference in 3:4–5 to the mystery, which to other generations was not made known, but which now has been revealed to his "holy apostles and prophets." "Apostles" refers to that rather limited group who were witnesses of the resurrected Lord and were authoritative carriers and interpreters of the Christian tradition (the Twelve, Paul, and a few others). These two groups are singled out because they are recipients of revelation (see also 4:11–16).

The "foundation of the apostles and prophets" is capable of several nuances. Theoretically it could mean the foundation the apostles and prophets laid, the foundation they have, or the foundation they make up.[55] Given that Christ Jesus is the cornerstone, almost certainly the intent is to refer to the foundation the apostles and prophets make up. They are *part* of the foundation on which the church exists.[56] This verse shows in personified terms the respect Paul and others had for the Christian tradition (cf. 1 Cor. 15:3–4; Col. 2:6–7). The teaching of the apostles and prophets is the basis on which the church rests. All Christians, as part of the building, are founded on the revelation and instruction conveyed by these people.[57]

Jesus Christ occupies a unique place in the foundation as the "cornerstone" (*akrogoniaios*). This designation may seem strange and inadequate to do justice to the role of Christ unless one knows the background and significance of the term. This is no ceremonial cornerstone in which items are placed and on which a date is stamped, as we often use the word. Nor does it refer to a keystone or capstone crowning the top of the building—despite the number of commentators who have chosen this option. In the LXX this Greek word occurs only in Isaiah 28:16, where it clearly refers to a foundation stone, and it does not occur in the New Testament except in quotations of Isaiah 28:16.

---

ple (see Manual of Discipline, 8.5–8). For a discussion of the relation of 1 Peter 2:1–10 and Ephesians. 2:19–22, see my "I Peter II.1–10: Its Formation and Literary Affinities," *NTS* 24 (1977): 97–106.

55. In grammatical terms, a subjective genitive, a possessive genitive, or a genitive of apposition.

56. This statement is one of the reasons some feel Paul did not write Ephesians. On whether this represents a later veneration of the apostles, see pp. 25–27 of the introduction.

57. No attempt should be made to make all the foundation passages in the New Testament agree. In 1 Corinthians 3:10–11 Paul refers to the only foundation that can be laid, Christ himself. In Matthew 16:18 Peter is the rock on which the church is built, and in Revelation 21:14 the walls of the new Jerusalem have twelve foundations on which are the names of the twelve apostles. Each of these figures of speech must be interpreted in its own context without being overpowered by the other contexts or being seen as correcting a previous picture.

Cornerstones in ancient buildings were the primary load-bearing stones that determined the lines of the building. Such stones have been found in Palestine, one weighing as much as 570 tons (see also 1 Kings 7:10).[58]

But the cornerstone image gained an importance far beyond its architectural connotations. Isaiah 28:16 was significant because it promised security in a time of destruction. Even if a flood came and washed everything away, the cornerstone provided a place of refuge. This verse was understood eschatologically in pre-Christian Judaism, as the Qumran references show.[59] In all probability the LXX had already understood Isaiah 28:16 as referring to the Messiah, an interpretation also present in the Isaiah Targum.[60] Early Christians found "the cornerstone" a fitting title pointing to the Messiah (see also Rom. 9:32–33; 10:11; 1 Peter 2:4–8).

The Old Testament stone quotations (Ps. 118:22; Isa. 8:14; 28:16) provided the early church with significant material for Christology, soteriology, and ecclesiology, which served to solve several theological issues.[61] Christ is not just another stone in the foundation alongside the apostles and prophets. His position is different. Whereas the apostles and prophets are mentioned because of their teaching, Christ is mentioned because of his person and work. He makes the whole building possible, including the rest of the foundation. He is the promised place of security on which the community of God is built.

Not only is the building built on Christ Jesus the cornerstone, the whole building exists *in him* as well.[62] Both 2:21 and 2:22 begin and end with "in" (*en*) prepositional phrases: *In* him the building is bound together and grows into a temple *in* the Lord; *in* him the Gentiles are built together with the Jews to be a dwelling of God *in* the Spirit (NIV, "by his Spirit"). The repetition with "in" underscores that all this union with God and other people takes place *in Christ.* He is the one who unites and in whose being God is encountered. Life

---

58. See "Temple Foundation Stone Discovered," *Christianity Today,* May 18, 1992, 52. The use of Isaiah 28:16 in 1QS 8.5–8 to refer to foundations is further argument against the meaning "keystone," which does not appear as the meaning of *akrogoniaios* until the third century A.D.

59. In addition to 1QS 8.5–8, see also 5.5; 1QH 6.25–27; 7.8–9.

60. Targums are Aramaic paraphrases of the Hebrew Old Testament.

61. In 1 Peter 2:4–8 they provide one of the most decisive statements of the letter, and in Romans 9:32–33 they provide the solution to the Jew-Gentile problem (much of chaps. 10–11 are a commentary on 9:30–33).

62. Unless *en* should be understood as "on" rather than "in." The addition of the article in 2:21 in some manuscripts to read *pasa he oikodome* (meaning "every building") is late, and the context rules out such a reading. Instead *pasa oikodome* is probably a Hebraism, meaning "the whole building." See discussion in C. F. D. Moule, *An Idiom-Book of New Testament Greek* (2d ed.; Cambridge: Cambridge Univ. Press, 1963), 94–95.

in Christ means unity with God and the other people in Christ, and the resultant union is the place where God chooses to reside.

Implicit already in the use of Isaiah 28:16 is that this building is a *temple.* Temple ideas are also present in 2:13—14, and 18, but what is implicit before becomes explicit here. God's people are God's temple. The ones formerly kept out of the temple now *are* the temple.

While 1 Corinthians 6:19 refers to the individual as the temple of God, usually (as here) the people are corporately God's temple (cf. 1 Cor. 3:16–17; 2 Cor. 6:16). The purpose of the physical temple in Jerusalem was to show that God had taken up residence with his people. The New Testament emphasizes the replacement of the Jerusalem temple with Christ and his followers. "One greater than the temple is here" (Matt. 12:6; see also John 2:19–22).[63] Note the Trinitarian focus of this temple discussion: In Christ and through the Spirit we experience the presence of God.

The temple is a "holy" temple because God dwells there; it is a temple set aside by and for God. The word "holy" (*hagios*) has already occurred in verse 19 as the word used for "God's people," to whom the Gentiles are joined. The temple is holy and the people who make up this temple are "the holy ones." *They* are set apart by and for God.

Once again Ephesians stresses that life is relational. In Christ separation is broken down and relations with God and his people are established. This is not merely some act in the past, but life with God in the present.

Bridging Contexts

A MAJOR ASSUMPTION in applying Scripture is that people in the ancient world were essentially the same as we are. We see the continuity from one generation to another, and we see ourselves in the text. This commonality is what makes it possible for us to take an ancient text and bring it into our context, recognizing, of course, differences between their world and ours.

Should we remember or forget? Ephesians 2:11 is unique in the New Testament, for it is the only text that explicitly tells us to remember our former plight. How does this message fit with Philippians 3:13–14, which tells us to forget what is behind? Actually, both texts have the same concern—a life shaped by Christ. Philippians emphasizes Christ as the focus and goal that determines all we do. In 3:5–11, however, Paul does the same thing he asks in Ephesians 2:11: He remembers his past and the reordering of his life to gain

---

63. See Bertil Gärtner, *The Temple and the Community in Qumran and the New Testament* (Cambridge: Cambridge Univ. Press, 1965).

Christ. In Ephesians he not only wants people to remember their former plight, but also what they have become.

Memory is a wonderful gift from God that enables life; without it true living is virtually impossible. Remembering structures our minds to live for God. It frames our identity and sets us on course for life in Christ. We need to remember sin, for part of sin's delusion is that it keeps us unaware of sin. We need also to remember the biblical stories and the content of the faith. In the Lord's Supper we remember Christ's death and resurrection, and we remember the change worked within us. Remembering is a way to deal with our pride and self-sufficiency and also to keep connected to God.

Old problems in new dress. The mention of circumcision, uncircumcision, blood, and Israel all seem foreign—if not barbaric—and are of little obvious relevance for us. But the problems described continue to be deeply rooted human problems that vex us all: alienation, division, name-calling, separation from God and his purposes, and hopelessness. As long as these problems continue, people will know loneliness, fracture, lack of trust, and discouragement. Note the description of sin as alienation, fracture, and purposelessness (2:11–12). From these problems come a host of other sins, such as envy, hatred, lying, conflict, abuse, murder, and war.

Note too how the problem of alienation was rooted in religious privilege. The text both assumes the legitimacy of Israel's privilege and sees that privilege as part of the problem. Much of the world's animosity and conflict is caused by religion, and a glance at church history shows painfully that Christians have been excessively guilty. But does a sense of privilege from God inevitably lead to arrogance and division? In applying this text we must ensure that privilege leads to unity, not division.

Ancient Judaism saw circumcision as the primary symbol of obedience to the Torah, of belonging to God, and of purity.[64] Old Testament faith and Judaism were always concerned with separation from the surrounding people, and practices such as circumcision, Sabbath keeping, food, and other purity laws marked out their differences. These distinctions created difficulties in social relations. The disdain that Jews had for the uncircumcised and impure exacerbated the problem, and, as one might expect, non-Jews retaliated with equal disdain and disparagement.[65] But Jewish practices grew out of the reality of God's election and purposes for Israel. The privilege Israel enjoyed was real; the arrogance and disdain were a failure.

Looking at this ancient problem is like looking in a mirror. The church too enjoys privilege, but has handled it no better. Conflicts within denom-

---

64. The role of women was ignored, except as they were joined to their families.

65. To be fair, we should point out that not all relations between Jews and Gentiles were bad.

inations, across denominations, and between Christians and non-Christians are commonplace. Circumcision is no longer the focus, but name-calling, disparagement, and alienation still occur. Too often religious practice is "in the flesh," merely human, made from human hands as fully as any physical circumcision. Not much progress has been made since Ephesians.

But the description of alienation resulting from privilege is only a part of 2:11–13. The focus on deprivation must also be considered. Much of the world still stands where these Gentiles stood—apart from God, with no involvement in his purposes, and with no hope. When God is left out of the picture, life really is bleak and boring. People stand on the sidelines of life, trying to keep fit and to be entertained. Little reason exists to focus on anything other than self, but that leads to alienation and division and ultimately to despair. People need to hear God calling them into the game; they need to hear God calling them to peace.

How can Christ bring us near to God? Must we still think of sacrifice as essential to bring us to God? Is *blood* still a necessary ingredient for salvation? How can Christ take human hostility into himself and bring us to God? Questions about Christ's death for us are difficult. They cannot be diminished, for at stake is the very heart of Christianity. The language of Ephesians is not archaic language that may be set aside, for it points to the fundamentals of the faith. Paul's discussion about Christ's saving death assumes a Christology and a faith that involves us with Christ.[66] *Christology is soteriology.* Half a Christology will not do, and if Jesus was just another Jew, his death may have been tragic or even impressive, but not saving. Also, if we are not bound to him in faith, he cannot bring us near to God. But *if* he was God's Son sent for us and if we are bound to him by the Spirit, then Paul's words have meaning.

Several facts are foundational:

(1) We can do nothing that will make ourselves acceptable to God.

(2) We deserve the wrath of God because of our self-centeredness and sin.

(3) In the ancient world sacrifice was universally practiced (and still is in many places),[67] which reveals the deficiency humans feel in relation to God.

(4) The sacrifice of Christ was the *end* of sacrifice—at least in places where Christianity had any effect.

These four facts stand true regardless of what one thinks about Christianity. If God does not reverse the human plight, there is no hope. But the message

---

66. See pp. 47–48, 56–57, 63–64, 100–102, 112–14, 117–19.

67. Various types of sacrifice existed in the Old Testament and elsewhere—such as sacrifices of thanksgiving, for forgiveness, to ward off danger, for communion, and for purification.

of Ephesians is that God in his love did. We may surmise other ways God could have dealt with sin—ignore it, for example, or require penance or purgatory—but, to say nothing else, all such options are too impersonal. In God's love "he became what we are in order that we might become what he is."[68] In Christ God drew alongside, entered into the problem caused by evil, took responsibility for evil, and bore its pain and consequence in his own being. Christ came as the representative human being, standing for us all. He came as the promised bringer of peace.

But is focus on *blood* necessary? There is nothing magical about the word "blood," despite the way it gets used by some Christians. The word cannot be ignored, but neither should it be overemphasized.[69] The blood is not important in itself, but for that to which it refers—the sacrificial death of Christ, which is central to the gospel. We are not free to deemphasize Christ's death, but we are free to find the best way to communicate the significance of that death for us.

The main problem in understanding Paul's theology of salvation at the end of the twentieth century is not the complexity of his thought. Rather, our society does not pay much attention to God, nor do people see any real need for God other than to provide quick fixes for minor problems. The solution is not to bash people into recognition of their sin, but to present God's call to unity in Christ and peace. Humans have an innate need to belong—both to God and to other humans—and the more we focus on ourselves, the more distorted life becomes. Sin and alienation must be defined, but the focus is on the call to be what God created us to be.

Who cares about Israel? This passage assumes the privilege of Israel and is one of the most important passages in the New Testament referring to Israel. Can we just forget about Israel as an unimportant detail in the story? Actually, the relation of Israel to the church is one of the most significant theological problems the early church faced, a problem that is treated to some degree in virtually every New Testament book. Why did not more Jews believe in Jesus? Were God's promises to Israel still valid and were Jews still elect?

This passage does not answer these questions. It values Israel's heritage and privilege, but speaks only of unity between Jews and Gentiles in Christ. In fact, it does not discuss unbelieving Jews (on which see Rom. 9–11). But *Christians must care about Israel* because God's work did not suddenly begin with the baptism of Jesus. God's purpose in Christ and his church started with cre-

---

68. The words are from Irenaeus, *Against Heresies*, Preface (see pp. 102–3, n.38, above).

69. "Blood" occurs only twelve times in Paul's letters, and four of those have nothing to do with atonement.

ation, focused on Israel, cannot be separated from Israel, and is equipped with the Scriptures of Israel. The church cannot cut itself off from its Old Testament heritage and the movement of God's purposes throughout history.

There is another reason this question must be asked. Dispensationalists and their opponents have often debated what Ephesians 2:11–22 teaches concerning the relation of Israel and the church.[70] Is the church now in Israel or is it something separate from Israel? Whereas Romans 11:17–24 says Gentile branches are grafted into Israel, this passage speaks of a new being, something that did not exist before, a "third race," as it were. But what continuity is there then between the old Israel and the new being in Christ? Was Israel removed and the church given its place? Did a remnant of Israel join Gentiles to create a new being, and if so, what about the other Jews? Does God have two groups of his people, both valid, but separate (and thus evangelism of Jews is unnecessary)?

Dispensationalists are eager to keep this text from saying Gentiles are now part of Israel. This text does suggest something new created by Christ, but caution is in order in treating the relation of Israel and the church. Paul was not attempting to answer our questions, and we must avoid letting our questions obfuscate the text. Three facts are clear in the passage:

(1) Israel is assumed to be in a privileged position.
(2) Now Gentiles share in the privilege.
(3) In Christ Jews and Gentiles are joined into one new being.

Beyond this, the text is silent; it does not address the issue of non-Christian Jews. Certainly implications should be drawn about the relation of Christians to Jews, as we will see. But wisdom in interpretation is often in knowing where to stop interpreting, and we ought not force this text to answer questions it does not treat. Rather, it should be joined to others like Romans 9–11 to form a biblical theology treating the subject, a subject that involves issues Paul himself had not fully worked out.

The new being that is created, however, is not the church, nor is it "a third race," even though this expression is both valuable and open to abuse. The new being is Jesus Christ himself, who as risen Lord incorporates Jews and Gentiles into himself. The fourfold emphasis on being *in him* in 2:14–16 requires this.

---

70. See Rader, *The Church and Racial Hostility*, 222–34; Carl B. Hoch, "The New Man of Ephesians 2," *Dispensationalism: Israel and the Church*, ed. Craig Blaising (Grand Rapids: Zondervan, 1992), 98–126; Andrew T. Lincoln, "The Church and Israel in Ephesians 2," *CBQ* 49 (1987): 605–24; Markus Barth, *The People of God* (Sheffield: JSOT, 1983). Barth's contention that Christ joins Gentile Christians to Jews (whether Christian or not) exceeds the subject of Ephesians, which is about Jews and Gentiles *in Christ*.

A dead end. This text is inappropriately forced into other theological battles as well. Since 2:20 speaks of prophets as foundational, some say this demonstrates that prophecy ceased after the apostolic period.[71] To avoid this conclusion, W. Grudem argued "apostles and prophets" should be understood as "apostles who are also prophets,"[72] which is unlikely. This whole discussion abuses the foundation metaphor and pushes the text outside its own boundaries. Whenever we go from the biblical text to the modern world, we must exercise special caution when dealing with metaphors. Sometimes the logic may seem obvious, when in reality the metaphor is pushed beyond anything the author intended. Metaphors are used for specific purposes *in context* and should be extended only in the direction of the original purpose. Ephesians 2:20 is only concerned to say the church is built on the revelation of the gospel through apostles and prophets. We may not extend this metaphor to solve the debate whether prophets still exist today.

If this barrier, then all barriers. Much of biblical application takes place by analogy. In bridging contexts, we must identify the theology operating in the text, place it in relation to other texts and theologies, and then extend it from the biblical world to our own. The theology operative in 2:11–22 is a theology of unity, in which the barrier between Jew and Gentile is destroyed and oneness is created.[73] Today, unless we were born in a Jewish or Palestinian home, we have little awareness of any barrier caused by Judaism. On the other hand, we are conscious of numerous barriers within our society and between our society and that of others that devalue, distrust, limit, and take advantage of other people. If the law in some way was the dividing wall in the ancient world, for us it is racial difference. The hostility between races, especially between blacks and whites, in virtually all countries continues as an embarrassment. Economic and gender barriers also create conflict and add to the alienation. Our world is filled with such barriers.

Did Christ's death abolish all the barriers? The barrier between Jew and Gentile was one of the most obvious in history. While more intermingling occurred between Jew and Gentile than might be expected,[74] the separation and distinction of Jews was clearly defined. Furthermore, this separation was grounded in commands from God. If *this* barrier has thus been set aside, what

---

71. See the discussion in R. Fowler White, "Gaffin and Grudem on Eph 2:20: In Defense of Gaffin's Cessationist Exegesis," *WTJ* 54 (1992): 303–20; R. B. Gaffin, Jr. *Perspectives on Pentecost: New Testament Teaching on the Gifts of the Holy Spirit* (Phillipsburg, N.J.: Presbyterian and Reformed, 1979).

72. Wayne Grudem, *The Gift of Prophecy in the New Testament and Today* (Westchester, Ill.: Crossway, 1988), 57–63.

73. Remember that unity is one of the main themes of the letter.

74. See John G. Gager, "Judaism as Seen by Outsiders," 105–13.

other barrier can be justified? If God does not show favoritism (Acts 10:34–35; Rom. 2:11), if all are created in his image, if God's purpose is unity, if we are to love even our enemies (Matt. 5:44), if Christ took the hostility into himself to destroy it, on what grounds can we justify keeping any barriers in place? Paul and the early church had already extended the unity in Christ to Jew and Gentile, to slave and free, and to male and female (Gal. 3:28). None of our barriers—our ways of devaluing, limiting, and taking advantage of others—has any basis.

The cross is the place where barriers are destroyed. Before the cross we know our own sin, and we cannot stand there without realizing all of us are without defense and have no claim on God. No one has higher value than anyone else. The ground at the cross is level. Any standing we have is God-given, not something that inherently makes us better than others.

An important problem, however, is our inability to think beyond what we already know. Why did Christians during the United States Civil War era on both sides fail to see the significance of Ephesians 2:11–22 for the slavery question? Were they caught up in debates about slavery and equality so that they neglected to remember Christ destroyed the barriers and created unity?[75] Do we assume—or love—the barriers so much that we do not hear the text? God's description of reality ought to be the definition by which we live.

But if barriers are removed in Christ, what about barriers with non-Christians? We must recognize that no barrier that rejects people for who they are is ever justified. All whom we meet are *potentially* people who will be in Christ and therefore one with us. The grace that has accepted us into Christ is extended to them *by us*. All people regardless of race or status—however defined—are to be valued, enabled, and treated justly.[76]

Can we have peace in this world? Similar to the foregoing is the problem concerning peace in this world. On this issue most of us feel like the author of stanza 3 of "I Heard the Bells on Christmas Day:"

And in despair I bowed my head:
   "There is no peace on earth," I said,

---

75. See Rader, *The Church and Racial Hostility*, 173–74, who points out that Ephesians 2:11–22 is not mentioned in publications and printed sermons dealing with the slavery issue. He offers several reasons why this happened, one of which is that people were more concerned about equality than unity, but can we ever really have equality without unity? For other painful evidence of the way Christians argued against the abolition of slavery, see E. N. Elliott, ed., *Cotton is King and Pro-Slavery Arguments* (Augusta, Ga.: Pritchard, Abbott, & Loomis, 1860).

76. One barrier does still exist: Separation because of sin is still required (see chap. 5). Christians may never be in union with evil. The difficult part is separating from evil without causing division, name-calling, and distrust or being guilty of arrogance.

> "For hate is strong, and mocks the song
>   Of peace on earth, good will to men."[77]

Paul here describes God's reality in Christ against which our reality is seen as an outdated perversion. We cannot deny the reality of this world, but we are defined by the larger reality God has established. Like everything else in Ephesians, peace too is now and not yet. Complete peace will not come until "all things are brought under one head" (1:10), but peace still defines us now. This peace cannot be reduced to a feeling of peace within or to peace of mind, for the text deals with human relations and even sees peace with God in terms of a united people ushered into his presence. "Christ is our peace" means we live in the peace he has established and conveys to us. Both the vertical *and* the horizontal dimensions of this peace are to be lived in the present.

From individual to corporate. In the treatment of 2:1–10 we saw that Christians can no longer view themselves merely as individuals. They are part of Christ and of each other. In 2:11–22 this theme is emphasized once again, with "one new being" and with the "body" and "building" imagery. The problem is that modern Christians—especially in the Western world—seem to know only individualism. We must change our outlook. This passage confronts our individualism and asserts our involvement with Christ and with those in him. We cannot separate our relation with God from our relation with other people. The two are so interwoven that they do not exist in isolation, even if we rightly argue the relationship with God is primary. The horizontal and vertical dimensions interact with and define each other. Even in approaching God in confession and repentance, we have already acted on the horizontal plane.

This text is not about people going to heaven or about the church as a group of individuals gathered for mutual support. As important as these are, the goal is for people to be joined to each other in Christ and given access to God in the present. As we will see especially in relation to 4:3, unity is a given from which we live.

The church is a corporate reality. Earlier we stressed that Christology is soteriology, but now it becomes clear that *Christology is soteriology is ecclesiology is ethics.* These theological categories are not separate subjects put into containers for analysis; they are aspects of the same reality of being bound to Christ. Christ incorporates people into his own being, his death, and his resurrection, and therein lies their salvation. But in him they are a corporate reality (a new being, a body, a temple), which results in a church of people

---

77. *The Covenant Hymnal* (Chicago: Covenant Press, 1973), no. 139.

bound to each other in Christ. Because they are bound to each other in him, they take their character from him and live out the fact that they belong to each other. This is the root of the love, care, and justice Christians are to show.

AS IN PREVIOUS sections, we have a text that does not specifically ask anything of us. No imperative is given regarding any act or attitude (other than remembering). All the focus is on the change Christ accomplished and the privilege of new life in him. At the same time, however, the relevance of this passage for Christian living and for the church is enormous.

Remember your identity. Memory enables life by providing an understanding of reality within which we live. We remember pain, enjoyment, people, information, and events in order to make appropriate choices for the present and future. Some memories we choose; others are burned into us by the sheer force of the event. Memories can be paths to success or scars that disable. Sometimes we choose to forget painful parts of life, but often only succeed in repressing the memory until a later, possibly more difficult, time. We also make choices in remembering as to how much attention will be given to particular painful or enjoyable events. Remembering is the way we name and process the past, the way we structure our minds to know how to live.

Paul asks that we remember the life-determining change Christ has brought in us—that is, the radical movement from being dead in sins to life in Christ, from being excluded to being included, for this movement is still at work in our lives every day. Such remembering gives attention to the continuing change at work in us and will not allow us to become lax or guilty of pride. Remembering is therefore the key to loving and worshiping God. Balance is required, however. We do not remember the former life for its own sake or to wallow in its memory. It no longer determines us. We focus instead on Christ and the change he has brought.

For some people past memories are so painful that they cannot be forgotten, and no suggestion is made that such memories can be easily erased. But Christians must know that the only event that defines us is Christ's death and resurrection, in which we are involved. We die to self—both the sinful self and the self sinned against—and rise to new life in Christ. Here too the now and not yet character of faith is present. The old reality still must be faced, but newness in Christ is the defining force.

A woman who has been raped cannot forget the violation against her, but must the violation continue as an open wound or scar preventing life? Or can life defined by Christ bring healing and wholeness? Does betrayal necessarily lead to cynicism and mistrust, or does definition come from elsewhere? Does sin define us or does Christ? We cannot always choose what happens to us, but we can choose—at least to some degree—what power it will be granted. If this sounds cavalier, a glance at 2 Corinthians 11:22–33 shows it is not. Paul was exposed to unbelievable suffering and humiliation; but for all its impact, Christ was still his defining reality, and some of his letters do not even betray that he has suffered.

Remembering requires attention; it does not happen automatically. To apply this text means that time will be given to thinking, reading, discussing, and learning about the change God has brought. Remembering will lead to prayer and an awareness of God's presence and his involvement in what we do.

A warning for Christians. Christians enjoy enormous privilege in being taken into the family of God, but such a thought is open to *serious* abuse, abuse so common that use of such language becomes problematic. Far too frequently Christians view privilege as something they possess, forgetting that the gift ought never to be separated from the Giver.[78] We possess nothing but the Christ to whom we are bound. Any privilege comes from him and is known only in him. When we forget this, we distort the faith and overestimate ourselves.

Ephesians 2:11–12 serves as a strong warning to Christians, for we are as vulnerable to the failures of the Jews as they were. Unfortunately, much name-calling takes place within the church. When we label someone pejoratively, we too are acting "in the flesh"—in a merely human way that does not involve God. We also have our religious badges that demean and exclude, just as circumcision did for the Jews. Our sense of privilege turns into a "holier than thou" attitude that makes healthy relations impossible. When we communicate division and disdain, are not our religious acts also "made from human hands"?

My own Southern Baptist denomination is torn by strife. Actions taken on all sides have *not* been done in a Christian manner. Do we not have to say, 'This is a *baptism* in the flesh, made from human hands"? Unfortunately, much Christian action falls in this category, but we cannot live as Christians while behaving in a non-Christian manner. If we do not show the same love and grace as the One into whose family we have been brought, we betray that we do not really belong in the home. We are still estranged from God while performing religious acts.

Application of this text occurs in humility and repentance, followed by serious family talk about how we communicate who we are. How can we keep

---

78. See pp. 100–101.

privilege, obedience, and righteous action from bringing division, disdain, and name-calling? "Holier than thou" attitudes are almost impossible to stop and are often unperceived by the "holy." We cannot draw people to Christ while inadvertently belittling them. Privilege should lead to thanksgiving, not arrogance. Once again a sense of grace is the key. Grace excludes pride and extends itself to others in need.

We belong. Throughout life, most of us have some sense of not belonging, and we feel unaccepted and inferior. The drive to identify with someone, some group, or some cause deemed important—even if it is only a sports team—is enormous. Such identifications make us feel important. We need to belong, to have some sense of fit in the world, and from a sense of belonging comes the ability to relate and accomplish things. Our own families are, of course, primary in giving us a sense of belonging.

This text says we *do* belong. Christ brought us home to God. We live in God's house as members of his family, and at the same time we are a house in which God lives (2:19–22). We belong with God and are involved in what he is doing. The other people in the house are family with us. This home defines us. Christ has given us place in his world, and from that sense of belonging comes a growing ability to relate and accomplish the tasks to which we are called. This texts asks that we remember where home is: We are at home with God.

From here all else in the Christian life flows. The church as a family of faith should have the feel of family. Family members care for each other, are committed to each other, confront each other, and sustain each other. A sense of family should shape our worship. Worship should not be like a production we watch; rather, we need the comfort and freedom of being involved in a family experience, joining together to communicate with God, to address and be addressed. No one should be allowed to feel like an outsider in the church; all people need to know they belong.

The barriers are down; Christians live with God. Consciously or unconsciously people—even those who believe in Christ—can think of God as distant and unapproachable. This lack of a sense of the nearness to God lies at the root of much of human failure. Yet even before faith, God is never distant from us, as Paul reminded the Athenians (Acts 17:27) and as the psalmist testified (Ps. 139:7–12). The language of nearness is, of course, metaphorical, and we need to distinguish language about God's presence prior to faith and our being brought near in Christ. In the former, God is the holy, gracious God seeking people, but his holiness is also an overwhelming presence. In Christ, however, we have been brought to God, and the barriers blocking access to him, such as sin, hostility, and the weakness of the flesh have been removed.

Peace, access, nearness, and reconciliation all emphasize that the barriers between God and us have been removed. But what does the text want us to do with this information? Nothing explicit is said, but several implications are present.

(1) We live with God and he with us. We communicate with God, and his presence shapes us. Once again faith is shown to be relational, not a decision or set of beliefs.

(2) Life, salvation, and resources for life flow from God to those with him. This is not a "health and wealth" theology, but a recognition that God is the giver of all good things.

(3) Worship and thanksgiving are a natural part of life.

(4) The character of God is our guide. What is implicit in this text will be made explicit in 5:1: Christians are to imitate their God.

The barriers are down; Christians are joined. The attitude of this world is best expressed in the phrase, "You're different from me, and I resent you for that."[79] We *create* barriers between races, nations, religions, genders, social and economic classes, denominations, schools, communities, teams, and families. Differentiation is necessary for identity, but the human tendency to create *barriers* is a distortion and a sin. Distinction and uniqueness do not have to lead to division. The erection of barriers results from the ways we attribute value, that is, by devaluing those who are different.

Even before being in Christ, humans have more in common than they do differently. All are made in the image of God, have the same needs, and experience the same distortion from sin. But especially in Christ no ground exists for barriers or divisions—not along racial, sexual, cultural, or any other lines. We are one with all others in Christ whether we like it or not. To maintain divisions is to deny what Christ has accomplished.

Application requires a change of mind. The markers that define us must give way to the *one* determining marker that says who we are—Christ himself. The other markers may be real, but they neither define us nor divide us from other people in Christ. All people stand with the same value before God, and we belong to the same family with other believers.

The race problem. Nowhere is this theology more important for modern Christians than in dealing with *racial hostility.* Christians of other races are part of us, and divisions cannot be allowed to continue. The racial barrier is like a festering wound in the body of Christ. We may no longer have separate drinking fountains such as I witnessed as a child—one marked "Whites only" and another marked "Colored only." Yet racial hostility boils just under the

---

79. Tom Wright, *Bringing the Church to the World* (Minneapolis: Bethany, 1992), 25.

surface in the United States and many other countries, and Christians contribute to the problem. Sunday is often the most segregated day of the week, for Christians worship along racial lines.

The perversion of both active and passive racism must be challenged and stopped. The church must be a place where people know the barriers have been removed, can find solace, and can deal with racial injustice. The witness of the church is at stake. When people are told either implicitly or explicitly that they are not welcome in a church because of their color, the church has become an absurd place.

Racism will have to be treated on two levels, both as a general societal problem and specifically within the body of Christ. Racism in any form is prohibited by the equality of all people before God and by his unrestricted love. But the theology of the body of Christ deals with the issue at another level. The point is not merely that all Christians are *equal;* rather, the point is that all Christians have been *joined,* which has far more significance and impact.

If the barriers are down and we are joined to other believers, then several responses are required from Christians. (1) Acceptance and *valuing* people of other races on an equal level is a necessity. An attitude that says in effect, "They are not our kind," destroys the body of Christ. Since all of us operate with such attitudes, an ongoing repentance is prerequisite.

(2) In addition, we will need *investment* in Christians of other races. We cannot accept and value what we do not know or care about. We need to demonstrate that other groups matter to us. The unity cannot be merely a theoretical unity, but must be put into practice.

(3) We need to seek *justice* for other groups as well. Questions about justice are often complicated—witness the debate over illegal immigrants—but the church should be leading the discussion about justice and compassion so that whole groups of people are not placed on a second tier. Racism has to be named, confronted, and rejected.

(4) Finally, some level of *sharing* among Christians must take place. Unity does not exist without involvement. Hands need to be joined in worship, in learning, in ministering to needs, and in evangelism. The most significant witness to the love of Christ lies in the ability of Christians of various races to care for each other and work together.

Male and female. From the ancient world on, barriers between the sexes were created for two primary reasons: to prevent abuse of women and because women are viewed as inferior. Today radical feminists, in reaction to centuries of abuse, have deepened the hostility between the sexes. Here too the witness of the church is at stake. Christians need to show that in Christ relations are different, that women are not devalued and are not to be used or abused, and that the barrier has been destroyed in Christ. Women should not have to fear abuse but should feel as accepted and valued as men are. Here, as else-where, the not-yet character of faith lived in this world may be all too obvi-ous, but the church must be the place where people experience the now in the presence of the not yet. Women must know they are fully part of the body of Christ and that barriers do not prohibit their full participation.

One of the most sacred sites for Jews is the so-called "wailing wall" in Jerusalem, a retaining wall from the temple mount in Jesus' day. Anyone who has seen this wall knows that a rail stands to separate men who pray on the left from women who pray on the right.[80] Churches are not so obvious, but Christians have for too long categorized women differently. This text will not allow the barrier to continue.

Many other barriers exist in our society, such as education, social stand-ing, and economics. The differences will not go away, but the church must think through the fact that the differences should not divide us or make any-one feel less valuable.

Two wrong turns. At times Christians have argued that unity in Christ is a "spiritual" reality and does not require involvement with other groups. Sep-aration of the "spiritual" from the "secular" cannot be tolerated. Such attempts avoid the implications of the gospel. That which is spiritual affects, rather directs, all of life. One has only to look at Paul's confronting Peter over not eating with Gentiles (Gal. 2:11–14); unity in Christ has to do with sitting at table together. The church cannot be allowed to exist in self-selected and self-serving groups.

Second, some have concluded that since the barriers are down, Christians need not evangelize Jews. The relation between Jews and Christians is a del-icate issue, both because Christians exist only because of their Jewish her-itage and because of the holocaust in Nazi Germany. From an exegetical standpoint, the unity about which the text speaks is unity between Jewish Christians and Gentile Christians—not unity between Jews and Christians. This is a unity *in Christ*. Paul certainly did not hesitate to seek the conversion of Jews, and neither should we, given the humility and respect that is needed for any work of evangelism.[81]

However, no ground exists for even a hint of anti-Semitism, a sin that too easily appears among Christians. The implicit message that Jews should be punished because they crucified Christ is theologically naive. The Jews *as a race* are no more responsible for the death of Christ than any other race, and

---

80. This segregation of the sexes has been a synagogue custom for nearly two thousand years. Whether it was in practice in the first century is uncertain.

81. Nor should modern Israel be given political privilege over Palestinians, as some evangelicals have often argued.

we should be careful in describing the crucifixion that Jews do not become scapegoats. They are like the rest of us, needing a Savior.

United, not uniform. Paul's emphasis on unity does not mean all Christians are alike. Unity in Christ does not negate differences, cultural uniqueness, or the value of culture. Jews in Christ do not become Gentiles, nor do Gentiles become Jewish Christians. Women do not become men, or vice versa, and people do not suddenly all have the same abilities. Paul's body theology assumes both unity and diversity (1 Cor. 12:14–26).

Once again, the issue of the relation of gospel and culture enters the discussion.[82] Enjoying one's own culture is to be expected, and we choose like-minded people for good reasons. The homogeneous principle of church growth, which has churches target groups culturally similar to themselves, is understandable. Communication requires similarity, and like attracts like. Worship is a cultural expression and has most impact when framed in culturally specific ways. No one should be surprised or find fault that blacks are more comfortable in black churches, Koreans in Korean churches, and whites in white churches.

But the barriers are down, and the homogeneous principle—for all its practicality—cannot guide the church. Cultural preferences must take a backseat to unity in Christ. The most important issue is always *identity*: What is the strongest defining reality for us—Christ or culture? Culture is important—indeed, a necessary part of the fabric of our lives—but Christ, not culture, gives the primary definition to life. Culture is the means by which Christ is expressed, but the message is Christ himself. Do ethnic churches exist to preserve a culture or to promote Christ? Often one gets the impression that the real center of all our churches is our culture, not our Lord. That attitude needs to change.

Churches need to be astute enough to know when they are using culture, when they are adapting culture, and when they must confront culture.[83] Churches must demonstrate that the barriers are down. That most churches are culturally monolithic is an embarrassment. Church members must show they care about other people in Christ, even if they are different culturally, economically, politically, or socially. A monolithic church in a multicultural context is a failure. Churches need to demonstrate unity with Christians of other cultures, to seek justice, and to evangelize across cultural and racial lines. We have to show the barriers are down.

The church is a peace institute. The peace discussed in this text is not about good inner feelings; it is about relations. Far too many people have

---

82. See p. 41.
83. See the classic discussion by H. Richard Niebuhr, *Christ and Culture* (New York: Harper & Brothers, 1951).

distorted ideas about religion, that religion is what they do when they are alone, quiet, and thinking of God. They forget that the vertical relation with God is bound to and expressed in horizontal relations with people. Note too that the text does not say, "He is *my* peace"; it says, "He is *our* peace." A church is a group of people who know this and embody peace in anticipation of that day when God establishes peace in all his creation. In the church God's work of peace has a beachhead and is already represented. Christians by definition are people of peace. That does not mean we are passive or quiescent. On the contrary, as people of peace we by necessity struggle for justice.

In our churches peace is rarely given value. We have assumed our culture's insecurity to such a degree that peace is relegated to end time eschatology. Premium value is placed on "doing it my way" and "believing as I say." Christians are marked more by division than peace. But if peace was a criterion by which Paul solved problems, then peace should have regulative force for us too. It should both rule our hearts *and* our churches. In the church peace should get a chance. Numerous schools for war exist, and both amateurs and scholars study wars. Few people study peace. The church should be a place where people study and practice peace. But again a caution is in order. Peace does not mean passivity. If Isaiah 57:21 reminds us "there is no peace for the wicked," then focusing on peace will mean focusing on righteousness and justice.[84]

Christians are a corporate group. Modern evangelicals tend to focus on Christianity as a religion of the individual. The failure of the church has often driven people to this option, but the New Testament knows nothing of "lone ranger" Christianity. The individual and the faith of the individual are both important, but the Christian faith is a corporate religion. When one is baptized into Christ, one is baptized into the body of Christ (1 Cor. 12:13; Gal. 3:27–28). Thist part of the reality of faith should not be neglected. People do relate to God as individuals, but the focus is corporate.[85] In the horizontal relation the vertical relation is lived out. The gospel needs to be presented in such a way that people realize its *sociological* dimensions.

The division in the church into so many groups is a scandal. I am not suggesting all parts of the church should agree. Nor is the goal to form structures of unity; rather, the goal is living unity in Christ. Far too often Christians are more interested in their brand of Christianity than in Christ. They are Lutheran, Baptist, or whatever before they are Christian, and any-

---

84. See the works in n. 20 and Wink, *Engaging the Powers*, 175–257.

85. God is present with individuals, but God is experienced in a qualitatively different way when Christians gather. Otherwise no need would exist for temple language or for such statements as, "Where two or three come together in my name, there am I with them" (Matt. 18:20).

one else is, at best, misguided. Without focusing on structures, must not the church focus on unity in Christ? Must not the church be both evangelical and ecumenical?

To focus on unity has nothing to do with being weak on doctrine. Unity is itself a *theological* necessity. Christians cannot sacrifice the essence of the gospel to attain unity, for that would not be Christian unity. Most of our divisions, however, occurred without justification and were usually accompanied by non-Christian attitudes and acts. We must be ready to tolerate disagreement as we enjoy unity. Obviously central tenets of the faith—such as the authority of Scriptures, the deity of Christ, and the death and resurrection of Christ—should not be diminished, for without these central features we no longer have a *Christian* church.

Holding staunchly to correct doctrine is not sufficient to defend the faith. Do we not as staunchly need to hold to Christian attitudes and practices and to unity? Why do the so-called defenders of orthodoxy have such a difficult time showing grace? Is it impossible to be both orthodox and magnanimous at the same time? Orthodoxy ought to make people gracious. The key is in seeing that both the content of belief and the conduct of belief are determined by Christ.

The church is centered on Christ. Communities can exist for a variety of reasons, but the Christian church exists only because of Christ and his purposes. Christianity is a religion centered on a person. The church gathers around the character of Christ, not the characteristics of the people. Apart from the significance of his death and resurrection, the church has no reason to exist. The church is a community and has traditions and rituals, but it is not about any of these things. The church is about Jesus Christ, and the other pieces of the picture exist to display the role of Christ in the church. It is possible to be Jewish and to observe events such as the Passover Seder without religious commitment to Judaism. The Christian community, however, has no other reason to exist other than Christ himself. He is our peace, the one in whom all are united, the one who gives access to God, and the cornerstone on whom the building grows.

Consequently, the activities of a church should reflect this central focus on Christ. Only then can believers fulfill their mission. This suggestion is not limiting, for Christ is the focal point of God's purposes and the one in whom all things are brought together (1:10). The church's agenda is not a collection of meaningful ideas and projects. The church's agenda is Christ, in whom all subjects are placed in order.

As a result, teaching and preaching about Christ must be the focus. This is implicit in Christ's preaching peace in 2:17 and in the mention of "apostles and prophets" in 2:20. Just as this whole passage emphasizes what Christ accomplished, so the church proclaims his message of peace both far and near and teaches people the implications of the change he brings. A church communicates Christ both in speech and action, or it has ceased to be a church.

The sociological dimensions of this text rule out any division of evangelism and social justice. Such a dichotomy should never have been allowed. Neither can evangelism be viewed as anxiety-driven speech-persuading decisions. Evangelism is the authentic living out of life with Christ in word and act. Unfortunately, churches too frequently become uncomfortable about presenting Christ and fall into a maintenance mode. They are the ones who need most to heed this text with its call to remember the change and its Christocentric focus on the privileges Christ brings.

The church is the people. Even when we know better, we tend to think of the church as either a physical structure or a denominational entity, both of which exist to produce programs. Such meanings of the word *church* are derived meanings. Even in the New Testament the word *ekklesia* is used of a non-Christian "assembly,"[86] and Paul may have intended no more than "assembly" or "gathering" when he applied the word to Christians. Neither physical structures nor denominations are necessary to have a church. The people are the stones that make up this building in which God dwells.[87]

My comments are not intended to disparage physical buildings or denominations. Conducive space enables worship and ministry, and organizations can facilitate tasks, but neither is the church. If we remember the church is the people, several implications follow. (1) Church is no longer perceived as a program that some people put on for others to watch. The people are participants, joining together to worship and to have fellowship with God, who is present with them as a group. (2) Ministry is for everyone, not merely the clergy. The people are the temple in which God dwells. (3) Value is placed on people. Sometimes the impression is given that people are dispensable, as long as the building is maintained and the programs keep going. The average church in the United States devotes the majority of its funds to its building and internal operations. What if we invested in people as much as in our buildings and systems?

An actor sitting in a theatre looked around him and said, "This is my church." Everyone has a church, the place you go for definition and to assert your allegiances. For some people it is a bar, for some a stadium; for Christians it is the place where Christ is the norm and where allegiance is paid to him.

---

86. E. g., Acts 7:38; 19:32, 39, 41; cf. Heb. 2:12 (NIV, "congregation").

87. Paul speaks of the church in universal terms, but Robert Banks is correct to say that local churches are to be viewed as tangible expressions of the heavenly church. See *Paul's Idea of Community: The Early House Churches in Their Historical Setting* (Grand Rapids: Eerdmans, 1980,) 47.

Ephesians 3:1–13

FOR THIS REASON I, Paul, the prisoner of Christ Jesus for the sake of you Gentiles—

²Surely you have heard about the administration of God's grace that was given to me for you, ³that is, the mystery made known to me by revelation, as I have already written briefly. ⁴In reading this, then, you will be able to understand my insight into the mystery of Christ, ⁵which was not made known to men in other generations as it has now been revealed by the Spirit to God's holy apostles and prophets. ⁶This mystery is that through the gospel the Gentiles are heirs together with Israel, members together of one body, and sharers together in the promise in Christ Jesus.

⁷I became a servant of this gospel by the gift of God's grace given me through the working of his power. ⁸Although I am less than the least of all God's people, this grace was given me: to preach to the Gentiles the unsearchable riches of Christ, ⁹and to make plain to everyone the administration of this mystery, which for ages past was kept hidden in God, who created all things. ¹⁰His intent was that now, through the church, the manifold wisdom of God should be made known to the rulers and authorities in the heavenly realms, ¹¹according to his eternal purpose which he accomplished in Christ Jesus our Lord. ¹²In him and through faith in him we may approach God with freedom and confidence. ¹³I ask you, therefore, not to be discouraged because of my sufferings for you, which are your glory.

THE SAME DESCRIPTIVE-DOXOLOGICAL style Paul has been using continues through this chapter. What he intended to do at this point was to explain again how he was praying for them, just as he had done in 1:15–23. But a glance at 3:1 and 14 reveals that, as in 2:1–5, Paul starts a thought, is diverted, and then returns to his original thought. In 3:1 he starts to describe his prayer for them, but the mention of "Gentiles" leads him to speak of his own apostolic ministry to the Gentiles and its significance. Then in 3:14 he returns to his prayer. Just as 3:14–21 is parallel to 1:15–23, 3:2–13 is in many ways parallel to 1:3–14. Both sections emphasize "administration,"[1] "grace," "revelation," "mystery," "glory," and "God's purpose."

Note particularly the prominence given to "grace" (vv. 2, 7, 8) and to words for revelation: "revelation" (v. 3), "revealed" (v. 5), "made known" (vv. 3, 5, 10), "preach" (v. 8), "make plain" (v. 9), and "mystery" (vv. 3, 4, 9). Note too the shift in pronouns from "I" and "you"/"your" in verses 1–10, to "we"/"our" in verses 11–12, and then back to "I" and "your" in verse 13. There are also close parallels between this passage and Colossians 1:25–2:3.[2]

Structure. The Greek text is made up of two long sentences (vv. 1–7 and vv. 8–13), with the resulting structure:

A. Paul the prisoner on behalf of the Gentiles (3:1)
B. Paul the steward of grace and servant of the gospel (3:2–7)
C. The purpose and significance of Paul's gospel (3:8–13)

M. Barth viewed 3:2–13 as commentary on 3:1, but they are more a digression than a commentary.[3] The NIV has placed verse 7 with verses 8–13 for convenience, for these verses explain verse 7. Considerable overlap exists between verses 2–7 and 8–13, for both focus on grace and revelation. Even though the revelation focuses on the mystery made known in Christ (vv. 4 and 8), neither Christ nor the salvation of the Gentiles is the real focus. Rather, Paul's message here has a higher purpose, the revelation of God himself. God is both the revealer and the One who is revealed (vv. 2–3, 8, 10). Note the use of the passive voice in verses 2, 3, 5, and 8, all of which are "divine passives" (the passive voice used to describe an action of God).

Paul the Prisoner (3:1)

"FOR THIS REASON" points back at least to 2:11–22, if not the whole of chapter 2. The gospel that gives life and includes the Gentiles is the guiding purpose in all Paul does. "I, Paul" is used in several of his letters as a way of emphasizing what follows (see 2 Cor. 10:1; Gal. 5:2; Col. 1:23; 1 Thess. 2:18; Philem. 19).

Where Paul was in prison is debated,[4] but whatever decision is made does not affect the reading of this letter. That Paul is the "prisoner of Christ Jesus"

---

1. 1:10 (NIV, "put into effect") and 3:2.

2. For the impact of these verses on the question of authorship, see the introduction, pp. 26–27.

3. Barth, *Ephesians*, 1:359–60. This section explains the character of Paul's whole ministry, not just his imprisonment.

4. The choices are Ephesus, Caesarea, or Rome, with either of the last two being possible and Rome being the most likely (see p. 29).

is important. He could have blamed the Romans or even the Jews for his imprisonment, but for him their involvement is incidental. How should "of Christ Jesus" be understood? Does he view his being in prison as the direct purpose of Christ for him so that, in effect, Christ put him in chains?[5] Or does Paul see his present situation as on behalf of Christ, as part of his service for Christ? Either is possible, but 6:20 and Colossians 4:3 seem to favor the latter.[6] In either case, Christ is the one who has laid hold on Paul.

The only reason why Paul was in prison was because he thought Gentiles had the same access to God that Jews did. If he had been content to be a Jewish Christian with a mission to Jews or if he had been willing to keep Gentiles on a lower plane, he would not have been in jail.[7] But the purpose of Paul's call was to bring about the obedience of faith among the Gentiles (Rom. 1:5; Gal. 1–2), and if faith was the key to salvation, both Jews and Gentiles were on the same plane.

Paul the Steward of Grace and Servant of the Gospel (3:2–7)

"SURELY" (3:2) DOES not suggest that the Gentiles have not heard about Paul's responsibility with the gospel. It means "if as I take for granted." Paul was responsible to administer God's grace to the Gentiles. "Administration" (*oikonomia*), related to *oikonomos* ("steward"), refers both to the office of being a steward and to the carrying out of the responsibility (the word is also used in 1:10 [NIV, "put into effect"]; 3:9).[8] Paul is a steward in charge of God's grace. If he fails in his task, the Gentiles will be deprived of God's grace.

In verses 7–8 "grace" itself is the gift given to Paul, while in verse 9 what is administered is the "mystery" (*mysterion*). "Grace" and "mystery" are closely related. Not only are both administered, but in 3:3 the administration of grace is directly connected with the revelation of the mystery. *Mysterion* occurs twenty-one times in the Pauline letters, six times in Ephesians (1:9; 3:3, 4, 9; 5:32; 6:19). As indicated above,[9] this term does not refer to something unknown. Rather, in a Semitic context it refers to what is known only because God revealed it. More specifically here, it refers to the revelation that the

---

5. Note how Acts 20:22–23; 21:4, 10–14 underscore both the Spirit's compelling him to go to Jerusalem (lit., 20:22 has "bound by the Spirit") and the prophetic warnings of imprisonment.

6. See also 4:1; Philemon 1, 9–10, 13; 2 Timothy 1:8. 16.

7. See also Romans 15:30–32 and 1 Thessalonians 2:14–16.

8. Elsewhere in Paul at 1 Corinthians 9:17 (NIV, "trust"), Colossians 1:25 (NIV, "commission"), and 1 Timothy 1:4 (NIV, "work").

9. See comments on 1:9, p. 53.

Gentiles are included in Christ as equals (see esp. 3:6). In Colossians 1:26 the mystery is the word of God,[10] though the next verse shows the focus there too is on the gospel for the Gentiles. Then in Colossians 2:2–3 the mystery is reduced to Christ himself, "in whom are hidden all the treasures of wisdom and knowledge" (cf. *mysterion* in Eph. 1:9, which focused on all things being brought together in Christ). We may conclude that *mystery* refers to the revelation that all things will be brought together in Christ, and specifically that Jews and Gentiles are brought together.[11] "In Christ" is key in understanding the mystery, for that phrase points to a double union—union with Christ and union of Jews and Gentiles in him.[12]

A previous letter? (3:3). Uncertainty exists about the intention of "as I have already written briefly." Reference could be to something written earlier in the same document or to an earlier document.[13] If we assume the readers had access to Colossians or Romans, we could argue that the reference is to an earlier document. However, in light of the difficulty with the address in 1:1–2, one can assume nothing about the recipients. Most commentators accept that Paul is referring to 1:9–10 or to 2:11–22,[14] and this is the safest understanding, even though it makes 3:4 seem unusual. If so, then verse 4 means, in effect, "If you have read 2:11–22, you see the insight I have into the significance of God's revelation in Christ."

The new revelation (3:4–6). "Mystery of Christ" (v. 4) can be understood as "the mystery about Christ" or "the mystery that is Christ."[15] Because of Colossians 4:3 the former seems more likely. The revelation is focused on Christ, but as Ephesians 3:6 shows, the more narrow focus is on the significance of Christ for joining Jews and Gentiles.

The idea of a revelation not made to previous generations but "now" (v. 5) revealed eschatologically (cf. v. 9) is paralleled in a number of texts describing the gospel,[16] so much so that some scholars speak of a "revelation schema."[17] It is striking that wisdom, gospel, mystery, ages, revelation, and

---

10. Cf. Romans 16:25–27; 1 Corinthians 2:1; Ephesians 6:19; Colossians 4:3.

11. See Chrys C. Caragounis, *The Ephesian Mysterion*, especially 118.

12. Similar to the double reconciliation in 2:16 between God and humanity and between Jews and Gentiles. See Stott, *God's New Society*, 117.

13. Cf. the use of the word in Romans 15:4.

14. See Caragounis, *The Ephesian Mysterion*, 99–100; Schnackenburg, *Ephesians: A Commentary*, 132, as representatives.

15. An objective genitive or an epexegetic genitive, respectively.

16. See Romans 16:25–27; 1 Corinthians 2:6–16; Colossians 1:26–27; 2 Timothy 1:9–11; Titus 1:2–3; Hebrews 1:1–2; 1 Peter 1:19–21.

17. E.g. *Lincoln*, Ephesians, 170. See my treatment of Romans 16:25–27 in "Gospel in Romans: A Theology of Revelation," *Gospel in Paul*, eds. L. Ann Jervis and Peter Richardson (Sheffield: Sheffield Academic Press, 1994), 292–96.

Gentiles are brought together in several of these texts.[18] In the New Testament the gospel is a gospel of revelation: God reveals himself as a saving God. Note also the Trinitarian focus of this passage.

The NIV wording "men in other generations" (v. 5) is a questionable translation of an unusual phrase, actually a double plural: "children [sons] of humans [men]" (cf. Mark 3:28, the only other occurrence of this phrase in the New Testament). While "son of man" can refer to humanity in general or to select individuals (esp. Jesus),[19] the plural refers to all humanity. This verse does not deny that in the Old Testament Gentiles were included in God's purposes,[20] but no previous revelation focused on the Gentiles being accepted by God on equal footing with Jews. The contrast heightens the significance of the eschatological revelation that has come "by the Spirit."

But while the revelation extends to all Christians (1:9), the foundational revelation has come only to certain select individuals. "Apostles" refers to the founding apostles who saw the risen Christ and were given insight about the significance of the gospel and the responsibility for handing it on.[21] "Prophets," clearly New Testament prophets, does not refer generally to prophets in the early church, but to those who had received revelation that helped frame how the gospel was to be understood and lived.[22] These people laid out the perimeters within which faith moves. Paul had a unique call, even though others worked among the Gentiles, but he was not unique in receiving revelation (see Acts 15:6–29; Gal. 2:1–10). Ephesians 3:5 suggests a significant number of people received revelation from God's Spirit, some of which may be reflected in hymns and confessional statements Paul adopted from the early church.

The primary emphasis of the revelation is the "withness" of the Gentiles, which is emphasized in the Greek text by alliteration (3:6: *synkleronoma kai syssoma kai symmetocha*—"heirs together, members together of one body, and sharers together").[23] The promises were formerly made to Israel, but now Gentiles are "heirs together with" (cf. also Rom. 8:17; 1 Peter 3:7) the Jewish Christians and receive a full share of all benefits. "Inheritance" language

---

18. Romans 16:25–27; 1 Corinthians 2:6–16; Ephesians 3:2–13; Colossians 1:25–2:3.

19. See LXX of Psalm 8:5 and Ezekiel 2:1 respectively.

20. See Genesis 12:3; Deuteronomy 32:43; Isaiah 2:2; 11:10; 49:6.

21. Because "holy" comes before "apostles" and "his" (NIV, "God's") comes immediately after, some think only the apostles are called holy (see Lincoln, *Ephesians*, 179; Schnackenburg, *Ephesians, a Commentary*, 133–34). This is an unnecessary conclusion. The NIV rightly takes "by the Spirit" with "revealed" rather than with "prophets."

22. See the discussion of this issue at 2:20, pp. 136–37.

23. Three of the fourteen "with" (*syn*) compounds in this letter occur in this verse. The NIV adds "Israel" to the text.

was a Christian way of talking about salvation—either in terms of God's inheriting a people or the people's receiving an inheritance from God.

Revelation that enlists (3:7). The revelation that comes in the gospel is not only so that people will understand, but that they may be enlisted in the service of the Revealer. Paul had been made a servant because of "the gift of God's grace." The gift obligates. "Grace" in this verse does not relate to Paul's salvation, but to his ministry. Through grace he became a servant of the gospel. Grace not only connects us to God and Christ and to each other, but it also enlists and empowers us. Paul himself experienced what he prayed for his readers (cf. 1:19; 3:16).

The Purpose and Significance of the Gospel (3:8–13)

IN 1 CORINTHIANS 15:9 Paul referred to himself as "the least of the apostles," while here he is "less than the least of all God's people."[24] For all his sense of the privilege of being an apostle, Paul had no great sense of his ability or of a high rank. He felt he should have been rejected because he persecuted the church, but he was chosen—a choice not based on his ability, but on God's grace. Anything he accomplished was a result of the power of God at work in him.[25]

To proclaim and to reveal (3:8b–11). Grace was given to him for three purposes: (1) to preach to the Gentiles the riches of Christ (v. 8); (2) to make plain the administration of the mystery (v. 9); and (3) to make the wisdom of God known to the rulers and authorities in the heavenly realms (v. 10). These are not three separate purposes, for all three focus on revelation. The first two may be essentially the same, depending on what interpretive decisions are made,[26] while the third is a result of the other two. When the Gentiles understand the riches of Christ, the church will be the place where the wisdom of God is made known to the rulers and authorities. In the end the three purposes are one—to make known the gospel in which God reveals himself as the God who saves and unites Jews and Gentiles. With "unsearchable riches of Christ" (3:8) Paul means the unfathomable or inexhaustible resources available in Christ—that is, the grace and power for salvation, for life, and for bringing all things into unity.

"To make plain to everyone the administration of this mystery" (3:9) is unclear. "Make plain" is the same verb as was used in 1:18 of Christians being

---

24. Some commentators suggest a play on Paul's name, since in Latin *paullus* means "little" (see Bruce, *The Epistle to the Ephesians*, 63).

25. See 1 Corinthians 15:8–10 and 1 Timothy 1:12–17.

26. Paul S. Minear, *To Die and to Live: Christ's Resurrection and Christian Vocation* (New York: Seabury, 1977), 94–95, distinguishes the audience in the first two, that the first purpose focuses on Gentiles, the second on the union of Jews and Gentiles.

enlightened. But who administers the mystery: Christ, God, Paul, or the church?[27] Most commentators think the reference is to Paul, given the similar language in 3:2–3 and in Colossians 1:25.[28] Paul felt a strong responsibility to make the mystery understood (note the parallel between vv. 2–5 and v. 9).[29] He wanted everyone to know the secret hidden in God but now made known, that the Gentiles are accepted by God as equals with Jewish believers. The mention of creation in verse 9 and the focus on God's eternal purpose in verse 11 underscore the continuity between the new creation in Christ and God's original creation and actions throughout history.

Ephesians 3:10 assigns a lofty and cosmic role to the church. It is the channel by which God's wisdom is demonstrated "to the rulers and authorities in the heavenly realms." As before, "heavenly realms" points not so much to a place as to a spiritual reality, the reality beyond what we see.[30] This description of the church's role has no equivalent elsewhere in Paul or in the New Testament. Several options are possible:

(1) The church makes known God's wisdom to good angels (see 1 Peter 1:12).[31]

(2) The church makes known God's wisdom to evil powers in order to bring about their conversion,[32] to announce their defeat,[33] or to cause them to marvel.

(3) The church makes known God's wisdom to human institutions and structures to transform their actions.[34]

(4) Some combination of the above.

---

27. Barth, *Ephesians*, 1:343, argues Christ has this responsibility. Lincoln, *Ephesians*, 184, says the reference is to God's act of administering to disclose his purpose.

28. The question whether "everyone" belongs in the text compounds the problem. If it belongs in the text, the focus is on Paul's responsibility for the gospel. If it does not, the focus could be on Paul's task of enlightening other *Christians* about *their* responsibility for the new revelation.

29. Cf. 1 Corinthians 4:1, where Paul asks that he and others like him be considered as stewards (*oikonomoi*, a word related to *oikonomia*, "administration," in 3:9) of the mysteries of God.

30. See pp. 46–47.

31. Stott, *God's New Society*, 124, quoting McKay, *God's Order*, 61. McKay thought both good and evil spirits were addressed.

32. Walter Wink, *Naming the Powers*, vol. 1: *The Powers* (Philadelphia: Fortress, 1984), 89, 93–96. G. B. Caird, *Principalities and Powers* (Oxford: Clarendon, 1956), 28, 81, had argued this earlier. While admitting the difficulty of his interpretation, Wink thinks the conversion of the nations demands revelation *to the angels* of the nations, his understanding of "rulers and authorities." In my estimation he has both assumed too much and overinterpreted the verse.

33. Schnackenburg, *Ephesians: A Commentary*, 140.

34. Barth, Ephesians, 1:365.

The focus in Ephesians on "the rulers and authorities" has to do with evil powers, not good angels or human institutions. This verse should thus be understood in the context of the display of God's glory even to those who oppose him. In 1:19–22 and Colossians 2:15, Paul announces the defeat of the powers in Christological terms, based on the cross and resurrection. Here he does not need to repeat this announcement. Rather, he focuses on the majesty of God demonstrated in the unity of Jews and Gentiles. The church's very existence and conduct are making known how great God's plan of salvation is—both to people and to the powers. This gives an unparalleled importance to the church.

"His eternal purpose" is literally the "purpose of the ages," which connects to "for ages past" in verse 9 and to the discussion of God's purpose in 1:9–11. Note the past tense "accomplished." The "not yet" part of faith is still there, but God's purpose has already been accomplished in Christ. What remains is an unfolding of what has already been established. Once again Ephesians is theocentric, focusing on what *God* has accomplished in Christ.

Privilege and perseverance (3:12–13). The text again returns to the privileges available in Christ. In 3:12 the NIV translation is aesthetic, but it weakens the force of the text. A comparison of the NIV with a more literal translation will reveal the difficulty.

> NIV: "In him and through faith in him we may approach God with freedom and confidence."
>
> More literal: "In whom we have boldness and access in confidence through *his faithfulness* [or faith in him]."

The more literal translation shows both the strength of the text and its connection to "access to the Father" in 2:18. The two nouns ("boldness" and "access") are joined together to express one idea, a thought close to Hebrews 4:16.[35] Paul's concern is not for access to heaven at some future day, but access to God in the present. Note also that the NIV has placed "through faith in him" at the beginning of the sentence, but in doing so loses the connection between confidence and faithfulness/faith. The Greek word *pistis* can mean both "faithfulness" and "faith." The NIV has understood *pisteos autou* (lit., "faithfulness/faith *of him*) as "faith in him."[36] A more convincing understanding does not place the focus on human faith at all, but on his (Christ's)

---

35. See also Hebrews 10:19, which speaks of having "boldness" to enter the Holy Place. The NIV uses "confidence" to render the word "boldness" (*parresia*) in both passages in Hebrews, but in Ephesians 3:12 "confidence" translates *pepoithesis* and "freedom" is used to translate *parresia*.

36. *Autou* as an objective genitive.

faithfulness.[37] Any confidence Christians have is in his faithfulness, not in our faith[38] (cf. Rom. 8:35–39).

The literal translation also makes the connection with verse 13 understandable. Because of access to the Father and confidence based in Christ's faithfulness, Paul asks his readers not to be discouraged about his sufferings for them. This is not to suggest that verse 13 relates only to verse 12, for "therefore" takes in all of 3:2–12, but verse 12 summarizes Paul's discussion. The gospel gives Jews and Gentiles alike access to God. The thought that Paul's sufferings were the "glory" of his readers may seem strange at first, but Paul viewed his imprisonment as part of his service for Christ, a service that exalted the Gentiles. If he was in prison for preaching to the Gentiles, someone was fighting for them and their position was being given attention (cf. Rom. 11:13; Phil. 1:12–30; Col. 1:24–27).[39] That he was in prison should not be discouraging. The discouraging thing would be that no one was willing to go to prison for the ministry to the Gentiles.

Bridging Contexts

THIS TEXT IS highly personal and focused on Paul's first-century responsibility. At first glance we may conclude this text is not too relevant for us and consequently we should hurry on to the next passage. This is, in fact, what often happens in commentaries on Ephesians. This is unfortunate, for while Paul's call and the revelation to the apostles and prophets cannot be duplicated, the theologies embedded in these verses are important for our lives. The gulf between Paul's description of the church and our present experience is embarrassingly large. Bridging contexts may well call for wholesale reconstruction from our end.

---

37. Barth, *Ephesians*, 1:347. This is part of a larger debate in Pauline theology over passages that could be rendered either "faith in Christ" or "faithfulness of Christ" (see Rom. 3:22, 26; Gal. 2:16; 3:22; Phil. 3:9). See the discussions by Richard Hays, "ΠΙΣΤΙΣ and Pauline Christology: What Is at Stake?" and James D. G. Dunn, "Once More, ΠΙΣΤΙΣ ΧΡΙΣΤΟΥ," both in *Society of Biblical Literature 1991 Seminar Papers*, ed. E. H. Lovering, Jr. (Atlanta: Scholars Press, 1991), 714–29 and 730–44, respectively.

38. The NIV has rearranged the order to avoid the thought that confidence comes from human faith.

39. Verse 13 can be understood in different ways: (1) I ask that you do not lose heart; (2) I ask God that I do not lose heart; (3) I ask God that you do not lose heart. The NIV has chosen the first option and uses the word "discouraged." The second option does not seem to fit with Paul's attitude in this context, but does deserve reflection (cf. 2 Cor. 4:1—one does not talk of not losing heart unless it is an issue). The third option also deserves consideration—in effect, a prayer that they will not lose heart.

A theology of grace for ministry. Paul speaks of grace in ways unfamiliar to us. He says he was given responsibility for the "administration" of grace, became a servant by grace through the working of God's power, and was given grace to preach to the Gentiles. Whereas we usually limit grace to God's gift of salvation, this text forces us to realize that *grace is also the gift of ministry*. The gift always comes as a task. Grace always brings responsibility; it never is merely privilege. This was already present in 1:4, but now we are told how it worked in Paul's life.

Paul viewed himself as a *manager of grace*. His ministry to the Gentiles was unique, but all Christians are to be managers of grace. All who have received grace should extend it to others (see also 4:7; esp. 1 Peter 4:10, which instructs all Christians to administer God's grace faithfully). To receive grace is to be taken into its service. Grace connects, enlists, and empowers. It will not allow us to be passive, for it is God's power at work in us (cf. also 1 Cor. 15:10). This is the theology of grace the church must recover.

A theology of hardship. Much about human suffering lies outside the concern of this text, but hardship *in ministry* is addressed.[40] Paul's imprisonment was both a hardship and a potential embarrassment. But surprisingly, he gives little focus to his difficulty. That is, Paul's theology of hardship does not focus on the hardship, but on his Lord, his gospel, and his people (cf. Phil. 1:12–30). His theology is aware of something larger than his own circumstances. True, his imprisonment was not life-threatening, but he was chained[41] and limited in what he could accomplish. Once again, the issue is that which defines. Paul's circumstances were attendant factors, but they did not define who he was. Only the gospel defined him.

Paul describes himself here as both the prisoner of Christ and a servant of the gospel; elsewhere he describes himself as a slave of Christ (e.g., Rom. 1:1). None of these titles would normally be desirable, but Paul uses them as badges of honor, expressing his allegiance to Christ. Both what he does and what happens to him are part of his service to Christ. Christ defines him, not his circumstances. If he is a prisoner, he is Christ's prisoner.

Hardship viewed positively. Clearly in 3:13 Paul views his hardship positively. Rather than be discouraged about it, he wants his readers to feel good about it. From other texts (e.g., Col. 1:24) we know he rejoiced over his sufferings for the sake of Christ. Two different theologies are at work behind the positive view of hardship here. (1) Paul rejoices in suffering because it is a means of identifying with the death and resurrection of Christ

---

40. Second Corinthians, Philippians, or Colossians 1:24–29 provide a broader description of hardship in ministry.

41. See 6:20; also Acts 28:20; 2 Timothy 1:16. Note too that in Philippians, he faced death with the same attitude.

on behalf of other people. To be heirs together with Christ assumes suffering on his behalf.[42] (2) Paul's particular hardship is evidence of God's wisdom and love in including the Gentiles in his purposes. It brings attention to his ministry. Paul can be positive about what he is experiencing and asks his readers to be positive because he views his troubles as a direct result of grace working in him. The privileges of working for God and having access to God far outweigh the difficulty.

Our hardship will probably not be like Paul's, but identification with the cross is not optional and is always costly. We cannot show self-giving love and serve ourselves. For us too, definition must come from Christ, not our circumstances.

A theology of revelation. God's revelation to Paul and others described in this passage is unique, limited to select persons in the first century, but it is still theologically relevant for us for three reasons. (1) Most obvious is the value of the gospel. The gospel is good news, revealed in order to change lives. It is not merely a good idea, but a revelation of God and by God, focused on his grace. This gospel shows God's eternal purposes and the new circumstances brought about by Christ.

(2) God is shown to be a revealing God. Despite what had been hidden for ages and despite the fact that God hides himself (Isa. 45:15) and cannot be seen (Col. 1:15), he makes himself known. Even if the ultimate revelation has been given by the Spirit and in Christ, neither Christ nor the Spirit have quit their work. Without being presumptuous, we should expect that God still makes himself known.

(3) This passage is important for a doctrine of Scripture. Markus Barth suggests that in this and similar texts Paul appears to canonize his own doctrine and writings and to prepare the way for a Christian canon.[43] Paul's letters were read in gatherings of local Christians. The early church had nothing definitive other than such letters, the Old Testament, the sayings of Jesus, and the words of early Christian prophets. Such a passage as this underscores the foundational character of the apostolic witness. The gospel as marked out by these early writings is the perimeter within which Christians lived their lives and understood their faith.

Revelation for ministry. Paul's ministry was founded on his conviction about revelation and focused on the proclamation of that revelation. The same is still true of Christian ministry today. It emerges from the conviction that God has revealed himself uniquely in Christ, and its main task is to make the revelation known. Paul's ministry had the twin purpose of proclaiming the

---

42. See Romans 8:17; 2 Corinthians 4:10–11; 13:4–5; Philippians 1:29.
43. Barth, *Ephesians*, 1:362. See the passages mentioned in n. 16.

good news of the unsearchable riches of Christ and of enlightening every-one about their responsibility for that revelation. This is still what Christian ministry is about. It is a ministry of the Word, is focused on the Word, and is driven and defined by the Word.

Revelation to the powers. The most difficult part of bringing this text into our day concerns 3:10. How do we make God's wisdom known to the powers? As discussed above, W. Wink understood proclamation to the powers to mean bringing about their conversion, even though he was not sure what this meant. In applying this text, however, he defines the powers in terms of institutions, structures, and systems,[44] and modern Christians are told to pro-claim to corporations that profit should *not* be the bottom line and that they have a divine vocation too.[45] Wink's message to corporations is legitimate and a direct corollary of the gospel, but it is not an application of 3:10. I suggest this is one place where application of the text does not focus on what is explicit—making known to the powers. Neither this text nor any other text addresses where and how we can address the powers. Instead, the applica-tion of this text is in the church fulfilling the role she is called to exercise. When the message of grace has its way and unity is established and practiced, then the powers will know the many-sided wisdom of God.

A wrong turn. Just as we saw in connection with 2:20, this passage does not have any relevance concerning the continuing role for apostles and prophets today. That issue must wait until our discussion of 4:11.

A theology of unity. Paul's concern for the inclusion of the Gentiles seems remote from any concern the modern church has. No one questions what the apostle fought for so strenuously. In fact, Gentiles have taken over the church, and the paucity of Jewish believers is an embarrassment. But once again Paul stresses the unity of the church, a theme that dominates chapters 2–5. Here his focus is on the revelation that Gentiles belong, that they are on the same footing as Jewish Christians and receive the same ben-efits.[46] This unity is grounded on being in Christ Jesus. Geography is iden-tity.[47] But if being in Christ made Jews and Gentiles one by definition, does it not do the same for us with all others who are in Christ? Are we not required to see that proclaiming the gospel includes insistence on unity as part of the message? Our divisions are not between Jew and Greek, but both our divisions and our individualism are attacked by the theology of unity in this text. To be in Christ is to be made one with all who are in him.

---

44. Wink, *Unmasking the Powers*, vol. 2: *The Powers* (Philadelphia: Fortress, 1986), 173; *Engaging the Powers*, vol. 3: *The Powers* (Minneapolis: Fortress, 1992), 8–9. See p. 163, n. 32.

45. Wink, *Engaging the Powers*, 68.

46. See the discussions on pp. 126–36 and pp. 142–43.

47. See pp. 115–19.

The "eschatological now" in verses 5 and 9–10 requires a focus on new life in the present. Unity is not some goal for the eschaton; it is to be lived now. Things are not as they always were. When we are taken into Christ Jesus, we become one body with other Christians, regardless of our differences. We are one with all in him.

Boldness in living with God. Why Paul was not frequently discouraged is amazing, given the frequent failure of his churches. He had his moments, as 2 Corinthians shows (see 2 Cor. 1:6–11; 2:13; 4:7–18; 6:4–10; 11:21–33), but he was convinced matters would work out well both for his churches and himself. Note Philippians, for example: Paul should have been depressed, but he wrote about joy. In all situations Paul had only one solution to the problem he faced: applying the gospel and its implications.

Paul was eager for his readers to share his confidence rather than be discouraged, and once again the gospel forms his approach. Their particular reason for discouragement is far removed from us, but discouragement is still a threat. The antidote remains the same—the gospel—and the church is in need of confidence as much as ever.

We live in "the age of relativity." Absolutes do not exist for many in our society, and truth is understood as truth for someone, while another statement may be truth for someone else. Such a view of truth is unacceptable and certainly offers no basis for confidence. Confidence comes from conviction. The biggest problem in bringing the boldness offered in this passage into our lives is that we are often not convinced of the truth of our own gospel. Possibly we have been too inattentive or the message has been too frequently distorted by the messengers.

God really does have a purpose for his creation and has revealed himself as a saving God. He gives grace so that people are joined to him as family, confident they belong, confident of his faithfulness, and confident of the final outcome. God has given us what we need to face the difficulties and joy of life: He has given us himself and his good news.

WHILE THE TEXT asks nothing of its readers except not to be discouraged over Paul's imprisonment, the description of the gospel and its privileges carries forceful significance for Christian living. Application of this text will almost certainly bring a badly needed transformation.

Value the treasure. Surely the most important application of this text is in reproducing Paul's attitude toward the revelation that has come in Christ. If we do not value the gospel as revelation from God for us, it will not impact our lives. All of us live out of a system of values, often so unconsciously that we cannot even analyze whether the values deserve to be valued. Christians have distorted value systems as much as anyone else. Value is assigned to religious entities, such as tradition, denominational politics, a particular cause, or the evangelical sub-culture. Too often Christians merely adopt the value system of the surrounding culture, but forget ultimate value. For us the one truly great value, the "pearl of great price," ought to be God's revelation in Christ. We need a conviction that God truly has revealed himself in Christ.

To value this treasure, we must refocus on the gospel. The gospel is not one item among many. It is all Paul had and all we have. The gospel of grace, of death and resurrection, of inclusion with God's people should be given central place. We need to be *gospel people;* that is what the word *evangelical* denotes.[48] We must give attention to the gospel, be defined by the gospel, and solve our problems by applying the gospel. Once again this calls for a distinction between gospel and culture, including the so-called Christian subculture. Our very independence is at stake. Focus on the gospel is the one exercise that allows us to evaluate culture and stand over against its distorting pressures.

More attention needs to be given to the study of this new revelation and its relation to the old. If this sounds like a simplistic approach, then we understand neither the gospel nor the significance of such words as "unsearchable" (3:8) and "manifold" (3:10). Nor is this to suggest a simplistic focus on "evangelistic" messages. Too often the church thought it was focusing on the gospel by preaching evangelistic messages, but in the process never proclaimed or knew the depth and extent of the gospel. The gospel is not merely about getting to heaven; it is about life now as well as in eternity. It is as much about discipleship as about initial conversion, as much about unity as about individual faith, and as much about new life as about forgiveness. Focusing on the gospel will require the recovery of a full-orbed gospel.

In urging that we value the treasure of revelation, I am not urging focus on a particular theory of revelation. Theories are fine, as long as we do not forget that the revelation is unsearchable and inexhaustible and that our theories are always inadequate. People do not have to use the same words—such as "inerrancy"—to value the treasure. To set up a particular expression as a necessary description canonizes the wrong material and only detracts from the revelation. What people need to know is that the gospel is truth from God (1:13). While some theories are inadequate, several others are legitimate and useful. But our theories must not become substitutes for the revelation itself. We study the revelation, not our theories.

---

48. This word is so debated and abused that often it becomes hardly usable.

The value we place on something determines the hardship we are willing to endure for it. We will expend enormous energy and resources to care for a person or a prized possession we value a great deal. Paul valued the gospel enough to go to prison for it. He asked Timothy not to be ashamed of him, but to suffer for the gospel along with him (2 Tim. 1:8). Do we value the gospel enough to endure hardship for it? Would we go to prison? Most of us will probably not face prison, but are we willing to suffer the hardship of being belittled, of study, of financial investment, and of personal risk? Are we willing to die and rise with Christ in service, to lose life in order to find it?

To value the revelation is also to be responsible for it. The world always seeks to redefine the gospel into something more acceptable, to shift the focus from Christ to a side issue. We have a responsibility to care for it, study it, share it, hand it on to the next generation, protect it from slander and redefinition, and live it. To value the revelation is to know we have something new worth listening to and talking about. No reason exists to be reticent about the good news; a healthy evangelism is a necessary result.

Grace that forces. If grace enlists and empowers, why is passivity so common in the church? Christianity is not a religion of works, but it is still very much a religion of action. A significant application of this text surely has to do with our understanding of the gospel and evangelism. For too long people have heard a message that said, "No action is necessary," and they have been content to be passive. But you cannot be Christian and passive. Ralph Waldo Emerson said, "Only so much do I know, as I have lived."[49] If that is true, much of the church knows nothing. We need a more substantial proclamation of the gospel than is heard in many churches, for grace has been so embarrassingly diluted that "cheap grace" is an overevaluation.

We must present the gospel as a gospel of action, for grace always brings responsibility. The gift cannot be separated from the Giver, and the Giver is a worker. We need a new understanding of grace, though understanding alone is not enough. Somewhere in the mystery of the relation between God and his people the human will remains important. We are responsible for our actions, and we must choose to act. In the gospel we find a new Lord to whom we give ourselves and from whom we take our direction. That involves our will. Grace comes as gift, but it enlists us and empowers us. We become stewards of grace, responsible for showing others how it works. Like all gifts from God, it is directed out to other people. Grace engages us, calls us, pushes us, develops us, and gives us a ministry. Ministry is the gift of God's

---

49. Ralph Waldo Emerson, "The American Scholar," *The Complete Essays and Other Writings of Ralph Waldo Emerson*, ed. Brooks Atkinson (New York: The Modern Library, 1950), 52.

power at work in us for managing grace. The application of this text is obvious: Get to work.

Ministry redefined. Such an understanding of grace leads to a striking redefinition of ministry. Two points should be made. (1) The task of ministry cannot be limited to the professional clergy, the "called." Grace calls *all* of us. No clergy-laity distinction can be tolerated, and responsibility for ministry cannot be left to the clergy. All Christians are to be managers of grace and servants of the gospel, even if some have unique responsibilities.

(2) Implicitly we think of ministry as our gift to God, but Paul thought of ministry as God's gift to him. When we take that seriously, it changes our perspective. Ministry is not drudgery to be endured or something for which God owes us, and it is certainly not a job to be acquired or kept. Rather, ministry originates in and is the expression of God's grace. Ministry is the free flow of grace from God through us to other people.

While this passage concerns all Christians, it is especially applicable to people in professional ministry. Ministers frequently feel so burdened and beaten that they have little awareness that ministry is a gift to them from God. Granted, people in the church often bludgeon them and needlessly make ministry burdensome, but just as certain is the fact that pastors have accepted a redefinition of their role that prevents them from managing grace. What if pastors went back to being stewards of God's grace given them? Churches and search committees often have enormous difficulty deciding what they want pastors to do. Should not the primary question be, "Can this person explain, demonstrate, and dispense grace?"

Once again grace assaults the human ego. All of us know good reasons why we are "less than the least of all God's people" (3:8), but usually such thoughts are misguided or false humility. A sense of grace will not allow us to escape because of past failure or to view ourselves as too small—or too large—for the tasks God assigns. Nor will it allow us to overvalue ourselves or diminish others, for it recognizes God is responsible for all success. In other words, grace gives confidence for life, a confidence based on God himself.

Live the unity. We cannot read this passage without being struck both by the emphasis on the unity of the church and the failure of the modern church in precisely this area. We know division, not unity—a theme that will return with force in chapters 4 and 5. Already we know what is required: We are to live unity. We are not asked to like other Christians, to be like them, or agree with them, but to recognize that we are one with them and share the same Lord and the same benefits. We may not write people off any more than one part of the body can dismiss another part. What this text underscores is that unity is not some nonessential, some afterthought, or some by-product of the faith, but it is at the heart of Christianity. The revelation that came in Christ was a revelation about unity. If we do not proclaim unity, we have not proclaimed the gospel. If we do not live unity, we have missed the gospel's impact.

The attitude we have toward others is foundational. Do our churches exhibit grace and receptivity so that people know they are valued as equals, or do we implicitly communicate arrogance and an attitude of superiority? The application of this text to racial problems is obvious and needed,[50] but other kinds of divisions exist as well. Many people entering a strange church (or even a familiar one) do not feel unity. What do churches communicate that silences unity? Do we convey by language or attitude a spiritual elitism or a cultural tone that creates obstacles for unity? What the church does should express unity, whether in worship, in observance of baptism and the Lord's Supper, or in mission. Differences in culture, race, music style, or traditions will be obvious, but what should be more obvious is the unity that exists in Christ. Groups may form around various interests or styles, but undergirding the groups must be a genuine unity drawn from a common commitment to Christ.

Unity is not the goal; it is a necessary by-product. Nor does unity come without definition. This is a unity based on Christ, but not so narrowly defined that other Christians of a different stripe are rejected. Reasons for separation do exist, and the definition of the gospel is at the heart of such reasons. Lamentably, however, for generations the church has been more concerned about division than unity. In most cases, divisions today occur over personalities, egos, and culture rather than doctrine. We need to redefine the church in terms of unity.

We live in a day when people go to church to see what they can get. Even worship is a self-serving activity. Christians should be trained to express their unity as part of their worship. Despite the problems, we are willingly and publicly to align ourselves with those who confess Christ. By our presence together we *protest* the divisions that exist. Christian unity demonstrates the wisdom of God's purposes, and the exercise of unity is part of our worship.

Attention to unity is first and foremost the responsibility of leaders of Christian groups. They are the ones who set the tone, make the explanations, and model what the group is to be. Unfortunately, leaders are too often either inept or misguided by their own understanding of power to be effective. All of our institutions have histories of leaders who have created division and discord. Each time it happens people are hurt and become cynical, and the institution is less effective. Christian unity should be a guiding force

---

50. See pp. 140–41, 144–45, 150–51.

in the shaping of institutions, hiring, training, and determining management styles. The world is waiting for Christians to begin to model what we say.

A corollary of the focus on unity is greater realization that *conversion is sociological*. It is always conversion into a group of people. This should change our outlook in two ways. (1) The implications for the way we do evangelism are enormous, for individuals and churches must be more aware that they either mirror Christ or distort the image and that they make it easy or difficult for people to come to Christ. Why would anyone want to come to a church marked by division? (2) We must take seriously that we are made one body with others in Christ. Christianity is a communal religion. It emphasizes *koinonia*, a joint sharing. An individual faith focused on "me and Jesus" cannot do that. Such individualistic approaches are nothing but another form of narcissism.

The church versus the church. Life often consists of the effort to make the ideal real. The picture of the church in Ephesians presents an ideal, but Paul was not an idealistic dreamer. He knew well the failures of his churches. But he never wearied of presenting the ideal to his readers. For Paul the ideal he described *was* the real. It was what God had established. We have been raised with Christ and made one. The divisions that exist are a distortion.

The church described in 3:1–13 is strikingly unlike the church we know. In our society the church is increasingly viewed as irrelevant, trivial, and ineffective. It is populated by a divided people who do not deal with the real problems of life. Many Christians either do not know the ideal or have given up attaining it. Others have been driven from the church by boredom or the lack of grace and unity. Is this the only church there is or does another one exist?

The churches Paul wrote were in most cases small house churches, insignificant groups by anyone's estimation. Yet he spoke of their multinational character and cosmic effect. Like other Jews, he thought creation was to reflect the unity of the Creator, and the community of the Messiah was to inaugurate an eschatological unity.[51] He saw them as "functional outposts of God's kingdom,"[52] as prototypes of God's end-time community, and as a witness to the powers. For most of us, the church is a place that puts on services. Somehow we must move beyond this and recover a sense of the importance of the church as the place where the purposes of God are embodied and the unity God seeks is practiced.

Live with confidence. Life is difficult. Suffering, evil, and death surround us. Discouragement and a sense of being beaten down frequently characterize

---

51. See Hanson, *The Unity of the Church in the New Testament*.
52. Lincoln, *Ephesians*, 364.

the way we feel. If we do not fall into denial, cynicism and withdrawal are the usual results. Yet this text suggests we should live confidently. Is it possible to be realistic and live confidently?

Too often Christians learn about confidence in Christ and attempt a spirituality of confidence as if to convince themselves. The effort usually fails, and the complaint comes:

> Now here you are with your faith
> And your Peter Pan advice
> You have no scars on your face
> And you cannot handle
> Pressure.[53]

Denial of the difficulties is not the solution. Paul knew the difficulties and was still confident. He looked clear-eyed into difficulty and knew it was not ultimate. No matter what the circumstances, Christ was still the one who determined who he was. Such conviction brings a "settledness" for dealing with any difficulty.

Hardship comes to all of us. Some hardship we choose in identification with the cross; some we do not choose, but cannot avoid. We go through hardship, but not alone. Discouragement can come, but it does not find a home. Christians enjoy access to God and are at home enough before God to be confident. Awareness of God and his gospel gives us optimism. We know that God is at work, even when undetected, that God's future triumph is already determined, and that no matter how bad circumstances are, we can only fall so far, for God is there to support us (cf. Rom. 8:35–39). Christians even *own* death and difficulty as part of belonging to God (1 Cor. 3:22–23). External circumstances are not then a cause for depression. Whatever happens and wherever we are, we are there with and for Christ, enjoying God's grace. That is our identity.

Are these just high-sounding words? What do we do when discouragement does come? Lament, and even protest, are legitimate responses, as the prophets and psalmists show. But they also show the reverence and humility by which lament is made and that the lament always ends in trust and worship. The key to discouragement is always in turning to God and his purposes.

Ephesians is optimistic and encouraging. The biggest threat of discouragement comes to readers of Ephesians in seeing how far modern churches are from what the author describes. Is it possible to be what Ephesians describes? Paul would say that it is already true; live it.

---

53. The words are from Billy Joel's song "Pressure."

Three wrong turns. Three errors need to be avoided in seeking to apply the comments about boldness. (1) Boldness to approach God should not be mistaken for presumption before God. Boldness and reverence, even a proper fear of God, go hand in hand. This is a boldness of belonging and access, of freedom before God; it is not an overconfidence about knowing God and his will or of praying presumptuously as if God is at our command.

(2) Confidence is not arrogance and should not communicate to others any thought of superiority. Boldness and humility also go hand in hand.

(3) Confidence should not be considered a path to passivity, as if nothing is left to do. An extreme example of misunderstood confidence occurred when a man got his truck stuck in the snow and after nine weeks starved to death because he thought God would take care of him. He could have walked a few miles to dry pavement and safety. This was not confidence, but lack of wisdom. Confidence enables work; it does not render us passive.

Live the paradox. In connection with this passage Barth describes Christian living as a paradoxical existence.[54] Paul was a prisoner, but was seated with Christ in the heavenly realms. He was less than the least, but a recipient of revelation. He found glory in suffering and knew both the now and the not yet. He emphasized both new creation and the eternal purpose of God who created all things. He knew what it meant to lose life in order to find it. The Christian life is a life of tension—creative, peaceful tension[55]— and of balance and depth.

Ephesians 3:1–13 is a rich text that will not allow simplistic answers to the faith. To live in Christ is to enter the complexity to which this text points, or as Paul might put it, the *fullness* found in Christ. Texts like this push us beyond the simplistic answers often disseminated in the name of Christianity. They also call us to risk life in the depth of grace. Go for it!

---

54. Barth, *Ephesians*, 1:357.
55. See C. F. D. Moule, "The New Life' in Colossians 3:1–17," *RevEx*, 70 (1973), 481– 493, especially 481–82.

Ephesians 3:14–21

FOR THIS REASON I kneel before the Father, [15]from whom his whole family in heaven and on earth derives its name. [16]I pray that out of his glorious riches he may strengthen you with power through his Spirit in your inner being, [17]so that Christ may dwell in your hearts through faith. And I pray that you, being rooted and established in love, [18]may have power, together with all the saints, to grasp how wide and long and high and deep is the love of Christ, [19]and to know this love that surpasses knowledge—that you may be filled to the measure of all the fullness of God.

[20]Now to him who is able to do immeasurably more than all we ask or imagine, according to his power that is at work within us, [21]to him be glory in the church and in Christ Jesus throughout all generations, for ever and ever! Amen.

THIS SECTION RESUMES the thought begun at 3:1, interrupted by the digression in verses 2–13. *If Paul had stopped praying after 1:23, he now reverts to the mode of prayer* to explain to his readers his desire for them. "For this reason" (v. 14) points back to the salvation and privileges described in chapter 2. Both in terms of content and structure, similarities exist between this prayer and the one in 1:15–23.[1] Connections also exist with the beginning doxology by a focus on love (1:4), glory (1:6, 12, 14), and the Spirit (1:13–14). Prominence is given to words for power, knowledge, the interior life, and fullness. Once again this passage is strongly theocentric and Trinitarian.[2]

Structure. The prayer falls into three clearly discernible parts, the introduction to the prayer (vv. 14–15), the description of the prayer (vv. 16–19), and the doxology (vv. 20–21). The Greek text of verses 14–19 consists of one long sentence, which the NIV has made into two sentences by dividing in the middle of verse 17. This division presupposes—rightly—a decision to take *"being rooted* and *established* in love" with what follows rather than as an independent unit. These participles are in the nominative case and modify "you"

---

1. See p. 70.
2. Note the parallels with Colossians 2:6–10.

in the next clause, since nothing precedes that they can modify.[3] The prayer is artistically and symmetrically arranged with "that" (*hina*) clauses and infinitives both before and after the participles "being rooted and established in love," which stand at the center of the prayer. Note how the passage unfolds:

> I kneel before the Father ... (v. 14)
>> that [*hina*] he might give you power to be strengthened[4]
>>> [infinitive] ... (v. 16)
>>>> so that Christ may dwell [infinitive taken as result] in your
>>>> hearts ... (v. 17)
>>>>> rooted and established in love [participles]
>>>>>> that [*hina*] you may have power ... "[5]
>>>>>>> to grasp [infinitive] ... (v. 18)
>>>>>>> and to know [infinitive] ... (v. 19a)
>>>>>>>> that [*hina*] you may be filled ... (v. 19b).

While we could understand the three "that" (*hina*) clauses as parallel, so that Paul prays for three things (the Spirit's power, Christ's indwelling, and fullness),[6] more likely Paul prayed for only one thing, the empowering of the Spirit. All else in the prayer explains the meaning and result of that empowering.

Father of All (3:14–15)

THE POSTURE OF kneeling in prayer is one of several postures described in the Bible.[7] In addition to showing reverence and the readiness to obey, it may show heightened feeling and intent, which certainly fits with the wording of this prayer.[8] Paul possibly alludes to Isaiah 45:23 ("Before me every knee will bow").[9] If so, what will be true of all in the eschaton is already taking place with Christians.

---

3. The only alternatives are to take these participles as nominative absolutes, which is unlikely, or as imperatives, which Barth does (see *Ephesians*, 1:371–72). Taking them with what follows shows also that verses 18–19 are part of the prayer rather than an explanation of the results. It is unusual for elements of a *hina* ("that") clause to precede *hina*, but see John 13:29; Acts 19:4; 2 Corinthians 2:4; Galatians 2:10.

4. NIV, "I pray ... he may strengthen you with power ... "

5. NIV, "have power," but a different word is used here than is used in verse 16.

6. Or possibly only the first two.

7. Standing for prayer appears to have been more common. For this and other postures, see Matthew 26:39; Luke 10:13; 18:11, 13; 1 Timothy 2:8.

8. See Robinson, *St. Paul's Letter to the Ephesians*, 82–83.

9. Ibid., 83. The word for "kneel" (*kampto*) occurs elsewhere in the New Testament only at Romans 11:4; 14:11; Philippians 2:10, the first quoting 1 Kings 19:18 and the other two quoting or alluding to Isaiah 45:23.

Paul again emphasizes God as Father. He refers to God as Father forty-two times in his letters, of which eight are in Ephesians.[10] No other description of God is used so frequently in the New Testament. No doubt this goes back to Jesus' teaching his disciples to address God as *Abba*, the Aramaic word for "father" used by both children and adults but considered by Jews to be too familiar to use without qualification in relation to God.[11] God is the Father of believers, but both a narrower and a broader use of "Father" also occurs. More narrowly God is viewed as the Father of our Lord Jesus Christ, which marks out the uniqueness of Jesus' relation to the Father.[12] In 3:15 (and 4:6) the broader sense occurs: God as the Father of all humanity.[13] The emphasis in Ephesians on a cosmic Christ and a cosmic role for the church is based in an understanding of God as a cosmic Father. The anticipation that all things will be brought together in Christ (1:10) presupposes that God is the Father of all.

English translations cannot easily show the wordplay between "Father" (*pater*) and "family" (*patria*). The NIV "his whole family" is more commonly rendered "every family" (NASB, NRSV), which appears to be the better translation (the NIV also adds "his").[14] Several alternatives exist for understanding "every family in heaven and on earth," but most likely it is an attempt to be as inclusive as possible to emphasize the cosmic scope of God's reign and purposes. Paul saw the divisions among the human race as existing under the one God. The implication for the unity the letter seeks is obvious.[15]

Prayer for Power to Know Christ and his Love (3:16–19)

THE MAIN INTENT of Paul's prayer is clear: He wants his readers strengthened by God's Spirit so that they may know intimately Christ's presence and love.

---

10. See 1:2, 3, 17; 2:18; 3:14; 4:6; 5:20; 6:23.

11. See Mark 14:36; Romans 8:15; Galatians 4:6; cf. John 5:18. See the classic treatment of this expression by J. Jeremias in *The Prayers of Jesus* (Naperville, Ill.: Allenson, 1967). Jews did refer to God as "Father," but usually with a qualifying genitive such as "Father of lights" or "Father of mercy."

12. See Romans 15:6; 2 Corinthians 1:3; 11:31; Ephesians 1:3; Colossians 1:3.

13. See also 1 Corinthians 8:6. Both this verse and Ephesians 4:6 draw on the *Shema* (Deut. 6:4), the primary confession of the Old Testament and Judaism that only one God exists.

14. The NIV translates *pasa patria* as "whole family," similar to the way *pasa oikodome* was understood as "the whole building" in 2:21. The normal way to understand this construction is with the word "every" (cf. "every spiritual blessing" in 1:3), but clearly one building is in view in 2:21.

15. *Patria* occurs elsewhere in the New Testament only at Luke 2:4 (NIV, "line") and Acts 3:25 (NIV, "peoples"), the latter in a quotation of the promise to Abraham that through his offspring "all nations on earth will be blessed" (Gen. 22:18). Allusion to the Genesis promise is likely for Ephesians as well.

If this happens, all else will fall in place. The ethic of chapters 4–6 has its foundation in this prayer.

This prayer and its doxology (3:20–21) are connected by the words "power" and "glory." Paul's prayer (v. 16) is for God to give *power* from his *wealth of glory* (NIV, "glorious riches"), and his doxology is about the One who has *power* to give more than we ask or think and to whom *glory* belongs (v. 20).

"Power" and "Spirit" are so commonly associated in both Testaments that they are virtually synonymous. The Spirit is the power of God at work in people.[16] Paul prays for his readers that the Spirit will be so strong an influence at the controlling center of their being that their lives will show it. "Your inner being" (v. 16) is not the same as the "new being" in 2:15 or 4:24. This is an unusual expression, occurring elsewhere only at Romans 7:22 and 2 Corinthians 4:16. The former might well be paraphrased "in the depths of my being," while the latter contrasts "outer being" and "inner being." The expression is synonymous with "heart," the controlling center from which life is comprehended and choices are made.[17]

Although the NIV begins verse 17 with "so that," the indwelling of Christ does not result from the Spirit's strengthening; it is the *manner in which* the Spirit strengthens. In other words, verse 17 explains verse 16. Christ indwells us through the work of the Spirit. The Spirit's empowering or indwelling and the indwelling of Christ are not separate things.[18] In 2:20–22, the church was called "a dwelling in which God lives by his Spirit." This lofty description of the church is now paralleled by an equally lofty description of the individual believer, who has experienced salvation and transformation. By the Spirit's work Christ takes up residence in the person. Paul prays here that Christ will permeate one's whole being. It is the equivalent of the command in 5:18 to be continually filled with the Spirit.

We know Paul preferred to speak of our being in Christ rather than of Christ being in us. Ephesians 3:17 is one of only five Pauline texts that speak of Christ being in us (the others are Rom. 8:10; 2 Cor. 13:5; Gal. 2:20; 4:19).[19] Of these Galatians 4:19 is closest to Ephesians 3:17: Like a woman in childbirth Paul endured labor pains until Christ was formed in them.

---

16. In 1:13–14 Paul emphasized that all believers are sealed with the Holy Spirit as a mark of their salvation and future hope. In 1:17–19 he prayed that the Spirit would make known how great God's power is.

17. Cf. Romans 5:5; 8:9–11; 2 Corinthians 1:22; Galatians 4:6; Ephesians 1:17–18. The attempt by Barth (*Ephesians*, 1:392) to understand "the inner man" as Christ is misguided.

18. Note that the Spirit can be called the Spirit of God or the Spirit of Christ (e.g., Rom. 8:9).

19. See comments above, pp. 56–57.

The NIV's "established" hides the similarity of this text to two others. If translated more literally as "rooted and founded," we note its closeness to both 2:20–22 and to Colossians 2:6–7. In the latter verse Paul instructs Christians to live in Christ, being rooted in him, built on him, and strengthened[20] in faith. Here in 3:17 he prays that the readers will be strengthened with Christ, who indwells them through faith, and that by being rooted and established in love, they will come to know love. The mixing of botanical and architectural images is not unusual.

"In love" in 3:17 could be taken with Christ's indwelling, but the NIV is correct to take it with "rooted and established." God's love is the wellspring from which believers are nourished and the foundation on which they find stability. Being rooted and established in love enables them to perceive love, and from knowing love they are filled with the fullness of God. Love is both the source and the goal. When Christ permeates people, they know they are rooted in his love. From the experience of love they know love and are transformed.[21]

Of the five words summarizing the Christian faith,[22] "faith" and "love" are explicit here, but grace is implied in verse 16 and "truth" and "hope" in verse 19. Love plays a central role in describing the believer's experience with Christ (cf. 1 Cor. 13:13).

Two different words for strengthening appear in 3:16 and 18 (NIV, "have power"). The Spirit strengthens by the indwelling Christ, who enables perception. Just as love is both the source and the goal, Christ is the goal (v. 17) and the source of the power of God at work in us (v. 19). Paul's concern for unity returns with the mention of "all the saints" (v. 18). While the text is about individuals knowing, it is not about individualistic knowing. At every turn Christianity is a corporate religion, and only as people comprehend together can they experience what God has for them.

How the four dimensions "wide," "long," "high," and "deep" (3:18) should be understood is more problematic than the NIV suggests. The Greek text does not have "is the love of Christ," but merely "... grasp with all God's people what is the width, breadth, height, and depth." Most commentators supply as an object "the love of Christ," though some suggest other options such as "the wisdom of God," "the fullness," or "God's purpose."[23] But since

---

20. A different word for "strengthen" than the one used in Ephesians.

21. Note also Romans 5:5, where the Spirit pours the love of God into our hearts.

22. See p. 59.

23. Schnackenburg, *Ephesians: A Commentary*, 152, suggests "wisdom"; Bruce, *The Epistle to the Ephesians*, 68, suggests "fullness"; Robinson, *St. Paul's Epistle to the Ephesians*, 176, suggests "God's purpose." C. Arnold, *Ephesians: Power and Magic*, 91–93, argues that no object is needed since the dimensions are an expression in the ancient world for supernatural power. Accordingly, he interprets the goal as comprehension of God's power.

verse 19 is essentially an explanation of verse 18, the goal is more likely that they will comprehend Christ's love.

The first half of 3:19 is a good example of an oxymoron (a combination of words that appears contradictory): Paul prays that they may know the love that is beyond knowing. This is language from someone who has been surprised and overwhelmed with Christ's love.

Love brings movement; it causes things. To know Christ's love is to be transformed by love and expanded into the fullness of God. The expression "all the fullness" occurs elsewhere only at Colossians 1:19 and 2:9, both indicating that all that God is dwells in Christ. We saw in connection with 1:23 that "the fullness of God" refers to the way God makes his presence and power felt.[24] In experiencing Christ Christians experience the fullness of God, his presence, and power. In experiencing that fullness they themselves are made full by Christ. That is, they partake of God's own being and are made like him. This is an ongoing process. The thought of Colossians 2:9–10 is parallel: God's fullness dwells in Christ and in him Christians are made full. The implication in Ephesians is that as believers encounter God's love in Christ, they will be filled with love. This same thought is put in the form of an imperative in 5:1–2.

The Doxology (3:20–21)

THE DOXOLOGY BRINGS the first half of Ephesians to a close at the place it began in 1:3, in giving praise to God. Doxologies in the form "glory to God" are frequent in the New Testament, though most are much briefer.[25] The use of "glory" in Ephesians and throughout the New Testament is fascinating. God is a God of glory (1:17; Acts 7:2), and his glory reveals who he is (John 1:14; Rom. 6:4; Heb. 1:3). God gives glory to Christ (John 17:22; Acts 3:13; 1 Cor. 2:8; 1 Peter 1:21) and people (Rom. 2:10; 8:30; 1 Cor. 2:7). Christians are transformed from glory to glory (2 Cor. 3:18). People are to do everything for God's glory (1 Cor. 10:31) and are to give glory back to God (Eph. 1:6; Phil. 1:11). In the eschaton further glory will be revealed (Rom. 8:18). "Glory" is a word that virtually encompasses the whole of Christianity. Here the focus is on the praise and honor that should be given God for his saving work.

---

24. See pp. 79–81.

25. Romans 16:25–27 and Jude 24–25 also begin "To him who is able" and are similar in length. All three doxologies begin identically in Greek (for other doxologies, see Luke 2:14; Rom. 11:36; 16:27; Gal. 1:5; Phil. 4:20; 1 Tim. 1:17; 2 Tim. 4:18; Heb. 13:21; 1 Peter 4:11; 2 Peter 3:18; Rev. 1:6; 5:13; 7:12; cf. also Luke 17:18; John 9:24; Acts 12:23; Rom. 4:20; Rev. 16:9).

This doxology is striking in its assertion that glory is given to God "in the church and in Christ Jesus throughout all generations, for ever and ever." No other passage mentions the church explicitly in a doxology, although other doxologies imply it because Christians are the ones giving the praise. To suggest that the church and Christ are accorded equal status is presumptuous. The passage only assumes an unending relation between God, his people, and Christ. The presence of the people with God, made possible by Christ, will be a cause for eternal praise. This is what Paul had in mind in 1:18 with the expression "the riches of his glorious inheritance in the saints" (see also 2:7).

In verse 19 the love of Christ is beyond understanding, and in verse 20 the activity of God is beyond expectation or thought. The heightened language throughout the prayer shows the depth of Paul's emotion. A wordplay occurs in the Greek text of verse 20 between "to him who is able" (*to dynameno*) and "power" (*dynamis*). Note the preponderance of words for God's activity, a theme that has marked the letter from 1:1.

This doxology sums up the intent of the first half of the letter. We should praise God for his astounding work in Christ Jesus. Paul's point is not merely that God is able to do beyond what we expect. Rather, this power is already at work in us (cf. the similar language in Col. 1:29, which describes God's work in Paul's ministry). God does not fit the limitations of our expectations. The language is reminiscent of Isaiah 55:8–9: God's ways and thoughts are exceedingly beyond our ways and thoughts. God is at work and eager to work in us to achieve his purposes for salvation.

Bridging Contexts

THIS PRAYER IS as appropriate to pray today as it was two thousand years ago, and its theological ideas are directly are applicable for our lives. The most difficult part in this process takes place on an emotional level. Paul's emotions soar and lead him to spiritual heights in worship. How can these emotions be transferred so that we feel the same impact for our own worship? Emotions come out of deep convictions and personal involvement. Unless the theology takes deep root, the emotions— while they can be faked—cannot be authentically reproduced.

Still praying. It seems obvious that this passage asks us, like Paul, to pray and praise. A theology with any conviction should drive us to prayer and worship. Theology is not for grand ideas and academics, but for expressing our relation with God. It is not merely talk about God, it is addressed to God. "Worship is an act of inner agreement with God."[26] Prayer is "the

---

26. Abraham Joshua Heschel, *Quest for God: Studies in Prayer and Symbolism* (New York: Crossroad, 1990), 18.

contemplation of the facts of life from the highest point of view. It is the solil-
oquy of a beholding and jubilant soul. It is the Spirit of God pronouncing his
works good."[27] This is what Paul does in 3:14–21. The highest point of view
is the realization of what God has done in Christ. In anticipation of the day
when every knee will bow to him, we do it now.

Ephesians as a whole is a lesson in worship. Like 1:3–23 the prayer and
doxology here are descriptive and theological in character, concerned more
with God than individual need. They are rooted in the character of God,
focused on Christ, and pointed toward eternity. They are wholistic rather
than myopic. In such prayers, the comments about God increase understanding and commitment. They draw us nearer to God and make us more
receptive to him.

The doxology invites us to meditate on God, the One who is much more
powerful than we anticipate. This is not an invitation to think up self-centered grocery lists of tasks for God to do. Rather, it is a call to realize God's
unanticipated power to effect change in us, in keeping with the power already
working in us.

God our Father. Once again we find a worldview in which God is at
work, a worldview that clashes with our normal expectations. The God of
Ephesians is involved in the lives of his people. The central message of the
Bible is that God lives with us. This message is present throughout the *whole*
Old Testament, from the Garden of Eden to the tabernacle, the temple, and
the destruction and rebuilding of the temple. The presence of God is heightened in the New Testament—a message that goes from the name "Immanuel"
at Jesus' birth (Matt. 1:23) to the promise of his presence until the end of the
age (28:20). In John's Gospel and letters believers *remain* with God and Christ,
and God and Christ with them (e.g., John 15:4–7). In Acts humans live,
move, and have their being in God (Acts 17:28). Paul's "in Christ" language
also underscores a theology of the presence of God. We need this theology
to motivate our Christian lives.

The focus on God as Father requires attention. We noted above three
ways this imagery is used: a narrower sense limited to Christ, the customary
sense in reference to believers, and in a few texts like 3:14–15 of all people.
We would do well to think of these as concentric circles, with Christ being
at the center, then believers, and then all humanity.

---

27. Ralph Waldo Emerson, "Self-Reliance," *The Complete Essays and Other Writings of Ralph
Waldo Emerson*, ed. Brooks Atkinson (New York: Random House, 1950), 162–63. Emerson
did not capitalize "spirit," and much of his emphasis on self-reliance is an overstatement.
Compare Heschel, *Quest for God*, 5: "To pray is to take notice of the wonder. . . . Prayer is our humble *answer* to the inconceivable surprise of living" (italics his).

For some people the image of God as Father is problematic. The inadequacy of human fathers often makes the image an obstacle rather than a help. Several commentators argue that God as Father is the archetypal image from which all fatherhood is defined—that the image is not applied to God from human experience, but to humans from God.[28] This argument has validity, but it is of little help to those who have experienced the failure of human fathers in destructive ways. The church must assist such people to recover what it means to call God "Father."

More problematic theologically is the use of such a patriarchal image to describe God. Modern feminist concerns work to redefine God or use matriarchal images in worship. The issue here is not the use of inclusive language on the horizontal level; we should make every effort to include all persons in worship and teaching. The problem arises over whether "Father" should be changed to a neutral term like "Creator" and whether God can be addressed as "Mother." This question is not unrelated to the first issue of the inadequacy of human fathers, for often women recoil against masculine language precisely because of the abuse done to them by men.

These questions are not easy, partly because of the conventions of the English language and partly because of the metaphorical character of all language. No adequate treatment can be given here,[29] but several comments are in order:

(1) The use of the title "Father" has nothing to do with maleness. God is not a man, and gender does not provide an appropriate description of God. The title "Father" has to do with origin, love, security, and care.

(2) While all language is metaphorical, matriarchal images for God in the Bible are rare and, when they do occur, are similes (using "like" or "as"), which seems to place them in a different category from the use of "Father" as a specific title.

(3) Although practice may be changing quickly, in English masculine language has the potential to be generic, but feminine language is specifically feminine.

(4) The use of *Abba* and the frequent use of "Father" by Jesus and throughout the New Testament (and the church's history) makes the term too

---

28. E.g., Robinson, *St. Paul's Epistle to the Ephesians*, 84.

29. Among numerous works on this subject, see Elizabeth Achtemeier, "Female Language for God: Should the Church Adopt it?" *The Hermeneutical Quest*, ed. Donald G. Miller (Allison Park, Pa.: Pickwick, 1986), 97–114; Roland M. Frye, "Language for God and Feminist Language: Problems and Principles," *SJT*, 41 (1989), 441–69; Paul K. Jewett, *The Ordination of Women: An Essay on the Office of Christian Ministry* (Grand Rapids: Eerdmans, 1980), 119–41.

important to cast aside. The relational aspects of "Father," "Son," and "Holy Spirit" are too important to be replaced by "Creator," "Redeemer," and "Sustainer."

(5) Use of feminine language for God is particularly open to abuse because of associations with birthing and nature, as is evidenced in ancient fertility cults, certain Gnostic sects, and in modern neopaganism associated with the new age movement. However, even biblical terms like "Father" can be abused and twisted away from their intent. Application of this title will need to be sensitive both to people and to the range of theological problems.

That God is the Father from whom every family is named means partly that we all have the same origin and value. We belong to a larger human family, all members of which, as the first part of their definition, owe their allegiance to God. We all belong to each other. The built-in arrogance of every race, nationality, and clan has no ultimate basis. In 2:11–22 racism was obliterated through the work of Christ. In 3:14–15 we are shown that racism never had any basis in the first place.

A life at work. This prayer assumes that the Christian life is not automatic. Life from God comes as a gift, but it is not magic. It is a life of engagement with God's Spirit, who makes Christ and his purposes known. Life is relational, and relations require time and investment. God intended from the first for humans to live in relation to him. With God's Spirit taking up residence in us, that intent is realized.

Paul's prayer does not spell out how the Spirit's work occurs. Clearly with regard to daily living, the Spirit comes as gift, just as initial conversion is a gift. Nothing we do can cause God's Spirit to merge with our spirit (cf. Gal. 3:2–3). But the implication that we do nothing is a colossal error. The Spirit will not empower unwilling, inattentive spirits.

Paul's prayer indicates God's people should be aware of the need for the Spirit, attentive to God's purposes and leading, at work on the interior life, and ready to be obedient. The entire letter—both the theological descriptions in the first three chapters and the ethical instruction in the last three chapters—assumes that instruction, understanding, decisions, and effort are all required for people to enjoy the work of the Spirit. The doxology in 3:20 emphasizes that God is at work in us, but implies that we need to be more aware and more expectant of his work. Ephesians 5:18 instructs us to be continually filled with the Spirit. We are responsible and active in this process. Passivity does not fit with Christian faith.

A problem. Paul prays for power and strength for his readers and asserts that God is both able and at work in them. This is a lofty goal and description. But if this is so, if the Spirit is supposed to empower Christians, why don't we experience this power more? Why are the church and its people so ineffective? This is a problem we must face, but only two answers can be given:

(1) The theology is wrong; it sounds nice, but God is neither able nor at work.

(2) The theology is right, but we abort the process.

In answer, the problem is with us, not with God. The Spirit of Christ does not work in us without our willingness, nor does he move us to the desired goal overnight. He lives with us, and this life is a growth process. We are finite, limited, and prone to failure. The real problem is that we do not *care* enough. We do not have the necessary discontent within ourselves that will lead to change.[30] We like the privileges without the bother. But nothing in this life happens that way. What the Spirit seeks is the willingness to hear. Faith does come by hearing.

The centrality of love. That love is structurally central in the prayer is no accident. To experience Christ is to encounter his love and to be put on a path of understanding love. Now we see how the hostility mentioned in 2:14, 16 was killed. The love of Christ destroyed both the hostility between humanity and God and that between various groups of human beings. The love of Christ is shorthand for the love of God experienced in Christ.

With good reason love is one of the five words summarizing the Christian faith.[31] In fact, the whole of Christianity is caught up in the words "truth" and "love," and as we will see, these two words dominate the second half of the letter. As both source and goal, love will define and regulate all Christian action. Therefore, love ought also to be central in our lives.

MOST OF THE application of this text flows easily from the comments in the previous two sections. Action is now required.

Learn to worship. This text requires us to place a priority on prayer and worship. We do not do either particularly well. To some degree the church of our day has forgotten how to worship. We find ourselves unhappy with traditions and older forms and unsatisfied with the superficiality of new music and practices. In too many cases the congregation become spectators. Churches should be much more intentional in learning about prayer and worship. Meaningful worship does not

---

30. St. Theresa of Lysieux said, "If you are willing to serenely bear the trial of being displeasing to yourself, then you will be for Jesus a pleasant place of shelter" (quoted by Scott Peck in *People of the Lie* [New York: Simon and Schuster, 1983], 11).

31. Along with grace, truth, faith, and hope; see p. 59.

merely happen; it results from attention, thought, and effort. More is required than worship planning. We need worship education and authentic worship experience. We need a worship that involves people, rather than one that asks them to watch. This rediscovery of worship presupposes a mature spirituality that can do the job. Ephesians provides both the theological resources and the models to begin the task.

God as Father. The fatherhood of God is the foundation that determines our responsibility to other people. We cannot ignore the needs of others if we share a common origin in God and a common value before him. We live in a world bloated with suffering and poverty. We cannot fix the problems of the world, and providing help to people is not easy. But the fatherhood of God requires us to care and get involved, to speak and act to help out.

In addition, the fatherhood of God will not allow us to draw a circle around Christians as the limits of our responsibility. We enjoy an unparalleled unity with those in Christ, but a broader unity with all human beings exists as well. We may not ignore non-Christians or relate to them by some lower standard. We are human first and then Christian, made authentically human by being Christian. Many things exist that are human and not Christian, but nothing is Christian that is not also human. We must do justice to our humanity in order to do justice to our Christianity.

In that vein the issue of racism must again be confronted. Two fatal blows to racism are encountered in Ephesians: (1) Christ's death, which destroys hostility and creates oneness;[32] (2) the fact that God is Father of us all. Racism is an enemy against which the church must speak and act. Not only is racism an attack on other groups, it is also an attack on God, for the people being disparaged are his people, people he created and about whom he cares.

But not God as male. As indicated above, I would insist on the importance of calling God "Father." At the same time the church should go out of its way to remind people that God is not male, something it has neglected to do. We do not need to compound the language problem by sloppiness in communication. Occasionally we should introduce prayers with words such as "You who are neither male nor female." Occasional use of biblical *similes* that use feminine imagery (e. g., Isa. 66:13) will help. Great sensitivity needs to be exercised in *caring* for people with appropriate language about God, avoiding both the error of bashing people with patriarchal imagery and the error of reimaging the faith. Both errors are idolatrous and in effect attempt to create God in our own sexual image. Our primary concern must be communication that will connect the biblical God to a hurting world. Language creates a world, a perception of reality, within which we live, and the world

---

32. See pp. 129–36.

we create should both honor God and extend grace to all those around us.

Permeated with Christ. The imagery of the text also challenges our conceptions about faith. Rather than a small Jesus tucked away somewhere in our souls, the text assumes the presence of one who gives shape and strength at the core of our being, who takes up residence in and redefines us. Nothing is wrong with the language of *Christ living in us*, even though I have deemphasized its use in favor of the much more frequent Pauline language of *our being in Christ*. Both ideas are powerful, and behind both stands the conviction that Jesus is Lord, the one to whom our lives are given and by whom they are determined.

If we are permeated with Christ, such cherished ideas as independence, self-determination, and self-fulfillment must be abandoned, at least as they are understood in our society. Christ's indwelling means we are not our own (cf. 1 Cor. 6:19–20; Gal. 2:20). W. Wink correctly described worship and prayer as reminders of "who owns the house."[33] Christians are to live as if they know Christ owns the house. Regarding independence, we are independent of everything but Jesus Christ, and on him we are totally dependent. Regarding self-determination, we in our uniqueness are determined by him. Regarding self-fulfillment, we seek to fulfill God's will. This negation of self, however, is in actuality a finding of one's true self in relation to God, for that is the purpose of creation. In losing life, we find it. In trying to keep it for ourselves, we lose it. True freedom and true self-actualization are found in life with Christ.

This is the language of discipleship. To be permeated by Christ is to be stamped by his character, to be clothed with him (Rom. 13:14). Such imagery underscores the way Christ shapes our lives. The thought that we can believe in Christ without being like him is absurd. If Christ's indwelling does not transform, we must question strenuously whether Christ is present. The application of the text of Ephesians requires us to test the validity of our faith (see 2 Cor. 13:5). Christians worry about the assurance of their salvation, and other Christians seek to remove all doubt. Maybe we should let doubt do its work. Maybe we should be more concerned about the validity of faith than the assurance of salvation. Honest doubt can be healthy.

Contemplation. Paul prays that the Spirit will strengthen our inner being. Philip Spener said, "Our whole Christian religion consists of the inner man or new man, whose soul is faith and whose expressions are the fruits of life."[34] Application of this passage involves contemplation and reflection. Rather

---

33. Walter Wink, *Engaging the Powers*, vol. 3: *The Powers* (Minneapolis: Fortress, 1992), 160.

34. Philip Spener's comment on 3:16, *Pia Desideria*, trans. Theodore G. Tappert (Philadelphia: Fortress, 1964), 116.

than merely chasing after our physical needs and desires, we must attend to our interior lives. Our inner being requires as much care and exercise as our physical bodies.

Moreover, Melanchthon's statement "To know Christ is to know his benefits" is mirrored in this text,[35] but is made more specific. To know Christ is to know *his love*. From knowledge of God's love an ethic of love will be shaped in the following chapters, but human love is not the concern here. We must experience God's love and the wonder and worship that result from it. That love provides the nurture and stability for life, which creates confidence and trust. The words for knowing imply meditation on the wonder of God's love, from which comes praise.

We should also contemplate God's power. The beginning of the doxology (v. 20) is in essence an invitation to consider how great God's power is. Again we see how much Christianity is focused on the mind. Ours is a thinking religion. Its goal is not abstract reasoning or academic pursuits separated from practical doing, but an informed mind that shapes life. The message of Ephesians requires heart, head, and hands. Christians need time for reflection, for remembering, for searching into matters too deep for knowledge. The suggestion not to bother with subjects too grand for comprehension is ill-advised. In being stretched by what is beyond us, we grow. Inquiry after the unknowable God provides the knowledge and wisdom we need for life.

Christians need a regular schedule of reading, thinking, discussing, and praying that informs them about faith and life and helps them grow a soul. Most of us think we are too busy for such time-consuming exercises, but the inner being is not strengthened by osmosis. Our busy schedules are often filled with secondary—if not needless—concerns. Some activities may need to be laid aside, but the contemplative part of faith is not one of them.

Your God Is Too Small. This was the title of a book written years ago by J. B. Phillips, a book that still merits attention.[36] That title could have been drawn from Ephesians 3:20. Surely this is the real problem behind the failure of Christians to understand and live their faith. The problem is theological; our image of God—the idol in our minds—does not merit contemplation, devotion, or obedience. Our God is too remote, disinterested, and inept. In fact, he is too much like us (cf. Ps. 50:21). We neither expect anything from him—unless it is a handout—nor are we engaged with him.

Our view of God can never include all that he is, and his ways and thoughts will always be far above us. But the God of the Bible is not too small. Here is the God we need for life. Our contemplation and learning

---

35. See above p. 82.
36. J. B. Phillips, *Your God Is Too Small* (New York: Macmillan, 1961).

always have one goal, that of the *Shema*—to love the Lord our God with all our heart, our soul, and our strength (Deut. 6:4–5). The goal is not knowledge about God, but knowledge of God, the experiential knowledge that leads to love for God. Such experiential knowledge changes behavior.

This is one reason why Ephesians is so *theocentric*. Paul wants his readers to know how great God is, how magnanimous and loving his acts are, how powerful he is, and what he has accomplished through Christ. If people understand how mighty, loving, and active God is, then true worship and transformation of life follow.

The path to knowledge. As important as study, contemplation, and discussion are, they do not provide the essential ingredient. The Holy Spirit is the key to the knowledge we need. He is the revealer, the one who makes known to us the "deep things of God ... that we may understand what God has freely given us" (1 Cor. 2:10–12). The power of the Spirit is less for great deeds than for great understanding, from which godly living flows. The Spirit's work is not independent of our activity or a substitute for our effort; rather, "the Spirit helps us in our weakness" (Rom. 8:26). He works with us to strengthen our inner being. We do not cause his activity; the point of 3:20 is that the power of the Spirit—the Spirit given to *all* believers—is *already* working in us. What we seek is our spirit being brought into line with God's Spirit's. What is required is the openness to allow God to work, the willingness to hear, and attention given to life with God.

Glory in the church. The exalted ecclesiology of Ephesians has important practical consequences. The church is not an optional part of Christianity. Rather, it is the place now and throughout eternity where God is given honor and glory. Just as Christ is the evidence of God's redeeming love, the church is the evidence of God's transforming and uniting power (cf. 2:7). An exalted ecclesiology is not the same as a glorified and exalted church. God is glorified, not the church, except in being the recipient of God's love. Church history is marred by too many times and places where the church thought it was exalted. Whenever the church felt it had power, it was most in danger. This is still true. The church exists for worship and service and must perform those acts with the same humility as her Lord. Then God is given honor and glory.

In writing this commentary, one of the most difficult tasks has been in dealing with the contrast between what Ephesians describes and the reality I and most Christians experience. So often the church demonstrates more evidence of human depravity than of God's transforming and uniting power. A common problem for Christians is finding a suitable church. So many people become so disillusioned in that search that they retreat to a controllable, privatistic faith.

No quick fix exists for the failure of the church other than the theology of Ephesians and the rest of the New Testament, but two points must be made. (1) Failure to meet with other Christians for worship and instruction is not a legitimate option. Individualistic Christianity does not exist. We need other people to help us understand God. (2) The current failure of the church cannot be tolerated. The church does not have to look like any of our present conceptions, but Christians must develop a better understanding of God, of faith in Christ, and of unity, and then put that understanding into practice. No doubt the biggest obstacle is the human ego, but should that obstacle be so determinative for Christians who gather around an empty cross? Christians in the pews as well as the pulpits need to protest the arrogance, superficiality, and division that mark our churches. We do not have to agree on all points to respect each other, to be driven by God's love, to recover the meaning of faith, to exhibit life in Christ, and to worship God.

God our Father,
    We acknowledge that we and every other person has his or her origin in you.
    We owe you our lives.
    Forgive us for the arrogance of thinking we are better or more important than other people.
    Let your Spirit work in us to strengthen us. We want your Spirit to merge with ours.
    Make the presence of Christ so real that we sense your love and live from your love.
    Help us understand how deep your love is so that it changes us into your very image.
    You who are all powerful beyond anything we can conceive, we praise you. Every accolade of worth we throw at your feet. You alone are God. From your worth all other worth is determined.
    For the gift of life in Christ we and all your people worship you. Together and forever we will sing your praise. Amen.

Ephesians 4:1–16

❧

AS A PRISONER for the Lord, then, I urge you to live a life worthy of the calling you have received. ²Be completely humble and gentle; be patient, bearing with one another in love. ³Make every effort to keep the unity of the Spirit through the bond of peace. ⁴There is one body and one Spirit—just as you were called to one hope when you were called—⁵one Lord, one faith, one baptism; ⁶one God and Father of all, who is over all and through all and in all.

⁷But to each one of us grace has been given as Christ apportioned it. ⁸This is why it says:

"When he ascended on high,
    he led captives in his train
    and gave gifts to men."

⁹(What does "he ascended" mean except that he also descended to the lower, earthly regions? ¹⁰He who descended is the very one who ascended higher than all the heavens, in order to fill the whole universe.) ¹¹It was he who gave some to be apostles, some to be prophets, some to be evangelists, and some to be pastors and teachers, ¹²to prepare God's people for works of service, so that the body of Christ may be built up ¹³until we all reach unity in the faith and in the knowledge of the Son of God and become mature, attaining to the whole measure of the fullness of Christ.

¹⁴Then we will no longer be infants, tossed back and forth by the waves, and blown here and there by every wind of teaching and by the cunning and craftiness of men in their deceitful scheming. ¹⁵Instead, speaking the truth in love, we will in all things grow up into him who is the Head, that is, Christ. ¹⁶From him the whole body, joined and held together by every supporting ligament, grows and builds itself up in love, as each part does its work.

Original Meaning

NO PASSAGE IS more descriptive of the church in action than Ephesians 4:1–16. Verse 1 marks a transition from the prayerful description of God's grace and salvation in the first three chapters to an explanation of the consequences of grace in chapters 4–6. As noted in our discussion of 2:10,[1] Paul's ethical instruction in Ephesians centers largely on the metaphor "walk" (Gk. *peripateo*; NIV, "live"). From 4:1 to at least 5:21 the ethical teaching is structured around this verb. Note the following:

> 4:1: "*walk* worthy of the calling with which you have been called"
> 4:17: "*walk* no longer as the Gentiles *walk*"
> 5:2: "*walk* in love"
> 5:8: "*walk* as children of light"
> 5:15: "Therefore be careful how you *walk*, not as unwise, but as wise"

To a large extent, 4:1–16 provides the framework and specific theological basis for what follows in 4:17–6:20.

We ought not overemphasize the distinction between the theological material in chapters 1–3 and the ethical instruction in chapters 4–6. While the ethical teaching in chapters 1–3 is nearly all implicit, chapters 4–6 contain significant and explicit theological teaching. Note that 4:17–24 is a theological description contrasting two ways of life, much like 2:11–22.

Throughout the New Testament, ethical imperatives are based on theological indicatives. Obedience is always a response to grace. God acts first, and humans respond. Just as *kerygma* (proclamation) and *didache* (instruction) cannot be separated, neither can the indicative and the imperative. Often the two blend together in the same text. The imperative can be a means of preaching the gospel, for ethical statements can contain the whole gospel[2] (cf. 5:1–2). In the passage before us, 4:4–16 provides theological support for the imperative in 4:1–3.

We learn the most about ecclesiology in Paul's ethical material, whether here in Ephesians, in Romans 12–15, or in the Corinthian correspondence. The present passage focuses on life, order, unity, and the purpose of the church, as well as its diversity and difficulties. All five words summarizing Christianity appear here.[3] In other words, ecclesiology and ethics cannot be separated.[4] As we have noted, Christology is soteriology

---

1. See pp. 94, 96, 115.
2. Barth, *Ephesians*, 2:453–57.
3. "Grace," "truth," "faith," "love," and "hope."
4. Barth, *Ephesians*, 2:451.

is ecclesiology is ethics,[5] and this understanding continues throughout the letter.

Prominence is given to "one," "body," "measure," "build up," and "love." The occurrences of "in love" in 4:2 and 16 form an *inclusio*, bracketing the entire section. That is, everything in this ethic is marked by love. As in the earlier sections, liturgical and traditional material supply the substance of much of the language (e.g., 4:4–6, 9–10), and long sentences continue. The NIV provides a paragraph division at 4:14, which hides the fact that 4:11–16 is one sentence in the Greek text.[6]

Structure. This section falls into two major sections: 4:1–6 and 4:7–16. The logic of this passage unfolds as follows:

A. Live your call focused on unity (4:1–6)
 1. Live worthy of your call by keeping the unity of the Spirit (4:1–3)
 2. Unity is motivated by theological oneness (4:4–6)
B. Each person has received grace to build up Christ's body (4:7–16)
 1. Grace has been given to each one (4:7)
 2. Psalm 68:18 is proof (4:8)
 3. Parenthetical comment on the ascension (4:9–10)
 4. People are given as gifts to serve and build up (4:11–16)
  a. Servants build toward maturity, unity, and knowledge of Christ (4:11–13)
  b. A mature and growing faith is evidenced by truth and love (4:14–16)

Live Worthy of Your Call Focused on Unity (4:1–3)

THIS SECTION IS a summary statement, almost a heading, on which the rest of the letter will comment. Only one imperative has appeared prior to this in the letter: "remember" in 2:11. The exhortation in 4:1–3 is specific and practical; but almost as if Paul needed to buttress the ethic more, he returns in 4:4–16 to theological concerns. The next specific, practical imperative will not appear until 4:25.[7]

Similar to 3:1, Paul strengthens his instruction by referring to his imprisonment. Whereas 3:1 had "the prisoner of Christ Jesus," 4:1 has, if translated literally, "the prisoner *in* the Lord."[8] He is in prison in the Lord, and from

---

5. See p. 146.

6. Note the parallels with Colossians 2:19; 3:11–12; note also that "you" is used in 4:1–6, "we" in 4:7–16.

7. Ephesians 4:15 could be taken imperativally, and 4:17 is a general imperative.

8. Given the importance of Paul's theology of being in Christ, the NIV translation "for the Lord" loses the impact of Paul's thought.

this position of honor he makes his ethical challenge. "Lord" occurs twenty-six times in Ephesians, twenty of them in chapters 4—6 (in keeping with Paul's tendency to use "Christ" in texts about salvation and "Lord" in texts about ethics).

With the translation "the calling you have received," the NIV loses the text's double emphasis on election (lit., "the calling with which you were called"). Paul reminds the reader of the description of salvation in chapters 1—3 and especially of the doxology in 1:3–14. If God's love is so great, if his salvation is so powerful, if God has granted such reconciliation, then believers should live accordingly. They should value God's love enough to be shaped by it. Note that "calling" is used of the salvation and responsibility of every Christian, not of the "professional ministry" or an elite group. This one call is for all Christians to live in accord with what God has done.

The English imperatives that follow in 4:2–3 are actually prepositional phrases ("with all humility," etc.) and participles ("bearing ... making every effort"). This is *not* a series of imperatives of equal rank. Even if the phrases in verses 2–3 are understood imperatively, they are subordinate to the one main imperative—"live worthy of the calling you have received." They describe *a life worthy of God's calling, which is marked by humility, gentleness, patience, tolerant love, and peacekeeping*. Attention goes first to the ego and then to loving relations. An understanding of God's work is always an attack on the ego, not to obliterate or humiliate the self, but to bring it into relation with God and to redirect its interests. In losing life we find it.

Humility, not surprisingly, is held up in all Paul's letters as a necessary component of Christian living. Even when the actual word is not used, Paul sought this virtue in his readers.[9] In several other letters he links humility and unity at the precise point he starts drawing ethical conclusions (e.g., Rom. 12:3–8; Phil. 2:1–11; Col. 3:12–15).

The word translated "be completely humble" focuses on one's thinking;[10] it means "lowliness of mind" as opposed to haughtiness (cf. Rom. 12:3; 11:20; 12:16). Thinking low was the attitude of slaves and was considered a negative trait among ancient Greeks, but the Old Testament and Judaism viewed it positively. The best commentary on this attitude is found in Philippians 2:5–8, on the self-emptying mind of Christ.

"Gentleness" (*prautes*), a forgotten virtue, shows up with regularity in Paul's ethical lists, which demonstrates the value he placed on it[11] (cf. Phil. 4:5,

---

9. See Galatians 5:26 and virtually all of 1 Corinthians (esp. 1:29–31; 8:1–3; 13:4).

10. *Tapeinophrosyne*, the word in question, occurs only in Paul's prison letters and always with a positive meaning, except for Colossians 2:18 and 23.

11. Note Galatians 5:23; 6:1; Colossians 3:12; 1 Timothy. 6:11; Titus 3:2.

which uses *epieikes* but is concerned with the same ethic). In 2 Corinthians 10:1 Paul uses both these words for gentleness to describe his own demeanor—a gentleness he says is characteristic of Christ.[12]

"Patience" (*makrothymia*) is also repeatedly present in Paul's lists of virtues. With justification, John Chrysostom explained this word from its etymology as meaning "to have a wide and big soul."[13] Patience is the exercise of a largeness of soul that can endure annoyances and difficulties over a period of time.

The NIV's "bearing with one another in love" sounds archaic and loses the force of the text. A more appropriate translation is "putting up with each other in love." The Christian life is a life of putting up with other people, and this tolerance finds its ability and motivation in love (cf. Gal. 6:2). "Love" and "putting up with each other" are intertwined and mutually explanatory. Both are ways of valuing the other person.

"Love" (*agape*) enjoys the other person, but it does not exist for enjoyment. It is not a feeling or emotion, but an act of the will. It exists only in relation to specific people, and it is always costly. The focus on love is an extension of the emphasis on love in 3:17–19. That is, the love experienced in Christ must be extended to others. The noun *agape* was rarely used outside Jewish sources and the Christian writings. A few secular occurrences are now known, but clearly Christians injected the word with new content to talk about love in relation to God—first love from God, then also love for God and for other people because of God. This love does not have its origin in human motivation; it is a choice made because of the love of God.

The focus on "one another" is significant. This word occurs forty times in Paul's letters. Christians are part of each other and are to receive one another, think about one another, serve one another, love one another, build up one another, bear each other's burdens, submit to each other, and encourage each other. Christianity is a God-directed, Christ-defined, other-oriented religion. Only with such direction away from self do we find ourselves.

Living worthy of the call also requires eagerness "to keep the unity of the Spirit." "Make every effort" (v. 3) translates a word meaning "be zealous or eager." We are asked to value unity, be attentive to it, and invest energy in it so that it is not threatened. "Unity of the Spirit" means the unity the Spirit gives or brings, but a whole complex of ideas stands behind this phrase as parallels and the verses that follow show. The same Spirit works in all Christians, baptizes them into the same Christ, and nurtures and leads them all (see also 1 Cor. 12:13; Phil. 2:1).

---

12. The NIV uses "meekness and gentleness of Christ" in 2 Corinthians 10:1. "Gentleness of Christ" can be understood as "gentleness that comes from Christ" or "a Christ-like gentleness."

13. See Chrysostom's homily on 1 Corinthians 13:4.

It is important to realize that unity is something given by the Spirit, not something we create. It is based in the oneness of God and the oneness of the gospel, which works the same for all people. While the theme of unity occurs often in Paul's letters, the actual word (*henotes*) occurs only here and in 4:13. Comparing 4:3 with 4:13 shows again the now and not-yet character of Christianity: In 4:3 unity is a basis, created by God, from which we start; in 4:13, it is a goal toward which we strive.

"Bond" (*syndesmos*, elsewhere only in Acts 8:23; Col. 2:19; 3:14) is related to *desmos*, which is used of prisoners being bound. "The bond of peace" can mean either "the bond that is peace" or "the bond that peace creates." In either case, we should think of the discussion of peace in 2:14–18. The unity we share in God's Spirit is based on that peacemaking act of Christ, which has created one new being and links Christians together.[14]

Unity Is Motivated by Theological Oneness (4:4–6)

THE CREED IN 4:4–6 may be adapted from a pre-Pauline confession, but it is more likely from a creed used in Paul's churches or one that Paul composed originally for this letter. Its theology is Pauline, especially since no other New Testament writer makes use of the body image.[15] The confession has a threefold triadic structure: (1) body, Spirit, hope; (2) Lord, faith, baptism; (3) one God and Father of all, who is over all, through all, and in all. Again we find material that is both Trinitarian and focused on *theology*.

Christians must maintain the unity of the Spirit because everything they hold of any significance they hold with other people. Seven items are preceded by the word "one," and in each case the oneness expresses both the uniqueness of the item and its foundational value for unity. All seven express the reality that there is only one gospel and that to believe that gospel is to enter into the unity it creates. Christianity is a shared faith. No separate or merely individual faith exists, nor is there a different salvation.

Not only does this section relate back to 2:14–18, but to 2:21–22 and 3:6 as well. There are not several bodies of Christ in different locales, but one body of Christ, and each local congregation is representative of that body. Behind the one body—one Spirit language is the theology of 2:16–18 and 1 Corinthians 12:13, in which Christians are joined into one body by the Spirit and given access together to God. In addition to having a common origin in the Spirit's work and a common existence in Christ's body, believers share a common hope, the common eschatological destiny of the gospel.

---

14. Why the NIV chose "through the bond of peace" is unclear; the text has "in (*en*) the bond of peace."

15. Compare the similar ideas in 1:18; 2:16, 18; also 1 Corinthians 8:6.

In 4:4 Paul repeats his focus on "the calling with which we were called" (cf. v. 1).[16] The similarity of verses 1 and 4 underscores that living worthy of one's calling will mean living in unity, for all share the same calling and are on the way to the same destiny.

The second triad (v. 5) likewise refers to chapter 2. In Christ the whole building grows into a holy temple "in the Lord" (2:21)—the only occurrence of "Lord" by itself in chapters 1–3. While the world may know numerous "lords" (1 Cor. 8:5–6), Christians know only one, and this implies that the one Lord is not going to give contradictory commands to his followers.

"One faith" looks back to the explanation of the gospel in 2:1–10, but reference here is not to the act of believing. "Faith" is used here by metonymy for that which is believed, the content of the faith. The statement means there is only one gospel.

No other explicit reference to "baptism" occurs in the letter, although an allusion to it appears at 4:22–24 (perhaps also 5:26).[17] Paul's main emphasis here is that the only baptism that exists is baptism into Christ (or into his body) by the Spirit (cf. also 1 Cor. 1:13; 12:13; Gal. 3:27). If people have the same Lord, believe the same gospel, and have experienced the same reality of being baptized into Christ, should they not live out this unity?

An even greater basis for unity exists in God, the "Father of all" (v. 6). The theology is close to that in 3:14–15. Surely the Jewish *Shema*—the confession that Yahweh is one (Deut. 6:4)—lies behind this verse (cf. also Rom. 3:30; 1 Cor. 8:6). The liturgical expression "who is over all and through all and in all" is paralleled in several texts, most notably 1 Corinthians 8:6 (though this text is different in that all things come *through Christ*). Variation occurs in the way liturgical expressions are applied.[18]

Each Person Has Received Grace to Build Up Christ's Body (4:7–16)

THE LOGIC OF this section is too closely united to be separated into two paragraphs, as the NIV does. Even in keeping the section as a unit the logic is not easy to follow, for 4:9–10 are parenthetical (cf. the punctuation of the NIV).

---

16. The NIV language hides the similarity of language between verses 1 and 4.

17. Despite this, some scholars suggest Ephesians was originally a baptismal homily. See especially John C. Kirby, *Ephesians: Baptism and Pentecost* (Montreal: McGill Univ. Press, 1968), who suggests Ephesians is for the renewal of baptismal vows, probably in the context of observing Pentecost.

18. See also Romans 9:5; 11:36; 1 Corinthians 8:6; 12:6; 15:28; Colossians 1:16; 3:11. Romans 9:5 has the only other occurrence of "over all" in Paul's letters, but whether he is referring to Christ or to God is debated.

Like other passages on the body (Rom. 12:3–8; 1 Cor. 12:12–31), Paul's concern for unity is balanced by an emphasis on diversity and the responsibility of each person. While not as explicit in Ephesians 4 as in other texts, this is clearly Paul's intent. Therefore, the NIV is correct to begin verse 7 with a mild adversative, "but," to ward off any wrong ideas. That is, unity does not mean that individuality and individual responsibility are lost. Unity reigns, but Christ does not work merely at the universal level. He works in the individual and gives grace to each person.

Once again "grace" has an unexpected meaning. It does not designate saving grace here, but grace for ministry, if indeed the two can be separated. Paul could as easily have written, "To each of us *ministry* has been given." Just as in 3:8 he spoke of the grace given to him to preach to the Gentiles, here in virtually identical language he writes of the grace given to each person to do the work of one's calling.[19]

Both Romans 12:3–8 and 1 Corinthians 12:4–14 serve as commentary on this text. Unity does not exist in the sameness of person or responsibility, but in origin from God, dependence on the one gospel, and destination with God. Within the unity grace is given to everyone so that each person has a different responsibility. As Romans 12:6 puts it, "We have different gifts, according to the grace given to us." Unity is maintained by diversity and variety.

"As Christ apportioned it" (v. 7) is literally "according to the measure of the gift of Christ." This does not suggest Christ gives only a small amount of grace to some, for he has lavished his grace on us (1:8). The identity of the gift[20] is uncertain. It could be grace (as 3:7), the Holy Spirit (as 1 Cor. 12:7), or Christ himself. Closer determination is neither possible nor desirable, for to speak of grace is to speak of Christ and the Spirit. The concern is to recognize the God-intended and God-empowered diversity of functions within the body of Christ.[21]

The word "measure" (v. 7; NIV, "apportioned") reappears in 4:13 ("the whole *measure* of the fullness of Christ") and in 4:16 ("according to the working in *measure* of each part"; NIV, "as each part does its work"). What is measured to each one is needed to make the full measure of the body of Christ.

In his quotation of Psalm 68:18 in verse 8, Paul is interested primarily in the last line, "and gave gifts to men." This provides scriptural verification that the ascended Christ gives gifts to people. This quotation differs from both

---

19. At least fifteen of Paul's 101 uses of "grace" refer to grace for ministry (see esp. Rom. 1:5; 15:15–16; 1 Cor. 15:10; 2 Cor. 9:8.

20. Paul uses *dorea*, not *charisma*, here, although 1 Peter 4:10 does use *charisma* in a similar statement.

21. Similar language occurs in Romans 12:3; 2 Corinthians 10:13; 1 Peter 4:10.

the Hebrew text and the Septuagint in that both have "you ascended," "you led," and "you *received* gifts" rather than "he ascended," "he led," and "he *gave* gifts."[22] The original psalm is about God's being triumphant, taking captives, and receiving gifts from people (or possibly receiving people as gifts).[23] This psalm was apparently used in connection with Pentecost and the commemoration of God's giving of the Torah.[24] Other passages using the ascent–descent motif also focus on revelation (see John 1:51; 3:13; Rom. 10:6–8). Paul understood the psalm of Christ's ascension, or he has at least adapted it to Christ's ascension. The "captives in his train," his victory parade, can be either believers (2 Cor. 2:14) or principalities and powers (Col. 2:15). In light of Ephesians 1:20–23 on the Lord's exaltation over spiritual forces, evil powers are probably in view. The word "gifts" may have a double referent. They are given to people in 4:7, but in 4:11 people are also given as gifts to the church. That people are recipients of grace makes them gifts to the church.

Parenthetical comment on the ascension (4:9–10). The mention of ascension in verse 8a motivates a parenthetical comment in the next two verses. Interpretation of these verses has been made difficult by the church tradition that has understood them of a descent into Hades. At issue is how one should understand the genitive "of the earth" (in the lit. translation, "He descended into the lower regions *of the earth*"[25]). Does this mean "the regions under the earth" or "the lower regions, that is, the earth"?[26] If the former, then a descent to Hades is the intent; if the latter three views are possible:

(1) Christ's incarnation
(2) Christ's descent in the Spirit at Pentecost[27]
(3) Christ's descent to the church alluded to in 2:17.[28]

The last view has little to commend it, and a descent to Hades is difficult to accept for this text or for any other. Paul nowhere else speaks of a descent

---

22. The quotation in Ephesians is similar to the Syriac and the Targum (an Aramaic paraphrase of the Hebrew Scriptures), although the Targum still uses the second person singular: "You ascended up to the firmament, O prophet Moses, you took captives captive, you did teach the words of the law and *gave* them as gifts to the children of men."

23. Possibly the psalm alluded to the Levites as given to God (see Num. 8:5–19; 18:6; Isa. 66:20–21). See Gary V. Smith, "Paul's Use of Psalm 68:18 in Ephesians 4:8," *JETS* 18 (1975): 181–89. If so, the application to Christian leaders would be that much easier.

24. See especially Lincoln, *Ephesians*, 242–44.

25. Cf. the NIV footnote: "the depths of the earth."

26. That is, is it a partitive genitive or a genitive of apposition?

27. This view has been popularized by G. B. Caird, "The Descent of Christ in Ephesians 4,7–11," *Studia Evangelica II*, ed. F. L. Cross (Berlin: Akademie-Verlag, 1964), 535–45. See also Lincoln, *Ephesians*, 246–47.

28. Abbott, *Commentary on the Epistle to the Ephesians and the Colossians*, 116.

into Hades, and it is doubtful whether 1 Peter 3:18–22 refers to such an idea either. In Ephesians the conflict with the powers takes place in the heavenly realms, and Christ's victory is by exaltation, not descent (see 1:20–23; 6:10[29]). The main focus with this theme is on the movement from heaven to earth, that is, on the Incarnation (see John 1:51; 3:13; 6:51).

The other two views of verses 9–10 (the Incarnation or Pentecost) both assume the words should be translated, "He descended to the earth below." While a reference to Pentecost fits the logic of the passage, it is difficult to accept, for this would surely be an enigmatic way for Paul to express it. Most likely, he is referring to the Incarnation: The one who descended in the Incarnation is the same one who has ascended and is now exalted over all things.

The apostle's real concern in this parenthesis is not the descent motif, but the ascent. The NIV translation "in order to fill the whole universe" may mislead in that it creates spatial ideas. The text says literally, "in order that he may fill all things." Whenever Paul mentions the ascension, he emphasizes Christ's authority and the fact that Christ encompasses all things and places them in their proper role. Nothing is outside his jurisdiction or excluded from the benefit and wholeness he brings.[30]

People are given as gifts to serve and build up (4:11–16). This section is one long sentence in Greek, in which two subjects are treated: the ministry that takes place in the body and the maturity this ministry is to achieve. The gifts Christ gives to the church are *people* to promote serving and building up. This text teaches both about gifts and about institutional order.

In reconstructing New Testament history scholars often suggest that the primitive church was controlled by the Spirit and *charismata* and that church order developed later. This is one reason why some see Ephesians as representative of an "early catholicism," for the author is more focused here on "offices," order, and tradition. This reconstruction is unfortunate, for while the focus on the Spirit could be lost, from very early in the church's history both the Spirit and human leaders were joined. This passage says no more than 1 Corinthians 12:27–31: No community can exist without leadership of some fashion, and the Spirit and institutional order are not antithetical.[31]

---

29. Any discussion of Christ's going to Hades to release Old Testament believers is motivated by theological issues in the church's history and not by the text of Ephesians. Other occurrences of the ascent-descent motif do not refer to a descent into Hades; only Romans 10:6–8 even suggests such an idea, but there the idea is that no one needs to descend into the "deep" (*abyssos*, the place of the dead) to bring Christ up.

30. See 1:10, 22–23; 3:19; Colossians 1:15–20.

31. The word "office," however, is probably too strong to describe any New Testament text on leadership.

Servants build toward unity and knowledge of Christ (4:11–13). This text does not set up a hierarchy of clergy and laity; rather, it speaks of people given to the church to assist its service and edification. The idea is not of gifts given to a special group, but of grace giving people to the church (cf. also 1 Cor. 12:28, where God appointed in the church first apostles, then prophets, then teachers; after these three, functions such as powers and gifts of healing are listed).

No function is listed in verse 11, but the same three categories of people are listed with two additions: "evangelists" and "pastors" (lit., "shepherds"), who are joined to "teachers," These last two form one category, for one Greek article governs both. In other words, the phrase meant "teaching pastors," and only four groups exist.[32]

The titles listed here do not necessarily mean the same in the first century as they do today, particularly with "evangelists" and "pastors." In fact, although all the titles refer to roles that proclaim the faith, the actual definition of the titles is difficult. Particularly in Paul's letters the evidence is limited. Moreover, the categories are not mutually exclusive. Theoretically at least, all of them could be applied to Paul (cf. 2 Tim. 1:11, which applies "apostle" and "teacher" to Paul along with "herald"; also Acts 13:1, which lumps "prophets" and "teachers" together as one group).[33] Any attempt at neat classification fails when the evidence is examined.[34]

"Apostles" has a broad semantic range in the New Testament. The background is the Jewish concept of agency, in which an agent goes out to represent a sender in the New Testament. Sometimes it means that someone is God's agent as a result of having seen the resurrected Lord.[35] At other times it refers to those who have the foundational ministry of setting out the parameters of faith, particularly because of their presence with Jesus or their activity in the early church.[36] At other times it means little more than an envoy of the church.[37] In at least one place (Rom. 16:7) the term is used of a woman.[38] But in most cases "apostle" refers to a person in a limited group of leaders who had a special authority and role; otherwise, Paul's strenuous efforts to defend his own apostolic office make no sense. Apostles were

---

32. Note the cadence set up with each title being preceded by "some" (*men* before "apostles" and *de* before the other titles). Neither *de* nor the article appears before "teachers."

33. Barnabas is listed as a teacher-prophet, but he is also called an apostle in Acts 14:14.

34. See Ernest Best, "Ministry in Ephesians," *Irish Biblical Studies* 15 (1993): 146–166.

35. Note Acts 1:21–22; 1 Corinthians 9:1.

36. This is how Ephesians uses the word (see 2:20; 3:5; also Acts 1:21–22; 15:2–16:4; Gal. 1:17–2:10).

37. 2 Corinthians 8:23 (NIV, "representatives"); Philippians 2:25 (NIV: "messenger").

38. The NIV translation "Junias" is unfortunate, for the name is clearly the feminine, "Junia."

specially authorized agents of God, responsible for explaining and disseminating God's good news.

"Prophets" likewise carries breadth of range. It can refer to prophets who had a foundational role along with the apostles (2:20; 3:5) or to people who were designated prophets in the life of local churches (Acts 13:1; 15:32; 21:9; 1 Cor. 14:32). While any Christian could prophesy (1 Cor. 14:31), occasional prophetic speech did not necessarily bring with it the label *prophet*. At times prophets predicted future events (Acts 11:27–28; 21:10), but usually they explained the relevance of the gospel and the will of God (see 1 Cor. 14:3–40).

"Evangelists" form a group about which little is known (the word occurs elsewhere only of Philip at Acts 21:8 and of Timothy at 2 Tim. 4:5). That evangelists were itinerants proclaiming the gospel is probably not correct. Paul urged evangelist Timothy to *stay* in Ephesus to build up the church there (1 Tim. 1:3), and the evangelist Philip had a house in Caesarea. No doubt, their primary activity was to unbelievers, but the evangelist was a "gospeler," someone who focused on proclaiming the gospel and its relevance. Such activity could be addressed to either believers or unbelievers (see Rom. 1:15).

While all Christians have a teaching responsibility (1 Cor. 14:26; Col. 3:16), some people were recognized as "teaching pastors" (more lit., "teaching shepherds") in the church and were compensated for their teaching (cf. Acts 13:1; Gal. 6:6; 1 Cor. 12:28; 1 Tim. 5:17). The figure of a shepherd leading and caring for sheep is a familiar Old Testament image applied to both God and human leaders.[39]

Verse 12 is made up of three prepositional phrases, which, rendered literally, reads: "*toward* the equipping of God's people *unto* a work of service *unto* building up the body of Christ." Do all three phrases describe the leaders, thus giving three purposes for which they were given to the church, or does only the first phrase describe the leaders, with the other two describing the people? To put the question another way, do the leaders do all three tasks or do they equip the people to do the work and building up? An understanding of the relation of clergy and laity is at stake. The NIV has rightly chosen the second option. The emphasis on each person receiving grace for ministry in 4:7 and the parallels in Romans 12:3–8 and 1 Corinthians 12:4–31 necessitate a focus on the involvement of all the people in the work of the church. Furthermore, the emphasis on "preparing" requires a complement. What are God's people being prepared to do if it is not to serve and build up the body?

---

39. This list is not a complete list of early church leaders; note, for example, "overseers and deacons" (Phil. 1:1) and "elder" (Titus 1:5).

"Building up" (or "edification") is an important theme in Ephesians (4:16, 29) and in Paul's ecclesiology. He uses the word fifteen times in his letters (in Ephesians, Romans, and 1 and 2 Corinthian).[40] It is the goal of personal ethics (Rom. 14:19), of corporate worship (1 Cor. 14:26), and of Paul's own ministry (2 Cor. 10:8). The focus is mostly on internal strengthening of the church, but building up the church by reaching out to unbelievers is also included.

While the first part of verse 13 may have implications for the end times, this passage makes more sense if understood of an attainable, expected goal for Christians in the present. Otherwise the focus on Christian maturity in verses 14–16 makes no sense. Paul's concern is that his readers will not be blown about like babies now, not after the parousia. The NIV's "attaining to the whole measure of the fullness of Christ" also points to Paul's concern about edification and maturity in the here and now—a faith that reaches an adult wholeness.

While unity is assumed as something given in 4:3, it is still something toward which Christians must work. "Unity in the faith and knowledge of the Son" is not merely unity in the ideas that we believe, but a unity resulting from the experience of receiving the gospel and living with Christ. This is not knowledge about Christ, but a firsthand relational knowing *him*. Our Lord wants us to have a "mature" faith (cf. 1 Cor. 13:11).[41]

A mature and growing faith, evidenced by truth and love (4:14–16). What is the connection between verses 11–13 and 14–16? The NIV has interpreted the conjunction *hina* temporally ("then" in v. 14), but purpose ("in order that") or result ("so that") is more likely. Although some see verse 13 as parenthetical with verses 14-16 connecting to verse 12, more likely verses 14–16 connect directly to the maturity mentioned in verse 13: Paul wants his readers to become mature *so that* they will not be carried away by erroneous teaching.

Immaturity is described as being "tossed back and forth" and "blown here and there," that is, being easily deceived.[42] Paul pictures a person who does not know where to find the source for truth and life and who is repeatedly

---

40. The related verb occurs nine times as well.

41. The NIV "become mature" represents the words "unto a mature man." A parallel should be drawn to the new being in 2:15, but even though both images are corporate, the intent is not the same. *Aner* is used here for "man" rather than *anthropos*, which was used in 2:15. Nowhere else is *aner* used to represent the church, and it is safe to say that the focus is on conveying the ideas of unity and maturity, not on maleness or church. James 3:2 uses this same expression to speak of the person who is mature enough to control the tongue.

42. Note the preponderance of words in verse 14 for deception: "cunning" (meant negatively in the sense of trickery, actually the word for playing with dice), "craftiness," and "deceitful scheming."

being duped by charlatans and tricksters. Several implicit contrasts are set up by the text:

(1) infancy versus maturity
(2) tossed about versus joined and held together (v. 16);
(3) deception versus speaking the truth (v. 15)
(4) of human origin versus from Christ
(5) crafty people serving themselves versus honest, loving people serving others.

With the transition to the description of maturity in 4:15, we encounter perhaps the most important ethical guideline in the New Testament, one that summarizes what Christian living is about: truth, love, and continual growth into Christ in everything.[43] The word for "truth" here is actually a verb; a literal translation is "truthing in love."[44] The thought that *truth is something one does* occurs in the Old Testament, in the New Testament, and in the Qumran scrolls.[45]

The Semitic concept of truth focuses on that on which one can rely. It is primarily a relational term for covenant loyalty and is sometimes translated by "faithfulness." A truthful person is one who lives out his or her covenant obligations, which includes both what is said and what is done. Therefore, *both* truth and love bind us to the other person, for we cannot live truth and violate covenant relations. Truth involves a true assessment of the facts and a consideration of what is real as opposed to illusion, but it is much more holistic than what is done with the mind. At the least, it joins the coherence of act and word with relational fidelity.

Speaking and living the truth of the gospel is set opposite the deceitful teachings that carry away the immature. Yet a broader concern for truth generally must be included. The truth of the gospel cannot be separated from truth generally, whether it is in explaining God's purposes or relating to other humans. That this broader concern is in mind is shown by the commentary on truth that follows in 4:21, 24–25; and 5:8.

The third feature of this ethical summary is the most important. We are to "grow up into [Christ]" in everything. Rather than a future as in the NIV,

---

43. Truth and love are emphasized in the rest of the letter, which should be no surprise, since they are two of the five words summarizing the Christian faith (along with grace, faith, and hope; see p. 59). Note the focus on truth and love in 4:16, 21, 24, 25; 5:2, 9, 25–33; 6:14, 23.

44. This verb occurs elsewhere in the New Testament only at Galatians 4:16.

45. See John 3:21 and 1 John 1:6, both of which have "do the truth" (NIV, "live by the truth"). In the Old Testament see Genesis 32:10; 47:29; Nehemiah 9:33 (NIV, "faithfulness" or "faithfully").

the main verb is actually a first person command: "Let us grow up [or increase] into him in all things." Living the truth in love is both the means of growth and the result of growth. As we live in the truth and love encountered in Christ (3:19 and 4:21) and express these qualities, we become more closely attached to Christ and more like him. The idea of growing into Christ may sound strange at first, but it is part of the "spheres of influence" theology so important to Paul and expressed by the phrase "in Christ."[46] Christians are attached to Christ by faith; as they grow, they are more closely brought into relation with him and into conformity with his character and his will.

The idea of growth provides an easy transition back to the body imagery, and the first thought is of Christ's role as head of the body. This is one of the few places the argument is plausible that "head" means "source."[47] However, the idea of source does not derive from the word "head," but from the fact that Christ as the exalted Lord is the source of life and all good things. "Head" here as elsewhere points to the fact that he is Lord (cf. 1:22). Because he is Lord, he has the power and authority to provide what the body needs.

The body image has already appeared several times.[48] In fact, Paul's comments here develop the ideas in 1:22–23. No other New Testament writer uses "body" metaphorically,[49] but for Paul it is a major term for explaining salvation, the church, and ethics.[50] Moreover, the language here is similar to the building language in 2:21–22. The building grows and the body is built up; in both people are joined together as a result of their connection to Christ (cf. also Col. 2:19). The body image conveys several ideas:

(1) An intimate relation exists between Christ and those who believe in him. They are bound to him and draw from him resources for life.
(2) Union with Christ joins people to each other.
(3) Each person has responsibility within the body to fulfill his or her calling.
(4) The body grows and is built up by the activity of each part and the sustenance that comes from Christ.
(5) Everything done in the body is done in the context of love.

---

46. See pp. 40–42, 47–48, 56–57, 63–64.

47. See pp. 78–79, 294–96.

48. See 1:22–23; 2:16; 3:6; 4:4, 12; it will appear again in 5:23, 28, 30.

49. With the possible exception of the Synoptic eucharistic sayings, depending on how one interprets them.

50. Of Paul's ninety-one uses of "body," only four appear outside Romans, 1 and 2 Corinthian, Ephesians, and Colossians. While "head" is used of Christ in 1 Corinthians 11:3, only in Ephesians and Colossians is a Christological understanding of "head" brought into relation with "body."

The words "every supporting ligament" present difficulty. "Supporting" (*epichoregia*) usually carries the meaning "supply" or "provision"; *aphe*, the word translated "ligament," is used more generally as "connection," and, at least later, as "joint." Thus, does Paul mean "every supporting ligament" or "every contact that serves for supply"?[51] While both ideas of being bound together and of supply are present in this syntactically difficult verse, the evidence leans in favor of translating this phrase "every contact for supply."

BRINGING THIS TEXT into our contemporary situation is relatively straightforward. Most of the ideas are familiar and as pertinent for modern readers as for the original ones. Yet both the theology of the text and the clash of its worldview with ours require consideration.

Why be ethical? Why should anyone be ethical? Parents, schools, and society are supposed to teach what people should or should not do. In many modern societies the effort is now a failure, and Christians and non-Christians alike lament the collapse of ethics at every level. Crime, abuse, and violence are common, and for many sexual ethics do not exist. But why shouldn't we all satisfy our needs and desires, regardless of who gets hurt? Fear of the police or of retaliation is not sufficient reason, for often the benefit of unethical action is worth the risk. Respectability is no motivation, for our society gives little value to respect. Some suggest we have to be ethical to make the system work, but why should people care about that? For many the system does not work.

As Paul implies in 4:1, all ethics are theologically motivated. Theology motivates application, for it understands the importance of the subject. Paul's ethic is primarily a Christological ethic, and this text begins to spell out what that means.[52] Remember: Christology is soteriology is ecclesiology is ethics. All ethics—and especially Christian ethics—are by necessity ethics of response. God acts in creation, in the Exodus, in Christ, through the Spirit, or in our own lives, and we respond to his grace.

Earlier in our society enough people had theological conviction to motivate ethical living; others assumed the ethic without knowing the theology. Now most know nothing about theology and have thus lost any basis for the

---

51. See Barth, *Ephesians*, 2:449; he translates is (426): "He provides sustenance to it through every contact according to the needs of each single part" (the only other New Testament passage with *epichoregia* is Phil. 1:19, "the help given by the Spirit").

52. Ethics are not necessarily Christologically based, or for that matter, even Christian. For example, ethics can legitimately be grounded in a creation theology, in the Old Testament covenant, or in eschatology.

ethical behavior. Rules never motivate ethical behavior; awareness of God does. Thus, to bring the ethics of this passage to today we must recover its theology. Pastors and teachers should not merely give Christians a list of do's and don'ts. They *must* give direction, but with the direction they must convey a theology that motivates life.

We need to recover a sense of the calling with which we were called. Most Christians have no sense they are called, but every Christian has been called by God as an act of grace and given every endowment needed for life. With the gift comes the responsibility. We must live out the reality of God's love for us.

In other words, theology is not some arcane subject for academics; it is basic training in understanding the gospel so that we know how to live.

Relations among Christians. All of life is relational—even when we think we are alone and independent. We need respect and attention from other people. Even if we turn away from people, our abilities, views, and often our very existence are dependent on others. Christianity is a relational religion, and this text, while not being a treatise on relations, says much about getting along with each other.

Positive relations are based on several factors: a shared identity in terms of family, culture, subculture, and race; shared experience; shared values; and respect.[53] Christian theology offers a strong basis for relations with other human beings purely because they are people created in the image of God. But relations among Christians have a broader foundation. They share an identity in Christ, the experience of Christ, and values determined by Christ. This is what Paul attempts to convey with his focus on unity and on the body. Most of the vices in the New Testament ethical instruction are sins that disrupt community, and most of the virtues promote community.

The ego is the main problem in relations, for therein lies the origin of feelings of inferiority and arrogance, of envy and greed, of prejudice and defensiveness, and of intolerance and abuse. As William Temple noted, pride is always the root of spiritual failure.[54] The solution is in a sense of God's grace, for grace prevents the ego from inflating its own significance.

Like ancient Greek culture, our society often views humility, meekness, and gentleness in negative terms (cf. v. 2). Humility too frequently is misunderstood as passivity and antithetical to success, but this is a distortion. Humility is not about drive, energy, or ability, but about valuing. It is an awareness that all we are and have is from God. The humble person refuses

---

53. Note that God's relation with us is not based on any of these, for his relation with us is based purely on grace.

54. William Temple, *Readings in St. John's Gospel* (London: Macmillan, 1939), 1:118.

to value self above others or to assign more privilege or importance to self than to others. Humility is essential for good relations and avoiding sin, so much so that Ignatius said, by it "the prince of this world is brought to nothing."[55] Egotism, on the other hand, is an idolatry of the self, the failure to realize that God is the pattern for life, not us.

Unity. Ephesians is the unity letter, but we do not value unity. Rather than making every effort to maintain unity (v. 3), we sacrifice it at the first airing of differences. We value differences more than unity or people. Christians have been more fearful of some ecumenical world structure than of fragmenting the body of Christ. Something about us wants to set ourselves apart from others, but is this too not a form of egotism?

Disunity originates in pride, as the Corinthian letters poignantly show. Denominations and movements are as guilty of egotism and arrogance as individuals. Nearly all denominations have been guilty of arrogance and parochialism and have succumbed to fights that ignore the gospel. Moreover, each denomination is divided into liberals and conservatives—no matter how liberal or conservative the denomination actually is. We do not have unity between groups, within groups, or in local congregations.

Most groups have insiders and outsiders. We talk about unity and community, but we do not have them. Paul Minear's words ring painfully true when he says we can hardly use Ephesians 4 "as a description of twentieth-century Christianity without crossing our fingers, or stifling a hoot of derision, or angrily challenging the hypocrisy in any church that piously parrots those liturgical phrases: 'you were called to the one hope that belongs to your calling' (4:4)."[56]

How can unity be established? It does not need to be established, for it already exists, given by God. It needs to be valued and maintained. Christ is not divided (1 Cor. 1:13). The community is not the source of its own existence; Christ is. He is the unity of the church, for the church only exists in him. Christology is ecclesiology.

This is not to deny the validity and value of differences among communities, nor should theological and cultural distinctions be ignored. Our concern is not for some organizational unity. Rather, the concern is unity *in Christ*, which carries with it an assumption of the biblical message about Christ as crucified and risen Lord. Christians do not need to agree on everything to have unity; we need to live the unity of a common commitment to

---

55. Ignatius, *To the Trallians* 4.2. He is talking about *praotes*, a variant spelling of the word translated "gentle" in Ephesians 4:2.

56. Paul S. Minear, *To Die and to Live: Christ's Resurrection and Vocation* (New York: Seabury, 1977), 92.

Christ. The formula of Rupert Meldenius popularized by Richard Baxter is still good guidance: "Unity in essentials, liberty in incidentals, and in all things charity [love]."[57]

The mission of the church is at stake. Unity and mission belong together. In 3:5–10 unity among diverse groups is at the heart of the gospel and evidence of God's power and wisdom. The mission of the church is crippled by the division among various groups. Unless we evidence unity, our witness does not deserve to be heard.

One baptism? Of all the affirmations of unity in 4:4–6, surely the most difficult to swallow is "one baptism." Can we even say these words when baptism has been such a cause of division? Yes, for only one baptism exists, baptism into Jesus Christ. Paul was not speaking about the mode or timing of a ceremony; he was saying no other baptism exists except baptism into Christ.[58]

The most difficult topic is rebaptism. If a person is baptized as an infant and then rebaptized as an adult, is that not a rejection of the validity of the former? On the other hand, if rebaptism is not allowed, is that not a rejection of belief in believer's baptism? No easy solution exists, but the key is the integrity and respect of the people involved. We do not have to agree on the theology of baptism to accept each other. Both sides need the freedom to state their convictions without demeaning those who disagree. Both should allow the freedom for the person being baptized to follow his or her own convictions. Both should recognize they follow much the same process: They do something at birth (baptism or dedication) and around twelve years of age (confirmation or a push for decision), and both seek the validation of an adult faith around eighteen. It is merely a question of when and how much water is used. Do we value our differences more than our unity in Christ? Paul chose unity.

The ascent-descent motif. One of the difficult sections to apply is 4:8–10, since its relevance is not immediately apparent. The key is in staying with the purpose of this material. Paul quotes Psalm 68:18 to provide verification that the ascended Christ gives gifts for building up his church. Verses 9–10 strengthen this message of the Lord's equipping his church for ministry.

The purpose of the text is to provide theological basis for Christ's work in the church. Application will focus on the expectation and obedience that come from this theological conviction about the lordship of Christ, his incarnation, and his investment in the life of his followers. If he is the Lord who gives gifts and fills all things, we should expect his involvement in our work and should be ready to obey.

---

57. See Richard F. Lovelace, *Dynamics of Spiritual Life* (Downers Grove, Ill.: InterVarsity, 1979), 296.

58. See 1 Corinthians 1:12–17; Galatians 3:26–28.

The work of the church. This passage does not describe all the work of the church, but it does contribute much to a theology of ministry. Most of the concern is for internally building up of church, rather than for mission outside the church. Thus it is incomplete, but no text should be seen as a comprehensive theological statement. For all its emphasis, Ephesians is still not a complete ecclesiology.

The responsibility of the individual. In far too many churches people come, listen to a preacher, and do little else. No wonder the charge has been made that the body of Christ seems to have one big mouth and many little ears! But that is not how Paul viewed the church. While it is true that some have a special responsibility to teach and preach, Paul stresses that every Christian is responsible to build up the church. We have all received grace for ministry and must live worthy of our calling. We are all expected to work to strengthen the church, and only as each person fulfills his or her calling is the church truly strong.

Those with special responsibilities to teach and preach are to equip others to serve, not do the service for them, and these people are not set in a separate category or given tasks that others are prohibited from doing. We must value the service of everyone in the church, and ordinary Christians must accept their responsibility and seek to fulfill their calling.

Gifts for ministry. The discussion of spiritual gifts is enriched by this passage. Some suggest grace is a new capacity for service that is given to each Christian at conversion, which must be discovered and exercised. Usually the argument is that while a gift is not the same as a talent, one finds it the way one discovers a talent: Be attracted to the gift, study it, try it, develop it, and exercise it.[59] Spiritual gift inventories supposedly help people find their gift. But this approach is naive and does not do justice to the biblical accounts. In fact, it is a self-centered approach. The New Testament never asks us to identify our gifts.

The New Testament language for gifts is used in surprising ways. Among various uses at least six categories of gifts should be mentioned.

(1) The basic gift (*charisma*) is eternal life in Christ (Rom. 6:23), and all other gifts exist because of this one.[60]
(2) The Holy Spirit is also a gift (often *dorea*) given to every Christian.
(3) One's own station in life is a gift (*charisma*), specifically marriage and celibacy (1 Cor. 7:7).
(4) Ministry is viewed as a gift (*dorea* in Eph. 3:7–8).

---

59. E.g., see Ray C. Stedman, *Body Life* (Glendale, Calif.: Regal, 1972), 38–39, 51–58.
60. See Ernst Käsemann, "Ministry and Community in the New Testament," *Essays on New Testament Themes* (Philadelphia: Fortress, 1982), 63–94.

(5) People are gifts (*domata*) to the church (Eph. 4:8, 11).

(6) Various activities are gifts (*charismata*), such as those listed in 1 Corinthians 12:28, the ones usually thought of as "spiritual" gifts.

This suggests we need a much broader sense of *gift* than typically is the case. To say a gift is something given at conversion and is different from a talent is wrong. The parallelism in 1 Corinthians 12:4—7 shows that a gift is the same thing as a working or a service; a gift is merely the way the Spirit works through a person for the good of the community. Consequently, no one should assume a gift is a lifelong possession.

In Ephesians 4:11 certain leaders are viewed as gifts to the church, but actually this is true of all Christians. All have received grace and have a responsibility to build up the church. As the Spirit works through each person for the good of the community, *each person is a gift* to the church. We would do well to have less concern about identifying gifts and more concern about being a gift, that is, about how the Spirit functions through us to strengthen the body.

Christian leaders. This text identifies Christian leaders whose work has to do with proclaiming the Word of God. Although the list is not intended to be exhaustive, questions arise about the importance of 4:11 in shaping the structure of the church in the modern world. Should these four areas be made offices? Are there still apostolic and prophetic offices today?

We should pay careful attention to the purpose of this text, the titles employed, and the differences between the modern church and the first-century church. After the first century "apostle" and "evangelist" were used rarely to describe leaders. In the Apostolic Fathers "apostle" occurs only at *Didache* 11.3, and "evangelist" does not appear. The word *apostle* could be used today only if it were stripped of its primary New Testament significance in referring to those who saw the risen Lord and/or helped map out the boundaries for belief. We still need people guarding the content of the faith, but the use of such a word today is pretentious and misleading. No basis exists for excluding prophecy in the modern church, although the use of the title for specific persons is likewise both dangerous and pretentious.

Verse 11 does not lay out a church order, and none of the four categories is a church office. It describes how Christ equips the church for service. The functions listed here overlap, but the important thing is to see that *they are all ministries of the Word.* Leaders must communicate the message. Any attempt to reproduce the church structure of the early church is bound to fail. No New Testament text lays out a church order, and an investigation of such titles shows no single or fixed order existed in the first century.[61] Moreover, the

---

61. See Kevin Giles, *Patterns of Ministry Among the First Christians* (Melbourne: Collins Dove, 1989).

needs of modern churches are different from those in the first century. Churches now are larger, have expanded ministries, and are set in a different cultural context. Much about structure and administration is *cultural*, and with the Spirit's guidance we should design structures suitable for our tasks.

A sound understanding of ministry is essential. At the center of all else is the ministry of the Word preparing a community for service. *Language creates a community*, and those who communicate the message of Jesus Christ create a community with a shared identity and shared values. Preaching creates a power sphere in which and from which people live, for language is the tool we use to shape reality. Preaching is the opportunity every preacher has to bring order out of chaos on the basis of the Word of God.[62] This order, an order based on the cross and resurrection, gives people the foundation and direction for service.

The role of the leaders is to serve the people; nothing of a hierarchy of privilege exists. Unfortunately, even though Christians talk about servant leadership, it rarely exists. Pastors do not really believe in servant leadership, for all of us in modern society have a difficult time separating leadership from exercise of the ego. Leadership often ends up being for the leader or the institution, but not for the people. But Christian leadership must be different. If the first part of fulfilling our call is humility (4:2), then this must be true first of leaders.[63] The servant leadership Jesus requires is only the application of the gospel to the task of leadership. If leaders cannot apply the gospel to themselves, they are not leaders.[64]

The body. The body image is difficult to bring into our age because of the complexity of Paul's thought. He intended more than that Christians are *like* the body of Christ. He used the body image to express the reality of oneness with Christ. His whole theology of salvation depends on this oneness. In 2:15–16 Paul said that Christ created one new being in himself to reconcile Jews and Gentiles to God in one body; we are members of his body (5:30). This language is an extension of Paul's "in Christ" thinking.

In Romans 12:5 (a text close to the thought of Eph. 4:16), Paul wrote, "We the many are one body in Christ, and individually members of each other"[65]

---

62. See the discussion of preaching in John William Beaudean, Jr., *Paul's Theology of Preaching* (Macon, Ga.: Mercer Univ. Press, 1988), 205–7.

63. See Matthew 20:25–28. 1 Corinthians 16:15–16.

64. See my discussion of these issues in "'Your Slaves—on Account of Jesus:' Servant Leadership in the New Testament," *Servant Leadership: Authority and Governance in the Evangelical Covenant Church*, eds. James R. Hawkinson and Robert K. Johnston (Chicago: Covenant Publications, 1993), 1:7–19.

65. NIV: "in Christ we who are many form one body, and each member belongs to all the others."

(cf. also Eph. 4:25). "The one and the many" is a phrase we should make part of our vocabulary. We are individuals, but our bond with Christ makes us one with him and one with each other. This is both a striking privilege and a responsibility. Christ fills all things and in the process binds us together. The word "religion," we should remember, is derived from the root for the word "ligaments" and refers to that which binds together. Unity and efforts to assist each other are necessary conclusions.

The necessity of truth. With truth, we must rebuild the structure from our end, for many of us are all too willing to sacrifice the truth. John's statement that people love darkness more than light is still true (John 3:19), and song writers, philosophers, and ethicists all lament the failure of people to be truthful. The plaintive chorus to Billy Joel's song "Honesty" expresses a universal feeling:

> Honesty is such a lonely word
> Everyone is so untrue
> Honesty is hardly ever heard
> And mostly what I need from you.

The ancient philosopher Diogenes went on a journey with a lantern looking for an honest man. Blaise Pascal complained that human life is nothing but perpetual delusion and that human relations are based on mutual deception.[66] Martin Buber wrote of the uncanny game of hide and seek we play in the obscurity of our souls in which the soul seeks to hide from itself.[67] Thomas Merton charged that our minds are deformed with a kind of contempt for reality, but that in defiling the truth we defile our own souls.[68] And in keeping with Genesis 3, Scott Peck has pointed out that evil always has to do with lying.[69]

These analysts do not exaggerate. Both with ourselves and with others we live by distortion. In China, for example, gambling is illegal, but in Beijing they have "horse intelligence tests" at a race track. Betting windows are ticket counters, payout windows are prize ticket exchanges, and gamblers are fun-seekers—all under a huge banner reminding everyone that gambling is strictly prohibited.[70]

For much of our lives we live "horse intelligence tests." The government passes out "disinformation," politicians make empty promises, "spin doctors"

---

66. B. Pascal, *Pensées* (New York: Random House, 1941), no. 100.

67. M. Buber, *Good and Evil: Two Interpretations* (New York: Scribners, 1953), 111.

68. Thomas Merton, *No Man Is an Island* (New York: Harcourt, Brace, Jovanovich, 1983), 190–91.

69. Scott Peck, *The People of the Lie* (New York: Simon and Schuster, 1983), 135.

70. *Chicago Tribune*, November 7, 1993, section 1, p. 3.

distort facts, and lawyers seek a perverted justice that prohibits truth, knowing that if the truth were told they would lose their case. Distortion pervades our society, from what we tell the IRS to what we tell lovers and friends. A recent book even argues truth is morally overrated.[71] Lying is so prevalent that it is the central element in TV sitcoms. It is easy to laugh at people living in distortion.

Christians too fall into this discounting of truth, but if evil always has to do with lying, then surely Christians must place an enormous premium on truth. Lying is costly. Lies destroy both a healthy self and healthy relations. Mental and spiritual health depend on our willingness to tell the truth. Several poignant statements about truth merit reflection:

> Mental health is an ongoing process of dedication to reality at all costs.[72]

> Truth matters. . . . In fidelity to truth lies human dignity. . . . In obeying the evidence of truth, no human being is humiliated—rather, he is in that way alone ennobled.[73]

> We make ourselves real by telling the truth.[74]

> The worth and integrity of an institution depends on its willingness to call things by their right names.[75]

Truth is the only place we live legitimately and freely. We avoid the truth for two primary reasons, two reasons that are the source of all sin: pride and laziness. Pride objects to truth, for it always seeks to present a more self-enhancing picture, and laziness avoids truth because it requires and creates work. The price, however, of avoiding truth is enormous. Lying destroys us, the people around us, and our relation with God and others.

Truth too can hurt, but that is why truth is the second word in Christian living and should not be not taken by itself. The first word is *grace*, which

---

71. David Nyberg, *The Varnished Truth: Truth Telling and Deceiving in Ordinary Life* (Chicago: Univ. of Chicago Press, 1993). Nyberg assumes there is so much deception that it is the backdrop against which an occasional example of pure truth-telling stands out.

72. Peck, *People of the Lie*, 162. See also the comment of Richard Restak, another psychiatrist: "Secrets, especially those we try to hide from our conscious selves, make the mind sick. Conversely, acceptance of unwanted thoughts robs them of their power to inflict suffering" (*Chicago Tribune*, December 1, 1991, section 5, p. 4).

73. Michael Novak, "Awakening from Nihilism: The Templeton Prize Address," *First Things* 45 (August/September, 1994): 18–19.

74. Merton, *No Man Is an Island*, 188.

75. Slightly altered from Wendell Berry, "The Loss of the University," *Home Economics* (San Francisco: North Point Press, 1987), p. 87.

enables us to face the truth. Together with love, faith, and hope, these five words give a foundation strong enough to deal with life. Truth is not to be applied by itself, nor for that matter is love. Truth and love are wrapped together. They are not antithetical; that thought never occurred to Paul. Rather, love rejoices with the truth (1 Cor. 13:6). When love and truth are kept together, true community comes into being.

TO THIS POINT in the letter the readers have been asked to do nothing except remember their past alienation and present acceptance in Christ (2:11). For three chapters they have been reminded of God's goodness and the marvelous salvation that is theirs. Now with all the force possible, readers are implored to live worthy of their calling.

Application requires accepting the challenge to live out our faith. So often Christianity is presented as if nothing is required of believers. We place so much emphasis on human weakness, on our inability to do anything profitable, and on the necessity of God's actions in salvation that no room is left for human responsibility. *The New Testament never gives this impression!* Human responsibility is wedded to God's action, but we *are* responsible. We must expect something of ourselves. If God's salvation is so good, live like it. This requires an act of the will and a determination to follow through. As Philip Spener said, "It is by no means enough to have knowledge of the Christian faith, for Christianity consists rather of practice."[76]

The metaphor "walk" (NIV, "live") suggests something controlled, enduring, and directed, not something frenetic or aimless. Short term effort is of no value; we need a lifetime of faithfulness mirroring God's call. None of this suggests we accomplish anything by ourselves, but life with God and by his help is a life of discipline and effort. We want discipleship without discipline; it does not exist. We seek what we can get by with, but the challenge is to do what we should, to live worthy of the call.

Our problem is that we have a million dollar salvation and a five-cent response. We seem unimpressed with God's salvation. We protest that no one can actually live worthy of this calling and express our fears of perfectionism. The text is anxious about neither; its concern is only that our lives are shaped by God's salvation. Right theology should lead to right conduct. Why is the process so frequently aborted? Is it because theology is threaded through the brain but never gets to the heart? Such belief is useless. Is our

76. P. Spener, *Pia Desideria*, trans. Theodore G. Tappert (Philadelphia: Fortress, 1964), 95.

knowledge only a source of pride? Our understanding of our call must be sincere and honest, going to the depths of our being. Then by a determined act of our wills and by the help of God's Spirit, our lives must be drawn into line with this call. We are called to receive and show grace.

Relational ethics. The virtues Paul lists in 4:2—humility, gentleness, patience, and loving tolerance—are probably not the first we would list in describing a life worthy of God's calling, but these are exactly what is needed. God's new society operates differently.[77] The key in all four virtues is getting rid of something first.

Humility. In order to have humility, *we must renounce self-centeredness.* A proper self-understanding is the most crucial ingredient for life. We are neither worms nor God; we are marvelous, relational creations in the image of God, intended for relation with God. Without God we have no meaning. Humans are intended to be something great, but in the process of trying to be that, we have become self-centered and self-seeking. We relive the plot of Genesis 3 each day of our lives. All of life's energy is directed toward self and its perspectives. We seek respect and want recognition, honor, and authority. We take assertiveness training, strive for superiority, and are encouraged to look out for number one. Our self-seeking evolves into jealousy and disparagement of others. But individualism and self-assertion are foes of Christian maturity.[78]

Give up self-importance and honor. At every turn Christian faith is an assault on our self-seeking. We are important, but we are not to seek importance. We are not the center, God is. All we are and have is a gift, so why should we boast?[79] Imagine how much easier relations would be if people knew from the outset that we sought their best interests and had no desire to belittle them or promote ourselves. Humility, this lowliness of mind, is a habit we develop. There are steps and exercises to humility,[80] but in the end humility is a continual awareness of God, of our own sinfulness and frailty, and of the equal value of all other persons.

Nowhere is humility more important and necessary than in pastors. They are to model the attitude for their people, but they are the ones *most likely to fail.* They are placed "on stage" to perform, are given authority, and are subjected to ongoing critical review. Any defect in self-understanding will be magnified beyond measure. Pastors should be the first in line to learn about and exercise humility.

---

77. *God's New Society* was the original title of John Stott's commentary on Ephesians.

78. Robinson, *St. Paul's Epistle to the Ephesians*, 101.

79. 1 Corinthians 4:7.

80. See Richard Foster and James Bryan Smith, eds., *Devotional Classics* (San Francisco: Harper, 1990), 178–83, 269–74. Confession, obedience, and rejecting the desire for distinction are obvious first steps.

Gentleness. In order to have gentleness, *we must renounce harshness and violence.* Rather than harshness, the lack of caring and receptivity, and the violence so often met in our world, we should practice gentleness. Healthy relationships cannot exist under force and threat. Some Christians present themselves as so brittle and hostile that no one wants to be around them. Even if they are right, they are repulsively right.[81] Gentleness conveys a sensitivity, a desire not to harm, and a valuing of the other person. With gentleness people can be nurtured.

While gentleness is important in all our relations, including the workplace and church, possibly the arena in which gentleness is most needed is within the family. So much emotional and physical damage is done within the context that should be the most loving. Children and spouses are crushed by harsh, demeaning language and by violence. We can say we meant nothing by it, but the damage will have been irreparably done. "Christian" homes are sometimes among the worst offenders. We need to see family members as if they were marked "Fragile, handle with care." Gentleness nurtures people, respects them, and allows them to drop defenses and deal more objectively with issues.

Patience. In order to have patience, *we must renounce the tyranny of our own agendas.* All of us have a sense of timing about when events should happen, one that rarely agrees with anyone else's sense of timing. Our society has taught us to "want it now" and expect to get it. The idea that we should not have to wait on anything or anyone is merely another form of self-centeredness. A lack of patience reflects a narrowness of soul. Patience is that largeness that values other people enough to give them room and time to fail, learn, and develop. While patience in daily schedules is important, it is especially necessary in allowing people space to mature at their own rate rather than expect them to do everything right and to do it now.

Tolerant love. In order to have tolerant love, *we must renounce our rights.* We focus on our rights, but rights—even though important—can be another form of damaging self-centeredness. As has been said, "Be careful of standing on your rights, for then God may stand on his." Insisting on one's rights never leads to healthy relations. People must be willing to forgo rights and put up with each other in love. Let us recognize that all of us are at times a burden and a pain. Since we are bound to other people in Christ, a choice must be made not to let them go.

Love is a choice, the act of caring enough to give attention to people. As often noted, the opposite of love is not hate, but indifference. You love first, then you learn to love. You choose to invest in other people, and this

---

81. The language is from Morris, *Expository Reflections on Ephesians,* 131.

commitment enables putting up with them. We thereby provide a platform for them to grow. More often than not, failure to provide such a platform leaves people with fewer and fewer good choices. How often has our failure to put up with someone driven them over the edge?

Putting up with in love is what families and friends should do. That means tolerating activities, choices, and inconveniences we do not like. No one knows that better than a parent of a teenager. Putting up with in love is also what churches should do. It may well mean tolerating music or worship styles that are not fully satisfying. It may mean going through a trying time with another person, but it will not allow writing the other person off.

Isn't this a little extreme? All this sounds too passive and weak. Where is the legitimate focus on being strong and aggressive, on having an agenda, and on confronting people that need to be confronted? If we try this humility approach, will we not be crushed and worn out by selfish and burdensome people?

On the contrary, this text tells us exactly what is necessary to fulfill God's call. A life worthy of the call is a life of fellowship,[82] which cannot take place apart from humility, gentleness, patience, and tolerant love. But these four activities have no relation to weakness; quite the opposite, they require strength and a clear-eyed sense of the goal. The refusal to exalt self does not lead to incompetence or passivity; rather, it means a person is strong enough not to require attention and pampering. One has resources from which to give, rather than being so fragile as needing constant support. One has the maturity and ability to care.

Nor is there any suggestion of allowing other people to be selfish, irresponsible, or burdensome. Love seeks justice and cares enough to confront, or it is not really love. The focus on speaking the truth in love in 4:15 (see below) is contrary to the thought that abuses by other people should be merely tolerated. Both speaking the truth in love and putting up with each other in love are required. If the thought occurs that a life such as this is weak and passive, note Paul's aggressiveness and confidence in telling his converts to imitate him or his strength in confronting Peter at Antioch and the churches of Galatia and Corinth.[83]

Unity in the body. If Christ has created peace and given us unity, then unity has to be part of our self-understanding. We are one with other people in Christ, like it or not. The exercise of our faith is an exercise of unity. You cannot have Christ to yourself. What we do in relation to each other

---

82. Foulkes, *Ephesians*, 116–17.

83. On imitation of Paul see 1 Corinthians 4:16; 11:1. On the conflicts mentioned see Galatians 2:11–14; then 1:6–9; 3:1–6; 5:2–12; and the whole of 1 and 2 Corinthians.

must grow out of an understanding of unity and be geared to produce unity. Therefore, unity in Christ is both the starting place and the goal (4:3 and 13).

We cannot be mature Christians by ourselves, for we cannot give ourselves everything we need for a life of faith. Christ could supply our needs directly, but instead he has chosen to grace other people so that they contribute to us and we to them. Grace comes from God, but it is also conveyed along horizontal channels.[84] Or, as F. F. Bruce put it, "The higher reaches of the Christian life cannot be attained in isolation from one's fellow believers."[85]

An emphasis on unity cannot be left to certain denominations or schools of thought, for unity is part of the gospel (see 2:14–18). Church leaders need to teach and preach about unity and find ways to communicate oneness within local congregations and among congregations. Other people in Christ are part of us and we are part of them (4:25).

At the same time, the individuality and independence of each person must be guarded. Unity does not mean sameness; in fact, unity is achieved through diversity. Nor does unity mean all Christians work under the same structure or always meet together. We must show mutual respect and be willing to engage in conversation, work, and occasions of worship. We all face the same problems in society and in our churches. Should not our common identity in Christ, our shared experience of Christ, our shared values, and mutual respect be given more attention than our differences—differences that in most cases are as much cultural as they are theological?

Reformation and renewal have often led to divisions; we need reformation and renewal that lead to unity. If a person names and follows Christ, I belong to that person, even if I do not like them. It is tough to agree with people and love them when we are alienated culturally, but is our commitment to Christ smaller than our commitment to our culture?

Wrong turn: Unity at any cost. On the other hand, the emphasis on unity does not mean unity at any cost. Unity is not the goal; unity *in Christ* is, the unity that comes from a shared faith and a shared knowledge of Christ. Therefore, there are limits to unity. The church and its unity are always Christologically and theologically defined.

Many of the divisions in modern Christianity have little to do with theology. Older theological battles have faded in memory so that many denominations no longer reflect the reasons they emerged. Many divisions occur as much for reasons of culture and personality as for theology. In fact, debate about theology would be an improvement! In some churches the theological base has become so diluted or distorted that little is left resembling

---

84. See Lovelace, *Dynamics of Spiritual Life*, 168.
85. Bruce, *The Epistle to the Ephesians*, 87.

a biblical faith—not least what has happened when radical feminism has tried to "reimage" the faith. No one should think of unity with heresy or immorality.

Are divisions not a necessary fact? How can we speak of unity when so many divisions exist—divisions that will not go away? Is there not value in divisions because no single group can reach the variety of subcultures in our society?

Yes, there is value in the plurality of groups, and that plurality will continue. At the same time, most Christians have more in common than differences. A single structure is not our goal. In Acts 6–8 the Hellenistic Christians in Jerusalem were not like the Hebraic Christians, and they certainly did not all meet together. Instead, our goal is awareness of a common bond, mutual investment in each other, and linking of arms to evangelize and to address mutual problems. Other Christians are not the enemy; they are part of us and share the same privileges and responsibilities.

Which of our differences actually *require* separation? Most do not. Even differences in belief about baptism do not require separation.[86] The Lord's Supper could be observed in ways that would allow all of us to be present at the table. The seven areas of theological oneness in 4:4–6 should make our differences pale in significance. It is time to emphasize our commonality.

Some evangelicals often fear discussion in particular with Catholics. As a matter of fact, evangelicals today have more in common with Catholics than they do with many mainline Protestants. Yet efforts of cooperation with Catholics and joint Evangelical-Catholic statements have brought criticism and alarm that cooperation will limit evangelism of Catholics. But do not all groups need evangelism? Southern Baptists—my own denomination, known more for its fights than its grace—have over fifteen million members, half of whom cannot be found. No group should proselytize, but I would not mind if Catholics led Baptists to Christ!

Is any one group really less sinful or more spiritual? Catholics have been guilty of intolerable abuses, but so have Baptists and every other group. Moreover, the lives of our people often differ little from those of non-Christians. Christians of all stripes divorce, commit adultery, have pregnancies outside marriage, are dishonest, and have problems of addiction. Should not all groups who believe in Christ say, "He is our peace," and live the unity he created by placing all of us in his body? Is it not possible to be both evangelical and ecumenical?

None of our visible churches is *the* invisible church, the body of Christ. Only God knows who is in the body, and we would do well to consider the

---

86. Some denominations actually permit either adult or infant baptism and immersion or sprinkling.

picture from God's side. Does God recognize denominations or does he see people in Christ? Live unity; keep the bond of peace.

Is this theology enough? Are the seven items mentioned in 4:4–6 enough? As long as one sees them within the context of Paul's writings and his intent, they are not minimalist descriptions. This is a full and mature Trinitarian theology, which focuses both on salvation in Christ and on God. Five of the seven words focus on salvation: one body, one Spirit, one hope, one faith, and one baptism. The cross and resurrection are not mentioned, but these five terms are shorthand for more detailed discussions of both the cross and res-urrection in 1:18–22 and 2:14–18. Eschatology and the triumph of God are included in "one hope," and Paul's monotheism is clear. God is over all and through all and in all (4:6), and Christ fills all things (4:10).

The emphases in this foundation for unity should determine the interests and shape of our theology. We should focus on the gospel and on what God has accomplished in Christ and place less stock in our ability to define the truth, for we all see through a glass darkly (1 Cor. 13:12). Humility is required first in doing theology. For too long we have allowed lower order items to cause division. We cherish eschatological timetables and the nuances of sys-tems and lose the focus on God's redeeming his people. Long ago Luther pointed out that truth is lost by disputing, which profanes the soul and causes neglect of what is important.[87] Theological clarity and precision are neces-sary, but when our explanations become the cause of division, we have not rightly understood our salvation.

Furthermore, that God is over all, in all, and through all (cf. also Acts 17:28) must be taken seriously, along with the focus on Christ's filling all things. No person or thing is beyond the reach of God. God and Christ are at work in the people with whom we disagree. Even if people are wrong or do not believe, they do not escape God's presence. God is still at work; he is still God—even if unacknowledged—and is still present and filling all things.

The work of the church. To say the church is ineffective and has lost its influence is an understatement. A drive through a community to look at its churches is rarely comforting. Mainline churches are dwindling away, and reactionary, conservative churches are often unable to deal with the culture. Christ is muted or distorted beyond recognition. More loyalty is paid to the evangelical subculture than the gospel. The pastor's prominence stifles the work of Christians and encourages self-promotion. This passage offers a blueprint for redesigning the work of the church and its leaders.

---

87. This statement is not in the translated works of Luther, but is quoted by Spener, *Pia Desideria*, 100.

To do so, Christians must break the monopoly the clergy has on the tasks of ministry. The body of Christ does not have two classes of members—clergy and laity—or two sets of expectations. Everyone has the same task of building up the body, even though responsibilities vary. Certainly some tasks are more appropriate to pastors and require professional expertise, but even with those tasks pastors should include and train church members. Ministry is the only profession that retains nothing to itself, gives away all its knowledge free, and invites those served to do the same work.[88]

The church must train people for various levels of ministry. And training is not merely for future clergy; all members are to be trained and enabled to do the work to which God calls them. The failure to train and enlist all believers shortchanges the grace of God (cf. 2 Cor. 6:1). Even baptism and Lord's Supper are not off-limits for church members, *if* the church recognizes their leadership and deems their conduct appropriate. The main issue is the integrity of the act.

Enlisting all members into the work of the church should not focus merely on acts of public worship or teaching. To suggest this only shows how narrowly we view ministry. The ministries of the people cover most of life—some of it the unnoticed ministry to family and friends and some of it more intentionally reaching out. Ministry includes quietly nurturing individuals, working with small groups, addressing problems in society, and providing care to people in distress. This is not do-goodism—which is not bad in itself—but an exercise of the grace of the gospel to build up the body. The entire body must be involved in the work of the body.

The work of the leaders. Application of this text also requires that we take more seriously the work of Christian leaders. The clergy cannot possibly do all that is necessary for building up and caring for the body. Our present practice has made ministry an impossible burden. We expect both too much and the wrong kinds of things from pastors, much of which should be done by other church members. Pastors are not hired to do the ministry, but to prepare the people to work, and pastors must be the first to expect work from parishioners. We must also stop viewing pastors as masters of ceremonies who conduct services for others to watch. Abraham Heschel complained of people who pray by proxy, letting their leaders do their praying.[89] Worship has not occurred if people only watch someone else do it. Pastors lead in worship, but worship only occurs if the inner beings of the people are engaged, strengthened, and involved.

---

88. That church members cannot officiate at weddings is due to legal constraints, not theological ones.

89. Abraham Joshua Heschel, *Quest for God: Studies in Prayer and Symbolism* (New York: Crossroad, 1990), 50–51.

What we *should* expect from clergy we rarely receive—the communication of God's Word to elicit and enlist the souls of people. That is exactly what Paul does in Ephesians: He focuses on the gospel and its effect. Many pastors get involved in all sorts of other activities and do not develop their knowledge and ability to explain the Word. Respect for pastors is low. Often they are no longer perceived to be leaders, for their expertise is not obvious. Pastors must be experts in the gospel—the broadest subject in the world—and its application to life, beginning with themselves. They need to train their people biblically. Without it, it is no surprise that so many have been duped by flashy televangelists. A pastor's job is to help people be productive with their own Christian work and service.

Doing the truth in love. The importance of truth cannot be overestimated. All three persons of the Trinity are linked with truth, the gospel is the word of truth, we are to speak and do the truth, and we are to worship in truth. Worship is telling the truth about God. Confession is telling the truth about ourselves. Counseling is a process of helping people deal with the truth. In the end we have no other activity but speaking and living the truth in love.

Application of these words focuses first on the gospel itself. We are to live the gospel, God's truth in Christ under which all other truth is subsumed. As we have seen,[90] the gospel expresses reality, so speaking the truth in love involves rejecting the pseudo-reality in which our society seeks to live and embracing what is really real—God and his work in the world. Living the truth in love is a *theological* act, by which the whole of God's message is incorporated. Ephesians takes a comprehensive view of God and humanity, moving from God's eternal electing grace to the fullness of time when all things are summed up in Christ. It has in view the once, the now, and the not yet. This is the reality that living the truth seeks to communicate, and it is the framework within which all other living of truth and love takes place.

Living the truth in love is no abstract exercise; it is personal, practical, and all-embracing. No other foundation exists for healthy living. We as humans prefer to live in delusion, hiding from ourselves and thinking we are better (or worse) than we are. We lie to ourselves, to each other, and to God. The entertainment industry consciously hides reality and creates an illusion in which people seek to live. As one actor said after being caught in a huge indiscretion, "I don't believe in truth. I believe in style." With so many lies, it is not surprising that people are like corks in storm-tossed waves, being carried in every direction (4:14). But sooner or later, the delusion falls apart, and we and our relationships suffer. We need to speak truth with God—even if it is

---

90. See pp. 61, 115–19, 146–52.

to express our doubts and fears—with ourselves, and with other persons, and then we need to *live* the truth.

People need some place where they can be accepted for who they are and can speak honestly about their fears, frustrations, and hopes. The church, not the local bar, needs to be the place where people can speak the truth in love and hear it spoken to them in love. Christians need to be communications majors. Knowing what to say and how to say it is never easy. Sometimes speaking the truth in love requires confrontation; sometimes it requires giving people room to find out for themselves.

Living the truth in love means embracing people in an unwavering commitment to truth. This commitment has a theological foundation in the gospel and knows as part of its own truth that we see through a glass darkly (1 Cor. 13:12). But in the humility of partial knowledge, what is known is not evaded. Truth is not used to harm, nor is love allowed to distort. Love rejoices with the truth (13:6). Both love and truth are needed for health and all relations.

Every couple should make an unbreakable vow to always speak the truth in love. Every parent and child should make the same unbreakable vow. Love may seem out of place in business ethics, but the guideline for business too is speaking the truth in love. Churches and pastors too have only the same path. Whether dealing with the shallowness of a self-proclaimed "good" person or with someone struggling with cancer, truth in love is all we have.

Speaking the truth in love may require confrontation, which many of us seek to avoid out of concern for our own security. But in a fallen world confrontation is necessary to love. The command to love one's neighbor as oneself is even preceded by the admonition, "Rebuke your neighbor frankly so you will not share in his guilt" (Lev. 19:17–18). Both patience and tolerance also have their roles. Wisdom is required to discern when service to others means speaking or "the ministry of holding your tongue."[91]

Living the truth in love requires confronting the lies society hands us. Alcohol is *not* required for a good time. Pornography *does* demean women, and *no*, the majority of people are not promiscuous. Poor people are *not* necessarily lazy. *None* of us is independent and self-supporting. All Christians are *not* hypocrites, and *no*, you cannot worship God just as well by yourself.

Moreover, church lies need to be confronted. When the Catholic Church annuls a marriage after thirteen years, two children, and a divorce because the man was not baptized, that is a lie that cannot be condoned. When various people seek to cover over sexual indiscretion or harassment by their leaders, they should be confronted. When denominations deny their gospel

---

91. Dietrich Bonhoeffer, *Life Together*, trans. John W. Doberstein (New York: Harper & Row, 1954), 91.

by vindictiveness and division, someone needs to say they are living a lie. Corruption flourishes because the culture exalts loyalty over integrity. Integrity is all we have worth fighting for.

The fight for integrity can be costly. People may lose their jobs if they speak the truth in love. Evil may resort to violence when its lies are debunked. But discipleship is always costly. Speaking the truth in love is a way to identify with the cross. But even when costly, integrity is still the only thing we have.

Handling conflict. Conflict is unavoidable in life and is never easy or pleasant. No automatically successful procedures exist, but this passage provides guidelines for handling conflict. In short, forget your ego, see to yourself first, and speak the truth in love. Show humility, gentleness, patience, and put up with people in love without an air of paternalism. Love and concern should be so obvious that other people know that they are not conditioned on agreement. Even if people have to go their separate ways, they can do so without violating their Christian character. If Christian attitudes cannot prevail in tense times, they have no claim to be genuine.

Concluding reflection. Application of this passage requires nothing less than a reformation of Christianity. We have strayed from the gospel as surely as if we had sold indulgences. Our individualism, ecclesiastical hierarchies, and lack of integrity do not match the calling with which we were called. We have lost our sense of the body of Christ. Be good stewards of his grace and fulfill your role in his body. Live the truth in love. It is not beyond you, for it is enabled by being attached to Christ.

> From the cowardice that shrinks from new truths,
> From the laziness that is content with half-truths,
> And from the arrogance that thinks it knows all truth,
> O God of truth, deliver us.[92]

---

92. Quoted in Henlee H. Barnette, "The Minister As a Moral Role-Model," *RevEx* 86 (1989): 509–10.

Ephesians 4:17–24

S O I TELL you this, and insist on it in the Lord, that you must no longer live as the Gentiles do, in the futility of their thinking. ¹⁸They are darkened in their understanding and separated from the life of God because of the ignorance that is in them due to the hardening of their hearts. ¹⁹Having lost all sensitivity, they have given themselves over to sensuality so as to indulge in every kind of impurity, with a continual lust for more.

²⁰You, however, did not come to know Christ that way. ²¹Surely you heard of him and were taught in him in accordance with the truth that is in Jesus. ²²You were taught, with regard to your former way of life, to put off your old self, which is being corrupted by its deceitful desires; ²³to be made new in the attitude of your minds; ²⁴and to put on the new self, created to be like God in true righteousness and holiness.

Original Meaning THIS IS THE fourth of the five explicit "formerly–now" contrasts in Ephesians.[1] It comes as an exhortation and provides commentary on 4:1: "Live [walk] worthy of the calling you have received." Paul grounds his ethical concerns in his theology. The result is one of the most poignant descriptions of sinful humanity and of conversion.[2] Note the oppositions:

former "Gentile" life versus present life
futility versus truth
darkened and ignorance versus taught
putting off the old being versus putting on the new
deceit versus truth
corrupted versus new creation
impurity and lust versus righteousness and holiness
separated from the life of God versus created to be like God

---

1. See p. 93.

2. Note the prominence given to words for the mind, ignorance, thinking, desiring, learning, truth, and sin. Parallels exist with 2:12, 15; Romans 1:21–32; Colossians 1:21; and especially 3:9–10.

With justification A. Lincoln points to the similarity of the "two ways" theology of Judaism and early Christianity.[3]

Structure. The Greek text of this section contains two long sentences, each comprising a paragraph in the NIV. Verses 17–19 appeal for a life different from the former sinful way of life, while verses 20–24 describe the transformation that has taken place in Christ.

The connection with the surrounding material should not be lost. Precisely because of the unity of the body and Christ's work within the body (4:1–16), the appeal to live worthy of one's calling is strengthened and expanded. The material that follows (4:25–6:20) is largely commentary on 4:17–24. Primary attention is given to the role of the mind in Christianity, to truth, and to sins involving sexuality, anger, the tongue, and covetousness. Paul's concern in this second half of the letter is to paint a clear contrast between the former life and the Christian life and in so doing to keep Christians from sin and from association with sin.

The Old Life of Futility (4:17–19)

THE GREEK WORD translated "I . . .insist on it" (v. 17) is literally "I testify" or "I declare." In contexts like this it has the connotation "urge" (cf. 1 Thess. 2:12). Paul expresses his appeal to his readers with increasing strength as the letter progresses. "In the Lord" adds authority to his appeal and virtually suggests his teaching comes from the Lord. The letter reaches a climax here. Paul's readers cannot go further without making an ethical decision. Here the die is cast. The rest of the letter will only take care of details.

Paul asks his Gentile readers not to live like Gentiles![4] This sounds strange, but obviously "Gentile" could be used both in an ethnic sense and in a moral sense, somewhat akin to the earlier flexibility of the English word "pagan." Jews divided humanity into two classes—Jews and Gentiles. While Paul could address them as Gentiles ethnically (2:11), he did not want his readers to be like the Gentiles among whom they lived. In the second century Christians would speak of themselves as a "third race" (a thinking already reflected in 1 Cor. 10:32).

Sin as futility of the mind. Paul's primary concern is not with a list of specific sins, but with a distortion and disorientation of the mind. Several expressions convey this thought:

(1) "futility of their thinking" (v. 17)
(2) "darkened in their understanding" (v. 18)

---

3. Lincoln, *Ephesians*, 272. The "two ways" are the ways of evil and of righteousness (see, e.g., Ps. 1).

4. For the structural dominance given to the word "live" ["walk"], see p. 194.

(3) "ignorance that is in them" (v. 18)
(4) "due to the hardening of their hearts" (v. 18)
(5) "continual lust" (v. 19)
(6) "deceitful desires" (v. 22).

The parallels with Romans 1:21–32 deserve careful attention. Both texts view sin as a malfunction of the mind. In Romans, a split in the knowing process causes alienation. Although Gentiles "knew God," they did not acknowledge him (Rom. 1:21). This refusal to "know what they know" is expressed in Ephesians as hardness of heart (contrast Paul's prayer in 3:19, that his readers will know what they cannot know, the love of Christ). Both Ephesians 4:17–19 and Romans 1:21–32 focus on willful futility, darkness, distorted reasoning leading to alienation from God, and resulting passions and desires that lead to uncleanness and sins. Sins are not the cause of the problem, but the result; the problem lies in the mind and in choices made against God. In Romans God gave people over to the desires of their hearts, whereas Paul uses the same word here to say they give themselves over.

The word translated "futility" (*mataiotes*) expresses meaninglessness, uselessness, worthlessness, or emptiness. The majority of the occurrences of this word in the LXX are in Ecclesiastes to express the meaninglessness of life. In the New Testament the word occurs elsewhere only in Romans 8:20 (NIV, "frustration") and 2 Peter 2:18 ("empty").[5] As M. Barth expressed dramatically, "With one single word Paul describes the majority of the inhabitants of the Greco-Roman empire ... as aiming with silly methods at a meaningless goal."[6]

Four elements in verse 18 trace the problem back to its source. (1) The Gentile way of life is meaningless because the Gentiles have no light to give them life and guidance. They are intellectually blacked out.[7] In the ancient world light was a universal symbol for understanding. In Judaism (cf. Ps. 36:9) and the New Testament light is used of life-giving relation with God (cf. Eph. 1:18; 5:8–14). (2) Darkness engulfs the Gentile mind because they are "separated from the life" God gives, who is the source of the light. (3) The Gentiles are separated from God because of deliberate "ignorance," which has taken up residence in their souls. (4) The Gentiles are ignorant because of their hardness[8] of heart. The heart is the source of all loyalties.[9] In this case,

---

5. The related adjective (*mataios*) occurs six times (e.g., 1 Cor. 15:17 ["futile"]; James 1:26 ["worthless"]).

6. Barth, *Ephesians*, 2:499.

7. Ibid., 2:500.

8. The root translated "hardening" is used for marble and for skin or bone that has no feeling. The NEB translation, "grown hard as stone," conveys the idea well.

9. Paul S. Minear, "A Theology of the Heart," *Worship*, 63 (1989): 247.

hardness of heart has prevented all loyalty to God. In sum, hearts made insensitive to God have set off a chain reaction that turned out the light and led to meaninglessness.

If verse 18 traces the problem back to its origin, verse 19 shows its outcome. "Insensitivity" in one direction leads to "sensuality" in another. This play on words in the NIV is not present in the Greek text, but it effectively communicates the intent of the passage. The triad of "sensuality," "impurity," and "lust" is paralleled in 5:3, with "sexual immorality" replacing "sensuality." The word translated "having lost all sensitivity" describes the callousness and numbness resulting from the hardening.

"Sensuality" (*aselgeia*), by implication, is the idol to which the Gentiles have given themselves. As in Romans 1:21–32, the loss of relation to God leads to uncontrolled, outrageous, sinful behavior, especially with regard to sexuality.[10] Although "every kind of impurity" covers numerous sins, the grouping of words in the various vice lists suggests that its primary reference is still to sexual sin (see Gal. 5:19). The translation "indulge" in 4:19 is too strong and may create the wrong nuance; it means merely "working" or "doing."

The word translated "continual lust" (*pleonexia*) means literally "the desire to have more."[11] Ephesians 5:5 and Colossians 3:5 equate greed and idolatry, a theme that is implicit here in 4:17–19. These verses reflect a Jewish understanding of idolatry as the root of all sin, and greed as the sin encompassing all sins (cf. Wisdom of Solomon 15:5–6). Impure activity is rooted in greedy desire. This word joined with "deceitful desires" in verse 22 and the "hardening of . . . hearts" in verse 18 make a strong accusation about the self-centered character of sin.

Learning the Messiah (4:20–24)

THESE VERSES PROVIDE as strong a contrast as possible between his readers' previous mental distortion and the truth, learning, and renewal of mind that occur in Christ. If the Gentiles' core problem is a distorted mind, the solution can only be a renewing of the mind, which is exactly Paul's understanding of salvation (cf. Rom. 12:2). He uses three images to achieve the contrast: instruction of the mind, changing clothes, and new creation. Paul seeks the same thing here as in 2:11—that believers will *remember* the contrast between what was *formerly* true and what is *now* true.

---

10. In other texts the NIV translates this Greek word as "lewdness" (Mark 7:22); "debauchery" (Rom. 13:13); "shameful ways" (2 Peter 2:2); "filthy" (2:7), and "lustful" (2:18). Other words for sexual sin often occur in close proximity.

11. The NIV usually translates this word "greed"; more traditional translations use "covetousness."

Knowing the Christ and Jesus (4:20–21). The wording of verses 20–21 is unusual, almost harsh, and the nuances of the text are difficult to convey. Literally, verse 20 reads: "You did not learn the Christ this way."[12] No parallel exists for learning a person. More is intended than mere learning facts about Christ. That is, the readers have been schooled in the Messiah. They know him, have firsthand knowledge of him, and know how radically different his life is from that of the Gentiles. The implication seems close to 1 Corinthians 2:16; they have, or should have, the mind of Christ.

In verse 21, Paul goes on to emphasize what they already know:[13] They know better than to live the life he described in verses 17–19, for they know the truth that is in Jesus.[14] The name "Jesus" standing alone is rare in Paul and seems to refer to the earthly Jesus and his life, death, and resurrection.[15] In this verse, Christ is viewed as teacher, subject, and the sphere of learning. "Heard of him" can be translated "heard *him*"[16] as a parallel to "know [the] Christ" in verse 20 (cf. 2:17). Also unusual is the statement they were "taught *in him*," but the intent seems to be that the context of their learning was their union with Christ.

"In accordance with the truth that is in Jesus" (lit., "just as truth is in Jesus") should not suggest information about Jesus. Paul's point is that Jesus embodies and encompasses the truth. Find Jesus and you find truth. Find truth and you find Jesus. Truth does not exist apart from him. This is not surprising, given the expectation in 1:10 that all things will be summed up in Christ. In sum, verses 20–21 describe encounter with Jesus and instruction from union with him so that truth is found in him. The following verses show that truth is revealed primarily in dying and rising with Christ.

Old being–new being (4:22–24). Verses 22–24 contain three infinitive phrases: "to put off," "to be made new," and "to put on," which may be interpreted in several ways. They could be taken:

(1) As complements of verses 20-21 to explain the content of Christ's teaching. The NIV has chosen this alternative and inserted the words "You were taught" to facilitate the connection.

---

12. Of 46 occurrences of the Greek word *Christos* ("Messiah") in Ephesians, 23 have the article (often used with proper names in Greek). No pattern emerges as to the significance of the use of the article. Its presence here may be insignificant, but it may also emphasize the whole divine plan as caught up in the Messiah.

13. The NIV should not be understood to suggest the readers had not heard of Jesus.

14. Lincoln, *Ephesians*, 271, suggests "Christ" in verse 20 stands for the Christian tradition, but this is unlikely, especially in view of the change from "Christ" to "Jesus" in verse 21.

15. See Romans 8:11; 1 Corinthians 12:3; 2 Corinthians 4:5, 10–11, 14; 11:4; Galatians 6:17; 1 Thessalonians 1:10; 4:14.

16. "Him" is in the accusative case, which can be understood either as "heard about him" or "heard him."

(2) As imperatives.

(3) As result ("you were taught so that you put off").

At issue is whether these transforming actions are viewed as past or still to be performed. Note the parallel in Colossians 3:9–10, where the command not to lie is based in the fact that the old being has already been removed. The intent in Ephesians may be the same, for these words are a theological reminder to motivate the ethical material that follows (note "therefore" in v. 25). Whatever else we say, this passage is evidence of Paul's frequent blending of the indicative and the imperative. His intent is to buttress his plea in 4:17 for a different lifestyle. Verses 22–24 show what the readers were taught, but the implication is that these words should also be put into practice.

A comparison of several texts demonstrates the strong probability that 4:22–24 is derived from a baptismal liturgy or at least a Pauline baptismal theology. Note the following:

> *Ephesians* 4:22–24: "You were taught, with regard to your former way of life, to put off your old self, which is being corrupted by its deceitful desires; to be made new in the attitude of your minds; and to put on the new self, created to be like God in true righteousness and holiness."

> *Colossians* 3:9–11: "Do not lie to each other, since you have taken off your old self with its practices and have put on the new self, which is being renewed in knowledge in the image of its Creator. Here there is no Greek or Jew, circumcised or uncircumcised, barbarian, Scythian, slave or free, but Christ is all, and is in all."

> *Romans* 6:3, 6: "Or don't you know that all of us who were baptized into Christ Jesus were baptized into his death? ... For we know that our old self was crucified with him so that the body of sin might be done away with, that we should no longer be slaves to sin."

> *Romans* 13:14: "Rather, clothe yourselves with the Lord Jesus Christ, and do not think about how to gratify the desires of the sinful nature."

> *1 Corinthians* 12:13: "For we were all baptized by one Spirit into one body—whether Jews or Greeks, slave or free—and we were all given the one Spirit to drink."

> *Galatians* 3:26–28: "You are all sons of God through faith in Christ Jesus, for all of you who were baptized into Christ have clothed yourselves with Christ. There is neither Jew nor Greek, slave nor free, male nor female, for you are all one in Christ Jesus."

Galatians 3:26–28 is the fullest form of this baptismal theology, but Romans 6:3–6 and 1 Corinthians 12:13 also refer explicitly to baptism. The litany of divisions set aside is present in Galatians, 1 Corinthians, and Colossians. Galatians and Romans 13:14 speak of being clothed with Christ, whereas Ephesians and Colossians speak of being clothed with the new being (cf. Rom. 6:6). The implication is clear: The new being is Christ himself (cf. Eph. 2:15).

This raises a question as to how "old being" and "new being" should be understood. Do these terms refer to the individual before and after conversion? Or should they be seen as *corporate* expressions for two ways of life?[17] While this latter option may sound strange, it merits reflection. Paul's theology is complex, and consideration must be given to his "spheres of influence" thinking,[18] his Adam-Christ typology,[19] his language for old and new being,[20] outer and inner being,[21] and new creation.[22] The corporate sense of "new being" in 2:15 and the view of all people as either in Adam or in Christ suggest a corporate understanding. But the other terms suggest an individual understanding, for 4:23 seems to have individuals in view (see also Col. 2:11). In the end, both corporate and individual aspects must be retained, though the individual understanding seems dominant. Even if the terms are taken corporately, the focus is on what *individuals* do in conforming to the corporate reality.

Paul's main issue here is transformation—change of identities. The language for "putting off" and "putting on" occurs in a variety of ethical contexts, including non-Christian sources.[23] "Putting off" and "putting on" are another way of expressing the ideas of dying and rising with Christ, which also appear in discussions of baptism and ethics (cf. Rom. 6:1–11; Col. 2:11–3:4).

The tenses in these three verses are important. The laying aside the old being (v. 22) and the putting on the new (v. 24) are both described by aorist

---

17. See Robert Tannehill, *Dying and Rising with Christ* (Berlin: Verlag Alfred Töpelmann, 1967), 24–25.

18. See pp. 40–42, 47–48, 56–57, 63–64, 102.

19. Romans 5:12–21; 1 Corinthians 15:20–22, 45–49.

20. Romans 6:6; Ephesians 2:15; 4:22–24; Colossians 3:9–10.

21. Romans 7:22; 2 Corinthians 4:16; Ephesians 3:17.

22. 2 Corinthians 5:17; Galatians 6:15.

23. In addition to the texts above, for "putting off" see Romans 13:12; Ephesians 4:25; Colossians 2:11; 3:8; Hebrews 12:1; James 1:21; 1 Peter 2:1; for "putting on," Romans 13:12; Ephesians 6:11–14; 1 Thessalonians 5:8. Even though baptism stands behind the imagery of "putting off" and "putting on," the idea of changing clothes should not be viewed as evidence of a baptismal ritual of literally changing clothes. Evidence for this practice does not appear before the second century. Lincoln, *Ephesians*, 284–285, gives helpful information on this subject and on the background of the language.

infinitives. This tense is used for *undefined* action;[24] it is merely mentioned without further specification. The most important issue is the contrast these words provide. The present tense, which shows ongoing action, describes the continual corruption of the old being (v. 22) and the continual renewing of the mind (v. 23).[25] Both items are important. The old being is in a state of ever-deepening corruption, and the Christian life is an ever-increasing renewal of the mind (see 2 Cor. 3:18; 4:16).

The old being fit the former way of living, and its ongoing corruption was fueled by "deceitful desires."[26] Paul's thought is related to 2:3, which spoke of disobedience caused by following fleshly desires, although no mention is made here of the ruler of the air. The old being is the human self without God, deluded and deceived into a downward spiral by fleshly desires. The solution requires ongoing renewal and a new creation—two phrases that we would have expected in the reverse order. But Paul's emphasis on continual corruption seems to have brought the corresponding emphasis on continual renewal first. Note Colossians 3:10, where the continual renewal *follows* the putting on of the new being.[27]

The NIV's "made new in the attitude of your minds" (v. 23) is literally "being made new in the spirit of your mind." The word "spirit" can mean "attitude" (2 Tim. 1:7), but more seems intended in Ephesians. Some scholars even take "spirit" as a reference to the Holy Spirit and understand Paul's intent to be the Christian mind guided by the divine Spirit.[28] But this is not his point in verse 23. He is concerned about the human spirit, that controlling center of our being and the means of our relation to God. This is the object of the continual renewal.

The language for the new being (v. 24) recalls Genesis 1:26–27 and the idea of creation in God's image. The image marred in Eden is being recre-

---

24. *Not* necessarily "point" action, as has been the traditional way of looking at the aorist tense!

25. The NIV does not communicate the continuing process of renewal. To do so is awkward—"to be being made new."

26. Lincoln's suggestion (*Ephesians*, 283, 286) that "deceit" should be seen as a genitive of origin yielding "desires which come from deceit" is possible, but less likely; yet if true, it would strengthen the argument that truth is the origin of righteousness and holiness in verse 24.

27. Ephesians and Colossians use two different roots to describe newness, and they use them differently. Ephesians 4:23-24 uses *ananeoo* ("make new") and *kainos* ("new"), whereas Colossians 3:10 has *anakainoo* ("renew") and *neos* ("new"). The two roots are used interchangeably in Paul's time, and no difference in meaning is intended, despite the proposal by Schnackenburg, *Ephesians: A Commentary*, 200.

28. See, for example, Schnackenburg, *Ephesians: A Commentary*, 200. Note Titus 3:5, which does speak of the renewal by the Holy Spirit (cf. also Eph. 3:16).

ated in Christ. This new creation is viewed as a work God has already accomplished and reflects the same ideas as 2:10. Whereas the old being fit the former life of living in lust (v. 19), the new being fits with God in "righteousness and holiness." These two nouns form a hendiadys—one idea expressed through two words. Literally, the text reads "righteousness and holiness of truth," which the NIV has understood as an adjectival genitive—"*true* righteousness and holiness." However, since truth is emphasized so much in this context (vv. 15, 21, 25) in opposition to lying and deceit (vv. 14, 22, 25), a genitive of source seems likely. Righteousness and holiness have their source in truth, the truth found in Jesus.

What will the new being look like with its righteousness and holiness? The focus on truth here and on Christ who gave himself indicate that the key characteristics of the new being are truth and love. The following sections will verify and illustrate this conclusion.

 CHANGE THE WORD "Gentiles" to "Americans" or some other relevant label, and we have little difficulty bringing verses 17–19 into our contemporary situation, for they are like a mirror. We see ourselves all too well. Verses 20–24 do require further examination, for the religious ideas they express are unexpected and almost too good to be true. Can we really do what they ask? We also need to process the theology of these verses, for better descriptions of depravity and conversion may not exist.

Human depravity (4:17–19, 22). Today only the naive doubt human depravity. Wars, conflict, crime, and moral decline provide unavoidable evidence. We may think *we* are basically good, especially in comparison to others, but all of us readily acknowledge something is out of kilter in the human psyche. Yet most of us do not feel as negative as this text. We do not admit that life is futile, that we are in the dark and cut off from God, ignorant and hard-hearted, and that we are given over to uncontrolled sensuality and passions. At the same time, neither do we think we can put off the old being and put on a new one. We do not admit the depth of the human plight or the wonder held out to us. The mediocrity of our thought neither requires action nor enables success.

Is the description too negative? Are these verses too absolute? How is it possible to think the human mind is futile—worthless—when humans have accomplished so much? And surely not all Gentiles were as bad as Paul says.

This passage does not reject value in humanity, and it must be read in keeping with its purpose. This is not a discussion about human worth, ability, or accomplishment, nor was Paul unaware that some Gentile philosophers wrestled with ethical questions and sought high morals.[29] The passage is a rejection of the Gentile way of life, not a rejection of the Gentiles as persons (which would be strange for one who saw himself as the apostle to the Gentiles, cf. 3:1). Paul's statements here are both a rejection of the dominant lifestyle of the society in which the readers lived and a call for them to reject it. Furthermore, these are generalizing statements that describe the conduct of those who cut themselves off from life with God.

Granted the intent of the text, it is not too negative. It is precisely on target. Christianity is a religion that emphasizes on the one hand the futility and distortion of humanity without God and on the other hand the value of humanity in God's eyes and with God. Christianity invites us to recognize we are vile, but it also invites us to desire to be like God.[30] It knows that human beings need a redemption they do not deserve, but also that God thinks they are worth redeeming. Only in facing the painful truth about ourselves is there hope for healing.

Rather than being too negative, when we are honest, we know this text describes each one of us. The theology of the verses 17–19 requires reflection in two major areas:

(1) Life without God is meaningless, for true life is from God.
(2) The human mind is twisted by an idolatrous self-interest.

(1) Our society usually ignores the age-old question of the meaning of life. We busy ourselves and entertain ourselves so we do not have to think. Diversions such as drugs, alcohol, entertainment, and work keep us from reflecting on life. But as wonderful as it is, life is short, painful, and—viewed from a human perspective—without much significance. If we are merely the accidental result of a "big bang," human existence is a cruel, cosmic joke, and no reason exists for ethical behavior. As one person put it, "You get sick and you die, so you have to keep busy." What would it matter if we did not exist? Humans are like grass in the desert, here today and gone tomorrow (Isa. 40:6–8). The writer of Ecclesiastes is right; life is meaningless. Without God in the picture, nothing on this earth can comfort us if we analyze it seriously.

(2) *Homo incurvatus in se* ("a human being curved in upon self") was Martin Luther's definition of sin.[31] Separated from God, human beings curl around

---

29. See the overreaction by Ernest Best, "Two Types of Existence," *Interpretation* 47 (1993): 39–51.

30. Blaise Pascal, *Pensées* (New York: Random House, 1941), no. 536. Pascal emphasizes these themes repeatedly. See especially numbers 139, 164, 171, 194, 418, 430, 494, 555, and 561.

31. See *Luther: Lectures on Romans*, trans. and ed. Wilhelm Pauck, The Library of Christian Classics (Philadelphia: Westminster, 1961), 218, 225, on Romans 8:3. See also the

themselves like shavings planed from a board.[32] Pride and self-centeredness cause hardness of heart, which in turn leads to choosing self instead of God. The result is an inversion that distorts. The lights go out and life is lived in futility.

Blaise Pascal's writings often seem to be reflections on our text:

- Pride takes you from God and lust binds you to yourself.
- The sensibility of man to trifles and his insensibility to great things indicates a strange inversion.
- Our own interest is again a marvelous instrument for nicely putting out our eyes.[33]

Pascal described a human as a reed, but a thinking reed, all of whose dignity is in thought.[34] The mind is the important element, but all dignity is lost when thought omits God and centers on self. Without God the mind is crosswired and without aim. Its energies go in the wrong direction. Pascal saw further that this inversion set up an internal war between the reason and the passions, so that we are always opposed to ourselves.[35] Lust is an insubordination of the flesh.[36] Our passions are never satisfied; we always want more. Even when we know actions are harmful to our bodies and relations, we still choose them. As ancient philosophers recognized, humans love their vices and hate them at the same time. They hate their sins and cannot leave them.[37]

By implication this text is about idolatry. We turn from God to the idol of self. We give ourselves to self and end up controlled by desires—desires that deceive by promising happiness, but never provide either satisfaction or fulfillment. Instead, they destroy. As Tom Wright points out, "idols demand sacrifices."[38] The cost is high to wholeness and to relations with people. The judgment of sin—at least in part—is that people are given over to their sins. Sin is its own punishment. Human beings need a higher calling than following passions.

---

treatment of John Loeschen, *Wrestling With Luther: An Introduction to the Study of his Thought* (St. Louis: Concordia, 1976), 43-58.

32. The image is attributed to Theophon the Recluse.

33. Pascal, *Pensées*, nos. 430, 198, and 82.

34. Ibid., no. 347.

35. Ibid., no. 412.

36. See Augustine, "On Continence," sections 5-9, *Nicene and Post-Nicene Fathers*, 3:381–83; "Sermons on Selected Lessons of the New Testament," Sermon 78, *Nicene and Post-Nicene Fathers*, 6:491–95. Pascal (no. 691) said, "Man has no other enemy than lust."

37. See, for example, Seneca, *Ad Lucilium*, Epistle 116; and cf. *Hippolytus*, 177.

38. Tom Wright, *Bringing the Church to the World* (Minneapolis: Bethany, 1992), 48.

Ancient Greeks like the Cynics and Stoics knew that desires corrupt and destroy life; they therefore sought to be free of desire. In fact, they viewed passions as diseases of the mind.[39] Living free of desire was considered the mark of wisdom and maturity. But no one can live free of desire, and the solution is not the rejection of desires, but their subjection to God.

Ephesians 4:19 could have been written this morning as a telling commentary on us. We give ourselves to trivialities and diversions. Our minds are given to sports, movies, and sitcoms to avoid thought.[40] Our self-centeredness alienates us from God. We do not acknowledge our need of God, do not have time for him, and if we think about him at all, our thought is juvenile. Having lost sensitivity to God and fellowship with him, we give ourselves to sensuality, trying through pleasure and especially through sexual avenues to recover that intimacy for which we were created. We are caught in an increasing downward spiral of serving ourselves. Pleasure and enjoyment are not illegitimate, but when they become the focus of life, they distort and corrupt.

Life is from God. The text implies that we need life from God. Human beings were never intended to live merely as individuals; we were created for relation with God. We are diminished when separated from what is greater than us—God. Without him, we lose our dignity. Lasting happiness does not exist apart from relation to him. We are restless until we rest in God.[41] What we need is not self-expression and self-satisfaction, but self-surrender and self-attachment to God, with whom all things are ours to enjoy (see 1 Cor. 3:21-22; 1 Tim. 6:17).[42]

Like 2:1-3, this passage is about depravity. The grim picture is not a rejection of humanity, nor a "total depravity" in the sense that nothing of value exists in humans. It is about a pervasive depravity that affects all our being and results from a skewered thinking that ignores God. Once again, by implication, sin is a bad trade. We have traded life with God for a corrupting, meaningless life with self.

The school of Christ (4:20–24). Paul's words assume that life is different for Christians; they state that an encounter with Jesus has changed things. Unfortunately, too many people claiming the title *Christian* serve self as fully as non-Christians. Their conversion is a stillbirth. They allow the non-Christian world to define life rather than the God who created them. All of

---

39. In much of Greek thought, the will of God is expressed by a single formula: "not to desire." See "θυμός," *TDNT*, 3:167.

40. More than fifty sitcoms appear on prime time TV each week.

41. This famous line is from Augustine's *Confessions* (1.1).

42. Cf. Abraham Joshua Heschel, *Quest for God* (New York: Crossroad, 1990), 57: "It is precisely the function of prayer to shift the center of living from self-consciousness to self-surrender."

us too often seek conformity to this world's scheme, or at least recognition from it. We must seek to apply the text both to Christians and to non-Christians. Verses 17–19 are not just descriptive of the "other folks." The text *is addressed to Christians* to make sure they do not live such a life.

We must also understand the strong language used here of contact with Christ. Paul's expressions for the depth of relation and union with Christ assume the kind of faith described in chapter 2.[43] This is not belief about Jesus, but an involvement with him and openness to him. Since he is the Lord who leads, the language of learning is natural. The truth that is learned is the truth of the death and resurrection of Christ, from which all other truth is understood. We identify with his death and resurrection by dying to self and rising to new life, which here are expressed as "putting off the old being" and "putting on the new."

Is conversion possible? This is a text about conversion.[44] Can we really put off the old being and put on the new? To ask this is to ask about the truth of Christianity, for if we cannot do so, the Christian faith is meaningless. No matter how nice its teaching, it will not deal with the core of our problem, our own sin. How can I put off what I am, my personality, and my desires?

Once again, this is an issue of our identity.[45] Conversion is a renunciation of a self-centered identity in favor of a Christ-defined identity. All that shapes us is given over to Christ, and his mindset of self-giving love becomes our mindset. *Conversion is the restructuring of a person's thinking by the Holy Spirit as the result of a direct encounter with the love of God in the person of Christ* (see 5:1–2; cf. Rom. 5:5; 8:5–9). Otherwise, we are not Christians. In effect, we take off what we thought was life and put on Christ. As Robinson commented, "He has displaced *me* in myself"[46] (cf. Gal. 2:20).

Desires are deceitful and powerful, however. Can humans lay them aside so easily? "Putting off" and "putting on" clearly call for us to act, but it is not merely human activity. All is done in union with Christ, the one to whom we are joined and who teaches and enables us, and his Spirit is the agent of renewal.[47] The text emphasizes both God's activity and human responsibility.[48] We put on what he has created (4:24). To ask how much is the divine

---

43. See pp. 104–5, 112–15.

44. See also the discussion on pp. 99–107, 117–19, 270–74.

45. See pp. 115–20.

46. Robinson, *St. Paul's Epistle to the Ephesians,* 108 (italics his).

47. Not on the basis of 4:23, but of 1:13–14; 3:16; 4:30, and other references to the Holy Spirit.

48. See Stott, *God's New Society,* 182; Barth, *Ephesians,* 2:542, who views humans as partners with God in a dramatic struggle. This passage betrays no fear of synergism, the idea that God and humans work together in the salvation process.

part and how much the human is to misunderstand the process. Salvation is totally the work of God in which we are totally involved. This alone does justice to the thought of being in Christ.

If this "putting off" and "putting on" is a one-time event, something done at baptism, why does Paul seem to imply his readers should do it again? Why is the old self with its selfish desires still so present? We continue as the same person with many of our same weaknesses, desires, and characteristics. Or expressed more poignantly, the old being is drowned in baptism, but the rascal can swim![49]

Biblical texts can be produced to suggest that change occurs at baptism, repeatedly throughout life, or at the end of time.[50] Once again the now and not-yet character of Christian faith is obvious. A change has already occurred, is occurring, and will be completed at the end of time. What happened at baptism is a real putting off of self and a putting on of Christ. If there is no transformation, there is no salvation. But this is *not* merely a decision or a one-time event. *Conversion is a process*, as the present tense of 4:23 shows convincingly. "Putting off" and "putting on" (or dying and rising) is the pattern by which Christians live. The dynamic by which we are saved is the dynamic by which we live and the completion of which we still await.[51] As M. Barth put it, change takes place every hour of a person's life.[52]

Two wrong turns. (1) If conversion is a process not completed until the end, any thought of perfectionism is misguided. This error fails to take seriously enough the depth of sin in our being or the impact of the sinful world in which we live. At the same time, rejection of perfectionism ought not be an excuse for dealing lightly with sin.

(2) People should not conclude that two equal beings exist in each Christian. Nor is this passage about two impulses, an inclination toward evil and an inclination toward good in each of us.[53] The text is about an old way of life and a new way, an old mindset shaped by the world and a new mindset shaped by Christ. Actually, this text is more about eschatology than anthropology, for it is about the newness the risen Lord brings into our present.

---

49. See Eduard Schweitzer, *The Letter to the Colossians*, trans. Andrew Chester (Minneapolis: Augsburg, 1976), 202, for a slightly different version.

50. At baptism, Galatians 3:27; repeatedly, Romans 13:12–14; at the end of time, 1 Corinthians 15:53–54; 2 Corinthians 5:2–4.

51. See 1 Corinthians 15:31; 2 Corinthians 4:10–11; Galatians 3:3.

52. Barth, *Ephesians*, 2:545.

53. Such as the evil *yetzer* and the good *yetzer* in Judaism.

THE APPLICATION OF this text is straightforward: Do not live like the Americans do with their futile thinking. Change the label if necessary, but you cannot conform to your society and its system of thought. In general, the more we conform to our society, the less we understand conversion. Paul here provides a theological understanding to motivate ethics, which 4:25–6:9 will apply to specific "practical" issues. Application of this passage, then, should focus primarily on the mind and on broader theological concerns.

Learn to think. If the problem is distorted reasoning, we need a wholesale restructuring of the mind. Other texts in Ephesians have emphasized the role of the Holy Spirit in this process (1:17–18; 3:16–17), so no thought exists of a depraved mind repairing itself. The light of the gospel shows the channels along which new thinking must run, and the Spirit engages our spirit in reordering life. We must learn to think for ourselves along Christian lines.

Our primary ethicists today are popular singers, actors, and talk-show hosts, and they have led us to ruin. Surely Christians have something better to say—*if* they think through the significance of the gospel. We must therefore analyze life and the gospel and take care of the interior life. The heart, the control panel from which life is ordered, must be continually made conscious of God and not merely of self. We must take time to think in communion with God, to reflect and meditate. Without attention to the interior life, no restructuring will occur.

Assessment of society. If conformity to our society is prohibited, an honest assessment of it is required. What evidence is there of futility and skewed minds, of hardness of heart, and of sensuality and corrupting desires? What is neutral in the society and what fits positively with God's purpose for humanity? Too often we assume the agenda that society sets is reality and, therefore, is the agenda for Christians as well. But we live in a society that is out of control. Its agenda places the self-interests of pleasure, recognition, and possessions as the goals of life. Concern for God and denial of self—although possibly admired—do not fit the system. But life is not about self-satisfaction; it is about relations both with God and with other people.

Probably the most obvious evidence of futility and sensuality is the entertainment media, which offers itself as the mirror of ourselves. Most of what is offered in movies and on TV is inane, time-consuming weirdness. To buy our time we are offered insipid humor, bizarre talk shows, and endless titillation. Little is instructive in a positive way. But the media do not provide merely a mirror of ourselves; they seek to shape us. In a recent newscast a

movie director said his intent with a romantic comedy was that all the view-
ers would race home and make love to their significant other.[54] Most people
going to movies are between the ages of 12–24, an important time when they
are being shaped morally and spiritually. They are presented with far too
much overt sex, promiscuity, sexual deviancy, and violence to women. Modernity—as one person put it—is rationalized sexual misbehavior. Furthermore,
humor, which is given such prominence, is no longer healthy and cathartic;
it is structured as a defense against depth.

Wilson Mizner reportedly said, "Hollywood is a sewer with service from
the Ritz-Carlton." He is correct. Forty years ago—when movies were relatively innocuous—Christians debated whether they should attend them.
Now when they are largely objectionable, we are no longer asking the question. Maybe it is time that Christians just said "No." Certainly the entertainment media can be used in constructive ways, but it rarely happens.
These industries cannot exist without Christian support, and application of
this text should influence Christians to withhold support from such a harmful industry. Don't live like the Americans.

The ignorance in our society is just as painfully evident. Apart from ignorance, how else can one explain addiction to alcohol, tobacco, drugs, and
gambling? How else can we explain the way women allow men to use them,
incest, abuse, fraud, the billion dollar industry of shoplifting, or numerous
other crimes. These and most other problems are the direct result of pleasure
and self-interest being given free rein. When desires become masters, they
are vices.[55]

The biggest ignorance of all is the failure to consider God and his claim
on our lives. Our society braces itself, occupies itself, and procrastinates to
avoid dealing with the "God" question. Any other subject is fair game, but
God cannot be dealt with straightforwardly. Education used to include religious instruction, but under the guise of separation of the church and state,
religious instruction is now prohibited. In the process we have raised a nation
of moral imbeciles. Why do we turn our backs on the reason for which we
were created and on our future?

Look to yourself first. Assessing society is not enough. Every person—the
Christian first—must be ruthlessly honest about his or her own depravity.
We cannot hide from it. Pride and pleasure seek to dominate everything we
do, including our most religious acts. Pride and self-interest are marvelous

---

54. Similarly, a novelist has been defined as a shaman who is offering his experience for
the use of the rest of the tribe. (Russell Hoban, *Chicago Tribune Magazine* [July 23, 1995], 8).
The same is true of actors and musicians.

55. Pascal, *Pensées*, no. 502.

instruments for putting out our eyes so that we never see the truth.[56] We need to endure the pain of close self-analysis and tell the truth both to God and to ourselves about our pride and self-interest. This is called confession. Only when we name our self-centeredness and own it can we lay it aside. Until then it owns us.

We must deal with our desires for material possessions. While much of the world does not have enough to eat, we want what we do not need. We gauge success by accumulation of money and possessions—positive and useful in themselves, but heavy baggage for life and terrible masters. We never have enough. The god "Desire" controls us and is never satiated.[57] The more control we give to desires, the more corrupting they become. Desires are not bad in themselves. They are God-given assistants for living, but they need a Lord. Give them one.

We must admit that Christians are just as much given to sexual desires as anyone. It is not enough to rail against sexual sin; we have to deal with our minds being crosswired and preprogrammed for sensuality. Christians and their leaders have failed miserably with sexual sin. Too often we have derided non-Christians, but have been embarrassingly mute in discussing sexual failures among believers. Sexual desire is enormously seductive because that is the one place where pleasure, pride, and power concentrate so heavily. We need to deal honestly with our sexuality and bring it too under Christ's lordship. Sexuality is a wonderful gift from God to be used appropriately, but it is a tyrannical lord if given control. The sacrifices this idol demands are destructive of self, of others, and of relationships, to say nothing of the church's witness.

Go to school. The focus on thinking is so central that application of this text requires investment in learning. Christians are learners; that is what being a disciple means. We are learners in Christ's school, learning from him and about him and being made like him. Whether the learning is formal or informal, it must be intentional (cf. also 1:17–18; 3:16–19).

The truth is that too many people claim the name *Christian* without ever learning what it means. That approach to faith is useless and further evidence of human ignorance. Others reach a plateau deemed respectable and go no further. Adult education among Christians lags and is ineffective, with only a limited percentage of adults being involved. Churches cancel Sunday School for the summer. But without learning, growth stops and worship shrivels.

The hunger for knowledge of Christ should be ever present and ever renewing. We have not been engaging enough, substantive enough, or honest

---

56. See p. 238. Or, as Art Spander said about a certain football player, "Egotism is the anesthetic that dulls the pain of stupidity" (*Sporting News* [August 22, 1988]).

57. Cf. a line from *Star Trek*: "Having is not so pleasurable a thing as wanting."

enough to keep people learning. Paul calls for continual renewing of the mind, and both individuals and the church through worship and instruction must see that it occurs. Pastors should be involved in teaching situations as much as they are in leading worship and preaching. This may require other people doing "pastoral tasks," but as 4:12 indicates, ministry is done by the people, not the leaders. A renewed focus on learning will require rethinking how learning is done best in the context of a specific community. The traditional Sunday School approach may not be the best procedure for many congregations.

Whatever approach is taken, all learning is costly, especially the learning in the school of Christ. Not only does it require time and investment, it requires change—the willingness to give up what we are in order to become what God intends. The subject of the learning is Christ, but two other words serve as commentary: sensitivity and truth. Since insensitivity and deceit are at the root of our problem, we need instruction in sensitivity—both sensitivity to God and to people. And with deceit causing distortion, our learning must focus on truth, on how Jesus is the embodiment of truth and on how all other truth relates to him.

In addition to churches taking seriously their teaching task, Christian higher education needs to be revamped. Despite the existence of several good Christian schools, Christian education in this country is largely a failure,[58] for basically it is secular education with food coloring. Christians have been lax about devising an approach that is truly Christian. Mark Noll begins his assessment of the problem by saying, "The scandal of the evangelical mind is that there is not much of an evangelical mind."[59] Superficial thought often reduces the gospel to banalities. How this happened in a faith that focuses on the mind and truth is a mystery. But we are at a point where the whole educational enterprise among Christians needs to be rethought. We need schools that do not sacrifice academic standards, but at the same time do not find their respect by jettisoning faith commitments. Intellectually gifted Christians should be challenged to consider academic careers, and donors should be encouraged to provide funds. Education is not peripheral to the church's mission; it *is* the church's mission.

Live your baptism. "Putting off" and "putting on" occur at baptism, but these are also continual activities in our lives as we seek to live our baptism. The mode of baptism is not the important thing; the theology of baptism is— the theology of living a changed life. For most Christians baptism has sig-

---

58. One has only to read George M. Marsden, *The Soul of the American University: From Protestant Establishment to Established Nonbelief* (New York: Oxford Univ. Press, 1994). Despite the fact that Christians started most of the private universities and colleges in this country, virtually no major Christian universities exist.

59. Mark A. Noll *The Scandal of the Evangelical Mind* (Grand Rapids: Eerdmans, 1994), 3.

nificance only as a rite of entrance. This is sad. Baptism is to be lived, or, as Martin Luther urged, we daily return to our baptism.[60] Christian living requires continually putting off the old being and putting on Christ. This is not an optional element for certain spiritual types; this is assumed for all Christians. Since we must be continually renewed, Christians need to give regular and frequent attention to the process, that is, to keep short accounts with God. Without attention it will not occur.

Unfortunately, we try to exempt certain parts of life from our baptism. We are like soldiers in a previous era who kept their sword hands out of the water when they were being baptized.[61] Or if we lay the old being aside, we at least want to remember where we left it. We are like King Claudius in *Hamlet*: "May one be pardon'd and retain the offense?"[62] If clothes make the person, we attempt to keep the uniform of the old being in the closet for quick changes. That will not work. We cannot keep the old being partially alive; Christ—the uniform of the new being—will not hang in the closet. It is never fitting for Christians to be "out of uniform."

In some ways, "putting off" and "putting on" achieve the same purpose. We put off a self-centered mind and put on the self-emptying mind of Christ. In other words, to live our baptism we need to learn how to die. Paul Minear suggests that instead of looking for evidences of rebirth, we should ask how many times a person has died. Rebirth without dying is Christian nonsense, and so is new creation without crucifixion.[63] Death—dying with Christ and to self—is necessary for Christian living. But dying is not the only part of the sequence. In putting on the new self, we participate in Christ's resurrection. Life is recreated in line with God's original intention. The new being is not merely absence of self-centeredness; it is taking on the character of God and his righteousness (4:24). What is intended is a life marked by truth and love as found in Christ, as 4:25–5:2 shows. That is not beyond human capability.

By way of summary:

(1) Don't live like the Americans with their futile thinking.
(2) Get your mind in order and make honest assessments.
(3) Be a Christ-learner ever renewing your mind.
(4) Die continually to self and its desires.
(5) Put on Christ along with his truth and love.

---

60. See Luther's *Large Catechism*, 4.84-86.

61. Mentioned by Walter Wink, *Engaging the Powers*, vol. 3, *The Powers* (Minneapolis: Fortress, 1992), 294.

62. William Shakespeare, *Hamlet*, Act 3, Scene 3.

63. Paul S. Minear, *To Die and to Live: Christ's Resurrection and Christian Vocation* (New York: Seabury, 1977), 155.

Ephesians 4:25–5:2

T HEREFORE EACH OF you must put off falsehood and speak truthfully to his neighbor, for we are all members of one body. ²⁶"In your anger do not sin": Do not let the sun go down while you are still angry, ²⁷and do not give the devil a foothold. ²⁸He who has been stealing must steal no longer, but must work, doing something useful with his own hands, that he may have something to share with those in need.

²⁹Do not let any unwholesome talk come out of your mouths, but only what is helpful for building others up according to their needs, that it may benefit those who listen. ³⁰And do not grieve the Holy Spirit of God, with whom you were sealed for the day of redemption. ³¹Get rid of all bitterness, rage and anger, brawling and slander, along with every form of malice. ³²Be kind and compassionate to one another, forgiving each other, just as in Christ God forgave you.

⁵:¹Be imitators of God, therefore, as dearly loved children ²and live a life of love, just as Christ loved us and gave himself up for us as a fragrant offering and sacrifice to God.

THE NEXT SECTION of this letter (4:25–6:20) serves as a commentary on 4:17–24. The first unit (4:25–5:2) details in practical terms what the Christian life described in 4:20–24 looks like. Then in 5:3–14 Paul describes what is excluded from that life, using the contrast between light and darkness. This is followed by a summary conclusion (5:15–21), which is itself made more specific by the House Codes (5:22–6:9). Finally 6:10–20 serves as a climactic appeal to stand against evil and for God.

The connection between 4:25–5:2 and 4:17–24 is explicit. In 4:25 Paul starts with "put off," the word used in 4:22, to show what putting off the old being means. Note also "no longer" in 4:28, which repeats the same word from verse 17. The concern in this section, as in much of the New Testament ethical teaching, is to reject what destroys community and promote what builds community.

The specific issues treated are truth, anger, theft, speech, and love. It is doubtful whether these injunctions tell us much about the actual behavior of the readers. True, the Corinthian correspondence shows that the early church had people who were still learning the most basic ethical lessons. But Ephesians is a general letter to a broad audience and does not reveal the author's awareness of any specific circumstances of his readers. If he had felt a need to correct known problems, he would have confronted them more directly. In all likelihood, then, these injunctions are a direct way to picture the significance of putting off the old being and putting on the new.

Paul's style changes in these verses to shorter sentences as he moves from theological grounding to ethical examples. He uses second person plural verbs throughout, except for 4:28 (third singular) and 5:2 (first person plural). He quotes or alludes to several Old Testament texts in this section: Zechariah 8:16 in 4:25; Psalm 4:4 in 4:26; Isaiah 63:10 in 4:30; possibly Psalm 40:6 in 5:2. Note also the parallels in Colossians 3:8–14. Once again the theology of this section is Trinitarian.

Structure. The chapter division at 5:1 is unfortunate, for the commands to imitate God and to love as those who have been loved in 5:1–2 continue the idea of forgiving as God has forgiven in 4:31. Ephesians 5:1–2 is best seen as the conclusion of this unit in the letter.

This section is not just a haphazard list of instructions. Instead, most of the injunctions are offered as contrasts between negative and positive ideas, and in most cases theological motivation is offered as to why the command should be observed.[1]

4:25: negative-positive ("Put off falsehood and speak truthfully")
　　　　motivation: "we are all members of one body"
4:26a: positive-negative ("In your anger do not sin")[2]
　　　　4:26b: positive (anger is limited)
　　　　4:27: positive (no foothold for the devil—or is this a motivation?)
4:28: negative-positive (stop stealing and work)
　　　　motivation: that you "may have something to share with those in need"
4:29: negative-positive (no unwholesome talk, rather, what is helpful)
　　　　motivation: "that it may benefit" (lit.: "give grace")
4:30: negative ("do not grieve the Holy Spirit of God")
　　　　This serves as *motivation* for all the commands.

---

1. Lincoln, *Ephesians*, 295, finds seven sentences in this block of text, five of which (4:25, 26–27, 28, 31–32; 5:1–2) have two exhortations followed by a motivating clause. This works for verse 25 only if the participle is taken as an imperative, but not for verses 26–27, and it ignores the motivation "as dearly loved children" in 5:1.

2. Literally, "Be angry and do not sin."

4:31–32: negative-positive (remove harsh traits and take on gentle ones)
    motivation: "as God in Christ forgave you"
5:1:   positive ("be imitators of God")
    motivation: "as dearly loved children"
5:2:   positive ("live a life of love")
    motivation: "as Christ loved us and gave himself up for us"

The seven *motivations* for ethics deserve attention.[3] The first three have to do with community—with involvement with others in the body and making contributions to them. In the last three Paul urges Christians to treat others the way God has treated them. The one in the middle urges us to avoid everything that displeases God. Whether this is intentionally central is unclear, but avoiding what is displeasing to God is surely the most important motivation.

For convenience sake we will treat this material in three sections: 4:25–27, which deal with lying and anger; 4:28–29, which are concerned with making a contribution to others; and 4:30–5:2, which serve as a general and summarizing statement.

Lying and Anger (4:25–27)

GIVEN THE FOCUS on *truth* in 4:15, 21, 24, it is no surprise that truth-telling is the first of Paul's ethical injunctions. The NIV translation makes three choices that merit comment:

(1) The imperative "put off" is actually a participle, which has legitimately been taken as an imperative, but the emphasis is on the main imperative "speak."
(2) The word "falsehood" is actually "the lie" (singular), understood in the sense "lying."
(3) The adverb "truthfully" is really the noun "truth," which makes the focus on truth even stronger than the NIV reveals. In doing so, the focus on truth is lessened.

The main imperative (lit.: "each speak truth with his neighbor") is a quotation from Zechariah 8:16. The motivation for telling the truth is that we are members of each other. Though the word "body" does not actually occur in this text, the NIV has added it because it is implied. Similar language occurs in 5:30 and in Romans 12:5, describing the body of Christ.

"In your anger do not sin" (v. 26) is a quotation from Psalm 4:4, which if rendered literally is, "Be angry and do not sin." Most commentators today accept that the first imperative is concessive or conditional: "Although [or if]

---

3. Possibly eight, if verse 27 is viewed as a motivation in parallel with verse 30.

you get angry, do not sin." This is the reasoning behind the NIV.[4] Some, however, still view this as a double command, placing a moral obligation on believers to be angry if the occasion requires but not to sin in that anger.[5] This may be reading too much into the verse since Paul's concern is the prevention of sin, not the obligation of anger. This verse may presuppose the possibility of anger without sin,[6] but its emphasis is not on "righteous anger." Rather, it is on preventing anger from causing sin. The danger of anger is evident in its being used as a beachhead for the devil, and verse 31 *excludes all* bitterness, wrath, and anger. Clearly anger does not fit well with the new being.

That the sun is not to go down on our anger is a way of saying that anger must not endure. It must be dealt with quickly and then set aside. The word "foothold" in verse 27 is literally "place." That is, we must not give the devil room in our lives to operate. Anger is one place of inroad for him, a Trojan horse for his attack.[7] In other words, anger usually leads to other sins.

To Harm or to Help? (4:28–29)

THESE TWO VERSES are bound together not only by the negative-positive contrast, but also by the words "need" and "good" (the latter of which the NIV translates as "useful" and "helpful"). Both verses show the "other" orientation of the new being as opposed to the previous self-centered and abusive character of the old being.

While stealing may have been common among slaves, by no means should verse 28 be thought as addressed to them. Theft then, as now, was a common problem. This verse may be the most striking description of conversion in the New Testament: "The thief is to become a philanthropist."[8] The person who did wrong in order to meet his own selfish desires must now work in order to contribute to someone else's need. This is a compelling example of dying and rising with Christ. The concern to address communal needs is reminiscent of the early church's community of goods.[9] In 1 Thessalonians 4:11 Paul urged believers to work with their own hands, and he also used this same language

---

4. The NIV uses the same translation in Psalm 4:4 as for this verse, even though the Hebrew word translated "anger" usually means "tremble" or "be agitated." Does the context of the psalm suggest trembling before God's presence or trembling in anger at human injustice? Paul uses the form of the text from the LXX.

5. See Daniel Wallace, ᾽ΟΡΓΙΖΕΣΘΕ in Ephesians 4:26: Command or Condition?" *Criswell Theological Review* 3 (1989): 353–72.

6. If that is not a violation of the Old Testament origin of these words.

7. Other texts speak of the devil's seeking an avenue of attack (cf. 1 Cor. 7:5; 2 Cor. 2:11; 11:14; 1 Tim. 3:7; 2 Tim. 2:26; 1 Peter 5:8; Rev. 12:9; 20:10).

8. Lincoln, *Ephesians*, 304.

9. Acts 2:45; 4:34–35; Romans 12:13; Titus 3:14.

of his own efforts to avoid burdening those to whom he preached.[10] His goal was for believers to be self-supporting *and* supportive of those in need. Note the contrast between "need" here and "desires" in 4:22 (cf. "lust" in 4:19).

The word "unwholesome" in verse 29 is used of spoiled fish or rotten fruit, but it is also used to describe stones that crumble. The metaphorical meaning connotes "foul" or "bad." Although obscene speech may be in mind (see 5:4), the concern for "building up" later in the verse suggests "destructive" language. "Building up" reminds the reader of Paul's concern in 4:16 to build up the body. With "may benefit" the NIV loses another connection with previous sections. Literally the text is, "that it may give *grace* to the hearers," which links especially with the grace given to each person for the benefit of the church (4:7). We receive grace from God for salvation (chaps. 1—2) and ministry (chaps. 3—4) so that we may extend God's grace to others.

Christian Ethics in a Nutshell (4:30—5:2)

THE LANGUAGE OF grieving the Holy Spirit (v. 30) is derived from Isaiah 63:10, where it describes Israel's rebellion. "With whom" could be "by whom" or "in whom," but the wording at 1:13 implies that the Holy Spirit is our seal guaranteeing salvation.[11] This verse marks the incongruity of grieving the one who is proof we belong to God and are destined for his future salvation. Why live contrary to him whose ownership seal we wear and in violation of our destiny? Here eschatology is brought to bear on ethics, and once again the double focus on present (now) and future (not yet) is expressed. This verse stands in marked contrast with what is said of the devil in verse 27. No room is to be permitted for the devil, but through the Spirit God is at work in us. The personal character of the Spirit is assumed.

Goodwill, not ill will (4:31–32). "Get rid of" is a third person passive imperative (lit., "Let anger, etc., be gotten rid of"), but this does not mean God removes sinful behavior instead of the readers. The focus in this passsage is on the responsibility of believers to act. Such acts of believers, of course, are presumed to be aided by the work of the Holy Spirit. "Anger" has already been treated in verse 26, but its importance is emphasized with two different words in verse 31 and by the association of anger with other words expressing ill will.[12] The word translated "brawling" suggests not physical violence, but "shouting."

---

10. See 2 Corinthians 4:12; cf. 1 Thessalonians 2:9.

11. In 2 Corinthians 1:21–22 God is the one who does the sealing.

12. Some distinguish the two words for anger by saying *thumos* is used of outbursts of anger, whereas *orge* is used of enduring anger, but in the LXX and the New Testament they seem interchangeable.

All the words in verse 31 are intended to express hostility and actions that destroy human relations. Note the grouping of five words (similar to Col. 3:5, 8, 12). Groups of five were traditional in ancient lists of vices and virtues. Some suggest a progression in the five words,[13] but this is uncertain. Bitterness is just as much the result of anger as its cause.[14] "Malice" may be the most important word, for it encapsulates the hostility the other words describe. The contrast between 4:31 and 4:2–3, the description of a Christian's calling, is striking.

In contrast to the badness and malice in verse 31, verse 32 calls for goodness, which applied to humans is understood as being "kind" (the same root is used for God's kindness in 2:7). Paul also calls for compassion and forgiveness. Goodwill toward other people is assumed for the new being. As elsewhere, treatment of others is grounded in God's treatment of us. Forgiveness (*charizomai*) is not Paul's usual language for salvation.[15] The idea of forgiveness of others being grounded in God's forgiveness is reminiscent of Matthew 6:12, 14–15; 18:21–35; Luke 6:36. Note again the focus on salvation taking place *in* Christ (cf. 2 Cor. 5:19).

Be like God (5:1–2). The command to imitate God is breathtaking to us, but it is a thoroughly biblical idea and not unusual in Jewish or Greek thought. Although other texts may not be this explicit, the Bible assumes that God's covenant people take their character from him. Leviticus 19 is perhaps the most striking text, for the Israelites are commanded to be holy because God is holy. At least fourteen times in that chapter a command to Israel is followed by the words "I am the LORD," to show that ethical action is determined by God's character.[16] Similarly, in Matthew 5:43–48 Jesus commanded his disciples to love their enemies in order to be like the Father and to be perfect as their heavenly Father is perfect.[17] Elsewhere Paul urges readers to imitate him or to imitate him as he imitates Christ.[18]

The second half of 5:1 shows why the command to imitate God is legitimate: The readers are God's children, whom he loves. These words point to the ideas of adoption in 1:5 and of family in 2:19 and 3:14–15. A person

---

13. Schnackenburg, *Ephesians: A Commentary*, 211.

14. The word only occurs in three other places in the New Testament: Acts 8:23; Romans 3:14; Hebrews 12:15. The verb form is used with similar intent in Colossians 3:19.

15. Other than the parallel in Colossians 3:13, Paul uses this word for forgiveness only in 2 Corinthians 2:7, 10; 12:13, all in reference to Christians forgiving each other. He also uses *aphesis* in Ephesians 1:7 and Colossians 1:14, and the verb *aphiemi* in this sense in Romans 4:7. For Paul, apparently words like "justification" or "redemption" were more comprehensive to express the concept of salvation.

16. Note also Leviticus 18:2–6 and 20:7–8.

17. Cf. Luke 6:36: "Be merciful, just as your Father is merciful" (see also 1 John 4:11).

18. See 1 Corinthians 4:16; 11:1; 1 Thessalonians 1:6; 2 Thessalonians 3:7, 9.

takes the characteristics of the family to which he or she belongs (cf. 1 Cor. 4:15–16). Since Paul's readers belong to God's family and, as his children, have received love, they should be like him and show love.

The imitation of God and his love is changed in 5:2 to the imitation of Christ and his love. Living in love sums up 4:25–5:1.[19] Love is the sphere in which the believer lives.[20] The standard by which Christian love is shaped and energized is the self-giving love of Christ on the cross. This verse is an important soteriological one, for it focuses on Christ's giving himself[21] rather than on God's giving or sending his Son, and on the death of Christ as a "sacrifice" (see also 5:25). Christ gave himself for us or on our behalf. As Ernst Käsemann stressed, Christ's death *for us* always covers two ideas: in our place and for our benefit.[22]

Christ's death is presented here as an example for our lives, but his death is never merely an example. With it comes a theology of atonement grounded in the love of God and Christ. Ideas of substitution, representation, and sacrifice are clearly present. In the Old Testament sacrificial system, smoke from an offering ascended as a pleasant smell to God,[23] which was a way of expressing God's pleasure at the worship being offered. The image is adapted to express God's pleasure in what Christ's death accomplished. Paul used similar language to describe the ministry of Christians (2 Cor. 2:14–16) or the gifts of others to assist him (Phil. 4:18).

Bridging Contexts

To BRING THE practical instructions offered here into our day requires no bridging in themselves; rather, they require obedience. As John Calvin noted, all correct knowledge of God originates in obedience.[24] Still, the theology of these verses requires reflection. We may need additional information, and we must consider obstacles to application. For example, is it ever permissible to lie? What of righteous anger? How can forgiveness and justice be held together?

How the author describes the new being is compelling: truth, no anger, no stealing, no destructive language, compassion, forgiveness, and love. This may not be the list we would have offered, for it seems rather basic and

---

19. Cf. Romans 14:15.

20. The NIV's "live a life of love" is literally "walk in love."

21. See also Galatians 1:4; 2:20; 1 Timothy 2:6; Titus 2:14.

22. Ernst Käsemann, "The Saving Significance of the Death of Jesus in Paul," *Perspectives on Paul* (London: SCM, 1969), 39. See p. 129.

23. For example, Exodus 29:18; Leviticus 1:9.

24. John Calvin, *Institutes of the Christian Religion*, 1.6.2.

simple. But with the twin anchors of truth and love the author is on target. Without these life and community are in shambles. Moreover, by prohibiting lying, anger, theft, and destructive language, Paul prohibits the sins that enable most others.

Some Christians worry about such specific directions for living, for they fear it may lead to legalism, but this thinking is far from the New Testament. Texts like this do not endorse legalism; they are descriptions of life in Christ, which is never without content. Christian living *requires* certain and specific actions. The Christian faith is not a passive religion; it is an aggressive pursuit of the productive and beneficial.

A relational, reflective ethic. Before dealing with the specific commands of this passage, attention must be given to the fact that the Christian ethic is a relational and reflective one. It is about covenant *relation* with God. God's Spirit is present in our lives and is grieved when we do not live worthy of the calling (4:1). We are carried along from within by a God who reacts to our behavior.

Relation with God establishes relations with other people. No matter how strenuous the effort, relation with God cannot be separated from relation with other people. The relational ethic is present in the body theology in 4:25 and implied throughout the passage. As Christians we are part of other believers, and we suffer or thrive with them. Until we take this interrelation seriously, we can never be what we are called to be. This perspective undergirds the necessity of building up others in Christ, both in what is said to them and in what we contribute to them materially. Insensitivity and hostility are not allowed.

Although Ephesians addresses primarily relations within the body of Christ, relations with non-Christians follow the same pattern. As pointed out earlier,[25] the same ethic applies to all people, even though the relation is different.

Ours is also a *reflective* ethic: We are to reflect God's attitude and acts toward us to other people. God is known in the cross and resurrection. He is not "out there" to dream about, but present to change lives. He is the standard for our actions, and that we are his children means we are to copy his acts. We have received grace and forgiveness from him, and we are to show these qualities to others. He loves, and we are to love.

With the allusions to Genesis 1:26–27 in 4:24, clearly Christians are to be image bearers, reflecting the image of God for the world to see. Shall we give self to self or to God? Shall we choose rebellion and attempt to take the place of God or choose obedience and be like God? The temptation in Eden was to be like God, which is strange, for humans already were in God's image.

25. See pp. 87, 145, 186, 188, 209.

In this text Christians are called to bear that image and show the world what God is like.

Of course, in many ways we cannot copy God; we cannot, for example, imitate his omnipresence or omnipotence, nor are we asked to. We are asked to imitate God's *character*. At issue is our behavior. The standard is high, but so is the privilege. Christians have God's Spirit with them (4:30) and belong in God's family (5:1). Such a lofty position requires that God's character be reflected in the way we treat other people. Copying God only means taking seriously who God says we are.

Truth. First and foremost, the new being tells the truth. Lying is no longer a resource in the Christian arsenal. For Christians truth is not a choice; it is a necessity.[26]

Lying is destructive both to the self and to relations with others. "By a lie a man throws away, and as it were, annihilates his dignity as a man."[27] The same is true for a woman. But it is not just the self that is destroyed. Since Christians are part of each other, as John Mackay has commented poignantly, "A lie is a stab into the very vitals of the Body of Christ."[28] How strange that one part of the body would deceive another part, as if the eye would lie to the foot about some danger it sees.[29] Lies distort reality and accompany every other form of wrongdoing.[30] They are usually motivated by self-enhancement or self-defense and usually come in bunches, for it is difficult to tell only one. The evil are people of the lie.[31]

The only place anyone can live meaningfully is with the truth. Truth is not an option in life. A free society cannot exist without truth, but neither can an individual be free without truth. "To obey the truth is to be free. . . . We do not 'have' the truth, truth owns us. . . . "[32] Truth—that which corresponds to the facts and on which we can rely—is both necessary and freeing (cf. John 8:31–32). Truth encompasses the totality of life, including relation with God. If God is real and has sent Christ, then living in truth requires living in relation with God, and speaking the truth includes communicating the reality of life with Christ. The issue is not just words, but an integrity marked by the coherence of word and act.

---

26. Truth has already been discussed in relation to 4:15; see pp. 205–6, 215–17, 225–27.

27. Immanuel Kant, *Doctrine of Virtue* (quoted in Sissela Bok, *Lying: Moral Choice in Public and Private Life* [New York: Pantheon Books, 1978], 32).

28. Mackay, *God's Order*, 174.

29. John Chrysostom makes this and similar points in his commentary on this text.

30. Note that in John 8:44 the devil is the father of lies.

31. Scott Peck, *The People of the Lie* (New York: Simon and Schuster, 1983), 66.

32. Michael Novak, "Awakening from Nihilism: The Templeton Prize Address," *First Things* 45 (August/September, 1994): 18–19.

Truth is particularly important for building community. Communities are based on mutual reliance, that people can be trusted for support. Once that trust is lost, it is difficult to recover. In speaking truth to our neighbor, we are saying, "You can rely on me; our relation will not mislead you or cause you harm. I will help you and my word will correspond to my acts." Healthy community cannot exist without truth.

Do we have to tell all the truth to everyone? The text is about speaking truth with our fellow believer, but that does not mean we can lie to someone else. Jesus' consistently rejected boundaries limiting the application of ethics.[33] Some religions permit lying to enemies, but Jesus requires disciples to love their enemies, which certainly excludes lying to them.

Philosophers and theologians have debated, however, the permissibility of lying in order to accomplish good, such as preserving life.[34] Obviously, who gets to define "good" is a major issue. Usually and appropriately attention is placed on a person's right to know. A murderer does not have the right to know where his victim is hiding. Therefore, many people would choose to lie to prevent greater sin. On the other hand, others—such as Immanuel Kant—have rejected the morality of *all* lying. Part of the problem may be our attempt to justify our "necessary" action in a sinful world, but even if one grants that avoidance of greater sin may in extreme cases require a lie, no easing of resistance to lying is legitimate. The lie-to-preserve-life syndrome is a slippery slope that soon permits lying to preserve *my* life *as I want it.* Are not nearly all lies based on the attempt to achieve good for someone? Again, a comment from John Mackay deserves reflection: "There is no place in the Christian ethic for the well-intentioned lie."[35]

This does not mean that we have to tell all the truth to everyone we meet. Privacy is a legitimate and necessary part of life. People do not have the right to know everything. That position overemphasizes community and ignores the boundaries of the individual. We are required not to lie; we are not required to tell all we know. What we communicate must be truth, and the subject matter and level of detail depend on the nature of the relation and discernment about what is healthy and beneficial. Truth must always be guided by love (4:15), but never sacrificed to it. Yet care is needed, for telling part of the truth can be a way of lying, and withholding necessary information can also be a deception. People can accept not being told information that is none of their business, but they seek trustworthy and beneficial relations. Of primary importance are the motives at work as the relation is lived out. The issue is integrity.

---

33. Note Matthew 18:21–22; Luke 10:25–37.
34. For an overview, see Bok, *Lying.*
35. Mackay, *God's Order,* 174.

Anger. This passage is frequently used to justify righteous anger. John Stott even argues from this text for *more* Christian anger.[36] His point is legitimate, and as we indicated in reference to God's anger in 2:3, "the person who does not get angry does not care."[37] Christians ought to get angry about injustice, poverty, racism, lies, and abuse.[38] Certainly not all anger is sinful.[39] But whether righteous anger is the implication of Ephesians 4:26 is doubtful. The text's primary intent is not to promote anger or even allow it, but to prevent it.

Human anger is usually destructive, and the New Testament attitude toward it is strongly negative. James 1:20 even says that human anger does not accomplish the righteousness of God. Furthermore, righteous anger is difficult to identify. No one feels his or her anger is unjust. In words similar to verse 27, Romans 12:19–21 counsels: "Give place to [God's] wrath." In other words, do not let anger give place to the devil to cause sin, and do not seek vengeance. Rather, give place to God's vengeance. Your task is to love your enemies.

The reason the New Testament deletes anger as an option is that anger is largely a self-centered emotion. Anger is a means of communicating what we care about—usually ourselves—and is an attempt at punishment. It is a chemical and physiological reaction to our displeasure that the world is not as we wish. It is also a choice we make, for we choose both what we react to and at what level the reaction will occur. "No one else can make us feel anger; we must own it ourselves."[40] We express anger only where it is safe, and virtually never to those we fear or respect highly. More often than not we cause harm when using anger. Seneca, who wrote the first known treatise on anger, said, "No plague has cost the human race more dear."[41] Like lying, anger destroys both the angry person—even physically—and community. Rather than focus on what displeases them, Christians should focus instead on how they will love God and the world.

The text assumes that people *will* make us angry, but anger must not take up residence. If given place, it infects and mutates into further resentment and

---

36. Stott, *God's New Society*, 185–87.

37. See p. 111.

38. On the other hand, Seneca cautions that the wise man [sic] will never cease to be angry once he begins, for every place is full of crime and vice. See *De Ira* 2.9.1. Stählin ("ὀργή," *TDNT*, 5:419) suggests that only two New Testament texts view human anger positively: Romans 10:19 and 2 Corinthians 7:11.

39. Jesus himself was angry; see, for example, Matthew 18:6–9; 23:13, 17, 33–39; Mark 3:5; 10:13–16.

40. See Janet Malone, "Exploring Human Anger," *Human Development* 15 (1994): 33–34.

41. *De Ira* 1.21. Seneca lived from 4 B.C. to A.D. 65.

hostility. If given place, it becomes the avenue the devil uses to cause sin. For that reason, it must be shown the door rather quickly.

What does this passage teach about the devil? The text here is brief, so thinking must draw on the broader discussions in 2:2 and 6:10–20.[42] Focus on the devil lurking to capture could lead to a misguided paranoia. Instead, the main point of the text is not to focus on the devil, but on our own anger, which is the root of the problem. On the other hand, those who ignore the devil gloss over the reality of evil as an enemy seeking an avenue of destruction. Scripture should be our primary guideline for the amount of attention given to any subject. If we follow it, the devil is given limited attention.

Productivity. All of us come into the world for a brief time, and we spend most of it yelling "Pay attention to me!" We feel justified in satisfying ourselves, even at cost to others. From the time we are old enough to recognize objects, we want what the other person has—if for no other reason, so that they will not have it. Ephesians 4:28 ignites a bomb under all our self-centered thinking. Our goal is not enjoyment; it is productivity so that we can give. We do not exist for ourselves, but for relations with other people and with God.

This simple verse is about theft, community, productivity, and stewardship. The Old Testament respect of property is affirmed, but property is to be shared, not held tightly. The community must be a need-discerning community. If a need exists, the community has a responsibility to help meet that need. This verse recognizes human needs as real and legitimate, as opposed to the illegitmiate and deceitful desires mentioned in 2:3 and 4:22. Needs are those necessities—material (v. 28) or immaterial (v. 29)—that enable life before God, whereas desires (v. 22) are needs distorted by self-centeredness, pulling us away from God.

We live in a society of takers, one that mocks the "Puritan" work ethic. But we have been created in the image of God to enter into his creative activity, that is, to work. In failing to be productive we fail to live up to our vocation as humans.[43] Possibly the strongest witness Christians can make is to become givers. The concern is not about giving money, which is at most ancillary to the text. The concern is working to benefit others.

Speech. Much of this passage is concerned with speech, which is the performance of a godly act. The first act recorded of God in Genesis is speech.[44] Speech is itself creative activity, for with it we create worlds—communities of shared discourse—and with it we frame the reality within

---

42. See comments at pp. 97, 109–11 and 347–54.

43. See Doug Sherman and William Hendricks, *Your Work Matters to God* (Colorado Springs: NavPress, 1987).

44. Stanley Walters, "The Voice of God's People in Exile," *Ex Auditu* 10 (1994): 81.

which we live. Specialists speak of "performative language," language we use to accomplish tasks or establish realities.[45] We fail to realize the power and dignity of language. Nearly all our language does things. Words are commitments,[46] and with them we enable and support or diminish and destroy.

Not only should Christians become communication majors, learning all we can about the process;[47] we should also be extremely careful how we use language. The assumption of verse 29 is that we either pollute or establish by the way we speak. Our authority is for building people up, not for tearing them down (2 Cor. 10:8).

Is forgiveness too wimpy? Even the secular world knows that forgiveness is one of the main features of Christianity. Two problems occur. (1) A gulf exists between our knowledge and our will. We know God's forgiveness, but do not have the will to forgive. Christians tend to be no better than other people—in fact, they may be worse. Offense turns to bitterness, callousness, and rejection. "Christians" go for years not speaking to relatives or friends, or churches split. But refusing to forgive is hazardous. Matthew emphasizes that our forgiveness is tied to our forgiving (Matt. 6:12, 14–15; 18:21–35). Moreover, refusal to forgive is a self-centered act and presumes a role in judging that is not ours. It devalues people and destroys relations. In the process, however, we devalue ourselves.

(2) But if we forgive, does not justice evaporate? In fact, isn't this whole section of the letter too wimpy? If we show kindness and forgiveness, will we not be run over by a hostile world? The text does not encourage naiveté about danger and violence in our world. But that is the precise reason that kindness and forgiveness are necessary. Sin breeds sin, and violence begets violence. Christians are asked to break the cycle by not retaliating, by not placing personal rights over other people. This is part of dying with Christ. Wimpy people should not apply for the job. The weak cannot forgive; only the strong have the resources to forgive, to give up self-defense. The Christian ethic requires strength and wisdom to know how strength is applied.

Nor is justice discounted. Of course, most of us want justice when *our* rights are violated, but we would like forgiveness for our own wrongdoing. Paul has already indicated how forgiveness and justice are both retained: Speak the truth in love (4:15). Justice is not a rejection of the other person,

---

45. See G. B. Caird, *The Language and Imagery of the Bible* (Philadelphia: Westminster, 1980), 20–25. Examples: "I pronounce you man and wife;" "This conversation is over;" and "You are not guilty."

46. Abraham Joshua Heschel, *Quest for God: Studies in Prayer and Symbolism* (New York: Crossroad, 1990), 25. See also p. 78: "A word has a soul, and we must learn how to attain insight into its life."

47. See p. 226.

but a statement of the truth, including an assessment of cost, restitution, and prevention. Forgiveness is not an absence of accountability. It is a refusal to let a past wrong destroy present relations. But is our concern for justice a concern for some external standard or a concern for people? Justice exists *for* people—even when it assesses punishment. That is why M. Zerwick could say, "Be merciful, if you want to be just."[48]

Sacrifice for sin. Perhaps the most difficult part of appropriating this section is the material on Christ's death. We have no problem agreeing that the human plight is desperate and that we deserve God's wrath (2:1–3; 4:17–19). But how can Jesus give himself for us, and are the sacrificial ideas valid? These issues have been encountered earlier in Ephesians, especially in 2:14–18.[49] The concern here is primarily to motivate the ethic.

The sacrificial ideas are important. Precisely because of the hostility and sin in the world, Jesus identified with the human plight and took on that plight and its punishment. He gave himself and in doing so developed a solidarity with humanity. That was his vocation.

This pattern of sacrifice describes God's taking away his own anger.[50] Our God is not a God who is removed from us, but a God who cares and who identifies with us. We have violated his commands and all he is, but he responds with self-giving love. The Father is not a remote being, appeased by the action of his Son.[51] Jesus died in our place (5:2), and we were involved in that death and in his resurrection. This self-giving love is evidence of God's own favor. The sacrifice is pleasing to God not only because of the obedience of Christ, but also because of what it does in restoring humans into relation with God. The focus on sacrifice is to show that God accomplished for us what we could not accomplish for ourselves.

APPLICATION OF THIS text is straightforward. It requires obedience. We begin with three general points: (1) Keep the pattern in view; (2) reject self-centeredness; (3) activate your will.

(1) If the Christian ethic is a relational, reflective ethic, we must always keep before us both the pattern of God's character and the reality of our relations. This is why images such as "in Christ" or "the body" are of such practical importance. We will not reflect what is not present to us, and we can-

---

48. Zerwick, *Epistle to the Ephesians*, 129.
49. See pp. 133–36, 141–42; also comments on 1:4–8; 2:4–7.
50. Cf. Ps. 78:38; 85:2–3.
51. In 1:6–8 God's grace sent his Son; in 2:4 the mercy of God brings life from death.

not copy what we do not see. Theology drives the ethic,[52] so the theology must be conscious and active. What motivates our obedience is not knowledge of correct action but awareness of God. Imitation of God is an overwhelming idea in the abstract, but experience of God's forgiving love makes imitation both necessary and natural.

(2) Awareness of our relations both with God and with other people is also the key to rejecting self-centeredness. None of the commands in this passage can be followed as long as the primary interest is oneself. Only when our attention is shifted to something greater than ourselves can we escape the prison of self-interest. If we are conscious that the Spirit is in us, marking us as belonging to God and therefore under his direction, service to self is blocked off. Similarly, awareness of oneness with other people will not permit inattention or mistreatment of them. If other people are diminished, we are diminished; if they prosper, we prosper with them.

(3) Obedience to these commands also requires a conscious choice and discipline, for they are contrary to our nature. Too often we allow our old nature to lead us into disobedience. We must grasp the imperative and choose obedience. This is not "works righteousness," for we make our choices in response to God and his presence, but human will and discipline are necessary. God works with us, not on us.

Integrity, integrity, integrity. If God is the pattern, integrity is the result. He is characterized by truth, and his people should be as well (see 4:15).[53] This means first of all that we discern truth in God. He is the source of truth by which we live. If taken seriously, this should separate us from much of our society, which seeks to live lies. The entertainment industry creates illusion and perversion and seeks to pass them off as truth. Our society asserts that immediate pleasure is the goal and denies the reality of death or judgment for our actions. The lies around us must be identified and challenged. For example, when a man says, "I am not willing to live a lie any more, so I will divorce my wife," he is not moving toward integrity.

Integrity requires a continual commitment to speak truth even when it is painful. But even in such situations, truth must be spoken in love. We cannot allow ourselves the privilege of deception. Our neighbors are part of us, and lying will only destroy both us and them. Whether in a court of law or at the kitchen table, Christians should not need an oath to insure veracity.

But do we not live by deception, trying to appear better than we are? If people know what we really are, will they not reject us? Maybe, but the depravity we know personally is also a depravity we all share and about

---

52. See pp. 208–9.
53. See pp. 206–7, 215–17 for the discussion of the application of truth there.

which we must be truthful. Otherwise, we hide behind masks of fake purity and never really deal with our sin. The text calls for a transparency, an openness guided by wisdom as to what is appropriate. Death is not a subject from which we can run, so why should we not discuss death more straightforwardly? Our sexuality often possesses us, so why should we not in the right context discuss it and deal with it? Why can't we be more forthright about our own egos? We do make ourselves real by telling the truth.

One of the ways we lie is by exaggeration. We want the story to sound a little better, our performance to be a little more admired, or the other person to look a little more ridiculous. But by exaggeration we distort reality. Some of the most guilty exaggerators are pastors, who use loud one-sided statements to make God look more wonderful and themselves more powerful. But God does not need exaggeration. People do respond to overstatement, but such language is ego-driven and detrimental to both witness and spiritual health. Pastors should lead the way in integrity of word by speaking the truth in a balanced way that does justice to all the truth, not just the pieces they want to emphasize.

This text pushes for integrity with property as well. You cannot put theft and imitating God in the same sentence. Self-centeredness says, "Take what you can get, no matter the method." God-centeredness marks out boundaries within which needs may legitimately be addressed. Rationalization is not permitted to justify theft, for no justification exists. Some theft is direct stealing of property, and in our society much of it is shoplifting or theft by employees. Other kinds of theft are closer to deception and lying. People steal by the way they deceive in business, in soliciting funds, in cheating on tests, or in reporting taxes to the government. Christians cannot allow themselves to be involved in any kind of theft, even when no one will ever know. At stake is our own self-understanding and our relation to God, to say nothing of our relation to other people and our ability to be witnesses to the integrity of God.

In many ways integrity is the subject of this whole passage. That is, the purpose of the gospel is to establish integrity in our being.

Helpfulness, not hostility. We live in a hostile world. All of us fear violence or mistreatment, so we tend to be watchful, guarding every inch of our rights. All of us have been wronged, which makes us aggressive in self-defense or so scarred we get revenge by harming someone else. The violations and failures that occur in all our institutions and movements push us to hostility and cynicism. Christians become defensive, suspicious, and vindictive. Talk about theology of the gospel does not root out our self-centeredness. Consequently, the openness the church needs is not there. It does not manifest the magnanimous grace of God.

"Hostile Christian" is an oxymoron. We must replace hostility with help-fulness. The primary place hostility and cynicism appear is in our families, the assumption being that those closest to us are responsible for the problem, have failed to solve it, or are easy targets for revenge. Chapters 5 and 6 of Ephesians will focus on the family, but this passage needs to be applied to families first. Where families are marked by bitterness, anger, shouting, or worse, violence, no one may speak of Christian faith. Usually our anger is in response to small things that do not really matter. And since anger is a choice to express our displeasure where no fear is present, anger is most often directed at the wrong people. The victims of anger are usually not its cause; they are merely people who are present and pose no threat—such as women, children, or people without power, the very people to whom we should guarantee safety.

Bitterness and hostility within the church must also be addressed. Cynicism, the first step toward bitterness, is often a defense against the insanity of the world and a means of coping, but it is also sin because it denigrates and closes off possibilities. Cynicism, it must be said, is one of the largest dangers for pastors and church leaders, for they know the failures of the church too well. Rather than being cynical about superficiality and failure, would it not be better to speak the truth in love and act appropriately? Can we be courageous enough to do that?

Clearly this text seeks the gentleness and tolerant love that were mentioned in 4:2. At bottom the issue is hospitality, the way we receive and care for people. Too often our demeanor communicates harshness and abrasiveness, or at best, indifference. Instead, people need to find in our presence receptivity and goodwill. They need to know that in the church they are safe and that resources can be found for assistance. The body of Christ consists of people who have traded hostility for helpfulness. Christians are builders, not destroyers. They are to be productive, addressing needs other people have. Their speech is beneficial speech,[54] and their acts beneficial acts. The goal is investment in people to build up community. We are not permitted merely to take care of ourselves.[55]

More harm than help? But the attempt to help can make matters worse. People become dependent on help and a drain on resources. Welfare systems become impotent and corrupting, and every church knows parasitic people who leach off the goodwill of Christians. Further, some people seem so broken they cannot be fixed. Does the idealism of this text really work?

---

54. Paul will treat the subject of speech more closely in 5:4 and 12 (see pp. 269, 276, 281).

55. See Deuteronomy 15–16, which argues against being tightfisted toward the poor and against appearing empty-handed before the Lord. Offerings are to be brought in proportion to the way the Lord has blessed.

Of course, it works. Not all needs will be met, and not all people can be "fixed." Human depravity and the brokenness of this world are powerful forces present until the day of redemption. Help can be given in unwise ways, but without help *no one* makes it. God called Christians to mutually edifying unity in Christ. That is both our task and our identity. We are to live productively and beneficially—which means that we must fight *for* what is right and good. If we do not, we will almost certainly have to fight later *against* what is wrong.[56] You fight for right by helping people.

The goal is not for some Christians to help others, but for all to help each other. All of us have needs the community is to address. Participation in the body of Christ does not allow some to avoid work or to take advantage. Where that occurs, truth must be spoken in love. People must take responsibility for themselves and help others—despite the problems. God cares, and because he does, his people care, even if their only recourse is to weep.

Words are easy; help comes at cost. Sometimes the needs of people are so deep that any thought of help is depressing. How do we help children with fetal alcohol syndrome or adults with neither the skills nor the desire to be self-supporting? Often the only possible avenue is a communal one. We cannot, of course, meet all the needs, but that we are blind to needs or unengaged in addressing them contradicts what it means to be in Christ.

Forgiveness. Forgiveness is grounded in God's forgiving us in Christ. Yet Christians seem unwilling to forgive, as the numerous divisions and conflicts in churches and families attest. How can Christians go for years holding grudges? Even if forgiveness is granted, we keep the offense available to use in future battles. As a country song puts it: "We bury the hatchet, but leave the handle sticking out!" We are also slow to forgive because it appears to ignore justice and restitution. But most of the time, refusal to forgive does not derive from some lofty sense of justice, but from self-centeredness. How foolish! As one person put it, "He who is unwilling to forgive breaks the bridge over which he too must pass." Moreover, standing on our rights before God is foolish, for God may then stand on his! The New Testament assures us that those who do not forgive are not forgiven. Ephesians 4:32 changes the "golden rule." We are asked to do unto others as God has done to us. We show whose we are by the way we act.

Forgiveness, however, does *not* ignore justice. God certainly did not, and once again the key is in speaking the truth in love. Forgiveness does not necessarily forget the offense—the pain may be too deep to forget—or ignore restitution. The nature of the offense determines the response. What forgive-

---

56. Heschel, *Quest for God*, 148, is strong in making this point. He points out that the failure to offer sacrifices on the altar of peace requires that they be offered on the altar of war.

ness does accomplish is the rejection of bitterness, malice, and revenge. We do not control the actions of others, but in choosing to forgive we establish control over our own responses.[57] We choose to value the other person despite his or her offense and to desire what is good for that person before God. Forgiveness also restores relations, or at least provides a foundation on which they can be restored. But forgiveness is a process and does not necessarily happen immediately. The nature of the offense and the maturity of the one forgiving will determine the length and character of the process. But forgiveness is necessary, and the process cannot allow bitterness to take hold and grow.

Keep short accounts. Christians are encouraged by this passage and others to keep short accounts with God. These accounts have to do primarily with how we have treated other people, so we need to keep short accounts both with God *and* other people. J. B. Phillips translated 4:26b as, "Never go to bed angry."[58] This is not only good advice for married couples and families, but for all of us. In short order we need to deal with anger, malice, and the need to forgive. Inattention to problems makes them worse.

Excellence, as defined by business experts, is doing a lot of little things well. Christians need to do a lot of little things well—keeping track, giving attention, and nurturing people. The habit of regular and frequent checks with God is necessary to determine whether we are grieving or pleasing the Spirit. Have we harbored anger and nursed grudges or been quick to forgive? Are we reflecting God's treatment of us, or do we have different standards for other people than those we require for ourselves? Are we givers and builders or takers and destroyers? To put it another way, if Jesus' self-giving sacrifice was a pleasing smell to God, do our lives provide such a pleasing smell, or is the smell rather foul?

By way of summary, to apply this text:

(1) Watch your tongue. Make it speak the truth, use it to build, not to destroy.

(2) Watch your hands and feet. Make them respect property and put them to work so you can give.

(3) You are part of those in Christ. Nurture people gently. Do nothing from malice and anger.

(4) You belong to God and his Spirit is in you. Treat others as he has treated you. Forgive and love.

---

57. Malone, "Exploring Human Anger," 38, who adds: "Thus, in forgiving others we empower ourselves."

58. *The New Testament in Modern English* (London: Geoffrey Bles, 1960).

Ephesians 5:3–14

Bᵁᵀ ᴬᴹᴼᴺᴳ ʸᴼᵁ there must not be even a hint of sexual immorality, or of any kind of impurity, or of greed, because these are improper for God's holy people. ⁴Nor should there be obscenity, foolish talk or coarse joking, which are out of place, but rather thanksgiving. ⁵For of this you can be sure: No immoral, impure or greedy person—such a man is an idolater—has any inheritance in the kingdom of Christ and of God. ⁶Let no one deceive you with empty words, for because of such things God's wrath comes on those who are disobedient. ⁷Therefore do not be partners with them.

⁸For you were once darkness, but now you are light in the Lord. Live as children of light ⁹(for the fruit of the light consists in all goodness, righteousness and truth) ¹⁰and find out what pleases the Lord. ¹¹Have nothing to do with the fruitless deeds of darkness, but rather expose them. ¹²For it is shameful even to mention what the disobedient do in secret. ¹³But everything exposed by the light becomes visible, ¹⁴for it is light that makes everything visible. This is why it is said:

> "Wake up, O sleeper,
>   rise from the dead,
> and Christ will shine on you."

Original Meaning

Eᵛᴱᴺ ᵀᴴᴼᵁᴳᴴ Pᴬᵁᴸ'ˢ subject is still Christian conduct, a shift clearly occurs at 5:3, which the NIV shows by a paragraph division and the use of the word "but."[1] Whereas 4:25–5:2 was primarily concerned with practices Christians should adopt, 5:3–14 focuses on what should be avoided: sexual sins, sins of the tongue, and covetousness. In fact, this unit is one of the lengthiest New Testament treatments of separation from the world.

Several connections exist between 5:3–14 and 4:25–5:2: "good," "truth," and sins of the tongue. Items given prominence are primarily a series of oppositions: darkness and light; deception and truth; fruit and lack of fruit; and hidden and revealed. Ideas of shame and partnership are also emphasized. In

---

1. Uncharacteristically, the Greek text has few connectives between the various injunctions in 4:25–5:2, which gives emphasis to the connective in 5:3 (an adversative *de*).

contrast to 4:25—5:2, there are no allusions to the Old Testament except for the confession in verse 14. Note also the parallels with Colossians 3:5—8.

Ephesians 5:8 deserves special attention, for it provides an effective summary of the whole letter, or for that matter, of Paul's theology. In addition to using "walk" (NIV, "live") in reference to ethical instruction, this verse has the "formerly—now" contrast, the idea of being in the Lord, and the blend between the indicative and the imperative.

Structure. This passage falls easily into two sections, but question exists about where the break actually occurs. The NIV places the paragraph division at 5:8, whereas the UBS Greek text places it at 5:6. Since verse 7 goes with what follows, the best explanation is that verses 7—14 form one paragraph with the latter half (vv. 11—14) providing commentary on the first half.[2] As in 4:25—5:2, theological motivation for obedience to the commands is interspersed throughout this whole section. The passage unfolds as follows:

5:3—6: Commands to avoid shameful sins
    5:3: Command to avoid sexual sin and covetousness
        Motivation: what is proper for God's people
    5:4: Commands to avoid sins of the tongue and, rather, to be thankful
        Motivation: Such sins are not "fitting"
    5:5: *Motivation for both commands*: Such sins prohibit inheriting the kingdom
    5:6: *Motivation emphatically restated*: the wrath of God is coming on the disobedient
5:7—14: The relation of Christians and the disobedient
    5:7—10: The Christian's nature should exclude association with the disobedient
        5:7: Command not to partner with such people
            5:8a: *Motivation*: formerly darkness, now light
        5:8b: Contrasting command: live as people of light
            5:9—10: Parenthetical description of life in the light
    5:11—14: Commentary on the distinction and on living as light
        5:11a: Command not to participate in their actions
        5:11b: Rather, even reprove such people
            5:12—13: *Motivations*: Shameful character of their works and the revealing nature of light
            5:14: *Verification*: Words of an early confession.

---

2. Note that Lincoln, *Ephesians*, 316—17, puts a paragraph break at verse 6 in his translation, but in his comments on structure says that this passage proceeds in two main stages: verses 3—6 and verses 7—14.

Avoid Shameful Sins (5:3–6)

SEXUAL SIN AND **greed.** The shift from Christ's self-giving nature in 5:2 to the self-indulgence of 5:3 is striking. The three sins mentioned—"sexual immorality" (*porneia*), "impurity" (*akatharsia*), and "greed" (*pleonexia*)—were already mentioned at 4:19. The second and third sins are the same in both passages, but the first sin in 4:19 is "sensuality" (*aselgeia*). Galatians 5:19 lists *porneia, akatharsia,* and *aselgeia* as the first explanations of "works of the flesh," all three apparently in reference to sexual sin.[3] The NIV does not show it, but "sexual immorality" and "impurity" are linked in 5:3 as a tandem (see also Col. 3:5). "Impurity" refers primarily to sexual sin, even with "of any kind" being added.[4] "Greed" is added as a separate sin, which can include sexual lust, but can refer to any kind of drive to "have more."[5]

Porneia is a broad word covering any sexual sin.[6] It can refer to incest (1 Cor. 5:1), promiscuity (1 Thess. 4:3), sexual relations with a prostitute (1 Cor. 6:13), or illicit sexual relations (John 8:41). It is also used figuratively of apostasy or idolatry because of the Old Testament image of Yahweh as the husband of his people (see Rev. 2:20–21). *Pleonexia*, "the desire to have more," here and in Colossians 3:5 is further identified as "idolatry." Behind this identification is a Jewish understanding of idolatry as the root of all sin and of greed as the sin encompassing all sins.[7] Greed motivates all other sins, and as J. A. Bengel has noted, is the highest act of revolt away from God.[8] Desire takes the place of God, for it, rather than he, determines life.

The words rendered "among you there must not be even a hint ... because these are improper for God's holy people" are literally "let [these sins] not be named among you, even as is fitting for holy ones." While some suggest Paul does not want these sins even mentioned (see v. 12), the NIV is right to take the expression as a forceful way of saying these sins are totally contrary to what it means to be a Christian. Both halves of the verse are intended to show how inappropriate sexual sin and greed are among those whom God has set aside for himself.

---

3. The same three in slightly different order appear in 2 Corinthians 12:21.

4. The word "impurity" can be used of any uncleanness, including literal or ceremonial uncleanness. See also Romans 1:24, where this word is used of sexual sin.

5. Note also that the verb form of this word is used in 1 Thessalonians 4:6 to describe sexual cheating.

6. Note Testament of Simeon 5.3: "Fornication is the mother of all evils: it separates from God and drives *those who indulge in it* to Beliar."

7. See Wisdom of Solomon 14–15, especially 14:12, 27–28. Testament of Judah 19.1 views love of money as a sure path to idolatry. Note that Paul's discussion of sin and the law in Romans 7:7–12 focuses on the command not to covet (cf. also Matt. 6:24; 1 Tim. 6:10).

8. J. A. Bengel, *Gnomon of the New Testament* (Edinburgh: T. & T. Clark, 1877), 3:102.

Sins of the tongue (5:4). This verse is an expansion of 4:29. The three words for sins of speech in this verse occur nowhere else in the New Testament, although cognates appear of the word translated "obscenity" (*aischrotes*; see, e.g. Col. 3:8). The root expresses that which is shameful or disgraceful; while the word could have a wider reference, its being paired here with two words on speech indicates that Paul's concern is about shameful and indecent language. "Foolish talk" (*morologia*) suggests speech from a fool (one void of understanding) and brings to mind the frequent condemnation of the fool in the Old Testament wisdom literature. "Coarse joking" (*eutrapelia*) usually has a positive meaning outside the New Testament, but clearly is negative here. It suggests something easily turned, a double *entendre*—speech innocuous in itself but turned to have an indecent intent. Such speech is not fitting for the believer.[9]

What is fitting for God's people is "thanksgiving."[10] The word group for "giving thanks" appears elsewhere in Ephesians only at 1:16 and 5:20, the latter referring to thanksgiving as a mark of being filled with the Spirit. Thanksgiving is an important component in Paul's thought. It is the basic attitude of the Christian, for it forces attention on God, his grace, and his desires rather than on one's own desires.[11] P. T. O'Brien suggests the term is a virtual synonym for the Christian life[12] (see esp. Rom. 1:21; 14:6; 2 Cor. 4:15; Col. 3:17).

Motivation in the form of warnings (5:5—6). "For of this you can be sure" is literally, "For this you know, knowing." Paul reminds his readers of information they already know, that sexual sin and greed are not fitting for God's people and that those who commit such sins will not inherit the kingdom of Christ and of God.[13] The language of inheriting is frequently used to

---

9. "Improper" in verse 3 and "which are out of place" (lit.: "things that are not fitting") in verse 4 reflect expressions popular in Stoic discussions (see also Acts 22:22; Rom. 1:28; Col. 3:18; Philem. 8).

10. The Greek text has a wordplay between thanksgiving (*eucharistia*) and coarse joking (*eutrapelia*).

11. Zerwick, *Epistle to the Ephesians*, 138.

12. P. T. O'Brien, "Thanksgiving Within the Structure of Pauline Theology," *Pauline Studies*, eds. Donald A. Hagner and Murray J. Harris (Exeter: Paternoster, 1980), 50–66, especially 62. He also points out that Paul uses thanksgiving language more than any other Hellenistic author, pagan or Christian, and that the thanksgiving language is close to what we normally understand as praise.

13. The alternative "kingdom of *the* Christ and God" in the NIV footnote reflects a debate about whether this text refers to Christ as "God." The Greek text has one article preceding "Christ" and "God." Usually this indicates one entity being referred to with the two words. However, the presence or absence of the article in Greek is not always easily explained, especially with names and titles. To assume that "God" is ascribed to Christ here

express what one receives or possesses as a gift from God (cf. 1 Cor. 6:9–10; Gal. 5:21).

The warning is strengthened in verse 6. Not only are practitioners of such sins excluded from the kingdom, but a more dire fate awaits them in the form of God's wrath. The word "comes" can be understood either of God's wrath exercised in the present world (as Rom. 1:18–32) or of God's judging wrath at the end of time. Some scholars argue that both present and future are intended, but the primary reference seems to be to wrath in the final judgment.

The wording of verse 6 is reminiscent of 2:2–3 and 4:14, 22. For that reason, M. Barth is wrong to read this verse as referring to Christians and the discipline of Christians.[14] Christians may be guilty of such sins, as the Corinthian letters show, but no evidence exists that Paul's readers were doing such sins. If they were, he would have addressed the issue more directly. This passage assumes a strong contrast between believers and unbelievers.

The exact nature of the coming wrath is not made clear in Paul's letters. He does not use words for "hell" such as *hades* or *gehenna*, and although insisting on the wrath and judgment of God, the apostle gives little explanation of what the punishment will be. The strongest expression of coming judgment is in 2 Thessalonians 1:8–9 ("everlasting destruction and shut out from the presence of the Lord "). Clearly the punishment is awful (Rom. 2:9), but Paul exercised considerable reserve in describing judgment, though this reserve should not be misinterpreted as doubt about its reality. Without the presupposition of judgment, one does not need to speak of salvation. At the same time, we should remember that—unlike this text—of approximately eighty references to judgment in Paul's letters, sixty of them are addressed to Christians.[15]

The Relation of Christians and the Disobedient (5:7–14)

DO NOT PARTNER with such people (v. 7). This verse functions as a heading for verses 7–14. The word translated "partners" (*symmetochoi*) is actually a compound form, "partners with" or "fellow partners."[16] The simpler form was

---

is hazardous, particularly when Ephesians does not make this point elsewhere (cf. 1 Tim. 5:21 and 2 Tim. 4:1, which use one article before God and Christ Jesus, surely with no intent of equation).

14. Barth, *Ephesians*, 2:566, 592–98. His comment that the author does not summarily condemn immoral people outside the church may fit with Paul's attitude in 1 Corinthians 5:9–13, but it does not do justice to Ephesians 4:17–19.

15. The estimation is from Herbert Braun, *Gerichtsgedanke und Rechtfertigungslehre bei Paulus* (Leipzig: J. C. Hinrichs'sche Buchhandlung, 1930), 44.

16. It is one of the fourteen "with" (*syn*) compounds in Ephesians. See pp. 136, 161.

used often for business partnerships, though not always in a technical, legal sense.[17] The compound form in Ephesians 5:7 occurs elsewhere in the New Testament only at 3:6: *"sharers together* in the promise in Christ Jesus." If one is joined to Christ and shares in him, one cannot share in the lives of those practicing sexual sin and greed (cf. 2 Cor. 6:14).

Live the light (vv. 8–10). As indicated above, verse 8 is a marvelous summary of much of Ephesians and of Paul's theology generally, but at the same time its content is shocking. The use of light and darkness themes in 1:18; 3:9; and 4:18 does not prepare the reader for the radical statement here. Other passages speak of disciples being the light of the world (Matt. 5:14) or having the light and being children of light (John 12:35–36). In addition, John 8:12 says Christ is the light of the world, and 1 John 1:5 asserts that "God is light." But we do not expect the bare statement, "You are light in the Lord." No text is as strong in its explanation of conversion.

The underlying thought is based on Paul's "spheres of influence" theology. People take on the character of the sphere in which they live. Once they lived in darkness and were darkness; now they live in the light and are light. They are not light in themselves, of course; they are only light "in the Lord." When they are in him who is the light, they too *are* light.

This verse is another clear example of the blend of the indicative and the imperative. The indicative statement virtually always comes first as a basis for the imperative. Therefore, the imperative is not wishful thinking, but a call to live out what the gospel says is true. The Christian life is always a call to be who God says we are. A life of faith is a life that takes God at his word.

The NIV "children of light" is a Semitic expression for "those who are characterized by light" (i.e., *"people* of light"). The parenthetical statement in verse 9 provides a quick summary of what such a life is like—"goodness, righteousness and truth." It reminds the reader of points already covered, especially in 4:20–5:2.[18] The ethic of the new life focuses on "good works" (2:10) or on what benefits other people (4:28–29). The new being speaks the "truth in love" (4:15, 25), has found truth in Jesus (4:20), and is created in "righteousness and holiness" of truth (4:24). The trilogy in 5:9 is reminiscent of the statement in Micah 6:8, that God requires human beings to act justly, to love mercy, and to walk humbly with God.

The ethic is always guided by "what pleases the Lord" (5:10)—a positive way of saying, "Do not grieve the Holy Spirit" (4:30). The word translated

---

17. The simpler form is used in Luke 5:7 of a business partnership and in Hebrews, usually in reference to sharing in or participating in Christ, the Spirit, or something from God.

18. The textual variant behind the KJV "fruit of the Spirit" is clearly inferior and appears to have been influenced by Galatians 5:22.

"find out" (*dokimazo*) means "put to the test, examine, or discern," in the sense "determine the validity of." Something that has passed the test is "approved" (*dokimos*). This word group plays an important role in Paul's ethical teaching. The renewal of the mind in Romans 12:2, for example, occurs so that Christians may discern what God's will is. Paul's prayer in Philippians 1:10 is that believers may have "smart love" to be able to discern what really counts. In 1 Thessalonians 5:21 readers are instructed to discern all things and hold to the good. The Christian ethic is largely an ethic of discernment.

Let the light do its work (5:11–14). The command in verse 7 not to partner with the disobedient is expanded in verse 11 with the command not to participate in their actions either. The NIV "have nothing to do with" instructs believers not to share in or participate with wrongdoing.[19]

The "deeds of darkness"[20] are "fruitless," meaning they are useless in producing what God desires. They fit the darkness; they do not fit with Christ. Such deeds produce nothing of value in God's eyes. If Christians are light, they cannot participate in such acts.[21]

The separation Paul calls for, however, is not so much a withdrawal as a confrontation. "Expose" (vv. 11, 13) often carries a nuance of correcting or convincing someone.[22] Whether the confrontation is only by conduct or also verbal is debated, though to suggest this passage has nothing to do with spoken confrontation is overly narrow. Although no guidelines are given for confronting, clearly Paul is not thinking of geographical separation and avoidance of contact, but of the refusal to participate in indecent actions. After all, contact with non-Christians is required if the light is to accomplish its purpose.

Apparently the shameful acts too indecent to mention refer to the sexual impurity treated in verse 3. Secret acts in connection with religious ritual could be in the background, but this does not appear to be the issue Paul addresses. He wants to convey the seriousness of these sexual sins without discussing the details of the depravity. The implication is that various possibilities exist for reproving acts without participating in their error.

Verses 13–14 are difficult because of the word *phaneroo*, translated "becomes visible" in verse 13 and "makes visible" in verse 14. This word usu-

---

19. Elsewhere this verb occurs only in Philippians 4:14 and Revelation 18:4, and its corresponding noun only in Romans 11:17; 1 Corinthians 9:23; Philippians 1:7; and Revelation 1:9.

20. "Deeds of darkness" could be understood either as an adjectival genitive ("deeds characterized by darkness") or a genitive of source ("deeds that have their origin in darkness"), probably the former.

21. The logic is the same as 2 Corinthians 6:14: "What fellowship can light have with darkness?"

22. See, for example, Matthew 18:15; 1 Corinthians 14:24; 1 Timothy 5:20

ally has the meaning "to make known," "to reveal"; it is the antithesis of something kept secret. The NIV rendering is understandable for verse 13,[23] even if the statement does not contribute much to the argument, but the rendering of verse 14 is problematic. Translated literally, verse 14a reads: "For everything that is revealed is light."[24] Predicate nominatives like this one are qualitative in nature. In other words, that which encounters the light takes on the quality of light.

The question that must be resolved is whether the "revealing" is merely negative (exposing people's sins) or whether a positive element exists as well, so that people are both exposed *and* transformed. The context seems to require both, and since the word translated "expose" also means "convince," this is understandable. The person who is exposed and convinced by the light is transformed. This is confirmed both by verse 8 and the confession in verse 14. F. Foulkes rightly sees three stages of the work of grace in verses 13–14: People are exposed; they allow themselves to be revealed; and then they become light.[25]

The context (the primary determiner of meaning) seems to require a translation such as:

All things exposed/convinced by the light are enlightened,
For everything being enlightened takes on the quality of light.
For this reason it says,
Get up, sleeper,
and rise from the dead
and Christ will shine on you.

The problem is that *phaneroo* does not normally carry the meaning "to enlighten," and interpreters should be cautious. Normally the word means "to reveal," "to be made known." On the other hand, to translate "Everything that is revealed is light" makes little sense. Instead of "enlighten," some commentators suggest "to illumine,"[26] but the effect is the same. The logic seems to assume that the light not only exposes, but also transforms (see 2 Cor. 4:6). In all likelihood we are dealing with proverbial statements about light, which lends to the logic being compacted (see also John 3:19–21; Rom. 13:11–14; 1 Thess. 5:4–8).

---

23. "By the light" could be attached to "exposed" as in the NIV or to "becomes visible." Either makes sense, but the connection with "exposed" is preferable.

24. This understands the verb form *phaneroumenon* as passive, as it is usually understood. If taken as a middle with an active meaning, the translation would be "everything revealing is light," which does not make much sense.

25. Foulkes, *Ephesians*, 154.

26. Lincoln, *Ephesians*, 330.

The last half of verse 14 is about Christ's transforming light. This is clearly traditional material, as "it is said" shows. These words are a confession or hymnic statement calling for people to wake up from their darkness and experience the transformation that the risen Christ brings. The wording may be drawn from passages on resurrection and light in Isaiah 26:19 and 60:1. Paul is describing the process by which darkness is turned into light and showing why the statement of 5:8 is true: Believers experience resurrection with Christ and are transformed by his life-giving light.[27]

"HERMENEUTICS IS THE very deciphering of life in the mirror of the text."[28] We decipher life by carrying on a dialogue with the text about our world and its world. The concepts in this passage are clear; the world we see is much like our own. Bringing its message into our generation will depend largely on *conviction* about the correctness and relevance of the text.

Our world mirrored. Ephesians has been called "the epistle for today."[29] Like much else in the letter, 5:3–14 could have been written to any of our present churches. Obviously the list of sins here is not exhaustive. No mention is made of violence, murder, or a variety of other transgressions. Paul's concern is not a comprehensive treatment of sin, but those sins by which his readers are most likely to be thrown off course. But why is so much focus placed on sexual sin, language, and greed? Sexual sin is the one place where pride, power, and pleasure are inordinately concentrated. If sin gains control, sexual immorality is often the result. Language and greed are so important because they are gateways by which sin finds entrance.

Modern Western society virtually idolizes sexuality, is obsessed with it, and is loathe to recognize boundaries for sexual expression. A recent news magazine lamented our loss of ethics by highlighting our society's loss of all sense of shame. Anything goes. In a later issue, however, the same magazine seemed to contribute to that very loss by discussing the increase of bisexuality in our culture in a way that promoted it, or at least approved of it.[30]

---

27. See 4:18 and the discussion on pp. 72–73, 230–31.

28. Paul Ricoeur, "Preface to Bultmann," *Essays on Biblical Interpretation*, ed. Lewis S. Mudge (Philadelphia: Fortress, 1980), 53.

29. Neil Alexander, "The Epistle for Today," *Biblical Studies: Essays in Honour of William Barclay*, eds. Johnston R. McKay and James F. Miller (London: Collins, 1976), 99–118.

30. See *Newsweek*, February 6, 1995, 20–21. Bisexuality was featured as the "cover article" of *Newsweek*, July 17, 1995, 44–50.

Sexual attitudes in the ancient Greco-Roman world were similar to today's, although at times more blatant. Often a double standard existed so that wives were expected to have sexual relations only with their husbands. Chastity by a woman was valued, but not necessarily practiced. Men, however, had various sexual outlets, as long as they did not commit adultery against another man's marriage. A famous statement illustrates the laxity: "Mistresses we keep for the sake of pleasure, concubines for the daily care of our persons, but wives to bear us legitimate children and to be faithful guardians of our households."[31] Cicero wrote approvingly of the legitimacy and antiquity of young men having affairs with courtesans.[32] Prostitution, homosexuality, and bisexuality were common; slaves were often abused sexually.

At the same time, we should not overstate the case for the ancient world. Not everyone was promiscuous, and various inscriptions attest to the value placed on marital fidelity. In addition, the frequent assertion that the worship of Artemis in Ephesus was associated with fertility rites is without evidence.[33]

Lax sexual standards do not fit with Christianity, whether in the first or the twenty-first century. Christians too easily adopt the sexual attitudes of the surrounding culture, but sexual sin will not mesh with life in Christ. What we do with our bodies matters because we belong to God. The argument that sexual intercourse outside marriage is legitimate was prevalent at Corinth, to which Paul reacted with astonishment: How could one join what is part of Christ with a prostitute? Sexual sin is a sin against one's own body (1 Cor. 6:15–19). The assumption behind such thinking is that sexual intercourse is far more than a physical act; it is a *psychical* act that binds two people into a unity and reflects the very image of God. Sexual intercourse answers the question, "To whom do you belong and whose image do you bear?" We cannot belong to multiple partners, particularly if we belong to God. On the other hand, sexual intercourse is *not*—as Christianity has often implied—dirty; it is a marvelous gift of intimacy from God to be used within the marriage covenant. To argue otherwise is to deceive with empty words (v. 6).

Greed, too, stares back at us from the mirror of the text. The desire to have more motivates both sexual sin and all other sins. In fact, sin has been described as seeking to get more out of life than God put into it. Even though

---

31. Demosthenes, *Against Neaera*, 122 (fourth century B.C.). Plutarch (first century A.D.) argued that a wife should not be angry if her husband had sexual relations with a paramour or slave, but should see that her husband respected her and did not share debauchery with her. See his *Moralia: Advice to Bride and Groom* 140B (16).

32. *Pro Caelio*, 20.48. He asserts that such affairs were never blamed or forbidden.

33. See Richard Oster, "The Ephesian Artemis as an Opponent of Early Christianity," *Jahrbuch für Antike und Christentum* 19 (1976): 28.

God has packed life full of good things, most of us are never satisfied. When desire for more takes over—especially with sexual relations—it distorts the mind, debilitates us, disrupts life, and finally becomes our master.[34] We say a person is lovesick for good reason: Greed makes us sick. Greed can also take control of our minds and distort us in the desire for possessions. It pushes us to acquire more money and resources. We never have enough. If lying is the enabler of sin, greed is its origin (cf. 1 Tim. 6:10).

We live in a society that encourages all forms of greed. The music and the entertainment media seek success by heightening sexual desire and displaying conspicuous consumption. The advertising industry uses sex to create and instruct other forms of greed. Self-centeredness is no longer merely a given; it is elevated as a desirable quest. The only goals most people know are pleasure and possessions, and for many that means life goes out of control. We have moved self-centeredness from a malady to a deadly contagious disease.

Obscenity, foolish talk, and coarse joking are ways we reinforce or court a godless lifestyle. These three categories cover everything from vulgarity to defiance of God to innuendoes. People may start using such language to prove they are tough and know the "ways of the world." But it is evidence that sin has taken up residence in their minds and that shame is being honored and embraced. It is a way to play with sin, but as G. B. Caird notes, where vice is regarded as amusing, the practice of it comes easy.[35] Or, as an ancient rabbi said, "Jesting and levity accustom a man to lewdness."[36] This passage is not, however, a rejection of humor, which can be engaging, creative, and enjoyable. Rather, it is a rejection of the talk of fools—those who are morally and spiritually perverse—and of humor as a way to play with sin.

Surprisingly, Paul offers thanksgiving as a catch-all description of the language that does fit Christ. This does not impose a narrow limitation on language; rather, it recognizes how determinative an attitude of thanksgiving is for life. When we acknowledge God and give thanks for life from him, responsibility to him is established and life is ordered away from self-centeredness and sin. Sin springs from ingratitude. Thanksgiving is an antidote for sin, for it is difficult to both give thanks and sin at the same time.

Judgment. Relatively few people in our society—Christians included—take judgment seriously. In popular eschatology expressed primarily at funerals of well-known people, everyone goes to heaven and continues doing

---

34. See Diogenes Laertius 6.66: "Bad men obey their lusts as servants obey their masters."

35. Caird, *Paul's Letters from Prison*, 84.

36. *Aboth* 3.14.

there essentially what they did here. Judgment has no place, or at best is reserved for murderous dictators. The naiveté is amazing.

We do not need a return to "brimstone" preaching, but we very much need a return to a focus on judgment. The parameters of Paul's comments on judgment mark the path. Judgment is taken seriously, but always in balance and without being overly descriptive. He never uses scare tactics, but the threat of judgment is explicit. Universalism is attractive, of course, but it is a lie.[37] If there is no judgment, no one needs salvation, and what we do does not really matter. There is a sense in which sin is its own judgment, which is reason enough to avoid it, but the real danger is end-time judgment and exclusion from life with God. If God does not respond with wrath to this world, he is not much of a God. He who does not get angry does not care.[38] God cares, and judgment is real.

Light in the Lord? Surely one of the most difficult statements to understand in this section is the assertion, "You are light in the Lord" (5:8). How can Paul make such a statement? He had written in Romans 7 that he himself did the opposite of what he wanted (to say nothing of what he knew about the Corinthians).[39] We could understand Paul if he had written, "You are part light and part darkness," or "Try to be light." But Paul took conversion much more seriously than we do. This is a statement about what people are *in Christ*. It is only in the Lord that they are light. The commentary on verse 8 in verses 13–14 shows what is intended. To have the light of Christ shine on us is to be transformed into what he is; to be in him is to take on his nature. The indicative states what is true: Christians are light in the Lord. Once again, this is a question of identity and the geography that determines identity.[40] Christ, in whom we live, determines our identity. From such a high understanding comes a high morality.

The imperative to live as people of light receives little explanation. Paul mentions goodness, righteousness, and truth parenthetically (v. 9), but his only directive here (v. 10) is to discern what pleases the Lord (discernment is also implied in determining what is proper in vv. 3–4). Once again we find a focus on the mind. Christians are thinkers who analyze conduct to see if it fits with their Lord.

Separation. The mark of Christian maturity is seen in the ability to explain and live what is meant by "separation." The text asks that we neither partner with the disobedient nor participate in doing works of darkness. Clearly

---

37. Stott, *God's New Society*, 197.

38. On the wrath of God, see pp. 111–12.

39. Depending, of course, on whether Romans 7 is autobiographical, but even if not, the point is valid.

40. See pp. 115–19.

participation in sin is excluded, but are we to avoid all contact with sinful people? A range of options is possible in dealing with this issue. In the ancient world, for example, the Essenes went to Qumran on the shores of the Dead Sea to separate from the defilement around them. Christians have sometimes chosen this path, but this is not what the text asks for. In fact, far too often when we think of separation, we think of geographical distance rather than distinction in lifestyle. "Separation" may indeed be the wrong word. It implies distance, but what the text seeks is distinction.

The problem, of course, is that when Christians try to separate from the world, they take the world with them wherever they go. The world is too much in us, and for all our separation, many Christians espouse the same values and lifestyles as non-Christians. Further, almost by necessity, we have to be involved with non-Christians in our jobs, our neighborhoods, and other parts of life. Separation has never been easy. In the ancient world Jews and Christians faced difficulty in earning a living because many jobs included belonging to a guild which paid dues to the local deities.[41] We must live in society but learn not to sacrifice to its deities.

The parallel discussion in 1 Corinthians 5:9–13 provides insight. Paul had written in a "previous letter" to the church in Corinth not to associate with people guilty of sexual and other sins. The Corinthians thought he was talking about immoral non-Christians, but Paul pointed out that he meant the immoral who claim to be Christians.[42]

The example of Jesus is similar. His biggest conflict was with the religious leaders, but he willingly associated with those considered immoral. We often do the reverse: We tolerate inappropriate "Christian" lifestyles and separate from non-Christians. We cannot share the gospel if we separate from unbelievers. The light is to shine in the darkness. The exposing in verses 11 and 13 presupposes contact with non-Christians. We separate from sin, not from people.

The injunction to expose or reprove sin means it is not enough merely to abstain from sin.[43] Christians have the responsibility to confront, though the text does not tell us how. Too often when we do confront, we do more harm than good. How we confront depends on our relation with those confronted. We do not have the right to force a Christian ethic on a non-Christian populace, especially if such ethics are theologically driven. At the same time we cannot be passive and avoid calling the darkness dark. By both

---

41. See G. H. R. Horsley, *New Documents Illustrating Early Christianity* (Macquarie University, 1989), 5:106–7.

42. Obviously this is important in discussing division within the church. We cannot live in union with those who claim to be Christians and live immorally.

43. Bengel, *Gnomon*, 3:103.

lifestyle and conversation we should be instruments by which the light does its work. The presumption of the text is that light is a power that transforms. To be an agent of the light requires wisdom and discernment. If discernment is required to find what is pleasing to the Lord, surely it is also required in thinking through how we relate to and confront the non-Christian world.

WE LIVE IN a society that is in a moral tailspin. In the 1950s our society feared communism and built massive weapons of destruction and bomb shelters to protect our way of life. No attention was paid to defending the moral fabric of society. But an "enemy" has infiltrated our institutions and our pastimes and damaged—or maybe destroyed—our moral framework. We do not need to overstate the problem, for much morality still exists, but it also is under attack. Too many people have lost all motivation for ethics.

Increasingly the problems of our society are major moral problems: sexual sins, violence, racism, and theft. Politicians use phrases such as "defining deviancy down" and "mainlining deviancy" to describe what is happening in our society. Television shows set for the family hours are now filled with adultery, promiscuity, and homosexuality. Violence is presented as something fun to watch. We have made rock stars, actors, and talk show hosts our ethicists and philosophers, but few of these people merit being heard. In the ancient world acting was a disreputable profession.[44] Despite the glitz, often it still is.

Christians buy right into this culture, seemingly unaware of the offense or its impact. Is it possible to pull out of this moral tailspin? Of course it is, if the light does its job. Few people are being convicted by the light because too often the light has chosen to go back to darkness. Society needs to be reformed, but first of all the church needs to be reformed.

Sexual sin. Our society has a major problem handling sexuality. The problems of adultery, promiscuity, and the like are bad enough, but the extent of the problem is revealed even more by rape, incest, and sexual abuse. Conservative estimates are that one in six women will be raped and that one in ten children is a victim of incest. Our legitimate desires for love and intimacy have gone haywire, and the pride, power, and pleasure coalesced around sexuality have destroyed all sanity and control. Modernity, as one person defined it, is rationalized sexual misbehavior, and the problem is that we

---

44. In Rome a senator was prohibited from marrying a woman whose parents had at any time been an actor (see Mary R. Lefkowitz and Maureen B. Fant, *Women's Life in Greece and Rome* [Baltimore: John Hopkins, 1983], 185, 188–89. See also Pascal, *Pensées*, no. 11, who felt the theater to be the greatest danger to Christian living.

do all we can to stir up the desire. Pornography and "phone sex" are both billion-dollar industries. Sexual discussions are among the most popular uses of computer on-line services. Standards of modesty and decency with regard to dress have evaporated. Language is distorted so that words like "sophisticated," "mature," or "gentleman" are used to describe sexual perversion, deviancy, and pornography.

But society also sends contradictory messages that reveal condemnation of such activity even while it is being embraced. We keep this material from children, but why, if it is so harmless? We fall for sexual titillation, but become indignant at any hint of sexual harassment. We accept the lack of sexual restraints, but the press crucifies politicians guilty of illicit sexual activity. The entertainment industry leads both the promotion of sexual promiscuity and—is it out of guilt?—the battle against AIDS. Once again sin is shown to be the failure to do what we know.

But what is wrong with pornography viewed in the privacy of one's own home? Besides demeaning people by viewing them as sex objects, pornography destroys by staying in the mind; it structures the brain in an illegitimate way. This is not just appreciation of beauty, but the feeding and embracing of lust. It gears the mind in the direction of inappropriate acts. It is both the first step to sexual sin and is sin itself. As Jesus pointed out strongly, what you do with your mind matters (Matt. 5:27–30), especially with regard to sexual sin. Furthermore, pornography is a devious monster that entraps men especially and becomes an addiction.

The passage before us with its rejection of sexual sin and its call for non-participation and confrontation needs to be applied directly—not just in society at large but also in the church. Incest occurs in church families, and adultery and promiscuity are often as prevalent in churches as in the rest of society. Unfortunately, pastors too are guilty. Pornography and other "industries of sexual sin" could not survive without "Christian" support. The only solution is repentance and a Spirit-filled vow not to participate. Do not go to it, do not rent it, do not read it. Do not allow the mind to dwell where it does not belong. Do not place yourself in compromising situations, and do not commit sexual sin of any type. Such sins should not even be named among God's people, for his judgment will be carried out on those who practice them.

In applying the text we must also probe beneath the surface of the text. What motivates so much sexual sin? Self-centered pleasure-seeking is a large factor, but disrespect for women is also a significant element. The more women are pushed down and viewed as inferior, the easier it is to use them for one's own benefit.[45] The more the opposite sex is viewed as something

---

45. For a more complete discussion see the comments on the husband-wife section, pp. 301–6, 311–17.

to conquer, the more likelihood of sexual sin. On the other hand, the more the opposite sex is valued as people created in the image of God, the less possible it is to engage in sexual sin. The surprising thing is that so many women allow themselves to be used. Their need for love must be enormous, but sexual sin is not the way to get love.

Language. The way we talk can be a way to engage in sexual sin. Language expresses being. By a "pornography of the mouth" we allow sexual sin to define life, and in the process we defile human sexuality and demean people. Obscene language is destructive. Christians have no business using such language, and most usually do not. On the other hand, some believers do adopt inappropriate language as a form of rebellion or to prove they are "with it." Sometimes they discuss sexual topics as if to get as close as possible to sin without actually being guilty, and some pastors seem all too eager to discuss sexual issues when counseling. We must be able to have frank and decent theologically driven discussions about sexuality, but we also must avoid catering to prurient interests, our own included. How we carry on such discussions reveals who we are. We cannot be light in the Lord and have our mouths expressing darkness.

"Foolish talk" seems primarily concerned with foolish talk of a sexual nature, but application of the text requires rejecting *any* talk appropriate to fools (i.e., those who are morally and spiritually perverse). This is not a rejection of humor, but of misguided humor. Humor is a gift, but it can be a form of egotism, escapism, or self-defense and can be used in harmful, belittling ways. Like all other gifts, the issue is how the gift is used. Is the humor creative, enlightening, and restorative, or destructive, debasing, and inane? *Any* destructive and purposeless speech falls under the indictment of this text, including what is done from behind pulpits. When pastors use emotionalism, exaggeration, and bombastic verbal bullying rather than sustained argument, they are guilty. It does not fit with the Lord.

Greed. Many Christians denounce sexual sin, but are mute when it comes to greed. Our society does not consider greed a sin, which only shows how easily evil deceives. Whether lust for sex, greed for materialism, or immersion in some particular interest, all greed is sin, for it allows something other than God to order our lives. The application of this text starts with the obvious greed of sexual lust, surely the most disorienting greed on earth. Second is the greed of materialism, the idolatry of possessions, of which most of us are guilty. Third is the greed for power. Following that is a variety of other sins inspired by greed.

Greed is clearly behind the consuming passion for gambling in our society. Theft and embezzlement are usually extensions of greed. Our addictions, whether they be dependence on chemicals or fascination with sports, are a result of greed. When a football fan says after his team upset another, "This is the greatest day of my life," that is idolatry of the stupidest sort. Any consuming passion that defines life is a form of idolatry displacing God's rightful place. The Christian community needs to be self-reflective, name the idolatries, repent of the greed, and reorder life with all its good things under God's control. The only solution to this problem is thankfulness that recognizes that God alone deserves allegiance and orders life.

Leave the light on. Max Lucado tells a story about some candles who refuse to be taken from a storage closet to provide light during an electrical storm. They all have excuses why they should not give off light. When the husband tells his wife that the candles won't work, she explains, "Oh, they're church candles."[46] Ouch! That the story even works creates pain.

The task of Christians is to leave the light on. We are light in the Lord and are to live as people of light. Too often the light shines only a few hours, and then it is life as usual. We may be light in the Lord, but we keep our reservations on the train to darkness. Evangelicals used to focus on personal sin and neglect social sins like racism or abuse of wealth. For the past decade or so, sin is viewed increasingly in social rather than personal terms. Neither extreme is acceptable. Sin is both personal and social. Part of our job is to resist sin wherever we find it. We resist it by leaving the light on.

Leaving the light on requires four acts:

(1) Live continually in the Lord, aware of him, determined by him, and discerning what is pleasing to him. Fellowship, a joint-sharing of life with Christ, enables us to be light.
(2) Refuse to partner with or participate in sexual sin, greed, inappropriate language, and forms of disobedience.
(3) Perform positive action, doing good, righteousness, and truth.
(4) Expose the darkness for what it is.

None of this happens automatically. As we have seen throughout the letter, Christians are expected to be strong and wise and to live aggressively in following Christ, rather than conform to their surroundings. Each of the four acts above requires deliberate choices and an investment of energy. As verse 15 will underscore, they also require wisdom.

But how can we show distinction without also displaying a holier-than-thou attitude? How can we avoid participation in sin without being reactionary, prudish, and judgmental? How can we avoid being destructive when we confront? As usual, the framing of the questions implies the answers.

---

46. Max Lucado, "Light of the . . . Storage Closet?" *God Came Near* (Portland, Ore.: Multnomah, 1987), 113–17.

Being holier-than-thou, prudish and judgmental, or destructive are failures of which the church has been guilty, but they are neither necessary nor acceptable. The solution has already been presented in the ethic of Ephesians. Paul's first ethical instruction is his call for humility, gentleness, patience, and tolerant love (4:2). If we exercise these qualities, negative results can be avoided. We can refuse to be involved in wrong practices and still care deeply for the people doing them. We can speak the truth in love even when confronting and rejecting disobedience to God.

In most cases people will agree that what they are doing is generally not appropriate or desirable, even if they have an excuse why it is permissible for them. The problems arise when our own egos get in the way and when people perceive that we do not really care for them. When we expose (or reprove or convince about) sins, we should be clear in our own theological understanding of the issues and of the reasons why specific acts are wrong. The darkness will not be exposed if the light does not know what it is talking about.

But what does the text really require of us? What does it mean not to partner with the disobedient? To limit the message to marriage and business partnerships with non-Christians is simplistic and legalistic. We live in a society in which the majority of people carry a Christian label; while such a label may satisfy legalism, it will not satisfy the text. Also, some non-Christians are less guilty of disobedience than some who call themselves Christian.

The text's main concern is *neither* fear of defilement by contact *nor* avoidance of non-Christians. Rather, it is that the light will be truly light and do its job. Certain actions do not fit with the light, and people of the light should not allow the darkness to define them. The issue again, as it always is with the gospel, is definition and identity.

Dark and disobedient acts do not fit the identity, and people of the light should not allow *any* situation where they will be defined by darkness. On the contrary, we must be light and show up the darkness for what it is, a kind of death. By our acts and speech we must call people from darkness to the light Christ gives. People may hate the light and choose darkness, but when they do, it should be because their works are evil, not because the light is offensive (see John 3:19—21). The light cannot be offensive for it produces goodness, righteousness, and truth. The light is the place where people find the grace to face the truth and be transformed by the light.

One cannot leave the light on without a continual process of discerning. The whole of life is directed by what fits with Christ, is pleasing to him, and is proper for his people. No legalism exists here. Life and relations with both Christians and non-Christians are not determined from some chart, but from living with Christ and deciding what should be done in personal issues and relations. "Separation," the distinction we are to embody, is something that comes from the center of our being. We live out the integrity of our own souls. We can only be light when we live the truth of our own relation with Christ. Leave the light on.

Ephesians 5:15–33

B E VERY CAREFUL, then, how you live—not as unwise but as wise, ¹⁶making the most of every opportunity, because the days are evil. ¹⁷Therefore do not be foolish, but understand what the Lord's will is. ¹⁸Do not get drunk on wine, which leads to debauchery. Instead, be filled with the Spirit. ¹⁹Speak to one another with psalms, hymns and spiritual songs. Sing and make music in your heart to the Lord, ²⁰always giving thanks to God the Father for everything, in the name of our Lord Jesus Christ.

²¹Submit to one another out of reverence for Christ.

²²Wives, submit to your husbands as to the Lord. ²³For the husband is the head of the wife as Christ is the head of the church, his body, of which he is the Savior. ²⁴Now as the church submits to Christ, so also wives should submit to their husbands in everything.

²⁵Husbands, love your wives, just as Christ loved the church and gave himself up for her ²⁶to make her holy, cleansing her by the washing with water through the word, ²⁷and to present her to himself as a radiant church, without stain or wrinkle or any other blemish, but holy and blameless. ²⁸In this same way, husbands ought to love their wives as their own bodies. He who loves his wife loves himself. ²⁹After all, no one ever hated his own body, but he feeds and cares for it, just as Christ does the church—³⁰for we are members of his body. ³¹"For this reason a man will leave his father and mother and be united to his wife, and the two will become one flesh." ³²This is a profound mystery—but I am talking about Christ and the church. ³³However, each one of you also must love his wife as he loves himself, and the wife must respect her husband.

PAUL'S NEXT SECTION actually extends from 5:15–6:9. Commentaries subdivide this material into shorter sections, but in doing so create misunderstanding. Four subjects are treated in 5:15–6:9: life in the Spirit (5:15–21), the relation of wives and husbands (5:22–33), the relation of children and parents (6:1–4), and the relation of slaves and masters (6:5–9). To divide the material this way, however, distorts the relation of the "house codes" (the material about relations in the house) to life in the Spirit. For this reason we will treat 5:15–33 as a single unit.

Ephesians 5:15–21 is a *summary climax* and a further development of what it means to "live a life worthy of the calling you have received" (4:1). In 5:15 we find the last occurrence of "walk" (NIV, "live"), the word Paul has used to define the Christian ethic. Like many other sections in the letter, these verses are strongly Trinitarian. Note the logical connections between verses 15–17 and 5:4 and 10. Note also the parallels in Colossians 3:16–19 and 4:5–6.

The structure of the passage. The key to understanding this text is an awareness of its structure, which is complex enough that a decision about where to make paragraph breaks is difficult. Failure to understand the structure has made this section one of the most misappropriated texts in the Bible. The problem is that 5:15–33 contains both the culmination of one section and the beginning of another, and any division within this section tends to distort.

The command "Be very careful, then, how you live" (5:15) is explained by three "not . . . but" contrasts:

(1) not as unwise, but as wise (v. 15b)
(2) not foolish, but understanding what the Lord's will is (v. 17)
(3) not drunk, but (NIV, instead) filled with the Spirit (v. 18).

The NIV hides the structure of the Greek text from this point on. Verses 18–21 are one sentence, with five participles explaining what it means to be filled with the Spirit, the last of which is "submitting to one another in the fear of Christ."[1] *The "house codes" that follow in 5:22–6:9 are explicit instances of submission within the body of Christ.* Any treatment of them in isolation from 5:15–21 leads to error.

A closer comparison of the NIV and the Greek text is instructive. The NIV uses five sentences with six commands to translate the one sentence in 5:18–21:

"Do not get drunk on wine" (v. 18a)
"Be filled with the Spirit" (v. 18b)
"Speak to one another with psalms, hymns, and spiritual songs" (v. 19a)
"Sing" (v. 19b)
"Make music" (v. 19b)
"Submit to one another out of reverence for Christ." (v. 21)

---

1. The NIV has made this into an independent sentence.

The NIV also has one participle ("giving thanks" in v. 20). But the Greek text actually has only *two* imperatives—"Do not get drunk" and "Be filled with the Spirit"—and *five* participles:

Speaking to each other with psalms, hymns, and spiritual songs
Singing
Making music
Giving thanks
Submitting to each other in fear of Christ.

While participles can be interpreted as commands, these five participles describe the *results* of being filled with God's Spirit. We may have chosen other items, but at least in this text Paul was content to describe Spirit-filled Christians as people whose lives are marked by singing, thankfulness, and mutual submission.

A transition clearly takes place in 5:22, but this section does *not* begin a new subject. The address to wives and husbands is *only an example of the mutual submission* mentioned in 5:21. In fact, the manuscripts followed by standard editions of the Greek New Testament do not have the word "submit" in the text; it is assumed and must be supplied from 5:21.[2] Since a transition does occur in 5:22, some translations start a new paragraph at this point. To do so, however, destroys the relation to the theme of mutual submission in verse 21. Other translations, like the NIV, start a new paragraph at 5:21 in hope of maintaining the connection, but in the process lose focus on submission as an essential mark of being filled with God's Spirit.[3]

An additional fact tying 5:22–33 to 5:21 is the repetition of the word "fear" in 5:21 and 33. (The NIV has translated the word for "fear" in v. 21 with "reverence" and in v. 33 with "respect.") Writers in the ancient world often began and ended sections with the same theme as a rhetorical device to bracket that section as a single unit.

Other aspects of the structure of this passage are also instructive. Three subjects are treated in 5:22–33: conduct of wives, conduct of husbands, and the relation of Christ and the church. The interweaving of the last with the first two makes the passage more difficult. Note the amount of space devoted to each of the three subjects:

---

2. Other manuscripts have added some form of "submit" to make the sentence smoother.

3. A translation that begins a new paragraph at 5:22 should at least start the verse with a phrase like "As an example of mutual submission. . . . " People must know that the submission of wives to husbands and the love asked of husbands are *both* examples of the mutual submission required of all Christians in 5:21. They also must know that submission is a *necessary* mark of the Spirit's work in a person's life.

> Address to wives: 5:22–23a, 24b, and 33b
> Address to husbands: 5:25a, 28–29a, (31) and 33a
> Relation of Christ and the church: 5:23b–24a, 25b–27, 29b–32

The relation between Christ and the church provides a model for a husband's conduct toward his wife. Contrary to the frequent use of this text only to address the conduct of wives, Paul focuses mainly on the conduct of the husbands and a theology of Christ and the church.

Christians Living on Target (5:15–21)

CAREFUL LIVING (5:15–17). The main statement in this section is verse 15a: "Be very careful, then, how you live"; the rest of verses 15–21 provides description of what that entails. Literally, the text says, "Watch carefully [or closely] how you walk." The word translated "carefully" carries the connotation of something done accurately, precisely, or given close attention.[4] The theme of verse 15b is virtually repeated in verse 17. To be wise is to understand the Lord's will, which restates verse 10 and corresponds with the Old Testament wisdom tradition that stands behind these verses. The call to live wisely is not a call for theoretical knowledge. It is a call for moral discernment and a practical skill in making decisions. The emphasis once again is on the mind and on careful attention to keep life on target, the target being that which pleases Christ and fits his purposes.

In verse 16 the NIV's "Making the most of every opportunity" is an interpretation of the phrase "redeeming the time." The Greek word translated as "redeem" is a compound form, an intensification, of the word that means "buy" or "purchase." It is used with reference to buying back a slave, but in the New Testament, except for this text and Colossians 4:5, refers only to Christ's purchasing salvation (Gal. 3:13; 4:5). Discussions about whether the meaning is an attempt to gain time or to ransom time from the bondage of evil are probably too literalistic.[5] The expression is a metaphorical way to speak of using time well. A good translation would be, "Buy up every opportunity." Time is going by, and evil will use it if Christians do not.[6] That the days are evil is a general description of the presence of evil in the world. "The Lord" in verses 17 and 19 refers to Christ (cf. vv. 8, 10, 20, all of which are Christologically significant).

---

4. Cf. Luke 1:3; Acts 18:25.

5. See the discussion of various possibilities in Lincoln, *Ephesians*, 341–42.

6. J. A. Bengel, *Gnomon of the New Testament* (Edinburgh: T. & T. Clark, 1877), 3:105, remarks that the opposite of redeeming time is losing time.

Life in the Spirit (5:18—21). Why Paul wrote "Do not get drunk on wine" is not immediately clear. The following alternatives merit consideration. He may have:

(1) been aware of a specific problem among Christians in Asia Minor, as appears to have been the case in Corinth (1 Cor. 11:21);
(2) felt a need to warn against the practice of some pagan cults that viewed drunkenness as a means of unity with the spiritual world;
(3) wanted merely to give a general warning against a dangerous and unacceptable lifestyle;
(4) wanted to provide a contrast with the control of the Spirit, which is his real interest.

No evidence exists to justify either of the first two options. The last two options seem to have motivated the command. From 4:17 on Paul has been contrasting the unacceptable behavior of the unbelieving world with that of God's people. To write against drunkenness was a convenient way for him to call to mind the destructive and unacceptable lifestyle of so many in the culture around them (cf. similarly, Rom. 13:12—13; 1 Thess. 5:7).[7] The contrast of drunkenness and worship or godly living has a long tradition.[8]

Drunkenness is further described as wasteful living (*asotia;* NIV, "debauchery").[9] Drunkenness is symbolic of the height of folly, the loss of direction, and the waste of a life without God.

The command to "be filled with the Spirit" is unexpected and unparalleled in the Bible. Gordon Fee rightly calls this imperative the key to all others and is the ultimate imperative in the Pauline corpus.[10] Possession of the Spirit is the mark of being a Christian (see 1:13—14). But if the Spirit is given to a believer at conversion and, indeed, is the agent of conversion, what does this command involve? Human beings do not control the movement of the Spirit, do they?

We can understand this command by examining other texts with this or similar ideas. If a text says people are filled with grief (John 16:6), joy (Acts 13:52), or knowledge (Rom. 15:14), we have no difficulty understanding that the emotion or knowledge *dominates* their being and *describes* what they are really like. If Acts 5:3 describes Ananias by saying Satan filled his heart, clearly Satan has dominated his impulses; any countervailing tendencies have

---

7. Note also the contrast of drunkenness and Spirit at Pentecost (Acts 2:13—15).

8. Note 1 Samuel 1:12—16; Isaiah 28; see Schnackenburg, *Ephesians: A Commentary,* 236.

9. In the New Testament this word occurs only here and at Titus 1:6 (NIV, "wild") and 1 Peter 4:4 (NIV, "dissipation"). An adverbial form of the word describes the behavior of the prodigal son in Luke 15:13 (NIV, "wild").

10. Gordon Fee, *God's Empowering Presence* (Peabody, Mass.: Hendrickson, 1994), 721—22.

been rooted out. The Scriptures also speak specifically of people being full of the Spirit: Jesus after his baptism (Luke 4:1), Stephen (Acts 6:5; 7:55), Barnabas (11:24). The seven chosen to serve Hellenistic widows were to be full of the Spirit and wisdom (6:3). Surely the intent is that the persons chosen should be characterized by wisdom and live in tune with God's Spirit. Paul's point, then, is that the Holy Spirit is the controlling influence motivating and directing the lives of believers.

"Fullness," as we have seen, is an important theme in Ephesians. Note the following:

> 1:23: Christ is the fullness of God who fills all things.
>
> 3:19: Christians are to know the love of Christ in order to be filled into all the fullness of God.
>
> 4:10: Christ ascended in order to fill all things.
>
> 4:13: Christians are to attain to the whole measure of the fullness of Christ.

"Fullness" expresses unity with the triune God and the completion that God's salvation brings. The call to be filled with the Spirit is a call to live in that unity and to enjoy the wholeness of life with God. Christians must allow themselves to be the place where the presence and the power of God are evident.[11] We are filled both by and with the Spirit.

The message of 5:18 is close to the goal of Paul's prayers in 1:17 and 3:16, that the Spirit will inform and empower his readers. Attention is here placed on the believers' responsibility to be receptive to the Spirit. While human beings do not manipulate the movement of God's Spirit, human responsibility is involved. Furthermore, Fee is correct to emphasize the communal focus of this text: The whole church is instructed to be filled with the Spirit.[12]

And Paul emphasizes that Christians are to be *continually* filled with God's Spirit (this is the force of the Greek verb). They are to be controlled not by wine or by anything else, but by the Spirit. We have choice in the matter, for the Spirit's transforming work in us is not done apart from human involvement.

Of the five participles describing life in the Spirit, three have to do with singing (5:19). This whole section is reminiscent of the initial doxology in 1:3–14. Singing is the natural expression of joy that God brings into a person's life. The presence of early Christian hymns (e.g., 1 Tim. 3:16; possibly Phil. 2:6–11) gives some indication of the importance of songs in the early

---

11. See pp. 136–39.
12. Fee, *God's Empowering Presence*, 722.

church. The purpose of singing is both praise to God and instruction of believers.[13]

Singing, then, has two audiences. Christians sing to each other, reminding each other about God's character and work in Christ, but they also sing to the Lord as a way of offering praise to him. In the parallel in Colossians 3:16 singing is addressed to God, but "Lord" here in Ephesians 5:19 clearly refers to Christ.[14] Hymns in Revelation are addressed both to God and to the Christ/the Lamb (5:9, 13; 7:10; 12:10), and the typical feature of hymns identified in the New Testament is their focus on Jesus as Lord. Later, in a famous letter written about A.D. 111, Pliny the Younger described Christians meeting early to sing antiphonally a hymn to Christ as to God.[15]

Whether any difference is intended between psalms, hymns, and spiritual songs is difficult to say.[16] In all probability no clear demarcation is intended. That people are to sing in their heart is not a request that people sing with feeling or emotion. Rather, "heart" refers to the controlling center of one's being: "Sing with your whole being" (which certainly includes the emotions). The issue is the *integrity* with which one sings, not the feeling. Words are not merely sung, they express the reality of the life in the Spirit.

In addition to singing, life in the Spirit is characterized by giving thanks (5:20). Many Christians lack appreciation of the importance of thanksgiving in the New Testament. Even more than Ephesians the sister letter to the Colossians stresses thanksgiving repeatedly (Col. 3:15–17; 4:2). As we have seen, Romans 1:21 views the failure to give thanks as the root cause of sin.[17] With such a theology, it is not surprising that thanksgiving is associated with life in the Spirit. Thanksgiving is the believing acknowledgment of God and his purposes for good in Christ. Obviously such giving of thanks points to a lifestyle and not just to spoken words.

Christians are to give thanks to God always for everything "in the name of our Lord Jesus Christ." "Name" is a way of referring to what the person stands for and has accomplished. Christians are to give thanks "on the basis of" who Jesus is and what he has done, or "in accord" with who he is. The

---

13. See also 1 Corinthians 14:26; Colossians 3:16.

14. As it does throughout Ephesians and especially in this chapter (vv. 8, 10, 17, 20).

15. *The Letters of Pliny*, 10.96.7

16. Some differentiate "psalms" as the use of Old Testament psalms, "hymns" as Christian hymns, and "spiritual songs" as either anthems of heavenly worshipers (cf. Rev. 5:9–10) or spontaneous Spirit-inspired singing (see Ralph P. Martin, "Ephesians," *The Broadman Bible Commentary* [Nashville: Broadman, 1971], 11:166). See also Donald Hustad, "Doxology: A Biblical Triad," *Ex Auditu*, 8 (1992): 9–13. Bruce suggests that "spiritual songs" refer to "unpremeditated words sung 'in the Spirit'" (*The Epistle to the Ephesians*, 111.)

17. See pp. 230–31, 237–39.

implicit Christology and Trinitarian focus of this section are significant, for the experience of the risen Jesus in worship was the first step to Christology. By the time any New Testament documents were written, a full blown Christology already existed.

This text is Christologically significant, for it is evidence of the worship of Jesus, of his being linked with God liturgically, and of the transfer to him of the title "Lord."[18] The early church was aware that in encountering the risen Jesus, they were encountering God. They did not merely equate Jesus and God, but they knew that in Christ the fullness of God was made known to them (e.g., 1:23; 2:21–22).

The last participle describing life in the Spirit is perhaps the most surprising. People led by the Spirit "submit to one another" (v. 21). Many are offended by the word "submission," as if it points to a passive, weak life dominated by a negative self-image, a giving up of control and free will. This is not Paul's intent, except for the fact that control for Christians has already been given over to Christ.

The Greek word *hypotasso* ("submit") literally means "arrange under." It is used of submitting to God's law (Rom. 8:7), of everything being subjected under Christ's feet (Eph. 1:22), or of younger men being subject to older men (1 Peter 5:5). Attempts to translate "submit" by "be supportive of," "be committed to," or "identify with" are unacceptable. It is important to note that this text does not ask some Christians to submit to other Christians. It asks *all* Christians to submit to *each other*. No privileged group is in view.

Submission is a crucial ingredient in Christian living (this theme is central in 1 Peter). Christians in Corinth were asked to submit to workers who had made themselves servants to the church (1 Cor. 16:16)—they were to submit to servants! Prophets were to submit to other prophets to whom revelation came (14:32). Submission was so important for New Testament writers because it described the self-giving love, humility, and willingness to die that are demanded of all Christians. For example, in Philippians 2:3 Paul rejects selfishness and asks that in humility people consider others as "surpassing" themselves. In the verses that follow he shows how Christ himself modeled such a life (cf. Rom. 12:3; Gal. 5:13).

Jesus repeatedly makes the same point: Whoever exalts himself will be humbled, and whoever humbles himself will be exalted (Matt. 23:12). Neither Jesus nor Paul was weak, nor did either acquiesce to anyone, but both knew what God requires. Christians are called to live in mutual submission, and *without mutual submission they cannot fulfill their destiny*. Such submission is a

---

18. When New Testament believers applied the title "Lord" to Christ, they also applied Old Testament texts referring to Yahweh to him.

strong and free act of the will based on real love of the other person (cf. 4:2). In the end, submission is nothing more than a decision about the relative worth of another person, a manner of dying and rising with Christ, and a way to respect and love other people. In fact, for Christians, authority and submission are the same thing.[19]

Also troubling in verse 21 is the statement that submission is to take place in *fear* of (NIV, "reverence to") Christ. This is the only time this expression occurs in the New Testament, and it is important Christologically when compared to the usual emphasis on the fear of God. In the Old Testament "fear" is a *covenant* word, a characteristic of those who *love* God. "Fear" and "love" are used almost synonymously to describe allegiance and obedience to God (e.g., Deut. 6:2, 4; 10:12; Ps. 103:17–18). The New Testament continues this meaning in describing God-fearers like Cornelius (Acts 10:2) and early Christians (9:31), or in describing Christian life and ministry (2 Cor. 5:11; Phil. 2:12).

For us the term "fear" is usually negative, and the biblical writers knew this negative use. But by and large they used it in a positive sense, for which there is no satisfactory English equivalent. Words like "reverence" or "respect" are too weak to capture the nuance intended. The positive sense of the fear of Christ points to his power and holiness and to the recognition that he is Lord and coming Judge. Such fear is the ground of both praise and obedience. We ought not forget that the one who is feared is the same one who "loved us and gave himself for us" in 5:2.

The House Codes (5:22–33)

"HOUSE CODES" IS the label assigned to those sections of Ephesians, Colossians, and 1 Peter that give instructions to wives and husbands, children and parents, and slaves and masters. While these same three relationships were frequently addressed by Greek and Jewish writers in somewhat stereotypical fashion, no source for the Christian house codes has been discovered, nor do Greek or Jewish writers use the same language as the New Testament writers. The specific wording of this material emerged within the church.

Christians had to treat these subjects, at least in part, because they were accused of destroying society with their focus on freedom, love, and following Christ. Non-Christians needed to know that this was not the case, and Christians needed to be taught the relevance of their faith for their

---

19. On this issue see my "'Your Slaves—on Account of Jesus': Servant Leadership in the New Testament," *Servant Leadership*, eds. James R. Hawkinson and Robert K. Johnston (Chicago: Covenant Publications, 1993), 1:7–19; "Authority and Submission," *Between Two Truths: Living with Biblical Tensions* (Grand Rapids: Zondervan, 1990), 81–94.

primary social relations. Unlike other house codes, Christian house codes focused not only on wives, children, and slaves, but also on the *responsibilities* of the more powerful persons (husbands, parents, and masters).

Instructions to wives (5:22–24, 33b). We must begin by emphasizing that the instruction to wives to submit to their husbands is only the first example of the mutual submission required of all Christians. The word "submit" is not even used in the Greek text of verse 22.[20]

Christianity brought with it significant change for women, and apparently their freedom was a source of offense to non-Christians. In Galatians 3:28, for example, Paul wrote that distinctions like male and female no longer determined value.[21] In 1 Corinthians 7:15 he counseled Christians that they did not have to stay with an unbelieving spouse who wanted to leave. That he would have granted wives such privilege would have been surprising to non-Christians, for the assumption of the day was that a wife would take the gods of her husband.[22] It is understandable, therefore, that in Titus 2:5, Paul instructed women "to be subject to their husbands *so that no one will malign the word of God.*"

What Paul meant by saying wives should "submit to [their own] husbands *as to the Lord*" is unclear. The words could mean (1) in a similar manner as the submission they give to the Lord, (2) as if the husband were the Lord, or (3) as part of their submission to the Lord. While it is hard to imagine Paul suggesting the second option, either of the other two would be legitimate, but the theology implicit in the third choice clearly underlies the text. The wife's relation to the Lord is the basis, motivation, and qualification of her submission to her husband. In verse 24 the words "in everything" indicate that all spheres of life are included in this submission, provided, of course, that it is in keeping with life lived "to the Lord."

Verse 23 is surely one of the most abused and debated texts in the New Testament. Its focus is *not* on the privilege and dominance of the husband, and Paul never intended to suggest that wives were servants, compelled to follow any and every desire of the husband. The text does not tell women to *obey* their husbands, nor does it give any license for husbands to attempt to force submission.[23]

The debate has intensified in recent years over the meaning of *kephale*, the Greek word for "head." Many have assumed that *kephale* means "boss," "per-

---

20. See p. 287.

21. On Galatians 3:28 see my treatment, "Galatians 3:28: Conundrum or Solution?" *Women, Authority, and the Bible* (Downers Grove, Ill.: InterVarsity, 1986), 161–81.

22. Other problems involving women are evidenced in 1 Corinthians 11 and 14.

23. The only time that "obedience" and "submission" are brought close is in 1 Peter 3:1-6.

son in charge," or "leader," since the word has those metaphorical meanings in English. And the Hebrew word for "head" (*ro'sh*) is often used metaphorically in the Old Testament for tribal leaders or other persons in authority.[24] The problem is that this metaphorical meaning is not common in Greek. Most of the time the LXX uses some other word (such as *archon*) to translate *ro'sh*. *Kephale* was used only sixteen times in the LXX to translate *ro'sh* when the idea of "authority over" is present (about 180 occurrences).[25] Consequently, some have suggested that the metaphorical use of *kephale* should be understood as "source." A few scholars have suggested a meaning such as "prominence" or, for Ephesians 5:23, "one who brings to completion."[26] Unfortunately, *no one* involved in this debate is objective and evenhanded with the evidence.

Although the debate will no doubt continue, the most important factor for determining the meaning is the *context* of Ephesians and Paul's other writings. The argument for "source" as the meaning of *kephale* is not convincing. Although it may mean this in a few extracanonical texts, it is rare. Furthermore, "source" does not fit well in most of the Pauline texts. Paul is not arguing in 5:22–24 that the husband is source of the wife as Christ is source of the church. Scholars appear to have chosen this meaning only to avoid negative connotations for the discussion of male-female relations in modern times. The use of *kephale* in 1:22 and Colossians 2:10, where the issue is the subjection of all things under Christ, precludes the idea of source as the meaning in those texts. Paul is not arguing that Christ is the source of the principalities and powers, but that he has authority over them. Some connotation of authority appears to be included in Paul's metaphorical uses of *kephale*.

Still, Ephesians 5:23 does not focus on authority, but on the self-giving love of both Christ and the husband. "Head" in this context suggests "responsibility for." The husband has a leadership role, though not in order to boss his wife or use his position as privilege. Just as Jesus redefined greatness as being a servant (Matt. 20:26–27), Paul redefines being head as having responsibility to love, to give oneself, and to nurture. A priority is placed on the husband, but, contrary to ancient society, *it is for the benefit of the wife*. The activity of both wife and husband is based in their relation to Christ and in his giving himself for the church.

Although Paul makes explicit the priority or responsibility of the husband, the text also assumes the oneness and equality of husband and wife in 5:28

---

24. See Numbers 1:16; Deuteronomy 1:13; 2 Samuel 22:44; Isaiah 7:8.

25. Depending on which manuscripts one follows, for there are variants.

26. An overview of the debate can be found in Wayne Grudem, "The Meaning of *Kephale* ('Head'): A Response to Recent Studies," *TrinJ*, 11 (1990): 3–72.

and 31. Both headship and equality must be given their due. As elsewhere, the truth is in the tension of the text.

The parenthetical statement in 5:23 that Christ is the Savior of the body (i.e., the church) does not mirror the husband's relation to the wife. The NIV does not show it, but 5:24 actually begins with a contrast ("but") to 5:23. Although the husband has responsibility for the wife's welfare, he is not her savior and plays no role in her salvation.

In the summary statement in 5:33 the wife is asked to "fear" (NIV, "respect") her husband. This provides a ring composition that recalls 5:21 and offers another way that the husband-wife relation mirrors that of Christ and the church. But there is no thought of terror or fear of harm. The translation of the Greek word used here as "respect"—if joined to love—comes close to the idea intended for the attitude toward husbands. A wife is to show recognition of her husband's role and responsibility. No doubt, the fear due Christ is far different from the fear due husbands. The latter do not love as greatly, are not inherently holy, and are not end-time judges.

Instructions to husbands (5:25a, 28–29a, 31, 33a). Since wives are asked to submit, one might expect the text would ask husbands to *rule* in an appropriate way. It does not; instead, it asks husbands to *love* and give themselves with the same self-giving love that Christ had in giving himself for the church. Both the directions to the wife to submit and to the husband to love only make specific commands that had already been given to all Christians in 5:2 and 21 (cf. 4:2).

Ancient sources, surprisingly, do not speak frequently of husbands loving their wives. Paul's words to women seem negative to us, but in his day they were surprisingly positive. Why he did not ask wives to love their husbands is unclear.[27] Is something different intended with the command for husbands to love than the command for wives to submit? No, for both commands are Christologically grounded and require giving oneself to the other person. In the final analysis, submission and *agape* love are synonymous. If anything, the stronger language is used of the husband's responsibility. The command for him to love his wife as himself is an application to husbands of the expectation of mutual submission required of all Christians (5:21).

In the ancient world husbands had relatively few obligations beyond providing food and shelter. They were free to do as they pleased, whereas wives were obligated to do domestic chores and to do what their husbands required. Paul's words change the picture dramatically. Rather than being guided by self-interests, the husband is asked to place the well-being of his wife first and to give himself to caring for her.

---

27. Titus 2:4 does, but uses different words from those in Ephesians 5:25.

Ephesians 5:28 applies the commandment to love one's neighbor as one-self (Lev. 19:18) specifically to the wife. Paul is not suggesting we must love ourselves before we can love someone else. Both the writer of Leviticus and Paul assume that a person will look after his or her own interests and welfare, and both seek the same for other people. In the end love is a matter of *justice* for the other person, but raised to the degree that one is willing to forego one's own rights, interests, and desires. Paul here assumes a theology of the oneness of the husband and wife based on Genesis 2:24 (see 5:31). Consequently, the idea of hating or neglecting one's wife is as strange as hating or neglecting oneself.

The words of 5:29 express a tenderness and nurturing expected from the husband so that the well-being and wholeness of the wife are assured. Verse 33 only repeats in an emphatic and personal way the command for husbands to love their wives. This love is not merely the natural love of a man for a woman. As wonderful as such love is, it is *insufficient* for the marriage relationship. Such love is not confined to feelings and attitudes; it involves a series of choices that expresses discipleship to Jesus Christ. The love required of husbands is *Christologically defined*. Christ's love motivated him to give himself for the good of the church. Husbands must follow the same pattern and love enough to give themselves for their wives.

The relation of Christ and the church (5:23b–24a, 25b–27, 29b–32). Often overlooked in this passage is Paul's mature reflection on salvation and the church. The marriage relation is seen as an analogy of Christ's love, his saving work, and his ongoing care for the church. Imagery from the Old Testament about the relation of God and Israel stands behind this use of the marriage analogy. Israel was viewed as God's marriage partner (see esp. Isa. 54:5–7; 62:4–5; the book of Hosea). Ezekiel 16:1–14 may provide the background for Ephesians 5:26–27, for it describes God as caring for, washing, marrying, and adorning Israel with splendor.

Verses 25–27, which explain how Christ is Savior (v. 23b), are often identified as confessional material borrowed from the early church. Such dependence on early church formulations is possible, especially because of some of the unusual phrases Paul uses here,[28] but it is often difficult to separate traditional material from Paul's own. The expression "Christ loved the church and gave himself for her" (5:25) is paralleled almost verbatim in 5:2 and Galatians 2:20. If this is confessional language, Paul has made it his own theology.

The importance of Christ's love in Paul's thinking cannot be overemphasized, nor should it be set over against the Father's love. In this letter God's

---

28. Note "cleansed with washing of water in a word" (5:26) and "glorious" (NIV, "radiant"), but on the latter, cf. 1 Corinthians 4:10.

love is the motivation for election (1:4) and salvation (2:4); Christ's love surpasses human knowledge (3:19) and is the motive of his sacrificial death (5:2, 25) and indwelling (3:17). The Father and the Son are unified in their love of humanity.

In addition to the sacrificial language of 5:25, Christ's saving work is described in terms of sanctifying, cleansing, and presenting. The choice of the language "to sanctify" (NIV, "make holy") a bride may seem strange, but these words were especially appropriate for Paul. The main emphasis in the word "sanctify" means "to set apart," which is exactly what one does in marriage—one's partner is set apart from all the rest. There are overtones here of Christians' being set apart to God.[29] In other words, the act of sanctifying does not refer here to Christian growth, although the "sanctify" word group can be used that way (cf. Rom. 6:19, 22). Here it is used as general description of salvation as a whole.[30]

Nor should the "cleansing" in verse 26 be seen as action prior to salvation.[31] Christ sanctifies and saves by cleansing; they are one and the same act (cf. 1 Cor. 6:11; Titus 3:5). Most scholars assume that Paul is referring to the cleansing of baptism in 5:25. But references to water or washing do not necessarily point to baptism, and a reference to baptism is unlikely, especially if Paul is drawing his language from Ezekiel (esp. Ezek. 35:25).[32] Nowhere else in the New Testament is *the church* baptized. While "cleansed with washing of water in a word" (lit. trans.) is a difficult expression, two ideas are in view: (1) cleansing brought about by the Holy Spirit, and (2) the role of preaching the gospel in bringing about this cleansing. The association of cleansing, washing, and the Holy Spirit is frequent in both Old and New Testaments.

The purpose of Christ's cleansing the church is "to present her" to God without blemish. In 5:26 Christ presents the church to himself, whereas in 2 Corinthians 4:14 God will present us with Jesus (to himself?). In Colossians 1:22 Christ presents believers either to himself or to God. Elsewhere Paul describes himself as presenting the Corinthian church as a holy virgin to Christ (2 Cor. 11:2). Obviously Paul could use the language of "presentation" in several ways and in reference both to the church in the present and at the end time. Future eschatology is clearly in mind in 2 Corinthians 4:14, but this passage and 2 Corinthians 11:2 seem to refer to the present.

The language about the church in this section is unusual. The church is given a focus as an entity *prompting* the work of Christ, not merely (as else-

---

29. In later rabbinic writings, "sanctify" was actually used of taking a bride in Jewish marriages

30. See 1 Corinthians 1:2; 6:11.

31. Note the alternative translation in the footnote of the NIV.

32. See the discussion in Barth, *Ephesians*, 2:691–99.

where) being viewed as the result of Christ's work. Here Christ loved *the church* and gave himself for it.[33] This does not mean the church is viewed as already in existence at Christ's death; rather, it is a way of reflecting on the significance of his death.

One of the most startling and powerful ideas about the church is expressed in 5:30–32. The union between believers and Christ is so real that Christians are *members* of Christ's body. In 4:25 Christians are said to be *members* of each other, and this mutual joining provides a theological motive for telling the truth. In 5:30 Christians are assumed to be so intimately joined to Christ that they are *part of him*.

Any explanation of Paul that does not do justice to a Christian's being part of Christ fails to explain his theology adequately. Ephesians itself can be conveniently summarized by these two expressions: part of Christ and part of each other. The "body" is not a vague ecclesiological concept for Paul; rather, it is a term that expresses the solidarity of believers with Christ. Surprisingly, the quotation of Genesis 2:24 is understood, *not* of the relation between husband and wife, but of the relation of Christ and the church (see Eph. 5:32; cf. also 1 Cor. 6:15). No doubt, the relevance of Genesis 2:24 to the relation of husband and wife is assumed, but the focus in Ephesians is on the solidarity between Christians and their Lord.

Paul describes this relation as "a profound mystery." While it is not impossible that "mystery" means "difficult to comprehend," this is not the way "mystery" is understood elsewhere, especially in Ephesians. Paul uses this term to point to a *revelation* from God, something one would not know had not God revealed it.[34] What Paul probably meant is this: "The revelation about Christ and the church is tremendous and profound."

EPHESIANS 5:15–33 CONTAINS three different kinds of material that require three different processes in bridging the contexts. (1) Verses 18–21 are *exhortation* that in most cases causes little difficulty in bringing into our generation. The language and ideas are not so historically or culturally rooted that they present significant problems. Nothing in them addresses a circumstance true only of the ancient world. However, as elsewhere, we must identify the theological assumptions driving the exhortations.

---

33. Elsewhere the language is that Christ gave himself for an individual (e.g., Paul in Gal. 2:20) or for "us" (Eph. 5:2). The change here is in keeping with the increased focus on the church throughout the letter.

34. Cf. 1:9; 3:9; see pp. 53, 159–60.

(2) The *house code instructions* to husbands and wives in verses 22–33 are rooted deeply in a different time and culture from our modern world. Bringing this section into today is a major task. Careful attention will need to be paid to the differences and the problems the text addresses.

(3) Portions of verses 22–33 are *theological descriptions* of Christ and the church. While they are as pertinent to the modern church as to any other, the language assumes a background of religious ideas and a theological framework. Both may require explanation.

Life in the Spirit (5:15–21). The theological implications of 5:15–21 are important. "Watch closely how you walk"[35] suggests a purpose and direction to life. Life is not aimless, nor is it a series of frenetic activities followed by down time. It is the steady progress toward the goal. The way has been marked out, as is underscored in verse 17 with "the will of the Lord." We must watch where we are going and make steady progress along the way. Verses 15–16 suggest a diligence about life and indicate that the journey is dangerous. We should watch closely because missteps are easy and the consequences disastrous.

Verse 16, with its concern for redeeming the time, reflects an urgency about life. Time is important, and it ought not be frittered away. Both a theology of life and a theology of time lie behind these brief exhortations.

The exhortations for wisdom and understanding drive us to consider the wisdom tradition in the Old Testament and Judaism. The main concern is not on the intellect, even if an intellectual emphasis is present. It is on wise living, on an understanding of God sufficient to produce insight into life and obedience. Wisdom involves considering all information in light of one's relation to God and acting on what one knows. As we have seen throughout Ephesians, the focus is on the mind and the process of discerning what the Lord wants.

Drunkenness (v. 18) was as real a problem in the ancient world as it is today, although it may not have been as pervasive. While wine was produced in large quantities, the variety and potency of alcoholic beverages were not as great as today. In addition, wine was often diluted with water. But alcohol was still a problem, and both Old Testament writers and ancient Hellenistic philosophers frequently warned against its abuse. Although a few groups in the ancient world condemned all consumption of alcohol, this text does not. Drunkenness is clearly a sin, but not all consumption of alcohol is sin. On the other hand, one does have to deal with the dangers of alcohol and the numerous problems it causes in our society. This is precisely one of the areas where we have to discern the will of the Lord.

---

35. NIV, "Be very careful, then, how you live."

Two portions of this text would have been as uncommon for ancient readers as for us: "Be filled with the Spirit" (v. 18), and "Submit to each other" (v. 21). The first was unusual, even though people knew about possession by evil spirits.[36] Yet we should not be surprised at this language if we have paid attention to Paul's teaching about the Spirit throughout the letter.[37] How it can be achieved today? By union with Christ, which is Paul's emphasis from the beginning of the letter. The Spirit is the one who conveys the presence of Jesus to us. Faith creates such a consciousness of the presence of God and Christ in us that we have heightened attention about God's desires and a sense of God's work in us to enable his will.

The idea of mutual submission would have been as offensive to people in the ancient world as today. Despite our nervousness over the word "submission," this text should not be watered down. Especially when the focus is on Christ as a pattern for Christian lives, the text confronts *both* ancient and modern cultures.

The text does not ask us to be "religious." The five participles do not call for trappings of piety that can be faked. Such a religious front is offensive to anyone seeking integrity. The text calls instead for a sense of God's presence that results in a spontaneous and authentic joy. Such joy may be expressed in a variety of fashions.

The relation of wives and husbands (5:22–33). Several factors point to the difficulty of bringing this message into our modern world. The very existence of house codes and the stereotypical focus on the three pairs (wives–husbands, children–parents, slaves–masters) points to the distance between this text and modern society. While we may be concerned about relations within the household, we do not have explicit codes, we do not have slaves, and we would not group wives, children, and slaves together as philosophers and ethicists did in the ancient world. The very form of the text is cultural. Furthermore, we would not ask wives to "fear" their husbands (v. 33). Modern society at least *talks* about equality of women, even though women are still frequently treated as lesser beings.

Most importantly, other biblical texts indicate that advice in the house codes was addressed to a *specific cultural situation*—the fear of some that Christianity was subversive. Any movement in the ancient world that threatened the social order was viewed as dangerous.[38] Titus 2:5 is revealing because it gives a reason why wives ought to submit: *"so that no one will malign* [lit., blaspheme] *the word of God."* Clearly the relation of Christian wives to their husbands was a source of scandal to non-Christians.

---

36. Seneca, *Moral Letters to Lucilius*, 41.1–2, speaks of God as a holy spirit indwelling us.
37. See especially 1:13–14, 17; 2:18, 22; 3:16; 4:3.
38. Judaism and the cults of Isis and Dionysus were also charged with being subversive.

Reading other passages sensitively indicates why this potential scandal was apparent. Galatians 3:28 gave equal value to women. Also, in a society where wives were expected to take the religion of their husbands, 1 Corinthians 7:15 assumed that Christian wives owed their first loyalty to Christ. If an unbelieving husband was content to stay married to a Christian wife, there was no problem; but if he chose to leave, the wife should let him go—and vice versa. That a wife had a greater loyalty to her religion than to her husband was no doubt shocking.

Other parts of 1 Corinthians 7 create tension with Ephesians 5:22–33 and consequently give hint that specific reasons have called forth the statements in the house code. Whereas the husband is head in Ephesians, 1 Corinthians 7:2–16 expresses a *mutuality* that is surprising. There Paul goes so far as to say that the wife has authority over her husband's body (7:4), and ten times he is careful to say explicitly about the wife what he says about the husband. Texts such as 1 Corinthians 11:2–16; 14:34–36 and 1 Timothy 2:8–15 are evidence of questions about the behavior of women in the early church. The *tension within the biblical text itself* indicates historically conditioned material. We must ponder both sets of texts for guidance.

Analysis of the other house codes in the New Testament shows a great deal of concern for testimony to unbelievers. Colossians 4:5 (parallel to Eph. 5:15) encourages Christians to walk wisely with respect to those outside the church (cf. 1 Cor. 10:32). Likewise, 1 Peter 2:12, 15; 3:1–2 encourage behavior that will stop slander against Christians and bring people to God. Such apologetic motivation must be considered in applying these texts in a society that views family relations differently.

Further indication of the difficulty of understanding the message of this text is provided by *historical research on attitudes toward women* in the ancient world. Women are viewed differently in modern Western civilization that in ancient Judaism and the Graeco-Roman world. The sources do not tell us equally about women in all social strata.[39] But what information we do have about women and attitudes toward them paints an *absolutely awful picture*. For example, one writer said women were the worst plague Zeus made. Another said, "The two best days in a woman's life are when someone marries her and when he carries her dead body to the grave." In Judaism women were not counted in the quorum needed for a synagogue and were ritually unclean during menstruation. One rabbi advised, "Do not talk much with a woman." Another added, "Not even with one's wife."[40]

---

39. For example, little is known about the life of women in the lower classes.

40. For good summaries of women in the ancient world, see Sarah B. Pomeroy, *Goddesses, Whores, Wives, and Slaves: Women in Classical Antiquity* (New York: Schocken, 1975); Leonard Swidler, *Women in Judaism* (Metuchen, N.J.: Scarecrow Press, 1976); Mary R. Lefkowitz and

By and large, women were viewed as inferior and were given relatively little freedom. Of course, their status varied in different places and times. Generally speaking, the farther west one went the better their lot, but even in Rome women were only in a slightly better position than their sisters in the East.

In a few places like Sparta and Egypt women were given greater freedom and responsibility. In most places, however, *if* they were allowed to live at birth, women were minimally educated, could not be witnesses in a court of law, could not adopt children or make a contract, could not own property or inherit, and were viewed, as both Aristotle and Josephus said, in all respects to be inferior to a man. They were seen as less intelligent, less moral, the source of sin, and a continual temptation (see Ecclesiasticus 25:13–26:27).

Respectable women—at least the ones described in our sources—were kept from public life. Typically, women lived in one part of the house and men lived in another. In many cases they did not eat meals together. In larger homes virgins spent most of their time in a section set aside for them. Conversation with people outside the house was kept to a minimum. For a woman even to do her spinning in her doorway was scandalous. Imagine how scandalous some would view the early church where both sexes met together in a house for worship and shared the Lord's Supper!

When girls married (usually about age fifteen or sixteen), they were expected to take the religion of their husbands. They were either under their father's, their husband's, or some other male relative's authority all their lives.[41]

Anyone who reads the New Testament texts about women without an awareness of the context will surely not apply them properly. We must take into account both this devaluation of women in the ancient world and the problems caused in the early church by the new freedom and valuation women found in the Christian faith. Are the statements made to wives so historically conditioned, then, that they can be ignored? In spite of what some Christians claim, the answer is "No." *All* statements are culturally and historically conditioned, some only more so than others.

While some texts have little or even no application for us,[42] no biblical text can be jettisoned or ignored. The issue is how they should be understood

---

Maureen B. Fant, *Women's Life in Greece and Rome* (Baltimore: Johns Hopkins Univ. Press, 1982); Ross S. Kraemer, ed., *Maenads, Martyrs, Matrons, Monastics* (Philadelphia: Fortress, 1988).

41. Marriages in the West were sometimes *sine manu*—"without hand," meaning that the wife did not pass to the husband's authority.

42. For example, Numbers 5:16–31 describes the testing of a wife with bitter waters. Mostly this text is a picture of the plight of women in the ancient world, and no one would

and applied. They point to a reality about God, humanity, and the relationship between the two that needs to be appropriated.

We have seen three important facts about the house codes:

(1) They were motivated by the desire to avoid slander on the church.
(2) They provided instructions on Christian conduct within the household.
(3) They addressed the same three groups that other Greek and Jewish writers addressed, but focused more on the responsibility of the husband, father, and master.

Slander from non-Christians about family relations is no longer an actual threat, although it will be where Christians have unhealthy family relations. The modern context still needs instruction for conduct within the family, but assumptions about the family are different. As before, the greater responsibility must still be placed on the persons with the most privilege.

Another question we must face is whether the statement that the husband is head of the wife is descriptive or prescriptive. That is, does this statement only tell us what is a fact in the ancient and/or modern sinful world, or does it express God's intention? Clearly the society described in ancient texts was patriarchal. Is this just the way life is in a sinful world? Or was headship already established in Eden before the Fall?[43] Despite the claims, nothing in Genesis supports such an idea. But then does Ephesians use male headship merely as a foil to teach something else? No answers are given in the text, but it is difficult to say Paul is only describing life in a sinful world when he compares the husband's headship to that of Christ. The fact that the husband is head is a *given* for Paul and for his society.

To some degree the same is still true. Our society is also patriarchal. If it were not, discussions about "glass ceilings," unequal pay, abuse of wives, and rape of women would not be so prevalent. The greater strength and aggressiveness of males often give them advantages and options denied to women. Further, women are more likely to be victims of the sinful abuse of male dominance. The issue *is* the abuse of power. The husband as head has a responsibility for the care of the wife in such a context. These comments do not suggest women are passive and cannot care for themselves; they only point to a responsibility given to husbands.

How do we determine what is normative in such a text? We must ask about its intention and its teaching about God, his salvation, and his purposes

---

suggest such a test today. Such texts are infrequent, though they are still instructive for understanding both the ancient world and the character of Scripture.

43. See "The Danvers Statement" printed as an advertisement of the Council on Biblical Manhood and Womanhood in *Christianity Today*, 33, no. 1 (January 13, 1989), 41.

for humanity. And as Luther emphasized, we must always answer these questions in the light of Christ and his work. This text is *not* intended to grant husbands a position of privilege or to teach that women are inferior. Its intent is to avoid offense to outsiders by encouraging mutual submission—a submission on the part of the wife and a self-giving on the part of the husband—with both partners having their lives determined by and motivated by Christ's own self-giving love. Still, a priority is placed on the husband, a priority that gives him a greater responsibility to care for his wife.

How far should the teaching of this text be extended? Does it have any relevance for women and men more generally? There are many more single people in our society than in the ancient world. What does 5:22–33 imply for them? This text is not about all women being submissive to all men. It is about mutual submission of all Christians to each other and of the submission of wives to their own husbands. It has nothing to do with the inferiority of women nor does it imply that women cannot function in leadership roles. On the other hand, I would suggest that the logic of the text directs Christian men to stand against the victimization of all women in our abusive world.

Does this text have relevance for decisions about the role of women in the church and ministry? The answer is "No,"[44] except for the fact that mutual submission gives all persons equal value. The passage is about mutual submission and family relationships, not about church leadership and what women may or may not do.

A crucial factor in understanding this passage is an awareness of the limitation of the text. The description in 5:22–33 assumes an ideal situation: Both partners are Christians and are eager to model their lives after Christ. This presents problems.[45] Why does Ephesians not address the problems in marriage relations? What is the relevance of this text when one or neither of the partners is a Christian? What if one or neither is willing to follow the will of the Lord? What if the relationship is abusive? The text provides no answers.

The "ideal" character of the description is required by the analogy between Christ and the church. This is not pastoral marriage counseling, and to treat it that way is short-sighted. The passage does model how the marriage relation should function, but it is only a foundation on which we can begin facing problems. An interpreter must develop a theology based on the ideal in this text and on other relevant texts—no text is to be interpreted in isolation—and then discern how that theology is to be applied to life.

A further factor may help in applying this text. The parallel discussion of the relation of slaves and masters in 6:5–9 is instructive, for there too an

---

44. Contrary to "The Danvers Statement" mentioned in the previous note.
45. The house code in 1 Peter and 1 Corinthians 7 both recognize less than ideal situations.

ideal situation is assumed in the directions given to Christian households. Slavery has long since been abolished, largely through the influence of scriptural principles. Just as we applaud the abolition of slavery, we need to ask how the world has changed for wives and how it needs to change further. What implications of the gospel still need to be worked out? What seems unlikely to change and what ought not change? How do we wrestle with the ideal in an ancient world, the ideal in our own, and the real problems we encounter? How should our lives be determined by the character of Christ and motivated by his self-giving love?

Paul did not directly attack slavery or the society's views on women. He focused on the gospel, a gospel in which "there is neither Jew nor Greek, slave nor free, male nor female" (Gal. 3:28). The differences still existed, but they had no value, for all were one in Christ and all had the same task of living lives determined and motivated by Christ. Paul did not work out all the sociological implications of his gospel. He did not have the time, nor was that the focus of his missionary efforts. He addressed some societal implications as required by his context and the problems of his churches. Other implications have been drawn only over centuries, and the task of understanding and applying the implications of the gospel continues today.

The relation of Christ and the church (5:22–33). This is an appropriate place to point out that theology is not done merely in the section on bridging contexts, but is present at all three stages of interpretation. In *understanding the original message* we focus on the theology explicit in the text or underlying the text. In *bridging* we seek the theology that spans cultures and contexts and is still pertinent. In *application* we determine how that theology takes root in our own context. We constantly must ask what the text teaches about God and humanity and adapt that teaching to life.

Specifically with regard to this text, the task of bringing the theological descriptions of Christ and the church into today's world must explain the significance of the metaphorical and religious language.

That Christians are the body of Christ will always cause difficulty. This concept expresses a unity and attachment to Christ similar to Paul's idea of being "in Christ." In fact, it is an extension of that language. Faith creates an intimate solidarity with Christ.

The marriage analogy likewise has its difficulties. Paul uses this analogy to convey the same idea as the body analogy: Christians are one entity with Christ, and accordingly he is to define the shape of their lives. For males, being the *bride* of Christ may seem strange, but neither males nor females should understand these ideas with sexual overtones. The oneness of the sexual union of a married couple merely illustrates the similar oneness of Christ and believers. Unfortunately, reading our own sexuality into our relation with Christ is a larger problem than most of us are willing to admit. Attraction or discomfort in relation to Christ and God are too easily enmeshed with an understanding of our own sexuality.

Further, we do not usually think of the church *submitting* to Christ, but this text does (5:24). Implied in such a statement is Christ's role as Lord and the church's need always to follow his leading and example. This text also focuses on Christ's activity for the church—saving it (v. 23), giving himself (v. 25), sanctifying and cleansing to present it pure and holy (vv. 26–27), and nurturing it (v. 28). Clearly we are to see the value Christ places on the church, the love he has for it, and his present work in it.

Other parts of the language are liable to misunderstanding or may sound foreign, but they are important for our lives. Most of us do not feel "holy and blameless," but that is what Christ seeks for us now (cf. Phil. 2:15). This part of this passage is not just for judgment day. It has in view Christ's present relation to the church and should have its impact in the present. That Christ sanctifies the church (v. 26) focuses on his setting the church apart for himself. As people set apart, Christians should live "set apart" lives, which is, of course, what the word "holy" means.

AS WE NOW seek to apply this passage, we must keep four questions in mind:

(1) How closely does the situation of the text correspond to today?
(2) What theology, explicit or implicit, should be appropriated?
(3) What will the practice of that theology look like in our present context?
(4) In what ways may that theology be applied to areas not addressed by the text?

Life with the Spirit (5:15–21). This text requires energy and effort on our part, for spiritual maturity only comes with work. If we are to watch closely how we walk, we must be attentive and self-analytical. Self-analysis can be stifling if out of balance, but Christians cannot expect to succeed in life with God without being honest with themselves and God about their chosen destiny. Any traveler inattentive to direction and progress will never arrive at the destination. We have already been asking ourselves: Do our lives grieve the Spirit (4:30)? Is our action an imitation of God (5:1)? Is it appropriate and fitting for those in Christ (5:3–4)? Does it please the Lord (5:10), and is it his will (5:17)? This section forces us to ask ourselves further questions about our Christian walk. Worship and prayer are the primary contexts where the pattern and goal for life are kept in view.

Time (5:16). The concern for time is given brief treatment in the text, but it is of enormous importance. Our society is the hurried society. We seem determined to pack as many activities into as brief a time as possible. We are too busy for life. We must reconsider how we use time. Most households in our society spend at least four to five hours a day watching TV, even though we may not care for what we watch. Other "diversions" take our attention too. But how much time do we give to life with God or to learning about that life? How much is invested in people or in doing something beneficial? We must not fritter away our lives on unproductive diversions and learn instead to invest time in our faith. The urgency and dangers implied in verse 16 are discussed in 6:10–20 as a spiritual conflict.

The will of the Lord (v. 17). Usually when Christians speak of discerning the will of the Lord, they have in mind God's will regarding major decisions about a spouse or a career. This is not what the text is about. The text is more concerned about God's intent for the way we live every day, about what is pleasing to him. Perhaps we would not have so much trouble in finding God's will for important decisions if we were more accustomed to discerning his will throughout life, making our lives conform to the pattern Christ has given.

What to do about alcohol? The text's prohibition of drunkenness obviously is directly applicable and possibly needed even more now than in Paul's day. Drunkenness has no place in the life of a Christian. How can we watch closely how we live if we are drunk? Consumption of alcohol is not necessarily a sin, but we surely must warn against its dangers and abuse.

Drunkenness—to say nothing of alcohol addiction—is a major problem in our society. This is clear in the problem of drunken drivers, of drunkenness as a form of escapism, of binge drinking (especially by students), and by our society's strange notion that to have fun we ought to get drunk. We spend a lot of time trying to get people not to drink and drive. If it impairs judgment so much, maybe we should just say, "Don't drink." Nothing makes more sense for a faith that emphasizes the development of the mind and human discernment.

The distributors and sellers of alcohol spend enormous amounts to persuade people to drink, while warnings of addiction and abuse are whispered. Why does our society complain bitterly about the abuses of the tobacco industry but say nothing about the alcohol industry? Consumption of alcohol has become acceptable for Christians, with the result that they too are guilty of laxness and over-indulgence. Drunkenness and addiction are not a mere innocent loss of control; they are the destructive waste of a life that ought to be lived unto God. Paul's real concern is the avoidance of "debauchery"—excessive and wasteful indulgence. If we as Christians choose to drink alcohol, we must make sure that it is a carefully monitored amount and that our witness is not compromised by our actions. The greater the abuse in a given culture, the less Christians should take part.

Obviously the prohibition of drunkenness extends to abuse of drugs, but it also applies to any excessive indulgence. Humans were created to live in relation with God, and any practice that diminishes a person's awareness of God and ability to respond to him and that suggests a life out of control stands under the indictment of the text. Surely society's excessive focus on materialism, beauty aids, cosmetic surgery, and spectator sports are all under indictment here.

Be filled with the Spirit (5:18–21). The text assumes the reader knows the importance of the Spirit and why we should sing and give thanks, but the command to be filled with the Spirit is not easily understood. It places emphasis on our action, whereas we are more accustomed to think of humans as passive instruments awaiting the working of the Spirit. We are so fearful of works-righteousness or of synergism that we have increased passivity. The New Testament does not share our fear, and God does not perform magic on passive instruments. Salvation is the work of God, but synergism is capable of being understood positively.[46] God calls for the human will to respond to his work and to be actively engaged with him. We must make choices for life with God if we are to appropriate this text, choices that involve the way we use our time, that open ourselves to God, and that make us willing to be transformed.

The Spirit's role in this cannot be overemphasized, for Christianity is a religion of the Spirit. All we are and have is a result of his work. The Spirit is not an optional add-on, a second work of grace, or a privilege of the elite. Rather, he is the agent of God's work in the world and is both the source and proof of conversion. To be in Christ and to be in the Spirit are virtually the same. In fact, the Spirit is the presence of Christ with the believer.

To ask us to be filled with the Spirit does not point to repeated charismatic experiences, as some claim. It is to ask us to focus our attention on Christ and his presence in us, to open ourselves to the continual transforming work of the Spirit so that the presence of Christ empowers and shapes our lives. The Spirit is to be the dominating influence for all Christians.

No text is a complete discussion of the subject it addresses, and 5:18–21 certainly is not a complete discussion of being filled with the Spirit. Still, the

---

46. See Philippians 2:12–13 or James 2:22. Exegetes in the early church combined divine intention with human efforts and had no difficulty with the idea of synergism. See Schnackenburg, *Ephesians: A Commentary*, 312.

teaching here is important. Whereas people often claim that being spiritual includes speaking in tongues, self-denial, mysticism, or religious exercises, this text points to singing, thankfulness, and Christ-like submission.

True spirituality is focused on the gift of life in Christ, is shaped by Christ, and overflows with songs that both explain to other people the reason for joy and give thanks to God. Such spirituality goes to the core of our being and cannot be produced by spiritual exercises, valuable though they may be. The text does not address changes in mood, but surely no one should expect that emotions are always at the same level. While emotions are always involved in spirituality, being spiritual does not depend on a level of emotional feeling.

Because of the dangers of emotionalism, many Christians—especially middle class, white ones—squelch any expression of emotion about life in Christ. As John MacKay points out, however, "nothing great ever takes place without emotion." He further warns against the danger of destroying faith in our attempt to stifle fanaticism.[47] The Christian life is not sedate. Emotionalism is an error, but we need emotion—passion—in our worship and lives. Without it we are not human. We need both peace and passion, both to be filled with the Spirit and disciplined by Christ.

The implicit Trinitarian Christology here is important. Early Christians sang to Jesus and gave thanks to God on the basis of what he had done. The early church did not start with a Christology and move to an experience with Jesus. They started with an experience of the risen Jesus, which led them to worship him. Christology grew out of their experience. The same is true for most people today. The experience of Jesus is the basis of worship and reflection.

Singing. Application of this text could lead to an artificial religiosity: People sing or say the expected words and hope that spirituality follows. The spirituality promoted by religious broadcasting often does just this, and in none too natural a way. But spirituality is the *cause* of singing, not its result. No one is asked to take on cultural religious trappings. People are expected only to express an inner joy Christ brings, even if they cannot carry a tune or even if they have to write new songs to express with integrity the reality they have found in Christ.

Thanksgiving. The second mark of the Spirit, thanksgiving, is given only perfunctory attention by most Christians, but it may well be the most important activity we do. As several people have pointed out, sin is basically ingratitude, and in Christianity, religion is grace and ethics is gratitude. The giving of

---

47. Mackay, *God's Order*, 177–78. For the second point he is dependent on Arnold Toynbee.

thanks is the first act after the recognition that we are not independent creatures but people who owe allegiance to God and have been blessed by him.

We need to affirm that all we are and have comes from God. Only then can we live lives of response to grace. The practice of thanksgiving is itself transforming. It is difficult for a person to be thankful and spiteful at the same time. It is difficult for a person to be thankful for his or her spouse and at the same time to be desiring another person—not impossible, but difficult.

Ephesians 5:20 asks that we always give thanks *for everything* in the name of Christ. Christians have sometimes felt compelled through texts like this to be thankful even in a tragedy, such as the death of a child. The result has been heartache for themselves and others. Surely such reasoning pushes the text beyond its intention. When the Bible uses "all" or "every," we must ask whether it is meant with or without qualification. Paul's intent is not that we are to be thankful for evil or tragedy. John Stott is correct in saying "everything" in verse 20 is hyperbole.[48] We are not asked to thank God for evil. Rather, we are asked to live out our awareness that all of life, even the "bad," is lived out under his control and in relation to him.

Submission. The most difficult part of this text for ancient and modern readers is the expectation that Christians will submit to each other (5:21). Some have argued that mutual submission is illogical, which it *is*, if viewed apart from Christ. However, if we understand the gospel, mutual submission makes perfectly good sense. What Paul has in mind is that Christians reject self-centeredness and work for the good of others. Submission is nothing more than a decision about the relative worth of others.

Our society emphasizes equality, but mutual submission is a much stronger idea. With equality, you still have a battle of rights. Equality can exist without love, but it will not create a Christian community. With mutual submission, we give up rights and support each other. Mutual submission is love in action. It brings equal valuing and is the power by which a *Christian* community establishes itself.

Mutual submission will not allow us to promote ourselves and our own interests, but neither does it make us "doormats" to be used by others. *Legitmate* submission cannot be coerced. The text assumes that everyone in the community is supported and enhanced. Where that does not take place, a person will have to be wise enough to discern whether to forego his or her own rights or seek justice. Christ's pattern of self-giving love does not mean that we can never seek justice for ourselves. Jesus did not acquiesce to Herod or the Pharisees, and Paul did not hesitate to defend himself or speak strongly to the Galatians or Corinthians. Submission will mean that even in seeking

48. Stott, *God's New Society*, 207.

justice, we are motivated by love for others in the community, rather than by love of self.

The relation of pastors and congregations is an obvious place where mutual submission needs to be implemented. In a wordplay on the word "submit," 1 Cor. 16:15–16 asks that people *arrange themselves under* (i.e., submit to) those who have *arranged themselves for service* to God's people. That is, they are to submit to servants. Pastors are servants of a church and should submit to the people, but they are not to be belittled or made subservient. From such a position they lead as they model the character of Christ. People in the church are to submit to the pastor, but not so that the pastor becomes a dictator to whom they acquiesce. Each is responsible to seek the benefit of the other as both live out the self-giving love of Christ.

Mutual submission should be applied to current discussions of worship styles. To insist that worship can take place in only one manner is myopic and limits the expression of the whole body. Mutual submission requires the humility to listen, tolerate, be taught, and be enriched by the worship of others, so long as it is within legitimate bounds.

A further place where mutual submission has application concerns money. Usually we allow our society to dictate how money is used, assigned, and hoarded. Mutual submission is disturbing to this society's dictates, for it requires reconsideration of how wages are determined and how wealth is shared. This raises difficult questions, but do not equal valuing and self-giving love have economic impact? Our wallets are not bracketed from mutual submission. Is not 4:28 with its command for the thief to work to have something to give an example of mutual submission? In particular, justice needs to be done to equal pay for women. Sadly, Christian organizations are among the worst offenders in underpaying female workers.

Mutual submission is to mark the relations of all Christians. This does not mean people will always agree, for they will not, just as Paul and Barnabas did not agree about Mark (Acts 15:36–41). Certainly it will not mean giving in to error, for there are times when one must *not* submit. Note Paul's refusal to submit to his opponents (Gal. 2:5) when the character of the gospel was at stake. But if the issue is not error, the gospel calls for the sacrifice of self-centeredness and the valuing and promoting of other people. As we have noted, greater responsibility belongs on the person enjoying privilege. Consequently, the mutual submission of rich and poor places added pressure on the rich, but with the realization that each makes a contribution to the other. In the end submission is nothing other than humility and the self-giving love of Christ.

To add the idea of the "reverence of Christ" to submission only compounds our discomfort. "Reverence" (lit., "fear") expresses a recognition of the holiness of God and an awareness of being bound to him by his love. Here it expresses a Christological basis for submission. Self-centeredness is jettisoned because one knows Christ is both loving Savior and coming Judge. Christ is a friend, but not just a friend. He is also Lord of the universe.

The relation of wives and husbands (5:22–33). Few issues create as much debate and disagreement as that of the status and roles of women, particularly as they relate to their husbands. We would do well to remember that no other relationship so mirrors God's relation with us and his purpose for us. The marriage relation is the most revealing of who we really are, and for those who are married, it is the primary relationship for discipleship. In a day when many young people are giving up on marriage, we need to hear this text.

Wrong turns. Too often men have concluded that women are theirs to control or treat as they like. The painful fact is that these verses have been used like a club to keep women in a defeated role. Christians and non-Christians alike know and use the statements "Wives, submit to your husbands," and "The husband is head of the wife," even if they have never read Ephesians 5. These statements have been misinterpreted to mean that wives always have a subservient role and that husbands always make the decisions. Women have been viewed as property that husbands may treat as they wish.

Even abusive behavior by husbands has even been justified on the basis of Ephesians 5:22–24. Pastors have been willing accomplices by telling women that they must submit. A book like James and Phyllis Alsdurf's *Battered into Submission*[49] presents in horrifying detail how distorted the interpretation of Paul's statements has become. Their book is not about wife abuse in general, though estimates are that one-third of all wives are beaten during the course of their marriage. Their book is—painfully—about wife abuse in *Christian* homes. Studies have shown that 18 percent of Christian wives report abuse of some sort by their husbands and about 5 percent suffer physical abuse. Men in more conservative denominations with traditional views of marriage are more likely to abuse their wives.

Such misuse of Ephesians 5 is scandalous and cannot be tolerated. Christians must take a much more forceful stand against wife abuse and against all denigration of women. Churches must not only speak out against the problem, but be much more willing to confront, instruct, and if necessary, to discipline members who are abusive.

The problem is broader than physical abuse. The attitudes of men about women, and specifically of husbands about wives, are often demeaning. Their

49. James and Phyllis Alsdurf, *Battered into Submission* (Downers Grove, Ill: InterVarsity, 1989).

comments may not be intended to hurt, but the truth is that husbands frequently belittle and ridicule their wives with comments about their level of intelligence, their worries, cooking, or habits. Wives, of course, are capable of the same sins, but husbands are more likely to engage in such belittling as a result their sense of being "head."

The abuse of women in the family is a manifestation of the sexual illness of our society. We live in a sex-diseased society that has developed manifold ways to debase women. Movies and TV focus on rape, violence, and "use" of women. One fourth of all the sex images in "cybersex" involve the torture of women. Virtually everyone agrees all this is terrible, but no one does anything, and "good" people still take part. Christians must separate themselves from such "entertainment" and from such treatment of women. It will not fit with Christ.

Some Christians have also distorted this passage by speaking of a husband's "umbrella of authority." So much emphasis is placed on the husband as head that he is seen as a privileged authority figure and wives are reduced to second-level status. In extreme cases wives are not even held responsible for their actions; their husbands are! Headship in this text has nothing to do with privilege; it is about the servant character of authority. Wives do have responsibility for their actions, and they also have equal value. Husbands are not bosses to be served, and wives are not their unthinking slaves.

What does it mean for us? We must once again emphasize that what is said to wives (and husbands) is only an example of the love and mutual submission required of *all* Christians and that the word "submit" does not even appear in the Greek text of 5:22. Wives *are* to submit to their husbands. That is, they stand in a giving relation to their husbands as their husbands do to them. But this text does not endorse a chauvinist mentality, with wives being servants doing all the work or agreeing to any request their husbands think up. All it asks is that wives give up self-centeredness, take seriously their mutuality with their husbands, and promote the benefit of their husbands. It underscores that no part of life may be excluded from the marriage relationship.

On the other side, headship does not give husbands privilege and superiority. Arguments from analogy about the headship of Christ and that of the husband cannot conclude that the headships are identical. Just as the fear due the husband is not the same as the fear due Christ because the husband and Christ are different, so the headship of Christ is different. He is Lord over all things; the husband is not *lord* over anything. The point of the headship analogy is the responsibility husbands have to give themselves to their wives as Christ gave himself for the church. They must be givers, not takers. Husbands are to give up self-centeredness and any privilege of being head in order to promote the well-being of their wives. They are to love their wives as themselves, recognizing that the unity of marriage makes their wives like their own bodies. Husbands should nurture and care for their wives so that they are established and enhanced. When wives are enhanced, so are husbands. The two partners are assumed to be one, mutually enabling each other.

The way Christian marriages are to function is therefore clear from this text. Both partners live first of all in, to, and for the Lord. The real head of the marriage is *always* Christ, and both partners are to live in mutual submission to each other, seek to promote each other within the purposes of Christ, and live out the oneness of their relationship.

Mutual submission means too that decisions are made by both partners for unselfish reasons. When disagreement occurs, the husband does not automatically have the deciding vote. In such cases, one partner may grant the other person's choice or both may agree to reject both options. Mutual submission may mean that one partner places career objectives on hold while the other completes an education. It may mean that one person gives up a satisfying job to enable a transfer by the other. It may mean no more than giving the other person freedom to make incidental choices for himself or herself.

It is obvious that this text addresses an ideal situation. What if the husband does not practice mutual submission and love? What if the husband only wants a servant? In the ancient world a woman would have had few choices, and for some women this may still be true. Peter urged wives to instruct husbands and win them to Christ by godly conduct (1 Peter 3:1–6). This too expresses an ideal, but it does point to the need for instruction for husbands.

When a woman enters a marriage relationship today, she does so in a far different way from in the ancient world where she may have had little say in the matter. She and her mate should both enter marriage wisely and with every intention of heeding their vows and living in mutuality. Mutual submission virtually eliminates divorce.

Whereas women in the ancient world had few options other than homemaker, women in our culture have almost unlimited lifestyle, career, and ministry opportunities. Our text does not imply some roles are open to women and others are excluded, and it certainly does not teach the inferiority of women. The increase in opportunities for women changes the way the responsibility of husbands functions. To derive from this text that women may not be in positions of authority is superficial reasoning. If husbands love their wives as themselves, they will both give and seek freedom, respect, and possibilities for their wives. They will support them emotionally and physically and make sure that there is justice in the division of labor in the household.

There are, of course, cultural variations in what is permitted to women. In some cultures women are no better off now than women were in the ancient world. What is the task of the church in these societies? Feminism must never be substituted for the gospel of Jesus Christ, but the church cannot allow the implications of the gospel to be muffled. The gospel includes a focus on the equality of all persons before God and in the church. The old valuations based on sex, race, and economic status can no longer define relationships. All Christians are called to live in mutual submission in the unity found in Christ. No matter what the cultural practice, Christian marriages should be different, and where necessary the sins of the abuse of power and insensitivity by husbands must be confronted.

To what point can the wife live out her Christian commitment and promote the benefit of her husband—and herself—when she receives no benefit in return? Where husbands (or wives) refuse cooperation in mutuality, difficult choices will have to be made. Sadly, one has to admit some circumstances make a marriage unworkable. If there is no mutuality, there is no marriage. If the relationship is abusive, either emotionally or physically, the wife *cannot* be asked to submit. She is asked to model Christ's love, not suffer or die at the hands of an abusive husband. She should be advised to remove herself from danger. Truth and justice cannot be ignored.

If a husband asks his wife to do something inappropriate for a Christian, again, she should not submit. Her attitude must be the same as the early church in Acts 5:29: "We must obey God rather than men!" Every human relation is experienced as part of our relation with God.

Since the text places greater responsibility on the privileged person and recognizes that the wife needs to be nurtured, Christian men ought to be particularly concerned to seek justice for women. With the pervasive mistreatment and injustice to women in virtually every culture, I am convinced that Christianity has both a responsibility and an opportunity to speak strongly for the justice of women. Christian men have a responsibility to support all women, single or married, without being patronizing in the process and without turning the responsibility into an opportunity for sexual exploitation.

Sexual intercourse. Paul's comments on unity in marriage, especially his quotation of Genesis 2:24,[50] make an important point about human sexual relations. As the parallel in 1 Corinthians 6:15–17 shows, Paul did not view sexual intercourse merely as a physical act. Rather, he viewed it as an incorporative act whereby two people are bound together and made one. The wife becomes part of her husband and for him to love her is to love himself.[51]

Dangers. There are dangers, however, in focusing on oneness and mutual submission. One danger is that a husband or wife may give so much atten-

---

50. Even though he applies this quotation to Christ and the church in 5:30–32.

51. The same thing could have been said of the husband's becoming part of the wife and of his being like her own body. The reason the text does not say this is because it focuses on husbands.

tion to the marriage partner that he or she ends up idolizing and fawning over the spouse (cf. 1 Cor. 7:32–35). The marriage relationship is only one relationship, and husband and wife do not enhance each other merely as individuals, but as Christians. The primary commitment of both is always to the Lord, and mutual submission within marriage is only an expression of commitment to the Lord.

A second danger is that so much attention is placed on oneness that individuality is lost. Despite oneness, husband and wife remain two different people with different purposes and callings from God. If dependence becomes overemphasized, one or both partners will be less productive, and the death of one spouse will create havoc in the life of the other.

The relation of Christ and the church (5:22–33). The Christology, soteriology, and ecclesiology expressed in this text are all important for the life of the church today. We sometimes get mired in the duties of the church and forget the role of Christ in the church. This text underscores both the love of Christ and the lordship of Christ. That *he* is head and the church submits to him ought to be a constant reminder that the church has no other agenda than that set and modeled by Christ. Pastors and church boards do not lead churches, other than to help them find the purposes of Christ. A greater sense that Christ leads the church, joined with mutual submission in finding his purposes, will move the church past many of its current problems.

Ephesians 5:25 points to the love Christ demonstrated historically on the cross, but verse 29 and the marriage analogy both point to the continuing love of Christ. He *still* nurtures and cares for the church, and the church will be much stronger if it is more conscious of his on-going love and presence. More time in church needs to be spent on experiencing Christ, worshiping him, and reflecting on identification with him, rather than just talking about him. The quotation of Genesis 2:24 in Ephesians 5:31 ought not be allegorized to refer to Christ's leaving the Father to come to earth. Paul is interested only in the oneness of Christ with the church.

Christ's saving work (vv. 26–27) also has a present focus. While the perfection of the church will not occur until the end time, Christ's work on the cross set apart and cleansed the church to be holy and without blemish in the present. In the doxology (1:4) God's purpose before the foundation of the world was that his people be holy and blameless (cf. Phil. 2:15).

Obviously one of the most difficult questions is why the church is so filled with imperfections. Do we take imperfections for granted or have we bought into an understanding of "cheap grace" that merely gives salvation, but requires no obedience? Paul knew, of course, the imperfections of the church, as the Corinthian letters attest all too well. But, as all of his letters and especially Ephesians 4–6 show, he repeatedly asked Christians to make true in their lives what God had done for them. Christians are to live differently because they have been set apart to God (cf. 5:26–27). The New Testament knows nothing of a salvation that does not change lives.

The church. The striking part of this text is surely its ecclesiology. Paul's "body theology" most frequently is used to describe the diversity of the church and the importance of each individual member.[52] In Ephesians and Colossians Paul develops his thinking so that Christ is now the head of the body. He focuses now on the relation of Christians to Christ as the one from whom all the body is energized and bound together (Eph. 4:16).

In Ephesians 5:30 the body theology finds its climactic expression. As members of his body, Christians are *part of Christ*: They are one with him and one with each other. Incorporation into Christ and participation with him are two of the great theological truths of this letter. Paul expects his readers to live with an awareness of being part of Christ.

We have seen earlier that this theology means *Christians can no longer view themselves merely as individuals.*[53] They are bound to Christ and defined by him. With that comes a sense of value and privilege and of Christ's presence and power for living. Oneness with Christ also brings a sense of mission and involvement in his purposes. We are not part of Christ merely for privilege, but for growth and service (cf. 4:16).

The ethical implications of this theology are immense. Mutual submission is merely a logical conclusion of Paul's understanding that Christians are part of each other. Oneness with Christ is the basis of *all* Christian ethics (cf. 1 Cor. 6:15). What sort of activities fit with being part of Christ? The character of Christ is not some external norm to which Christians are to aspire, but the framework of their being. How can they *not* put into practice their oneness with him? No hint of perfectionism is intended, but being part of Christ is a transforming privilege.

Such reasoning goes far beyond usual explanations of the gospel. The first step in appropriating this text will be in changing our evangelistic ideas. Any proclamation of the gospel is inadequate that does not show people the need of and the possibility of oneness with Christ and of being part of him. Such a diminished gospel will never provide sufficient ethical motive.

This text is of obvious importance for understanding the marriage relation, but that theme fades from center stage. The primary focus is on the relation of Christ and his church. The key themes are the love of Christ and the oneness of Christians with him. That relation drives all other Christian relations, including that of husband and wife.

---

52. See Romans 12 and 1 Corinthians 12.
53. See pp. 63, 117, 146–47, 149–53.

Ephesians 6:1–9

CHILDREN, OBEY YOUR parents in the Lord, for this is right. [2]"Honor your father and mother"—which is the first commandment with a promise—[3]"that it may go well with you and that you may enjoy long life on the earth."

[4]Fathers, do not exasperate your children; instead, bring them up in the training and instruction of the Lord.

[5]Slaves, obey your earthly masters with respect and fear, and with sincerity of heart, just as you would obey Christ. [6]Obey them not only to win their favor when their eye is on you, but like slaves of Christ, doing the will of God from your heart. [7]Serve wholeheartedly, as if you were serving the Lord, not men, [8]because you know that the Lord will reward everyone for whatever good he does, whether he is slave or free.

[9]And masters, treat your slaves in the same way. Do not threaten them, since you know that he who is both their Master and yours is in heaven, and there is no favoritism with him.

Original Meaning

THESE VERSES CONTINUE the House Codes that started in 5:22. Paul almost certainly drew from well-known early Christian teachings in framing these sections. He could have treated numerous relations or problems, but these topics were chosen because they are traditional and because Christians—like Jews—were seen as subversive elements in the society and especially as a threat to the family structure.[1] Christians needed to show they did not threaten order and decency. The very form of the Christian house codes is an apologetic to turn aside slander and accusations.

That Christians were seen as a threat to the household structure is understandable. As we have seen, women were told to submit to their husbands "so that no one will malign [blaspheme] the word of God" (Titus 2:5).[2] A similar statement occurs in reference to slaves: Slaves should consider their masters worthy of full respect "so that God's name and our teaching may not be slandered [blasphemed]" (1 Tim. 6:1). Such slandering could arise because Paul had set aside valuations based on whether one was free or a slave (Gal.

---

1. See pp. 293–94, 301–2.
2. See the discussion of this issue on pp. 293–94, 311–17.

3:28), wrote about slaves being freed by Christ (1 Cor. 7:21–23), and made slaves brothers of their owners (Philem. 15–16). Slaves, like wives, often would have been expected to adopt the gods of the family, which would have created further conflict for Christians. And regarding children, several of Jesus' sayings placed allegiance to him over allegiance to the family.[3]

Paul did not merely adopt the society's instructions to these three groups. Rather, he laced his instructions with theological motivations, just as he did in treating other ethical issues. In addition, and unlike non-Christian house codes, he addressed the subordinates directly—not just their privileged superiors. They were full participants in the community and would have heard the letter being read publicly. Paul also placed restrictions on the husbands/fathers/masters and instructed them about their responsibilities in the light of the gospel. He assumed the cultural framework about authority and then subjected it to reorganization by a higher commitment to Christ.

In in 6:1–9 Paul applies his ethic described in 4:25–5:21 to the household relations. Note the following connections:

> "right" (6:1) and "proper" (5:3), "fitting" (5:4; NIV, "out of place"), and "righteousness" (5:9)
> "exasperate"(*paraorgizo*, 6:4) and "angry" (*orgizo*, 4:26–27, 31)
> "the will of God" (6:6) and "the will of the Lord" (5:17)
> "good" (*agathos*, 6:8), and "useful" and "helpful" (*agathos*, 4:28–29)
> the topic of future judgment (6:8–9 and in 5:5–6)[4]

Note also the close parallels with Colossians 3:20-4:1.

Structure. The structure of this section is straightforward.

6:1–3: Instruction for children to obey their parents (6:1–3)

> 6:1a: *Motivation:* This is right (v. 1a)
>
> 6:2–3: *Verification and further motivation* from Scripture: Honoring parents brings prosperity and long life

6:4: Instruction for fathers to teach children

6:5a: Instructions for slaves to obey their earthly masters

> 6:5b–7: Fourfold description of their service, each with an "as" phrase[5]

---

3. See Matthew 10:21, 34–37; 12:46–50; 19:27–29; Luke 9:57–62; 14:26.

4. In addition "nurture" (*ektrepho*) is used in 6:4 and in 5:29 (NIV, "bring them up" and "feed" respectively) and "fear" in 6:5 and 5:21, 33 (NIV, "reverence" and "respect"). Note the "not ... but" contrasts in 6:4, 6, similar to those in 5:15–18.

5. The NIV loses the parallels by using "as" in verse 5, "to win their favor" (for "as pleasing men") in verse 6a, "like" in verse 6b, and "as" in verse 7. All four "as" phrases uses the Greek word *hos*.

6:5b: with fear and trembling in sincerity ... *as* to Christ

6:6a: not serving the eye, *as* pleasing men

6:6b: *as* slaves of Christ, doing the will of God ...

6:7: wholeheartedly, *as* serving the Lord ...

6:8: *Motivation*: The Lord will judge everyone according to their works

6:9: Instruction for masters to do the same things to them

6:9b: *Motivation*: They share a common Master in heaven, who shows no favoritism.

Instructions to Children and Parents (6:1–4)

CHILDREN AND SLAVES are told to obey, a conscious shift from Paul's direction for wives ("submit") and a recognition that children and slaves had even less status than women. All relations in the house codes are redefined by relation to Christ.

"Obey your parents in the Lord" does not mean "obey your Christian parents."[6] Rather, it means to obey as part of one's relation to the Lord. The meaning is virtually synonymous with "as to the Lord" in 5:22 or 6:6. That obedience to parents "is right" means essentially that it is right from a Christian perspective. This phrase has the same impact as "these are improper" and "which are out of place" in 5:3–4. The sexual sins described there are wrong because they do not fit with life in Christ. In other words, Paul never argues merely ethically, even if his ethical conclusions might be the same as his society's. Instead, he argues theologically from a Christian framework. That children should obey their parents was a given in his society, but for him it was "right" because of their relation to Christ.

"Children" could be understood to include adults, for a father in that society maintained authority in the family until he was about sixty years old or even until his death. Yet although adult children were expected to honor their parents, the concern of the text seems to be on young children, for they are still in the process of learning and being shaped (cf. v. 4).

The command for children to honor father and mother is quoted five other places in the New Testament.[7] The source of the quotation is identified in the NIV margin as Deuteronomy 5:16, but the LXX form of Exodus 20:12 (also an account of the Decalogue) is virtually the same as the Deuteronomy text. Neither of them is exactly like the text of Ephesians.[8] The use of

---

6. A few manuscripts omit "in the Lord," possibly to avoid the thought that obedience was confined to Christian parents.

7. Matthew 15:4; 19:19; Mark 7:10; 10:19; Luke 18:20.

8. Cf. the similar wording in Deuteronomy 22:7.

this command and of other Old Testament texts as motivation throughout the ethical teaching of Ephesians shows that the law has not been set aside.[9] We may find Paul's teaching on the law difficult, but *he* did not think he was abolishing the law.[10]

The intent of the Old Testament promise of a long and good life had to do with life in the land of Israel, which God had given his people. Honoring parents was an essential foundation for God's covenant people (note Lev. 19:3). Paul omits the focus on Israel, however, to make the statement more general and proverbial. God's promise is based on the presumption that obedience to parents leads to order and stability. This promise applies to the community and is not a guarantee to the individual.[11] This passage should not be spiritualized to refer to future life.

The Greek word for "fathers" in verse 4 can mean "parents," but more likely Paul is turning attention specifically to fathers. Fathers had legal control of children and were responsible for their instruction from about age seven. Girls did not normally receive formal education, but were taught household duties. Leon Morris is probably correct in saying it is significant that Paul wrote "children" instead of "boys."[12] Girls were valued less in ancient society, but Paul did not accept such a limitation.

In the ancient world fathers had absolute control and were sometimes harsh; that is why Paul includes the warning against provoking children to anger. The verb used for "exasperate" is rare and appears elsewhere in the New Testament only at Romans 10:19 (NIV, "make you angry"). The noun form occurs only in the prohibition of anger in Ephesians 4:26.

"Bring them up" does not do justice to the notion of care expressed by the verb, particularly since Paul's previous use of the verb in 5:29 (NIV, "feeds") conveys the idea of "nurture." "Instruction" translates a word that often connotes "warning" or "admonition," but "training and instruction" is probably an instance of two nouns expressing one concept, explaining the teaching that fathers are to do. "Of the Lord" is ambiguous. Most likely, it means that the instruction is subsumed under and determined by the Lord.

---

9. Despite 2:15.

10. The objection is sometimes made that this is not the first commandment with promise, since the second command in the Decalogue assures God's love to those who keep his commands. This is a rather pedantic objection, for the assurance of God's love with the second command comes in a description of God, not in a specific promise, and the broader law seems to be in view, not just the Decalogue.

11. See similar statements in Deuteronomy 4:40; 22:7; Psalm 55:23; Proverbs. 9:11; 10:27.

12. Morris, *Expository Reflections on Ephesians*, 192.

Instructions to Slaves and Masters (6:5–9)

THE GREEK WORD translated "master" (*kyrios*) is usually translated in the New Testament as "Lord," in reference either to Christ (as in v. 4) or to God. That is why the qualification "earthly"[13] is required in verse 5; it also is important in verse 9, where a wordplay between "masters" and "their Master" exists.

On the one hand, the directions given to slaves removes any suggestion that this new faith upset the cultural order; on the other hand, *these verses are still extremely subversive.* Slave owners may have been pleased with the service they would get, but in the process they lost control, for slaves now had a higher allegiance than to their owners. Slaves no longer belonged to their owners, did not really serve them, did not merely do their will, did not seek to please them, and were no different from them. They were slaves of Christ, served him, and did God's will, and the slave owners were to treat them the same way as slaves were to treat owners. The idea that in dealing with human beings they were really dealing with Christ is reminiscent of Matthew 25:40: "Whatever you did for one of the least of these brothers of mine, you did for me."

This section makes specific to slaves (and masters) what was asked of everyone in 5:10, 17, 21: pleasing the Lord, doing his will, and mutual submission. To apply mutual submission to slaves and slave owners was a startling redefinition of slavery. In 1 Corinthians 7:21–23 Paul even told slaves that slavery should not matter, that they were Christ's freed people, that both free and slave were slaves of Christ, and therefore that they should not be slaves of humans! The ease with which Paul made these points was based on his conviction that slaves, their owners, and he were all slaves of Christ. He referred to himself frequently as a slave of Christ, which should not be surprising insofar as Christ himself took the form of a slave.[14] The background for this theology is already in the Old Testament (see esp. Lev. 25:55).

In verse 5 we again meet the difficulty of understanding the word "fear" in the ancient world,[15] but to this word is added "trembling" (NIV, "respect and fear"). The combination of these two words is traditional and should be seen as an intensification.[16] Some suggest that the respect and fear are paid to God rather than the owners, but this is unlikely. Paul used this same combination in 1 Corinthians 2:3 to describe his demeanor in coming to Corinth and in 2 Corinthians 7:15 to describe the church's reception of Titus (see also

---

13. Literally, "according to the flesh."

14. See especially Romans 1:1; 2 Corinthians 4:5; Philippians 2:7

15. See pp. 293, 296, 312–13.

16. Of the five occurrences of "trembling" in the New Testament, four are connected to "fear."

Phil. 2:12). The combination expresses deference in a relationship, not actual quaking (cf. also 1 Peter 2:18).

Slaves are asked to serve "in sincerity of heart" in both verse 5 and verse 6.[17] "When their eye is on you" (v. 6) translates a compound word that means "serving the eye." The slave is not to play to a human audience. In effect, verses 6–7 comment on verse 5, each verse repeating the point that slaves serve Christ, not other human beings. Slaves were notorious for being lazy and for lying. Neither avenue remained as an option for Christian slaves.

The primary motivation for this ethic is the final judgment (cf. 5:5–6). Paul assumes here that judgment is according to works, the consistent expectation of the whole Bible (cf. esp. Rom. 2:6–11, though this section deals with equality in judgment for Jews and Gentiles, not for slave and free). Other New Testament texts also reject valuations based on being slave or free.[18]

That masters are asked to treat their slaves "in the same way" is cryptic, but still shocking. For them to follow this instruction, they would have to treat their slaves with respect and fear and with sincerity of heart as to Christ. That alone should have abolished slavery for Christians! Owners would also have to give up playing to audiences and do the will of God as slaves of Christ. Moreover, just as slaves had to give up slacking off, masters had to give up threatening, which fits neither service to Christ nor the life of humility and gentleness called for in 4:2–3. This ethic moves beyond the Golden Rule, that is, beyond treating others as we want to be treated; it instructs us to treat others as we would treat our Lord.

A structural parallel exists between the knowledge slaves have about judgment (v. 8) and the knowledge owners have of a common Lord in heaven, who shows no favoritism. Every thought of privilege evaporates before Christ.

BRINGING THE SECTION on slaves into our age is more difficult than the section on children. Slavery is foreign to us, while the relation of parents and children is essentially the same, even if attitudes are radically different. However, the foreignness of the grouping wives-children-slaves ought not be glossed over. Only by facing the patriarchal structure of the ancient world and the reasons these topics had to be treated will our eyes be open sufficiently to apply the text.

---

17. The NIV uses "heart" in both places, but a more literal translation of verse 6 is "from the soul."

18. See 1 Corinthians 12:13; Galatians 3:28; Colossians 3:11.

Children and parents (6:1–4). In both the Jewish and Greco-Roman world, honoring parents was second only to honoring God. In fact, some writers said parents were like gods to their children.[19] Honoring parents was expected as an ethical starting point, an expectation New Testament writers shared.[20]

The power of fathers was almost unlimited in the Greco-Roman world. They determined whether a newborn baby had the right to live or die, and many baby girls in particular were abandoned to die. Fathers could and did sell their children, especially girls, into slavery. They could punish them as harshly as they wished, work them hard, or even put them to death. Public opinion served as restraints and real family love was common, but the abuses are chronicled. Ecclesiasticus 30:1–13 is representative of attitudes in the ancient world: A father who loves his son will whip him and beat him often while he is still a child (vv. 1, 12). A father should not pamper his son, play with him, or share in his laughter (vv. 7–10).[21]

In many sectors of this ancient society people did not desire marriage or children, both for economic reasons and for the bother involved. The situation was so bad toward the end of the first century B.C. that the emperor Augustus passed laws against adultery and excessive spending and laws that encouraged marriage and children with monetary rewards.[22] Women who could afford to do so often hired wet-nurses to breast feed their babies, and as children got older slaves or hired teachers helped care for them.

Our society may be less harsh in its statements, but the attitudes and diversity of the ancient world are strangely mirrored in our own. The bother and expense of marriage and children still cause many to reject both. Parents do not have the free rein fathers in the ancient world did, but in far too many homes children are subjected to constant abuse—anger, violence, and sexual abuse. We perpetuate cycles of violence; hostile homes produce hostile children. Our problems within the family are even greater than in the ancient world, for little pressure exists today for children to honor parents. Teenagers are expected and even encouraged to be disrespectful and rebellious.

---

19. See Philo, *Special Legislation* 2.225: "Parents, in my opinion, are to their children what God is to the world"; Josephus, *Against Apion* 2.206: "Honor to parents the Law ranks second only to honor to God."

20. See Romans 1:30; 1 Timothy 3:4; 2 Timothy 3:2; Titus 1:6; cf. Old Testament texts mandating death for rebellious sons (Lev. 20:9; Deut. 21:18–21).

21. This passage does not even comment on girls. Lincoln, *Ephesians*, 395–402, provides a good discussion of attitudes concerning children and fathers. See also Jane F. Gardner and Thomas Wiedemann, *The Roman Household: A Sourcebook* (London: Routledge, 1991).

22. See Mary R. Lefkowitz and Maureen B. Fant, *Women's Life in Greece and Rome* (Baltimore: John Hopkins Univ. Press, 1982), 180–81.

But the text instructs children to obey and honor their parents. What this means in practical terms will depend on the age of the child and the integrity of the parents. Obedience will be different for a five-year-old and a twenty-year-old, even though honor may be much the same. Especially in our culture the freedom of young adults is a given, but even with that freedom honor of parents should remain.

The text assumes an ideal, but what if the reality is far worse? The less integrity a parent has, the more difficult honor will be. At times honor may even be reduced to honor for the "office" of parent rather than the person. Showing honor should never require distorting the truth. The guideline here, as everywhere, is speaking the truth in love. Where the parents' will conflicts with God's will, again the attitude of the early church is the right path: "We must obey God rather than men" (Acts 5:29). All application of this section must remember that these commands are an application of the larger ethic of Ephesians to a specific area. The whole letter is the framework for applying these instructions.

As in all relations, anger is out and nurturing is in. This is the body theology applied to the home. Concern for the anger of children is emphasized because of the destruction it causes in the family. At the same time, too often children are the targets for the hostility or threats from parents because of their potential for greater success. Jealousy and contempt lead to children being belittled and blocked, but in the process the parents destroy themselves. Again the issue is the use of power. Will it be used positively to enhance or negatively to destroy?

As in earlier sections, this text underscores the importance of teaching. Christians are to be nurturers, especially in their own homes. But the emphasis placed on teaching cannot be confined to the family. The church also has a responsibility to teach and nurture children. The text implies a value on children that should not be taken lightly. They are not to be ignored or merely tolerated, but cared for and instructed about life in Christ. If stewardship is the proper management of assets, Christian stewardship should focus first of all on nurturing children. Neither the church nor the family has an asset more valuable than its children.[23]

Slaves and masters (6:5–9). Not only is slavery foreign to us, but our understanding of it has been determined by nineteenth-century slavery in the United States. This increases our difficulty in understanding why the early church did not call for a wholesale rejection of slavery.

---

23. One further point, despite occasional claims to the contrary (cf. George Stoeckhardt, *Ephesians*, trans. Martin S. Sommer [St. Louis, Mo.: Concordia, 1952], 250), this text is irrelevant for a discussion of infant baptism.

In the Greco-Roman world slavery was so much a part of life that hardly anyone thought about whether it might be illegitimate. Only the Therapeutae, a Jewish sect in Egypt, and perhaps the Essenes, rejected slavery in principle. It was considered an economic and practical necessity, an assumed part of life as much as birds and trees. Scholars are reluctant to hazard estimates about the numbers, but as many as one-third of the people in Greece and Rome were slaves. In addressing them Paul was addressing an enormous number of people. People became slaves through various avenues: birth, parental selling or abandonment, captivity in war, inability to pay debts, and voluntary attempts to better one's condition. Race was not a factor.

No doubt for many slaves life was harsh and cruel, but their circumstances depended on their owners. They did not merely do menial work; they did nearly all the work, including oversight and management and most professions. Many were educated better than their owners. They could own property, even other slaves, and were allowed to save money to buy their freedom. No slave class existed, for slaves were present in all but the highest economic and social strata. Many gained freedom by age thirty, especially in urban areas. Even after gaining freedom, however, they were still under obligation to their former owners in times of need.

Laws attempted to prevent gross abuse of slaves, but owners did have free rein to treat slaves as they wished. Some were loved and treated like family, but they had no rights. Others were treated cruelly, and if owners wanted to torture, crucify, or kill slaves they could. The main limitation of physical abuse was the loss of value in the slave. Threat and violence were assumed necessary to control slaves. In a Jewish framework slaves were somewhat better off, and the Old Testament prohibited Jews holding other Jews in permanent slavery.[24] In the Greco-Roman world slaves were often dehumanized. Aristotle, for example, said that the free man rules over the slave because the slave has no deliberative faculty and is a living tool. He considered it inappropriate to speak about justice with regard to slaves.[25]

Ephesians 6:5–9 describes an ideal situation. What would Paul have said to slaves who were being sexually abused or asked to perform unlawful acts, possibly against their will?[26] A glimpse into the difficulty is provided in

---

24. Jews could buy another Jew who sold himself into slavery for only six years; then he had to go free (see Exod. 21:2–11). Women were not released after six years; if they were purchased, it was for marriage.

25. Aristotle, *Politics*, 1253b5, 1259b3–1260b6; *Nichomachian Ethics* 5.1134b, 8.1161ab. For information on slavery in the ancient world, see "Slavery," *The Anchor Bible Dictionary*, ed. David Noel Freedman (New York: Doubleday, 1992), 6:65–73; Thomas Wiedemann, *Greek and Roman Slavery* (Baltimore: John Hopkins Univ. Press, 1981).

26. Publilius Syrus wrote, "It is counted as a virtue to do wrong for one's master's sake" (maxim 534; see Gardner and Wiedemann, *The Roman Household*, 46).

1 Peter 2:18–25, which instructs slaves to submit even to harsh masters and to hold on to their convictions even when they suffered unjustly. These Christians were called to take their identity from Christ, regardless of the circumstances. Revolt was out of the question, but their lives were to be a quiet protest and a witness to a higher calling.

For the early church to advocate revolt would have been the death of the Christian movement. Slavery and other social issues were not their focus; the gospel and its description of life were.[27] They did not work out the sociological implications of the gospel except where it related to reception of the message and relations within churches. But as they presented life in Christ, they put in motion a process that would eventually destroy slavery. The painful fact is that it took far too long to accomplish the job, and the attempts by Christians to defend the legitimacy of slavery in the nineteenth century are disturbing.[28]

This forces us to question whether we too simply assume the necessity of the structures of our society. People are still being dehumanized and tyrannized by relationships and employers. While not slaves, they are enslaved by our economic and social system. We are prone to throw up our hands and say, "That's the way it is." Like Paul, we must find ways to say, "The slave is your brother," so that the system is subverted by the way people are valued and nurtured. Churches should lead the way in such thinking.

But the attitudes of people in such situations need to change too. Many people are caught in the system or are underemployed, but need the jobs they have. They tend to become resentful and uncooperative or passive, waiting for some external force to remedy the situation. What Paul tells slaves is directly relevant. Our jobs and our role in the culture do not determine who we are. We live in, to, and for Christ in all we do. Moreover, our value and identity do not derive from our circumstances, but from Christ. By directing all our actions to Christ, all of life—even the most mundane parts—is elevated to meaning and service to God.

The message of this text obviously moves from ancient slavery to modern employer-employee relations, but it pushes us far beyond that. Its theology concerns who we really are, what motivates us, whom we seek to please, and how we use power. Every part of life is redefined. No action or relation is seen by itself, and nothing is treated at merely a surface level. Everything we do involves a direct encounter with Jesus Christ. *He is the origin and the recipient of every act.* If this is true, no act is mundane and no person

---

27. Note also, however, that no theological defense of slavery is offered in the New Testament.

28. See E. N. Elliott, ed., *Cotton Is King and Pro-Slavery Arguments* (Augusta, Ga.: Pritchard, Abbott & Loomis, 1860).

is unimportant. Power must be used for him, not against him. And all of us stand on equal footing with the same Lord, who cares deeply how we treat each other and will hold us accountable.

 THE VERY FORM of this text is an indictment of modern-day churches. As passages like this show, early Christian congregations were made up of a cross-section of society, but the usual valuations of the society were rejected. In most of our churches the valuations of society are retained so that no real cross-section comes together. We have churches for different socio-economic groups; we do not draw people to a common place where hierarchies and valuations are set aside and people know they stand on equal footing before God. As long as a church is a "group of our kind," it fails its mission. Application of the text requires creation of a place where grace is evident and all people come together as equals.

Parents and children (6:1–4). The text addresses children first because that is the subject of the traditional house codes. Ideally parents should be addressed first, for they nurture long before children can obey. This text is an attempt to bring into the home the ethic of 4:1–5:21. Humility, tolerant love, and mutual submission belong first of all in the family.

Unfortunately, too many people, including Christians, have a public and a private persona. They appear as warm, congenial, righteous people in public, but are demons at home. We are our worst selves with the people closest to us. Christians should have only one persona, or we are no longer living in truth. We need to live tirelessly the humility, tolerant love, and mutual submission of the gospel both in private and in public. The most important witness we have is at stake—the witness within our families.

Life is painful when children turn their back on the Christian faith of their parents, but it is tragic when the misconduct and hypocrisy of their parents has caused them to do so. Integrity of faith starts in the family.

Parents. Being a parent is a hard job, but if God grants a person the privilege, nothing in life is more important. As brief as verse 4 is, the instructions cover a lot of ground: nurture and do not exasperate [or make angry]. The practical consequences of this instruction include:

(1) creating a context of grace, love, support, respect, and encouragement
(2) always speaking the truth in love
(3) attending to the material and emotional needs of children
(4) teaching, enlightening, warning, holding accountable, and disciplining, all as part of life lived to Christ; giving them a theology

(5) giving experiences, especially in work and in caring for others

(6) refusing to put down, demean, or damage them (shrill and angry speech does not belong)

(7) rejecting jealousy and contempt

(8) granting freedom within legitimate boundaries

(9) avoiding unhealthy pressure or expectations

(10) refusing to live through the children.

All of this takes time, communication skill, and discipline. Care of children is never an afterthought. In our society frequently both parents work outside the home, and children suffer. Christian parents need to think through this issue and how schedules can be arranged so that children receive attention. Communication skill is required, for children are constantly changing and every child is different. Without attention not only to what is said, but how it is heard, the relation will not flourish.

Then, as the guidelines suggest, parents discipline themselves first.[29] They need to have good mental health, for their children's lives depend on it. It is never too late to implement these guidelines, but they should start when the child is an infant. Mental illness is by and large caused by an absence of or defect in love that a child requires.[30] The feeling of value essential for good mental health is acquired in childhood and is difficult to find later in life.[31]

The teenage years do not have to be times of rebellion and disrespect. In fact, they can be some of the most enjoyable years, for teenagers are old enough to enter into discussion and participate in a range of activities that smaller children cannot. Parents should affirm repeatedly that they are on their children's side; they should be *for* their children. They are not the enemy. No one is perfect, but families can work together to enable each other.

A wrong turn. Focus on children, however, can become an idolatry of children or a wrongful indulging of them. Both of these lead to heartache. Like all else, being a parent is subsumed under life in Christ. Children are not the goal of life, but a context for living out life in Christ. The family is the primary place for discipleship.

Children. In effect, children are asked to give back what their parents give them: respect and love within the framework of their commitment to Christ. By obedience they give attention to parents, express their gratitude, and seek to assist. This is still the proper response for Christian children.

Obedience should never be blind obedience. The ideal situation within the text assumes the parents' request is legitimate, but sometimes parents are

---

29. Stott, *God's New Society*, 249.

30. M. Scott Peck, *The Road Less Traveled* (New York: Simon and Schuster, 1978), 175.

31. Ibid., 24.

insensitive or misguided in what they ask. Children too must learn to speak the truth in love, and their obedience to parents cannot mean disobedience to Christ. The most difficult circumstances for Christian children involve parents who are antithetical to Christianity or who are not emotionally balanced. Families are not only the primary place for discipleship; sometimes they are the most trying place. But even in extreme cases children must still love and respect their parents.

This is true not merely for small children and adolescents. In the ancient world, obligations to parents extended to death. We will not show obligation in the same way, but adult children must still honor their parents. Honor requires care and attention. Even totally independent children can and should learn from parents—and teach them—throughout life. Granted, past sins or present demeanor sometimes make relations intolerable, but for good or ill our psyche is tied up with our parents. We are rarely whole without being whole with them. Admittedly, circumstances sometimes are so bad that direct communication is harmful, but we need to find ways to address each other, honor our parents before God, exercise forgiveness, and speak the truth in love. Vengeance and punishment cannot be the goals, for they do not fit with the cross of Christ.

In our day, possibly the crying need in honoring parents has to do with care for the aging. We do not do it well, and no easy answers exist. Institutional help is sometimes necessary, but many institutions for the elderly leave a lot to be desired. If honor involves care and attention, we cannot marginalize and forget elderly family members by removing them from sight.

Slaves and masters (6:5–9). The application of the teaching on slaves and masters is obviously relevant for work relations, but it actually involves every relation and act. No relation is merely a relation; it is a context for relating to Christ. No job is merely work; it is a context for serving Christ.

Relations with people. The first application of this text concerns the way we understand ourselves and others. Society sends signals that declare our relative value and tell us where we fit in the hierarchy, but this text gives a different system of valuing. The hierarchy does not exist. We all have roles and tasks, but they do not render people more or less valuable. We all have the same Lord and face the same judgment. Arrogance and feelings of inferiority are out of place, as is favoritism. If God does not show favoritism, neither should we. We typically show favoritism to the rich and powerful, but little respect for the poor and powerless.[32] Both are sins.

It is so easy for us to demean people we consider to be "low on the totem pole." We do not have slaves, but we do have "service personnel" and people

---

32. Cf. James 2:1–13.

who "do not count." It is easy to dehumanize and tyrannize them. We "chew them out" when we are unsatisfied. We view them as faceless numbers when the time comes to downsize. By lack of attention, body language, or attitude we communicate to them, "We do not really care about you." Yet such people are as important as any "star" or power-broker, and our Christian witness depends on how we treat them. We must relate to them as if we were relating to Christ.

Application of this text also lifts people out of dehumanizing situations and gives them control. Others may seek to dehumanize them, but they have a high calling: They serve Christ. They do not work in response to some authority figure, but because they seek to do the will of God. No human controls them, for they serve the Lord Christ.

What we do matters. The most important application of this text is the realization that we are *slaves* of Christ. The language should not be dampened. We belong to him and serve him. If we take seriously that he is the origin and recipient of every act,[33] all our work takes on meaning and our treatment of people changes. Work will be done with care, not just to get by. People will be nurtured, not used or ignored. With this consciousness we come close to mirroring the creative activity of God. This requires a fundamental change in handling life.

For example, a worker with an airline could do enough to get by, but in the process neglect safety hazards or maintenance problems. That is an ethical issue and certainly not fitting with Christ. His work is not merely a job, but an opportunity to demonstrate integrity and obedience. By knowing that he serves Christ, he must make the plane as safe and efficient as possible.

A teacher could easily go through the routine, present material, give tests, and go home. Everyone would agree the teacher had fulfilled his or her contract, but it would not be enough. If the teacher teaches as to Christ, teaching is no longer a job; it is the care and nurture of souls. It is excellence of thought joined to the value of a person.

A waitress could give menus, take orders, bring food, and clean up. Maybe it would be enough, but if she serves as to Christ, she values herself and the people she serves.

A man sells papers in the street. He can take money and give papers, and no one will care. If he knows he serves Christ, he cares for people and values them even if they do not value him. What he does is important—not irreplaceable perhaps, but important.

But this is not a text solely to keep the lowly happy and working hard. The people who buy the papers are to relate to the man selling them as to Christ.

---

33. Cf. Colossians 3:17.

There are no people whom we may treat as unimportant. Even those without importance are important, and we are to treat them as we would Christ.

What we do and how we do it matters because all of life is lived in, to, and for the Lord. By necessity we are to reflect his love and truth. People and tasks are to be handled with care, for that is what the Lord requires.

To what audience do we play? Most people spend their lives seeking respect and admiration from a poorly defined audience. But as interests become focused, the audience becomes more defined. We choose the sector we want to impress. We act in direct response to the audience we think is watching. The more we care about the audience, the more diligent we are. We work hard if the boss is watching. We dress carefully if certain people will see us. We guard our tongue in certain groups. But if the audience is not present, neither is the effort. This is why we demean some people but go overboard to impress others. With the first we do not care about the audience; with the second we do.

Christians are asked to remember only one audience, the audience always present and to whom we are accountable—God. We are not to play to a secondary audience, and we are not to seek to impress another constituency. We are to honor God by living in truth and love.

Ephesians 6:10–20

FINALLY, BE STRONG in the Lord and in his mighty power. [11]Put on the full armor of God so that you can take your stand against the devil's schemes. [12]For our struggle is not against flesh and blood, but against the rulers, against the authorities, against the powers of this dark world and against the spiritual forces of evil in the heavenly realms. [13]Therefore put on the full armor of God, so that when the day of evil comes, you may be able to stand your ground, and after you have done everything, to stand. [14]Stand firm then, with the belt of truth buckled around your waist, with the breastplate of righteousness in place, [15]and with your feet fitted with the readiness that comes from the gospel of peace. [16]In addition to all this, take up the shield of faith, with which you can extinguish all the flaming arrows of the evil one. [17]Take the helmet of salvation and the sword of the Spirit, which is the word of God. [18]And pray in the Spirit on all occasions with all kinds of prayers and requests. With this in mind, be alert and always keep on praying for all the saints.

[19]Pray also for me, that whenever I open my mouth, words may be given me so that I will fearlessly make known the mystery of the gospel, [20]for which I am an ambassador in chains. Pray that I may declare it fearlessly, as I should.

Original Meaning — THROUGHOUT THE LETTER Paul has described the privilege and wonder of life in Christ and implored his readers to live in a way suitable to such privilege. From 4:17 on he has been urging his readers to stand against the pagan lifestyle around them. Gross sins should not even be named among them, and they should separate from and reprove the darkness. Their homes should reflect the unifying and self-giving character of the gospel. All this requires determined effort, for the darkness is still very present.

Now in the last section of the body of the letter, Paul sets forth an effective summary and challenge. Readers need to be prepared, as if for battle, for right living does not just happen and opposition is certain. Except for the discussion about darkness in 5:8–14, Ephesians has presented an ideal situation. Marriage, for example, was described in the ideal terms of believing and loving husbands and wives. Slaves and masters were believers who related in integrity and mutual submission. Now the presentation of the ideal is dropped. Paul acknowledges the reality of evil as an active force and seeks to motivate his readers to make real—even in the midst of evil—all that the letter has been saying about their identity in Christ.

Those enamored with rhetorical criticism in New Testament studies identify this section as the *peroratio*, the final section of a speech that sought to recapitulate and to arouse to action.[1] Whether New Testament documents fit into technical rhetorical descriptions is debatable, but the intent of a *peroratio* is precisely the purpose of this last section—to expand and reinforce, to recapitulate and arouse to action. Of course, any good speech or writing seeks to conclude with a clinching argument that motivates the audience.[2]

The degree to which earlier concerns of the letter are brought back to the reader deserves emphasis. Note the following correspondences:

power in 6:10–11 and in 1:19–20; 3:7, 16, 20
"put on" in 6:11, 14 (NIV, "in place") and in 4:24
"the devil's schemes" in 6:11 and "deceitful scheming" in 4:14; "do not
    give the devil a foothold" in 4:27 (cf. 2:2)
evil spiritual forces in 6:12 and in 1:21; 3:10
"darkness" in 6:12 and in 5:8, 11
"heavenly realms" in 6:12 and in 1:3, 20; 2:6; 3:10
"the day of evil" in 6:13 and "the days are evil" in 5:16
"truth" in 6:14 and in 1:13; 4:15, 21, 24, 25; 5:9
"righteousness" in 6:15 and in 4:24; 5:9
"the gospel" in 6:15 and in 1:13; 3:6
"peace" in 6:15 and in 1:2; 2:14–17; 4:3
"faith" in 6:16 and in 1:15; 2:8; 3:12, 17; 4:5, 13 (cf. 1:13, 19)
"salvation" in 6:17 and in 1:13 (cf. 5:23)
"the Spirit" in 6:17–18 and in 1:13–14, 17; 2:18, 22; 3:5, 16; 4:3–4, 30; 5:18
"the word" in 6:17 and in 5:26 (cf. 1:13 [with *logos* instead of *rhema*])
prayer in 6:18–20 and in 1:15–19; 3:14–20
"saints" in 6:18 and in 1:1, 15, 18; 2:19; 3:8, 18; 4:12; 5:3
"boldness" in 6:19–20 and in 3:12 (NIV, "freedom" and "fearlessly" respec-
    tively)
"mystery" in 6:19 and in 1:9; 3:3–4, 9; 5:32.

---

1. See the treatment by Andrew Lincoln, "'Stand, Therefore . . .' Ephesians 6:10–20 as *Peroratio*," *Biblical Interpretation*, 3 (1995): 99–114; also in his commentary, *Ephesians*, 432–41.

2. Rhetoricians described what effective communication is and taught people accordingly. Many people were astute enough to be effective without being trained in rhetoric.

The list is impressive and hardly coincidental. Paul does not recapitulate everything in the letter, but clearly he wants to remind his readers of new life in Christ and its effect.

The attempt to arouse to action is achieved by a stirring use of battle language. Metaphors of battle were (and are) common. The Old Testament and the book of Revelation are full of such imagery to describe God's own work, whether in defense of, or judgment against, his people.[3] As we will see, the wording to describe the armor is drawn mostly from Isaiah.[4]

The closest analogies to this text are speeches from generals motivating their troops for war. One of the most interesting of these is in the "War Scroll" from Qumran, a battle plan for the end time in which a priest, chosen especially for the occasion, is to give the speech. The language of this scroll is not metaphorical, for the Essenes believed that a literal war would occur in which their own camp would be besieged, but God and his angelic hosts would join them against the nations and the devil and his hosts. The sons of light, the Essenes, would defeat the sons of darkness, the enemies of God. Note its words of encouragement:

> Be strong and valiant; be warriors! . . . Be brave and strong for the battle of God! For this day is the time of the battle of God. . . . The God of Israel lifts his hand in his marvelous might against all the spirits of wickedness. . . . For the God of Israel has called out the sword against all the nations, and he will do mighty deeds by the saints of His people. (1QM 15.8–16.1)[5]

No dependence on Qumran is suggested, but just as the priests wanted to motivate warriors for a literal battle, Paul wants to motivate Christians for the battle with evil.[6]

---

3. See, for example, Genesis 15:1; Exodus 14:14, 25; Deuteronomy 1:30; 3:22; 33:29; Joshua 10:14–15; Psalm 18; 35; Isaiah 42:13–25; Jeremiah 21:3–7; 46; Revelation 2:16; 6:2–8; 9:7–19; 19:11–16.

4. Wisdom of Solomon 5:17–23 may also have been part of the formative background, for it describes the armor of wrath God puts on and adopts "breastplate of righteousness" from Isaiah 59:17. The word for "armor" there is the same word as in Ephesians 6:11, 13— *panoplia*. See also Ignatius, *Letter to Polycarp* 6:2, which uses language of battle equipment in an exhortation toward Christian living. In the New Testament, see Romans 13:12; 1 Thessalonians 5:8. Whereas Ephesians has "the breastplate of righteousness" and "the helmet of salvation," 1 Thessalonians 5:8 has "putting on faith and love as a breastplate, and the hope of salvation as a helmet" (see also Rom. 6:13; 2 Cor. 6:7; 10:3–4).

5. The translation is from G. Vermes, *The Dead Sea Scrolls in English* (Baltimore: Penguin, 1962).

6. Note also Exodus 14:13; Joshua 1:6–9; 1 Samuel 4:9.

Note the prominence given to the word "stand," occurring four times in verses 11, 13–14,[7] and to words for power in verse 10, the verb *dynamai* (NIV, "can" in vv. 11 , 16; "able" in v. 13), "armor" (vv. 11, 13), and "fearlessly" (vv. 19–20).

Structure. Three imperatives—"be strong," "put on the full armor of God," and "stand" (vv. 10–11, 14)—dominate the text; the rest is explanatory. Verse 10 functions as a heading for the whole passage. Verse 11 explains that we are strong in the Lord when we put on the armor he provides. Verse 12 shows why strength is needed, and the command to put on God's armor is then repeated (v. 13) and explained (vv. 14–20). Only two imperatives appear in the Greek text of verses 14-20—"stand" in verse 14 and "take" in verse 17. (Participles are used to convey the other main ideas.) Some begin a new paragraph at verse 17, some, such as the NRSV, at verse 18, and still others, like the NIV, at verse 19.[8]

A schematic of the structure is helpful.

Heading: "Be strong in the Lord and in his mighty power" (v. 10)
Means of achieving the goal: "Put on the full armor of God" (v. 11a)
   Purpose: "so ... you can ... stand ... against the devil's schemes (v. 11b)
     Explanation of the problem: "For our struggle is ... against the spiritual forces of evil (v. 12)[9]
Repetition and explanation of the means of achieving the goal: "Put on the full armor of God" (v. 13a)
   Purpose: "so ... you may ... stand"
Call for commitment: "Stand" (v. 14a)
   (Four participles explaining the means by which we stand)
     "with the belt of truth *buckled* around your waist (v. 14 b)
     "*putting on* [NIV, "with"] the breastplate of righteousness" (v. 14b)
     "with your feet *fitted* with the readiness that comes from the gospel of peace" (v. 15)
     "*taking up* [NIV, "take up"] the shield of faith" (v. 16)

---

7. The first occurrence in verse 13 ("stand your ground") is actually a compound form, meaning "stand against" in the sense "oppose" or "withstand."

8. In the first edition of the UBS Greek text verses 14–20 are one long sentence. Logically verse 18 shifts to the subject of prayer, but grammatically it is dependent on verse 17, which causes debate about the flow of the text. The NIV started a new paragraph at verse 19 because the logic shifts to prayer *for Paul,* but grammatically verses 19–20 merely continue verse 18. The NIV has inserted the word "pray" in verse 19; the text has only "and for me."

9. Robert A. Wild, "The Warrior and the Prisoner: Some Reflections on Ephesians 6:10–20," CBQ, 46 (1984): 286–88, argues that 6:12 is the central element in 6:10–20 because it is flanked on both sides by the command to put on the armor of God. This places too much emphasis on verse 12.

Call to be equipped: "Take the helmet of salvation and the sword of the Spirit" (v. 17)[10]
(Two participles explaining how we take the helmet of salvation and the sword of the Spirit):
"*praying* [NIV, "pray"] in the Spirit" (v. 18a)
"*being alert* with all perseverance and petitions for all the saints" [NIV, "be alert and always keep on praying for all the saints"] (v. 18b)
Request for prayer for Paul for two purposes:
"that . . . words may be given me" (v. 19)
"that I may declare [the gospel] fearlessly" (v. 20).

Be Strong Against Evil (6:10–13)

BE STRONG (VV. 10–11, 13).[11] Since Ephesians is about power for living in Christ, it comes as no surprise that the concluding exhortation has this emphasis. The passive form of the verb ("be strong") indicates that this empowering is something done to Christians, not something they do themselves; its present tense shows the empowering is continual. This is not instruction for a quick fix, but for a life spent drawing strength from Christ. To be strong in the Lord means to know his strength and to draw closer to him. It is an exhortation to act on what is known.[12]

The words translated "his mighty power" (v. 10) are the same as those translated "his mighty strength" in 1:19. There Paul had prayed that the readers would know the greatness of God's power; now he exhorts them to use this power.

"Put on the full armor of God" (v. 11) recalls the command in 4:24 to "put on the new self, created to be like God in true holiness and righteousness."[13] Putting on the new self is in essence the same as putting on the armor of God. The "armor of God" can be understood as the armor that God provides, the armor that God himself wears, or even the armor that is God himself. The language describing the armor in verses 14–17 is drawn from Isaiah 11:5; 52:7;

---

10. Paul uses participles to describe the armor until verse 17, where the imperative "take" is used. Some suggest the shift is from items requiring human effort to those that are pure gift, but this is unlikely. The other pieces of armor are no less gifts, and human effort is also involved in taking the helmut of salvation and the sword of the Spirit. Possibly these two pieces of the armor are more comprehensive, encompassing all other gifts. In any case, Paul emphasizes salvation and the Spirit by the grammatical shift. Faith is also emphasized by the insertion "In addition to all this" (v. 16).

11. "Finally" could be understood as "for the remaining time," but more likely it serves to introduce the conclusion of the letter.

12. Similar exhortations appear in 1 Corinthians 16:13; 2 Timothy 2:1 (see also Phil. 4:13; Col. 1:11; 1 Tim. 1:12).

59:17. While the Old Testament background suggests that the intent is the armor God wears, in the end all the armor language is a way to talk about identification with God and his purposes.[14] Some of the armor—truth, righteousness, and salvation—suggests we are to put on God or at least the characteristics of God. The idea is therefore close to 5:1: "Be imitators of God." Only by taking on the characteristics God reveals can we be strong.

An English translation cannot easily show it, but the imperatives throughout this section are plural. We usually interpret them as if they were addressed to individuals, but without denying their relevance for individuals, we should understand them as Paul's instructions for the church collectively to put on God's armor and stand as one person (cf. Phil. 1:27).[15]

The necessity of standing against the devil's schemes is assumed. To "stand" connotes strength, stability, and success in a conflict or difficulty.[16] Mention of the "schemes" of the devil reminds us of the trickery and subterfuge by which evil and temptation present themselves in our lives. Evil rarely looks evil until it accomplishes its goal; it gains entrance by appearing attractive, desirable, and perfectly legitimate. It is a baited and camouflaged trap. As Paul puts it in 2 Corinthians 11:14, Satan masquerades as an angel of light.[17]

The content of verse 11 is repeated in verse 13 with slight changes. The singular "day of evil" is interpreted by some as a reference to an outbreak of evil just before the end time, but the focus of the text is on life in the present. The meaning is "any time evil is encountered." The intent with "after you have done everything" is not clear, but probably refers to everything related to putting on the armor (detailed in vv. 14–17).

The struggle with spiritual forces (v. 12). The word translated "struggle" occurs nowhere else in the New Testament and is not frequent in other writings. It refers primarily to wrestling, but can be used more generally of a fight or battle. "Flesh and blood" is a Semitism for "human." What Paul means,

---

13. The NIV uses the same expression, "put on the full armor of God," in both verse 11 and 13, but different Greek verbs are used. In verse 13 Paul uses *analambano*, "to take up" (the same word reappears in v. 16 in the statement, "take up the shield of faith").

14. Note the similarity of Isaiah 52:1.

15. Especially those in non-Western cultures react against an individualistic approach. See Gottfried Osei-Mensah, *Wanted: Servant-Leaders, the Challenge of Christian Leadership in Africa Today* (Achimota, Ghana: Africa Christian Press, 1990), 67. Martin Kitchen, *Ephesians* (London: Routledge, 1994), 112–28, offers an extended but not always convincing argument for this view.

16. See Romans 11:20; 14:4; 2 Corinthians 1:24; Galatians 5:1; Philippians 4:1; Colossians 4:12; 1 Thessalonians 3:8; 2 Thessalonians 2:15; 2 Timothy 2:19. Similar urging to resist the devil and be strengthened by God appears in James 4:7–8 and 1 Peter 5:8–10.

17. Elsewhere Paul warns of Satan's temptations and complains of his obstacles (1 Cor. 7:5; 2 Cor. 2:11; 11:3; 12:7; 1 Thess. 2:18).

therefore, is: "Our struggle is not with human beings, but with evil spiritual forces." This is the only place in the New Testament where the Christian life is described in this sort of language.

Of the four expressions used for spiritual forces in verse 12 only "rulers" and "authorities" appear in the earlier list of five terms for spiritual forces in 1:21.[18] We are not to conclude that seven categories of demonic spirits exist; rather, both passages pile up terms for emphasis and rhetorical impact. The two new terms do add detail linking these forces to darkness and evil. "Powers of this dark world," if translated more literally, would be "world rulers of this darkness" and is reminiscent of 2:2 and 5:8–11.[19]

As indicated in our discussion of 1:21,[20] precise identification of the various expressions is impossible because of the ambiguity and paucity of the terms. *Attempts to rank spiritual forces is groundless and fanciful speculation.*[21] All four of the expressions in 6:12 point to the same reality; the fourth is perhaps the most descriptive and helpful—"the spiritual forces of evil."

The use of the term *spiritual* for evil forces is somewhat surprising. This is the only time in the New Testament that this word has a negative connotation, but a negative use is understandable given the frequency with which the word "spirit" is used for evil spirits in the Gospels and Acts or occasionally for a spirit contrary to God's purposes.[22] Paul even used the word "god" in reference to Satan in 2 Corinthians 4:4.

More surprising still is that the struggle takes place "in the heavenly realms." This does not mean a struggle in heaven, even though Job 1–2 and Revelation 12:7–17 could provide a background for such an idea. Nor should we think of an area lower than heaven but higher than the earth.[23] Rather, as elsewhere in Ephesians, this phrase refers to the *reality* that encompasses life in relation to God, including both what God has given and what believers are called to do.[24]

---

18. The word translated "power" in 1:21 is not the same word translated "powers" in 6:12.

19. "World rulers" is a word used of the planets in astrological speculation, the thought being that the movement of the planets controlled life on earth. The word was also used for Zeus and for emperors.

20. See pp. 76–78.

21. Such as Mark I. Bubeck's hierarchical explanation that the most powerful evil spirits are principalities, then powers (less independent and powerful), rulers of darkness (lower grade officers), and demons. See his *The Adversary* (Chicago: Moody, 1975), 72–73. See also C. Peter Wagner, ed., *Engaging the Enemy: How to Fight and Defeat Territorial Spirits* (Ventura, Calif.: Regal, 1991), 38, 48.

22. See 2 Corinthians 11:4; 2 Thessalonians 2:2 (NIV, "prophecy"); 1 John 4:1–3.

23. See Schnackenburg, *Ephesians: A Commentary*, 273; Hendriksen, *Exposition of Ephesians*, 273, for this view.

24. See pp. 46–47, 163.

Those who live in Christ have been given every spiritual gift and are made alive and enthroned with Christ (1:3; 2:6) in the heavenly reality. His own enthronement in the heavenly reality—God's reality—includes the subjection of every power (1:20). Believers have the task in this unseen reality to make God's wisdom known to the spiritual powers (3:10) and to stand against them (6:10–13). Our enthronement with Christ above the powers determines how we live on earth. Our struggle reflects the heavenly reality, which means we struggle against *subjected* powers. The powers may rule darkness and evil, but we as Christians no longer live there (5:8, 16).

Since verse 12 explains standing "against the devil's schemes" in verse 11, Paul was surely not thinking about structures of evil such as government, law, or social conventions. Rather, he thought of personal spiritual beings seeking to disrupt life as God intended it.

The Armor of God (6:14–20)

THE ARMOR DESCRIBED is that of a heavily armed Roman foot soldier, though as already indicated, the terms for armor and their spiritual associations are drawn from Isaiah. Paul uses this analogy because of the influence of the Old Testament, the picture it presents, and its rhetorical effect. The meaning would not be different if he had written, "Put on truth, righteousness, readiness, and faith, and take hold of salvation and the gospel." Speculation about the connection between specific "virtues" and specific parts of the armor is not helpful, especially when the breastplate and helmet are associated with different qualities in 1 Thessalonians 5:8.

Do the pieces of armor in verses 14–16 represent gifts from God or our obedience to God? That is, for example, do we belt on God's truth or the practice of truth? Both are true, but which did Paul have in mind? The separation of gift and task should not be made so starkly, and M. Barth is correct in pointing out that all the theological terms mentioned here are relational terms. They have to do with the covenant.[25] Each one points to a reality about God that determines human action. The nuance varies from item to item as to whether focus is more on God or on the believer.

A decision about "the belt of truth" is the most difficult, but the other three items in verses 14–16 ("righteousness," "readiness," and "faith") emphasize a human response to God's saving work. This passage *is* an appeal for human action. Clearly, "righteousness" in verse 14 does not refer so much to the gift of righteousness (Rom. 5:17) as to righteous acts by believers (see

---

25. Barth, *Ephesians*, 2:796.

4:24; 5:9).[26] "Salvation" and "the word of God" in verse 17, however, are clearly gifts from God, which at the same time enable and motivate human obedience.

A decision about the belt depends on which previous uses of "truth" are determinative. Belting on the truth alludes to Isaiah 11:5, which describes the "Branch," the Davidic deliverer, who has righteousness as a belt and truth (NIV, "faithfulness") as a sash. If the meaning in Isaiah is determinative, focus is on doing what is right and keeping faith with the covenant promises. More likely the context of Ephesians is determinative, but truth is used in this letter both with reference to God's truth revealed in the gospel (1:13; 4:21) and to truth as right living and speaking in the new being (4:15, 24–25; 5:9). I seriously doubt whether Paul would separate these two aspects of truth. To belt on truth means to be strengthened by God's truth in the gospel and to resolve to live truth.

The NIV uses "belt" to convey the idea of "tying around the waist"—the idea of "girding" in the ancient world, which is often associated with tying up long robes and designates readiness for action.[27] For soldiers, reference is probably to a leather apron-like covering tied around the waist to protect the lower abdomen.[28]

The "breastplate of righteousness" is from Isaiah 59:17, which describes God's putting on armor to come in judgment. Paul was not writing about judgment, but the fact that the new being is created to be like God (4:24). To put on the breastplate of righteousness means that Christians are to reflect the righteous character of God in their actions.

"Feet fitted with the readiness that comes from the gospel of peace" (v. 15) is adapted from Isaiah 52:7, which describes the messenger of good news. Usually this is understood in terms of willingness to share the gospel, but the intent is broader than sharing the good news. "Readiness" pertains to all of life. Knowledge of the gospel should make people alert (v. 18) and ready for life. Christians have been taught in the school of Christ. They are careful about their speech and actions. They do not live in the dark. They live wisely, redeeming the time and understanding the will of the Lord. Such people not only share the good news, but they are also agents of peace and love, ready to do the whole will of God. The paradox of armor given to those commit-

---

26. Barth (ibid.) argues that righteousness should be understood as a gift, because of its background in Isaiah 11:1–9, but the use in Ephesians suggests otherwise (as does 1 Thess. 5:8, which speaks of the breastplate of faith and love, surely pointing to human actions).

27. See Luke 12:35; 1 Peter 1:13

28. Barth, *Ephesians*, 2:777, maintains instead that the allusion to Isaiah 11:5 indicates reference is to a special belt designating an officer.

ted to a gospel of peace reminds the reader that the language is metaphorical.[29]

With the shield Paul has in mind the large shield Roman infantry used to protect their whole bodies. Such shields were four feet tall and two and one-half feet wide and were constructed of leather stretched over wood, reinforced with metal at the top and bottom. Especially if soaked in water, they were effective in stopping burning arrows.[30] When overlapped with the shields of soldiers on either side, they provided effective protection. They were not merely defensive, however, for a line of soldiers with interlocked shields and weapons poised could push right through enemy ranks.

Obviously "the shield of faith" is especially important for Paul, given his additions before and after this expression.[31] That faith protects is not to suggest that humans protect themselves by their power to believe. As shown earlier,[32] to speak of faith is not to focus on human belief, but on the faithfulness of God. What protects us from the arrows of the evil one (i.e., any temptation to error or wrong) is our relation with God.

"The helmet of salvation" (v. 17) is also from Isaiah 59:17, again describing God's own armor. M. Barth suggested the helmet is a ceremonial helmet, a helmet of victory, which indicates the battle has already been won,[33] though this is questionable. In Isaiah God strapped on a breastplate of righteousness and the helmet of salvation to bring righteousness and salvation. But in Ephesians, the believer puts them on to do righteousness and to receive salvation. God's salvation is the ultimate assurance of protection. From the treatment of salvation earlier in the letter, this salvation is both present and future (cf. 1:10; 2:5–8; 4:30; 5:5).

With the sword of the Spirit a change occurs. With the earlier pieces of armor, the second element identified the first. For example, the belt was truth. With the sword of the Spirit, this is not the case, for the sword is the word of God. The Spirit is the one who empowers the sword.[34] Throughout Scripture God's word is the instrument by which his power is shown.[35] The wording here may be influenced by Isaiah 11:4.

---

29. Both "shield" and "sword" are also metaphors. They are used in the Old Testament of God's protection and judgment respectively (Ps. 3:3; Isa. 34:6), though that does not seem to be Paul's main focus here.

30. Arrows were often dipped in tar and set aflame just before being shot.

31. "In addition to this" (v. 16) is literally "in all things" and could mean in every situation.

32. See pp. 104–5.

33. Barth, *Ephesians*, 2:775.

34. The sword in mind is the short, straight sword of Roman infantry, effective for close combat.

35. Whether generally (as Isa. 55:11; Heb. 4:12) or for creation (Gen. 1:3; Ps. 33:6; Heb. 1:3), healing (Ps. 107:20), judgment (Isa. 11:4), or salvation (John 6:63). Cf. Isaiah 49:2; Revelation 1:16; 2:12, 16; 19:15.

"Word of God" does not refer to the Bible but to the gospel message. The Greek word used here (*rhema*) usually refers to a teaching or prophetic utterance or, more specifically, to the gospel.[36] This identification does not place all the focus outward on proclaiming the gospel. The gospel empowered by the Spirit is the means by which the well-armed Christian is protected and empowered for life. That includes sharing the good news, but is much more comprehensive.

The NIV translation and paragraph division of 6:18-20 loses the sequence of thought. Prayer (v. 18) is not just the next command given, and while some translations and editions of the Greek New Testament start a new sentence here, this loses the connection with the preceding ideas. As indicated above, the words translated "pray" and "be alert" in verse 18 are participles, not imperatives. Some would connect these participles all the way back to "stand firm" in verse 14 and see them as describing how all the armor is acquired. Theologically this makes sense, but grammatically it is unlikely. The most obvious connection is to "take" in verse 17, which is reinforced by the repetition of "Spirit" in verse 18. The intent is to underscore the *demeanor* of those who take the helmet of salvation and the sword of the Spirit. The well-armed soldier in Christ's army, by definition, is continually praying in the Spirit and alert.

Whether prayer is a seventh piece of equipment is debated.[37] Grammar suggests it is not, or else being alert, which is a parallel to praying, would have to be considered a piece of the equipment as well. But the question is irrelevant, for whether it is a piece of the equipment or the demeanor with which the equipment is worn, neither prayer nor being alert is optional for believers. By definition, to be Christ's soldier is to pray and keep alert.

"Praying in the Spirit" does not refer to speaking in tongues.[38] Rather, it should be seen in connection with other passages on the Spirit in Ephesians, especially 3:16 ("may strengthen you ... through his Spirit in your inner being) and 5:18 ("be filled with the Spirit").[39] The Spirit communicates God to us, and through him we receive all gifts and empowering from God.

The instructions to pray and be alert are paralleled elsewhere in the New Testament.[40] By using "always" the NIV tones down an emphasis on perseverance in verse 18. Prayer combined with perseverance is, in fact, the way

---

36. See especially Romans 10:8, 17; 1 Peter 1:25.

37. Fee, *God's Empowering Presence*, 730, argues it is; Lincoln, *Ephesians*, 451, argues it is not.

38. As Fee argues in *God's Empowering Presence*, 730–31. For similar phrases see Jude 20; cf. John 4:24; 1 Corinthians 12:3; 14:16

39. Romans 8:26 is also instructive: "We do not know what we ought to pray for, but the Spirit himself intercedes for us."

40. See especially Matthew 26:41; Mark 14:38; Luke 21:36; Colossians 4:2. In 1 Thessalonians 5:6–8 the encouragement to be alert precedes the armor imagery.

to keep alert. Note the similar instructions in Philippians 4:6–7, with the result that people will be guarded by God's peace.

No sharp distinction is intended between "prayers" and "requests." By using both words Paul only sought to emphasize prayer. The word translated "requests" is used again in the second half of verse 18 but translated "praying." Prayer is the focal point of this verse, mentioned four times; the word "all" is also used four times, one of which the NIV translates as "always." With this repetition Paul underscores how important prayer is for all of life. The believer's entire life is one large prayer to God. In keeping with the corporate focus of the letter, the prayer is not individual and self-centered, for the readers are to pray for all God's people.

Just as Paul started the letter by praying for his readers, he closes by asking them to pray for him (vv. 19–20). Paul frequently requested prayer for himself at the end of his letters (cf. Rom. 15:30–33; Col. 4:2–4; 1 Thess. 5:25; 2 Thess. 3:1–2).[41] Except for 1 Thessalonians 5:25, his request was for the advancement of the gospel, not for his own benefit. With the attention he has placed on the privilege of speaking for Christ (Eph. 3:8–10) and on the power of speech (4:29), it is not surprising that he requests prayer for God's help in his effort to present the gospel. If God's help is needed in praying (Rom. 8:26), surely it is needed in explaining the good news.

The word translated "fearlessly" is actually "openness" or "boldness." When used in reference to speech, it means frank, uninhibited speech, such as that of a free person, who is not concerned about reprisal. It should come as no surprise that this same word is used at the end of Acts to describe Paul in Rome under guard, boldly and without hindrance preaching the kingdom of God (Acts 28:31). The boldness desired here is expressed forthrightly in Romans 1:16: "I am not ashamed of the gospel."

"Mystery of the gospel" does not mean some mysterious part of the gospel. As indicated earlier,[42] "mystery" does not mean something "unknown" or "mysterious," but that which is unknown until it is revealed by God. The words "of the gospel" explain the content of the revelation. A helpful translation would be, "make known the revelation that is in the gospel."

---

41. Verses 19–20 do not fit easily into a theory of a pseudonymous author. The explanation that the author adopts the persona of Paul as part of the device of pseudonymity is not convincing. See Lincoln, *Ephesians*, 453, 455. His attempt ("Stand, therefore ... ," 108) to explain this as impersonation to enliven the *peroratio* on the basis of remarks by Quintilian, a first century rhetorician, is a misappropriation. Quintilian was not referring to pseudonymity, but to the use of dialogue by which the readers or hearers knew the words of someone else were presented, as the examples he gives show. See Quintilian, *Institutes*, 9.2.29–37. Either Paul seeks prayer for himself, or someone seeks to mislead the readers into thinking he does.

42. See pp. 53, 159–60.

Because of the gospel, Paul was an ambassador in chains (cf. 2 Cor. 5:20, where Paul describes himself as "Christ's ambassador"). The word "ambassador" was used of a legate of the emperor. Paul's claim to being an ambassador is virtually the same as saying he is an apostle. As the representative of Christ, he has been sent with a message. This emphasizes the dignity of his work, but instead of respect and honor, he has received chains and imprisonment (cf. Acts 20:28; 2 Tim. 1:16). M. Barth suggests a play with the word "chain." On festive occasions ambassadors wore ornamental chains as a mark of the prestige of their countries. Paul's chain is a fitting symbol of his crucified Lord, but it also underscores the evil of this world.[43] Implicit in this self-description is a message to the recipients not to misread the situation or be embarrassed by his imprisonment.

APART FROM THE discussion of spiritual forces, even though the language may sound foreign, we should have little difficulty in bringing the ideas in this section into our lives today. Though we do not wear armor, we are accustomed to seeing police in full riot gear, with virtually the same logic of protection—equipment belts, bullet-proof vests, boots, shields, helmets, and weapons. What we lack is a sense of the *need* for protection, which is related to the understanding of spiritual forces.

Be strong in the Lord. We know that human relationships convey strength through encouragement, commitment, support, and help. Being empowered in the Lord is that and much more. Throughout Ephesians the idea of being in Christ has dominated Paul's thinking, and this theology is still being worked out at the end. Christians live in the Lord and are so close to him that they draw from the resources he possesses as risen Lord (1:19–20; cf. 3:16–17, where Paul prays that the Spirit of the indwelling Christ will strengthen our inner being).

This is not some magical idea of power, and contrary to what Simon Magus thought (Acts 8:18–19), power is not the goal. The goal is a life in relation to God. Power is not for impressive acts, but for living obediently. Clinton Arnold rightly contrasts a "substance" view of power in the ancient world with the relational view of power emphasized in Ephesians.[44] Power is not a current to be turned on and off. It is a continual, relational empowering that results from living in Christ. Nor is this a power to be used to our personal advantage. The power has one purpose: to enable us to stand with God and against evil.

---

43. Barth, *Ephesians*, 2:782.
44. Arnold, *Power and Magic*, 36–39, 73.

Put on. The metaphorical language of putting on various qualities is clear (cf. the similar language at 4:24). We say, "Clothes make the person," meaning that a person's clothes both define them and reveal who they are. Similarly, to put on a quality such as truth is to be determined by that quality. The issue again concerns identity. The Christian's identity is to be shaped by truth, righteousness, readiness, faith, salvation, and the gospel message.

What shall we do about the devil and evil spirits? Bringing verse 12 into our age is difficult, to say the least. Our world—whether Christian or non-Christian—is schizophrenic in its attitude toward the devil and the demonic. Much of our culture rejects any such idea as archaic nonsense, while the rest has an excessive fascination with the idea. Of course, throughout history nearly all cultures have believed in the demonic, and apart from the Western world, still do. But, just when we thought belief in demons would go away, it has come back with force.

We almost need the demonic to explain the extent of evil in the world. What makes a fourteen-year-old sexually molest and kill a four-year-old? Can humans be that depraved by themselves? What makes one ethnic group attempt genocide on another—be it Germans, Cambodians, Serbs, or Rwandans? Are people so depraved or is the demonic responsible? Even those who reject demons feel that malignant forces operate against them and use terms for the demonic to explain their feeling.

Furthermore, evil presents itself in ways so personal and beyond us, so contrary to us, that belief in the demonic is natural. People confess, "I was not myself when I did that." We develop a sense that evil is beyond our ability to cope and that something outside us is seeking to control us. As Leonardo Boff points out, "Evil has never been experienced in a vague, abstract form."[45] It approaches so powerfully and personally that we cannot help but suspect another presence. As Walter Wink notes, something or someone leads us to posit Satan's existence. Beliefs may be matters of debate, but the experience of Satan is a brute and terrifying fact.[46]

If the New Testament texts on the demonic are not just ignored, two primary options for interpretation and application emerge.[47] Either the rulers and authorities are demythologized and understood as the determining *structures* of life, or they are understood as *literal demons* responsible for all or much that goes wrong. As usually presented, neither approach is satisfactory.

---

45. Quoted without reference by Lawrence S. Cunningham, "Satan: A Theological Meditation," *Theology Today*, 51 (1994): 359.

46. Walter Wink, *Unmasking the Powers*, vol. 2: *The Powers* (Philadelphia: Fortress, 1986), 11, 26.

47. See the discussion of 1:21 and 2:2 on pp. 76–78, 84–86 and 96–98, 109–11.

If demythologized, the rulers and authorities become historical, biological, political, and societal structures that determine life negatively and oppress individuals. Application then is directed against materialism, the corporate and political world, bureaucracy, nationalism, militarism, social convention, and similar determiners. Those stressing the social impact of the gospel often find this option attractive. This demythologizing step has been relatively easy since the Bible uses "rulers and authorities" of human leaders.[48] Moreover, the *theology* of opposition to structures is correct, if not taken to an extreme, for structures can indeed be "demonic" in their effect. But that theology does not emerge from this text, for Paul had evil beings in mind, as the relation of verse 12 to verse 11 shows.[49] Some people legitimately adapt this approach by arguing that literal demons work through the structures.

If, on the other hand, the text is understood of literal demons, the tendency is for so much focus to be placed on the demonic that demons appear everywhere and are responsible for everything wrong. This is even worse and leads to disastrous consequences.

What is reality? The question is about the nature of reality, and our first response should be to express humility of knowledge. In the end we do not know about the existence or non-existence of evil beings. Evil we know; beings we surmise. Is the language for the devil and demons a personification of what was felt so personally as the presence of evil, or is it by necessity about real evil beings? Paul thought he was describing real beings. Do we still need the devil and demons? Or do we use the devil (and God) only for areas we do not understand?

On the one hand, the question of the existence of evil beings is unimportant, for we all know the existence and presence of evil. On the other hand, we cannot bracket the ontological question of the devil's existence, as W. Wink does, without treating the question of God's existence on the same playing field.[50] There is one major difference, however. God is an essential player in the universe; the devil and demons are not. We do not need them, and one day they will be removed.[51]

---

48. See Luke 12:11; 1 Corinthians 2:8 (cf. Luke 20:20).

49. For a critique of interpreting this language as structures, see Stott, *God's New Society*, 267–75; Arnold, *Power and Magic*, 169–82; Peter T. O'Brien, "Principalities and Powers: Opponents of the Church," *Biblical Interpretation and the Church: The Problem of Contextualization*, ed. D. A. Carson (Nashville: Thomas Nelson, 1984), 110–50.

50. See pp. 109–10.

51. As indicated earlier (see p. 110), why is it relatively easy for people to believe in a beneficient being (God) or beings (angels), but so much more troublesome to believe in the devil and demons?

Our attempts to answer the question about reality are revealed in our worldview. Four questions have to be answered:

(1) Are there immaterial realities beyond the material and natural world, beyond our senses? Christians say "yes." To limit ourselves to the material world raises problems both in explaining the material world and in dealing with the anomaly and meaninglessness of human existence. The problems are so large that we virtually implode upon ourselves.

(2) If the immaterial is real, how do material and immaterial relate? Several options exist. (a) There are two separate realms, with the natural world being a mirror of the supernatural (as in animism, where earthly circumstances reflect a reality in the spirit world). (b) There are two separate realms, with the spiritual world having little or nothing to do with the material world (as in Gnosticism, deism, and other forms of separatism). (c) There is only one realm for material and immaterial, in which God and the devil are both present and involved in the lives of people. The biblical witness affirms this third option forcefully.

(3) What is the relationship of good and evil? Again several options exist. (a) In cosmological dualism, good and evil, God and the devil, are equal and opposing forces. Much in our society assumes this paradigm, but it is not biblical. (b) Evil controls the world and God the heavens. (c) God is the only real and legitimate Lord, and evil and the demonic are illegitimate usurpers. The biblical witness insists on this third option.

(4) How powerful is evil? Again, the biblical witness is clear. Evil is a reality, even a threat, but there is no reason for alarm or anxiety. God's victory is certain. Sin will not win and is not Lord. This is not even a fair fight, for the resurrection has already demonstrated the outcome.

This last question is of major significance, for many people give the devil far too much respect. We speak of the devil as if *it* were omnipresent, omniscient, and omnipotent—terms that apply exclusively to God. If people admit the devil is not omnipresent, they then suggest *it* has hordes of demons as representatives. Ephesians 6:11–12 is one of the few texts that explicitly connects the devil and the rulers and authorities,[52] but the Bible does not describe the world as filled of demons.[53] The human preoccupation with the devil assaulting individuals is another form of egotism in which we see the cosmic battle of the universe centered on ourselves.

---

52. See also Luke 11:11–13 and texts like Matthew 25:41, which speak of the devil and his angels.

53. The only basis of such an idea is found in the accounts in Mark and Luke of the Gerasene demoniac (Mark 5:1–20; Luke 8:26–39; cf. Matt. 8:28–34). Both accounts use both the singular and the plural to refer to the demon(s) (cf. also Matt. 12:43–45; Luke 11:24–26).

To put the question another way: Who has power and to what are we vulnerable? The Bible instructs us to fear God, not the devil or demons. We should not fear being possessed or afflicted by the demonic, though we must be aware of the devil's schemes to delude us and cause us to sin. The concern of Scripture is *ethics*, not demonization. Paul's concern in 6:10–20 is the same as in 4:27—that by our inattention to life we give place to the devil, who will lead to sin.

The fundamental issue in discussing the demonic is the glory of God.[54] To whom are legitimacy and power ascribed by the way we live? To the degree we give the demonic credence, to that degree it has control. As H. Schlier put it, "Christ has left the devil only what power unbelief allows him."[55] Powers rule to the extent people let them rule. They do not deserve attention; they deserve avoidance. They may be real, but they do not determine life.

The New Testament focuses on the devil and demons for only *two* purposes: to say evil and death are defeated, and to warn us not to be beguiled by evil. Everyone knows about evil and death; Christians are people who believe Christ has already conquered both.

Other biblical evidence. A closer look at the biblical evidence verifies that the Bible cares about the demonic only to make the two points above—evil is defeated and we should not be caught by its schemes. The Old Testament has hardly any treatment of the demonic. Nowhere does the Bible treat the origin of evil or the fall of Satan.[56] By theological necessity we assume the fall of a created being,[57] but no text describes it. The lying serpent merely appears in the garden to cause sin.

In the Old Testament Satan is mentioned on only three occasions, and the devil never.[58] The only instance of possession by a spirit is in reference to Saul,[59] and no certainty exists that the same phenomenon is meant as with unclean spirits in the New Testament. A few other texts may be relevant, such

---

54. See Timothy M. Warner, "An Evangelical Position on Bondage and Exorcism," *Essays on Spiritual Bondage and Deliverance*, ed. Willard M. Swartley (Elkhart, Ind.: Institute of Mennonite Studies, 1988), 79.

55. Heinrich Schlier, *Principalities and Powers in the New Testament* (New York: Herder and Herder, 1961), 58.

56. Unlike the speculation of Thomas B. White, "Understanding Principalities and Powers," *Engaging the Enemy*, ed. C. Peter Wagner (Ventura, Calif.: Regal, 1991), 60. (Isa. 14 and Ezek. 28 *both* describe earthly kings.)

57. Note Colossians 1:16, which asserts that Christ created the rulers and authorities. Limited evidence of rebellion by angels against God appears in 2 Peter 2:4 and Jude 6.

58. "Satan" is mentioned in 1 Chronicles 21; Job 1–2; Zechariah 3. "Demons" are mentioned twice in connection with idolatry, similar to 1 Corinthians 10:19–21 (see Deut. 32:17; Ps. 106:37–38).

59. 1 Samuel 16:14–23; 18:10; 19:9.

---

as Isaiah 34:14 (which speaks of "night creatures") and Daniel 10:13 (which refers to the "prince of the Persian kingdom"), but how to interpret those texts is open to debate. Texts that speak of a "spirit of prostitution" (Hos. 4:12) or a "lying spirit" (1 Kings 22:19–23) do not refer to literal demons any more than a "spirit of timidity" does in 2 Timothy 1:7. Evil is real in the Old Testament, but the demonic gets small billing.

In the first-century world, both Jews and Gentiles focused more on the devil and demons than the Old Testament did. Jewish speculation about evil developed considerably in the intertestamental period, possibly in reaction to the crimes of Antiochus Epiphanes.

In the New Testament the evidence is surprising. Talk about possession of spirits or demons is confined to the Synoptic Gospels and a few chapters of Acts.[60] Sickness and demon possession were clearly distinguished in the New Testament, though some physical problems, such as speechlessness, were associated with demon possession.[61] The purpose of the focus on the demonic in the Synoptics (and Acts) is to demonstrate that the kingdom of God has broken in to defeat evil (cf. Matt. 12:28).

Paul speaks of "demons" only at 1 Corinthians 10:19–21 and 1 Timothy 4:1. In fact, he delivered people to Satan, not from him (1 Cor. 5:5; 1 Tim. 1:20). Furthermore, the gift of "discerning spirits" (1 Cor. 12:10; cf. 1 John 4:1) is not about detecting the presence of evil spirits, but about the ability to discern the validity of a statement from a prophet (see 1 Cor. 14:29–32).[62] This is not to suggest Satan or evil spirits are a small issue in Paul. As G. B. Caird points out, some mention is made of the rulers and authorities or Satan in every Pauline letter except Philemon.[63]

The concern to warn against evil is enormous, but evidence about the demonic is limited. Is there so much focus on the demonic in the Synoptics because of the climactic spiritual battle caused by Jesus' coming? Are things different since his coming with regard to the amount of demonic activity? If we accept that evil spirits do exist, three options are open:

(1) Demonic forces are as active now as they were in Jesus' day.
(2) They were defeated by Christ and are no longer active.
(3) They were defeated, and their activity is limited.

---

60. See Acts 5:16; 16:16–18; 19:13–16. In John the only occurrence of the language is in accusations that Jesus has a demon. John does speak of Satan, the devil, and the ruler of this world.

61. See Mark 1:32–34; 9:17; cf. Luke 13:10–17.

62. See Fee, *God's Empowering Presence*, 171–72.

63. G. B. Caird, *Principalities and Powers* (Oxford: Clarendon, 1956), p. 9.

Certainty is not possible, but the last option is most likely in view of the distribution of the New Testament evidence and texts like Luke 10:18 and Revelation 12:7–17.[64]

A disastrous wrong turn. Many evangelical churches have undergone a significant but misguided change. As a result of the so-called "third wave of the Spirit," many are focusing more frequently on the devil, demon possession and exorcism, territorial spirits,[65] and the issue of binding demons. The exegetical and theological thought supporting this change is superficial.[66] Often the language bears little resemblance to that of the New Testament. Should anyone speak of "hordes of demons" or the "swarming presence of Beelzebub and his minions"? Should anyone attempt to list 323 types of demons or describe territorial spirits in a particular locale? Where is there evidence to substantiate what people "discern" about spirits? Is it fair to say a "spirit of greed" entered California during the gold rush and still lurks around San Francisco?[67] All this sounds great to a society enamored with Star Wars and video games, but according to the Bible greed comes out of the human heart.

With regard to demon possession, why do most cases involve women while the demons are masculine?[68] Why is this phenomenon so closely aligned with mental and psychological illness? Some claim that spirits enter through traumatic hurt, repeated acts of sin, the occult, inherited spirits, or pacts made by one's parents.[69] True, the occult, Satanism, and drugs are often associated with demon possession, but what evidence suggests spirits can be inherited? Does the Bible teach us to cleanse our genealogical past?

We are also told that the natural defenses of sound healthy minds, emotions, and wills protect against demons.[70] All this sounds more mental than demonic. If trauma and unstable parents are avenues for the demonic, then

---

64. See Everett Ferguson, *Demonology of the Early Christian World* (Lewiston, N.Y.: Mellen, 1984), 170–74.

65. The idea developed from Daniel 10:18 that specific spirits control specific geographical areas. By naming or binding the spirits, the area is supposedly released to accept the gospel.

66. An attempt to rectify this is a collection of essays in *The Kingdom and the Power*, eds. Gary S. Greig and Kevin N. Springer (Ventura, Calif.: Regal, 1993); against this movement are the essays in *Power Religion: The Selling Out of the Evangelical Church?* ed. Michael Scott Horton (Chicago: Moody, 1992). The attempt to reject any "signs of power" after the apostolic age is as equally misguided as the overemphasis on power.

67. For such ideas and language see the essays edited by P. Wagner, *Engaging the Enemy*.

68. Wink, *Unmasking the Powers*, 63.

69. See Robert T. Sears, "A Catholic View of Exorcism and Deliverance," *Essays on Spiritual Bondage and Deliverance*, ed. Willard M. Swartley (Elkhart, Ind.: Institute of Mennonite Studies, 1988), 108–10.

70. Warner, "An Evangelical Position on Bondage and Exorcism," 83.

people suspected of being demon possessed are more victims of abuse than perpetrators. The connection with mental illness and the use of counseling in addition to exorcism is understandable.[71] But why do demons manifest themselves only with these poor, broken victims? Why do spirits not manifest themselves in the *really* evil—the Mafia, drug lords, corporate managers who cheat the poor, or senators who abuse women? Walter Wink is correct; discussion of demons is vastly overbilled and overindividualized.[72]

This new focus on demon possession, territorial spirits, and binding Satan is wrong. It is also strange that what is claimed as a movement of the Spirit focuses so much attention on the devil. In the process the biblical doctrine of creation is demeaned, for material objects become residences for demons. Possibly all the talk about demons and binding Satan is for people to be aware of evil and to build up their own courage, both of which are legitimate. But the extremism with language has led virtually to a return to animism.[73]

So what do we say? First, we should remind ourselves of several facts: (1) We always see through a glass darkly, so that we do not have ultimate answers when it comes to the devil and demons. Particularly with regard to the human mind, so much remains to be learned about how it carries on its own struggles with evil, abuse, and the fractured world in which we live. (2) We do not have to agree on this subject. This is not the gospel. (3) Careful and critical analysis is needed of both biblical texts and assertions about experiences with the demonic. Much of the "proof" smacks of loose thinking about anecdotal cases. We cannot ignore experience, but we can evaluate it theologically.

Often people move quickly from phenomena to ontology, from claims and experiences to statements of existence. Much that the ancient world (and some of the modern world) thought was demonic possession we can explain as mental illness. Other phenomena we might explain by a better understanding of the physical world. Still, as most admit, a "residue" of cases, including some in the present, seem to require seeing evil spirits as a piece

---

71. See several of the articles in Swartley, ed., *Essays on Spiritual Bondage and Deliverance*, especially "Jane Miller's Story and Testimony" and "The Case of Jane: Psychotherapy and Deliverance," 174–91, which tell of the painful childhood and life of a woman in therapy who underwent several exorcisms while in therapy. We should distinguish demon possession from split personality disorder, whereby a personality fragments for self-defense. Furthermore, nearly all discussions of demonic possession proceed on an assumption that humans are composed of body, soul, and spirit. Despite its convenience, I find it questionable that this trichotomous view can be substantiated biblically. First Thessalonians 5:23 cannot be the only text we read with regard to the human makeup.

72. Wink, *Unmasking the Powers*, 63.

73. Animistic cultures think of a high God removed from the earth, leaving humans to fend for themselves in battling other spirits. Focus on the demonic is similar.

of reality.[74] However, they are a small piece and should not be made the focus of Christian attention.

The point has often been made that Satan's greatest weapon is to convince the world *it* does not exist. That is probably true. But why do we need to know about *its* existence? Only to avoid being duped by evil.

THROUGHOUT EPHESIANS THE message has been addressed to the mind and the will. Paul sought informed action from his readers; he asked for a serious response. To apply this text, we too must be spurred to informed action. Ephesians is great material for meditation, but the only appropriate response is an energetic obedience.

Be strong, alert, and ready. The command to "be strong in the Lord" presumes that God is eager and willing to provide strength and that any lack of strength results from our neglect. It assumes also that empowering is not automatic, but comes as we seek a closer relation with Christ. It is a choice we make about the relative importance of life with Christ.

This command also assumes that we need strength. For all its joys, life is hard and full of difficulties, challenges, and traps. Some of these come from illness and death, some from what other people do, and some from our own egos. Whatever the circumstance, however, life in Christ requires our entire being. Both the standard and the challenge are lofty, but so is the help. The strength supplied is the strength of God's own Spirit.

If you seek a religion to make you comfortable, despite all its focus on peace and benefit, Christianity is not it. This is no religion for the weak or the lazy. Passive Christians cannot do the will of God; the very label "passive Christian" is an oxymoron. A battle is going on, and contrary to our deception, we do not live on neutral turf. We either live for God or against him. The choices we make either reflect God's character or the character of sin. As Leon Morris points out, you can drift into sin, but not into righteousness.[75]

For most of us, this means our goal is wrong. We seek a carefree life. It does not exist. Our conceptions of life and especially of retirement must change. Life's goal is not on "golden pond," and Christians are not called to tranquillity. We are called to peace, yes, but peace in the midst of struggle. This peace does not render us inactive; it makes us ready to do God's will.

---

74. See the treatment by Scott Peck, *People of the Lie* (New York: Simon and Schuster, 1982), 182–211, especially 183: "Genuine possession, as far we know, is very rare. Human evil, on the other hand, is common."

75. Morris, *Expository Reflections on Ephesians*, 200.

We need most of all a sense of urgency, an awareness of the conflict, and a sense of our own danger. Yet many of us are guilty of fraternizing with the enemy. If driving defensively is necessary in our cars, surely keeping alert and avoiding error are necessary in life, most of which is far more hazardous than driving a car. Christian living requires attention. Pay attention.

As a society, we have spent *trillions* of dollars arming ourselves against aggression from other countries. Radar, stealth bombers, aircraft carriers, night vision goggles, missiles, and a host of other offensive and defensive weaponry are designed to protect our way of life. Military personnel track every conceivable avenue of attack to make sure we are safe. On the local scene we hire police forces and security guards, put up lights and fences, and put locks on doors. But for all this readiness, we post no guards to secure our moral life or the morals of our society. No one tracks avenues of attack. As a result, our "way of life" is being destroyed. The attacks have come in our schools and universities, in music and movies, in law courts, and in churches. Christians have been so unprepared they have not even noticed they have been taken prisoner.

The ability to be strong and to be ready depends on one thing—an awareness of two realities, the reality of this world and the reality "in the heavenly realms" of life with God in Christ. Most of us are aware only of the world in which we live. We are determined by its definitions, interests, and forces. Awareness of the reality of God gives perspective from which to assess this world and to know that it does not measure up, that evil is present, and that change is required. To be determined by God, his definitions, and his Spirit is to be made strong and ready. The text asks, "In which reality will you live?" and calls us to take a stand against the evil of this world and to be like God. That is the purpose of the gospel. The gospel as both gift and challenge strengthens and makes ready. Live it.

Powerful, but not militant. Maybe it does not need to be said, but too often the church has misunderstood its metaphors of battle as license for violence. Our battles are carried out by standing firm against enticements to evil, not by destroying people. The statement in verse 12 is important: Our struggle is not with humans; they are not the enemy. To do evil to people does not fit with the Christian faith. We may not suddenly forget tolerant love, patience, and peace when we encounter people doing wrong. We still are defined by and armed with truth, righteousness, readiness, faith, and the gospel, not ill-will, slander, anger, and violence. The way we carry on our battles is the most eloquent witness to our faith.

Obviously such comments have direct relevance for the way Christians respond in arguments over social issues like abortion and homosexuality.

Our society's acceptance of these practices is wrong,[76] but if we act in unchristian ways in rejecting sin, what have we become? Violence cannot be used to achieve good. An ancient Jew put it well: "The person trying to do right by violence is like a eunuch desiring to seduce a young woman" (Ecclesiasticus 20:4). Whether absolute pacifism is an option in a sinful world is debatable, but that Christians must be people of peace is not. The church's history is littered with painful and atrocious violations of its own gospel. Never let it happen again!

Fear no evil. The dustcover of a recent Christian novel asserts, "Fear no evil is no longer an option." Novels may be fun reading, but from a theological perspective, such a comment borders on blasphemy. How different from the tone of the psalmists, Jesus, and Paul! How different from Martin Luther's comment on the devil, "One little word will fell him."[77]

One of the key ingredients for Christian living is a balanced perspective on evil. On the one hand, evil cannot be taken lightly; it is a destructive power against which we need vigilance. On the other hand, evil and its personalities are obvious frauds. According to the New Testament, Satan is more an annoyance than a great overpowering force. The threat of danger exists, but this enemy is defeated, is not in control, and is limited in power. Does God fear evil or the devil? The thought is ludicrous. But the armor God uses to defeat evil is given to us. Why should we fear? We should experience courage for living because the enemy has been defeated.

Evil is a trap. How can we do justice to the threat of evil without magnifying its role? What is evil anyway? Evil is a violation of boundaries and an assigning to ourselves or things values that we and they do not possess. It is a rebellion against God and the boundaries and values he designated. The Ten Commandments and other ethical teachings in the Bible mark those boundaries and values placed on God, parents, property, life itself, the use of our bodies, facts, and other people. Evil entices us to change the boundaries so that God does not receive the allegiance we owe and so that property, life, and the dignity of others is redefined in our favor. Evil has its roots at the center of our being in our attempt to obtain the best for ourselves. This is why evil is a trap; it always looks like something good for us, but it does not ask about God or other people, and it does not ask about long term effects. In the process the boundaries and values by which God orders life are distorted.

The spiritual forces of evil in Ephesians are trap setters, seeking to delude us into shifting the boundaries. Some traps we recognize easily, for we see the paths to destruction worn down by previous captives. Other traps we

---

76. This is not to make light of serious questions about the legitimacy of abortion in cases of threat to the mother's life, incest, or rape.

77. From the third verse of "A Mighty Fortress Is Our God."

hardly notice, for we have accepted the revaluing. In most cases our choice is not between obvious evil and something good but between two seemingly good and right options. As Walter Wink points out, Satan watches our inclinations and throws us to the side to which we are leaning. Discerning God's will is difficult in a field where Satan appears prepared to suit up for either team.[78] Evil traps us with the good, only slightly out of bounds. Each choice slightly out of bounds redraws the boundaries until nothing remains of God's intent. That is why evil is deceptive and why we need to be alert.

Do not focus on evil or the devil. I believe in the demonic, not out of necessity, but because the text requires it. But I am not particularly helped in believing in the demonic, for with or without that belief, I still have to deal with evil. But the goal is to avoid evil, not focus on it. Christians often make the error of giving the devil way more than *it* is due. The devil is more interesting to them than God, and *it* gets more attention. This is a twisted kind of idolatry and the very thing evil wants. If you are fascinated by evil, you will be enticed by evil. The New Testament instructs us to be alert and stand against the devil by standing for right, and *it* will run away.[79]

Focus on evil or the devil has several negative consequences, among which are:

(1) Attention is diverted from God to evil.
(2) Responsibility for evil is shifted from our own depravity to something outside us.
(3) Confession and change are made more difficult.
(4) Our sense of strength and courage is diminished.

By focusing on evil we destroy ourselves; by focusing on God we find life and protection. God deserves our attention; evil does not. In asking us to put on the armor of God, the text directs our attention away from evil and to God and his purposes.

But what of demon possession and exorcism? Humans love the bizarre and unusual, so it is no surprise that demon possession fascinates Christians and non-Christians alike. Evil is often so real and overwhelming and so personal that belief in demon possession is understandable. Clearly the New Testament assumes the reality of demon possession, at least within certain parameters, and the church has tried to deal with this phenomenon. Both the Roman Catholic and Anglican orders of worship have services for exorcism.

On the other hand, caution is required in approaching this subject. Exorcism is not listed as one of the gifts of the Spirit, and as indicated above, the

---

78. Wink, *Unmasking the Powers,* 33.

79. In addition to this passage, cf. James 4:7; 1 Peter 5:8–9; and the temptation narratives of the Gospels.

gift of discerning spirits is about false prophets, not detecting the presence of demons. In addition, Scripture gives no criteria for determining demon possession. *If* we could relate 1 John 4:1–3 to this subject—which is by no means sure—the only criterion would be Christological. Further, by any reasonable estimation, if demon possession exists, it is rare.[80] For the average Christian to be enmeshed in this subject is nonsense. I do not mean to be cavalier in diminishing this subject, for to those who believe strongly in demons, they are very real. But the New Testament evidence does not encourage a focus on demons and exorcism, nor does modern medical science.

Caution is also required because a focus on demon possession is destructive. To suggest that a person is possessed disables the self-understanding and ability of that person to deal with the problem. He or she no longer feels responsible for the problem. Certainly no one is helped when well-meaning but naive Christians suggest an epileptic or a child with fetal alcohol syndrome has a demon. Also, glib responses such as "When in doubt, cast it out" betray an intolerable ignorance about both Christianity and humanity. Often efforts at deliverance are quick fixes that do not last.[81] The possibility of demon possession should be approached with the greatest caution, and preferably only with the aid of Christian psychiatric help.

Two further points should be made forcefully. (1) People must see themselves as responsible for their own evil. Some people like the idea of being demon possessed, for then they are not responsible and do not need to confess and repent. (2) People should be warned to stay away from the occult, Satanism, and similar practices. The correlation between those dabbling in the occult and experiences labeled as demon possession is high.[82]

Can Christians be possessed or oppressed? The New Testament betrays no thought that a Christian can be demon possessed, and it makes no theological sense to say a person can have the Spirit of God and another spirit. Christians need to be concerned about the legitimacy of their faith, not about whether they can be possessed.[83]

Whether Christians can be oppressed is a different problem and depends to some degree on what is meant with "oppressed." Paul obviously felt his thorn in the flesh was a messenger of Satan (2 Cor. 12:7) and that Satan

---

80. See the comments by Peck in footnote 70.

81. See the article by Joe D. Wilmoth, "After Deliverance, Then What?" *Leadership* (Summer 1991), 68–70. One cannot help but wonder whether "deliverance ministries" are not emotional jolts that may or may not have long term effect.

82. Note Paul's concern (1 Cor. 10:19–21) about participating with demons in eating food sacrificed to idols.

83. The opposite position is argued by C. Fred Dickason, *Demon Possession and the Christian: A New Perspective* (Wheaton, Ill.: Crossway, 1987). He goes far beyond the biblical evidence, and his viewing tongues as an entrance for demons is erroneous.

blocked his visit to the Thessalonians (1 Thess. 2:18). Martin Luther at one point was so aware of the devil that he threw an inkwell at him. The question is one of focus. To speak of oppression by demons places focus on the demonic and suggests it is stronger than it is. A series of unhappy coincidences in a fallen world does not prove demonic oppression. The New Testament does not encourage such thinking. Rather, it encourages us to think of Christ and the strength he provides. Evil is a real threat, and we do well to realize the presence of evil in our own depravity rather than worry about the devil and demons.

Pray at all times. Christians do not need to worry about evil, for they know how to pray. In a similar passage in Philippians 4:6–7 Paul instructed his readers: Don't worry about anything, pray about everything, and the peace of God will guard your hearts. Be alert, yes, but don't worry or fear.

Prayer is the key ingredient in being strong and alert. When we pray in the Spirit, the Spirit is interactive with us. As a result, we are empowered and instructed by the Spirit. We put on the armor of God by being in communication with God. Like a radar beam that keeps a plane on track, prayer keeps us alert and in line with God's purposes.

Praying *in the Spirit* is different from just praying. Most people pray, if religious surveys can be trusted, but most of our prayers tend to be "wish lists" and prayers for protection. Praying in the Spirit involves engagement with God and assistance from the Spirit that takes us beyond our immediate concerns. True prayer is a comprehensive activity, involving a variety of modes from praise to lament, from confession to obedience, and from contemplation to intercession.

All of life is to be prayed, not just lived. That is why Paul instructs us to pray in the Spirit "on all occasions" (6:18). We cannot spend all of life "having our quiet time," but we can be continually in communion with God. Christians are not merely to experience their joys and problems, but to assess them in dialogue with God. Prayer is a kind of spiritual breathing.

What we must do is keep the channel open, aware of God and our relation to God. Too easily, we greet God in the morning or over a meal, but do not interact with him the rest of the day. Specific times of prayer are crucial, but all of life is to be prayed.

In addition, prayer is not "life with me and God." It is a means of being aware of the world and a larger set of relations. We do not merely pray for ourselves, but for all God's people, and by extension, for all of God's world. Prayer also reminds us of our need for the prayers of other people. We are not in this life alone, but are supported by a community of faith. If Paul felt that need, we should too. By prayer we are kept from being provincial, by prayer we express our love and concern, and by prayer we involve ourselves in the purposes of God.

Such a theology of prayer also assumes that life is not predetermined, that our concerns are important to God, and that God cares and responds to us. Prayer gives a significance to life, for what we do is important if our communion with God has the potential to change results. Again, balance and caution are needed, for prayer is not magic taking on the universe. We pray because we are engaged with God moving through life, and our life and conversation with God do change things.

Representatives of Christ. Paul viewed himself as Christ's ambassador with a special responsibility to communicate the gospel. While other Christians do not have the same task he did, the very fact that we live in Christ makes every Christian a representative of Christ. Our Lord is made known by the way his people act. In the section on slaves and masters we saw that Christ was the recipient of every action.[84] That we are his representatives underscores that he is also the *origin* of every action. When our behavior is not representative of Christ, then we have failed to live worthy of our calling (4:1).

As was clear in Paul's case, recognition and status do not validate the role, and circumstances—even tragic ones—do not diminish it. Validation comes through living in relation with Christ, acting in accord with his character, and speaking in ways that articulate the gospel clearly. We must take more seriously the representative aspect of our faith. Christianity is not only about getting to heaven; it is about living with and for Christ. We stand with and for him as we relate to other people. Once again we find a theology that views life as wonderfully meaningful.

Evangelism. The focus on the gospel throughout the letter makes Ephesians a primary source for thinking about evangelism. The emphasis on this issue at the end of the letter underscores its importance in Paul's eyes. The word of God—the gospel message—is not merely a means of protection (v. 17); it is also something to be shared. Evangelism is not *a* task of the church; it is the only task, for all we do is supposed to make Christ known. Such statements obviously do not limit evangelism to specific statements about the gospel, but neither do they provide a basis for evangelism to be unintentional. Christians—especially evangelicals—are "gospel people."

We do not need guilt about evangelism, nor do we need a sense that we always have to say something "Christian" to people we meet. Instead, we need an integrity of life with Christ that is guided by him and the wisdom to know how and when to speak. For all the importance that speaking obviously has in explaining the good news, integrity of life with Christ is more

---

84. See p. 328.

important. Most of our society has heard far too much talk, but has not seen the life of Christ actually lived out.

Our intent and prayer should be the same as Paul's. Paul felt a necessity to reveal who Christ is and set his mind on doing so.[85] We should do the same. As strange as it seems, when our lives reveal his, they take on a dignity and meaning impossible elsewhere. We *do* find life by losing it. Paul also knew he needed the right words and freedom of expression and asked his friends to pray accordingly. We still need to pray for wisdom and the freedom to say the right things. Then we need to do it.

---

84. The NIV "as I should" in verse 20 is literally "as it is necessary."

Ephesians 6:21–24

🍃

TYCHICUS, THE DEAR brother and faithful servant in the Lord, will tell you everything, so that you also may know how I am and what I am doing. ²²I am sending him to you for this very purpose, that you may know how we are, and that he may encourage you.

²³Peace to the brothers, and love with faith from God the Father and the Lord Jesus Christ. ²⁴Grace to all who love our Lord Jesus Christ with an undying love.

THE HEADING IN the NIV for this section—"Final Greetings"—is a misnomer. Paul does not greet anyone. Rather, this section has two purposes: to affirm Tychicus and the additional message he will deliver (vv. 21–22), and to close the letter formally with a benediction/blessing extending peace and grace to the readers (vv. 23–24).

Tychicus, the letter carrier (6:21–22). The instructions concerning Tychicus are paralleled almost verbatim in Colossians 4:7–8. This is the most extensive similarity between these two letters.[1] No other parallel between them exceeds seven words.[2] That someone copying from Colossians would suddenly copy verbatim here is not convincing, especially since Ephesians 6:23–24 is so unlike the closing of Colossians. Comments about the letter carrier do not appear in Paul's other letters, except for the commendation of Phoebe in Romans 16:1–2, which serves a different purpose. These instructions make sense only if Tychicus really is the letter carrier for both Colossians and Ephesians. In all likelihood Colossians, Ephesians, and Philemon were all written about the same time and carried by Tychicus to their recipients.

While a courier system existed for official mail, private letters were carried by private messengers or were sent along with people known to be traveling to the desired destination. The closer the relationship between the letter carrier and the sender, the more the former would be expected to give additional information and explanation of details.

---

1. There are thirty-two words the same; within them, Ephesians adds "what I am doing" and Colossians "and fellow servant."

2. Excluding verses 1–2, where stereotypical phrases show correspondences of seven words in 1:1 and eight in 1:2.

The description given for Tychicus is used of Paul's other close helpers.[3] Both Tychicus and the readers are called "brothers," the only two occurrences of this word in the letter—a common designation by Paul for his fellow workers and Christian friends. At least in some cases the plural form is used generically to include both men and women. The word underscores the bond and sense of family early Christians felt. The NIV translation "dear brother" is a bit archaic. Literally, the text has "beloved brother"; we might say "valued friend."

At the beginning of the letter Paul described his readers as "the faithful in Christ Jesus." Similarly, at the end of the letter Tychicus is described as a "faithful servant in the Lord," underlining the importance of both faithfulness and the idea of being in Christ. The theology of life in Christ not only determines Paul's understanding of salvation and ethics, it also describes how he sees his Christian friends.

Relatively little else is known about Tychicus. Acts 20:4 indicates he was from Asia and accompanied Paul on the trip to Jerusalem to take the collection from Gentile churches for the Jewish Christians. This was, of course, the trip where Paul was arrested and incarcerated. According to 2 Timothy 4:12 Paul sent Tychicus to Ephesus. It is hard to believe this is coincidental. Titus 3:12 mentions the possibility that Tychicus will be sent to Titus.

The word translated "encourage" in verse 22 carries several nuances (this word is translated "urge" in 4:1 and "comfort" in 2 Cor. 1:4). Paul was in prison, but rather than seeking encouragement for himself, he gives it. This also gives insight into the purpose of the letter: Ephesians is a letter of encouragement.

The closing benediction (6:23–24). No other letter closing is like this one. All of Paul's letters end with grace bestowed on the readers, and several of them extend peace or love.[4] The benediction here is fuller and more liturgical than most, which is not surprising, given the liturgical character of the whole letter. Note the double occurrence of the expression "Lord Jesus Christ" and the four major themes of the letter brought back to mind: peace, love, faith/faithfulness, and grace.

Twelve of Paul's letters have the greeting "grace to you and peace from God" at the beginning.[5] All his letters conclude with a grace benediction, and several either include peace in the closing benediction or have some

---

3. See Philippians 2:25; Colossians 1:7; 1 Thessalonians 3:2.

4. On "peace," see 2 Corinthians 13:11–13, which may be the closest to Ephesians; Galatians 6:16; 2 Thessalonians 3:16. On "love," see 1 Corinthians 16:24 (Paul's love) and 2 Corinthians 13:13 (God's love).

5. In 1 Thessalonians the greeting is merely "grace to you and peace." The Pastorals are slightly different.

focus on peace at the end of the letter. But no other letter has the expression "peace . . . from God" or "love . . . from God" at the end. This is an obvious effort to underscore God as the source of the peace and love that is extended.

The NIV translation "and love with faith from God" is problematic. This translation is not impossible, but it raises two questions. (1) Is the text saying "May God show you his peace and love," or "May you show God's peace and love"? In benedictions we would expect the former, but "with faith" forces the second question. (2) What does it mean to say "May God show you love *with faith?*" Is this an attempt to say faith is a gift from God too? If faith focuses on human faith, then maybe love does as well.[6]

A comparison of other blessings of this type shows clearly that grace, love, and peace—and sometimes mercy—are standard items in blessings and that the reference is to God's gifts and character being conveyed to the recipients.[7] In other words, Paul is saying, "May God continue to reveal his loving nature to you." The benedictions are prayers that God or Christ will be present and active in the people's lives (see 2 Thess. 3:16). With regard to love at least, the benediction is essentially the same as the prayer in 3:19, that the readers will know Christ's love.

But what does "with faith" mean then? It could be an abbreviated way of emphasizing the importance of human faith, but a neglected alternative is more likely. Remember that the word translated "faith" also means "faithfulness," depending on the context. If the focus is on the love and *faithfulness* that come from God and Christ, the passage makes better sense. This option would be translated: "Peace to the brothers and love with faithfulness from God the Father and the Lord Jesus Christ." This recalls the emphasis in 1:3 that God has blessed us with every spiritual blessing in Christ as well as the focus on the faithfulness of Christ in 3:12.[8] If this translation is correct, verses 23–24 focus on both the faithfulness of Tychicus and the faithfulness of God and on both the love of God and the love of believers.

A second translation difficulty comes at the end of verse 24. If translated literally the text reads: "Grace be with all those loving our Lord Jesus Christ in immortality."[9] These words emphasize the necessity and value of

---

6. Meyer, *Ephesians,* 555, understood love as a "moral element" because reference to divine love would not fit with faith.

7. See e. g., Romans 15:13; 1 Corinthians 1:3; 2 Corinthians 13:13; Galatians 6:16; 2 Thessalonians 3:16; 1 Timothy 1:2; Jude 1:2.

8. See pp. 46, 164–65. See also 1 Timothy 1:14, the only other occurrence of "with faith" and one that also seems to refer to Christ's faithfulness.

9. A negative version of this statement appears in 1 Corinthians 16:22: "If anyone does not love the Lord—a curse be on him."

loving Christ, but what is the intent and connection of "in immortality"? The NIV has taken "in immortality" as a description of those who love the Lord and translated the phrase as "with undying love." The KJV has "in sincerity";[10] the NEB has "grace and immortality." The problem is primarily understanding where "in immortality" should be connected. Several possibilities exist:

(1) Connect the words to "loving," as the NIV has done.
(2) Connect them to "grace," as the NEB has done.
(3) Connect them to "the Lord Jesus Christ," emphasizing that Christ already reigns in immortality.
(4) See them merely as a general and cryptic way to refer to the eternal consequences of the gospel.[11]

The third option seems the most likely, both grammatically and theologically. With this focus, readers are reminded of Christ's exaltation (1:20–23), of their own position with Christ (2:5–6), and of the promise that all things will be summed up in Christ (1:10). God's grace does not depend on our undying love, but on his faithfulness to his promise.[12]

Bridging Contexts

APPLICATION OF THE instructions concerning Tychicus have little relevance today. The benediction is directly relevant, but adds little or nothing not encountered earlier in the letter. The main transferable values in this section come in the care Paul had for his Christian friends and in the glimmers of theology expressed in his desire for them. Paul cared deeply both for Tychicus and for his readers. That Paul viewed Tychicus, his helper, as "in the Lord" bestowed a dignity on him and on the relationship that no other expression can match.

The benediction also carries a theology. The focus in the letter and here is on God and Christ as the source of the peace, love, faithfulness, and grace the readers need for life. The benediction reminds us that God provides what believers need through Christ, which is where the letter started in 1:3. Focus is also placed on human response with "all who love our Lord."

---

10. This should be excluded, for the other six occurrences of the Greek word all refer to immortality.

11. See Robinson, *St. Paul's Letter to the Ephesians*, 138; Caird, *Paul's Letters From Rome*, 94.

12. See Ralph Martin, "Ephesians," *The Broadman Bible Commentary*, ed. Clifton J. Allen (Nashville: Broadman, 1971), 177.

WE TEND TO ignore the relevance of texts like this. Their application may be limited, but they still are significant in shaping how we view God and ourselves. Paul's view of his friends and his concern for them deserve to be copied. By viewing other Christians as in the Lord and by desiring God's gifts for them, we change the way we relate to them. We cannot extend God's peace and love honestly to people we do not care about.

Perhaps the most important application of the text is the reminder that God and Christ are the substance of life. They are the willing source of what we need to live, and all God expects from us is a loving response.

In many ways the benediction is an appropriation of the entire letter. God has provided all you need in Christ; therefore, live worthy of the gift!

Scripture Index

Scripture Index

Subject Index